American Military History

Now in its third edition, *American Military History* examines how a country shaped by race, ethnicity, economy, regionalism, and power has been equally influenced by war and the struggle to define the role of a military in a free and democratic society.

Organized chronologically, the text begins at the point of European conflict with Native Americans and concludes with military affairs in the early twenty-first century, providing an important overview of the military's role on an international, domestic, social, and symbolic level. The third edition is fully updated to reflect recent developments in military policy and the study of military history and war and society, thus providing students with a foundational understanding of the American military experience.

This book will be of interest to students of American history and military history. It is designed to allow instructors flexibility in structuring a course.

William Thomas Allison is Professor of History at Georgia Southern University. He earned his Ph.D. at Bowling Green State University and teaches courses on American military history, the Vietnam War, and war and society. He has been a visiting professor at the U.S. Air Force Air War College, the U.S. Air Force Command and Staff College, and the U.S. Army War College, and has served on the editorial board of the *Journal of Military History*, on the U.S. Army Historical Advisory Committee, and as vice-president of the Society for Military History. He is the author of several works, including *Military Justice in Vietnam: The Rule of Law in an American War*, *My Lai: An American Tragedy*, and *The Gulf War, 1991*, and is the series editor for Modern War Studies at the University Press of Kansas.

The late **Jeffrey G. Grey** was Professor of History at the Australian Defence Force Academy. He earned his Ph.D. at the University of New South Wales and held several visiting professorships, including the Major General Matthew Horner Chair in Military Theory at the U.S. Marine Corps University. His numerous publications include *The Commonwealth Armies and the Korean War: An Alliance Study*, *A Military History of Australia*, *Australian Brass: The Career of Lieutenant-General Sir Horace Robertson*, and *'Up Top': The Royal Australian*

Navy in Southeast Asian Conflicts, 1955–1972, as well as volumes for the Centenary History of Australia and the Great War series. He served as president of the Society for Military History and on the editorial boards of the *Journal of Military History*, the *Journal of the Australian War Memorial*, *War in History*, and the *Australian Army Journal*, as well as editor for *War and Society*.

Janet G. Valentine is a retired Associate Professor of Military History at the U.S. Army Command and General Staff College. A scholar of the Korean War and citizenship and military obligation, she earned her Ph.D. at the University of Alabama and worked as a historian for the U.S. Army Center of Military History, the U.S. Air National Guard History Office, and the U.S. Department of Defense Joint History Office, and has held teaching positions at the University of North Florida and Mississippi State University. She has served on the editorial board for the *Journal of Military History* and the advisory board for H-WAR.

American Military History

A Survey from Colonial Times to the Present

Third Edition

William Thomas Allison, Ph.D.
GEORGIA SOUTHERN UNIVERSITY

Jeffrey G. Grey, Ph.D.
UNIVERSITY OF NEW SOUTH WALES/AUSTRALIAN DEFENCE FORCE ACADEMY

Janet G. Valentine, Ph.D.
U.S. ARMY COMMAND AND GENERAL STAFF COLLEGE

 Routledge
Taylor & Francis Group

NEW YORK AND LONDON

Third edition published 2020
by Routledge
52 Vanderbilt Avenue, New York, NY 10017

and by Routledge
2 Park Square, Milton Park, Abingdon, Oxon, OX14 4RN

Routledge is an imprint of the Taylor & Francis Group, an informa business

© 2020 Taylor & Francis

The right of William Thomas Allison, Jeffrey G. Grey, and Janet
G. Valentine to be identified as authors of this work has been asserted by
them in accordance with sections 77 and 78 of the Copyright, Designs and
Patents Act 1988.

First edition published by Prentice Hall 2007

Second edition published by Routledge 2016

Library of Congress Cataloging-in-Publication Data
Names: Allison, William Thomas, author. | Grey, Jeffrey, author. |
Valentine, Janet G., author.
Title: American military history: a survey from colonial times to the present/
William Thomas Allison, Ph.D., Georgia Southern University; Jeffrey
G. Grey, Ph.D., University of New South Wales/Australian Defence Force
Academy; [and] Janet G. Valentine, U.S. Army Command and General Staff
College.
Description: Third edition. | New York: Routledge, 2020. | Includes
bibliographical references and index. |
Identifiers: LCCN 2019058336 (print) | LCCN 2019058337 (ebook) |
ISBN 9781138735774 (paperback) | ISBN 9781138735804 (hardback) |
ISBN 9781003001232 (ebook)
Subjects: LCSH: United States–History, Military.
Classification: LCC E181 .A33 2020 (print) | LCC E181 (ebook) |
DDC 055.00973–dc23
LC record available at https://lccn.loc.gov/2019058336
LC ebook record available at https://lccn.loc.gov/2019058337

ISBN: 978-1-138-73580-4 (hbk)
ISBN: 978-1-138-73577-4 (pbk)
ISBN: 978-1-003-00123-2 (ebk)

Typeset in Bembo
by Swales & Willis, Exeter, Devon, UK

Visit the companion website: http://www.routledge.com/cw/Allison

For Jeffrey Grey
(1959–2016)
Mentor, colleague, friend

Contents

Preface

The American military experience is so distinctly woven into the history of the United States that it is, at times, difficult to separate the two. Such a notion is perhaps uncomfortable for some historians, but the fact remains that although American history has been shaped by race, ethnicity, economy, regionalism, power, and myriad other influences, so, too, has this experience been tremendously shaped by war and the struggle to define the role of a military in a free and democratic society.

Since colonial times, the people of America, including Native Americans, have spent a great deal of time at war. Well over one million Americans have perished in these wars. Americans have fought for land, trade, freedom, slavery, prestige, empire, democracy, and humanity, as well as vanity and hubris, to list but a few. Over time, the American people and their government have developed a distinctive way of thinking about, preparing for, and fighting wars. It is an exercise fraught with risk, sacrifice, and challenges that is always difficult and painful to undertake. And yet, we continue to make war.

War, naturally, plays a central role in this textbook, and in several instances, chapters are devoted solely to conflict. Other issues and events beyond war, however, also characterize the American military experience. The struggle between the tradition of militia and the need for a standing army, the evolution of civil–military relations, the advent of professionalism in the military, the nonmilitary uses of the military, and the military's role in democratic society as a tool of international and domestic power, a social institution, and symbol of American prestige abroad are all also part of this experience. To gain a holistic appreciation of American military history, these themes and others must be examined in the context of American history.

This textbook is meant to serve as a foundation for undergraduate courses in American military history. The content and style are intended to appeal to undergraduate students who may or may not be history majors. In providing such fundamental themes and content, the text is designed to allow instructors flexibility in their own course design, be it through lectures, supplemental readings, or other methodologies. The book is organized chronologically, beginning with European conflict with Native Americans and concluding with military affairs in the early twenty-first century. Each chapter also includes a brief list of books for further student reading. Obviously, the book lists are not meant to be authoritative or definitive, but instead representative and appropriate for undergraduates to explore some topics further. Individual instructors would undoubtedly add to or delete from the books offered in each chapter. Again, the purpose is to provide the student with a foundation and give the instructor flexibility. Appropriate maps and illustrations are added to provide additional context for the student. This new edition includes updated images and maps, as well as content throughout that reflects the exciting recent trends in historical scholarship, especially war and society studies.

We are grateful to Kimberley Smith, Zoe Forbes, Emily Irvine, and all of the generous and helpful people at Routledge/Taylor & Francis. They have been supportive and enthusiastic throughout the process of putting together this new edition. We are also indebted to the several reviewers—instructors from all sorts of institutions who use this textbook—for their constructive criticisms and corrective suggestions. They have helped improve this new edition. With that, however, we are the final arbiters of the content presented and take full responsibility for any errors or omissions therein.

This new edition, however, is bittersweet. Our co-author and friend, Jeffrey Grey, passed away suddenly in 2016. While he is deeply missed as a mentor, colleague, and friend, his presence looms large in this new edition. From the very beginning, when we began putting together the first edition in 2005, Jeffrey insisted that the role of a military in a free society be an overarching theme throughout the book. We have maintained that theme here, not only because it is so significant to understanding the American military experience, but, too, because Jeffrey believed so much that students should appreciate this delicate balance between the arbitrary nature of military service and the liberties we value as a free society. We dedicate, then, this new edition to the late Jeffrey Grey.

1   The First American Way of War

Introduction

When English settlers arrived to colonize the Atlantic seaboard of North America in the early 1600s, they found a most threatening and inhospitable environment against which they would struggle for decades to establish permanent settlements. From the English viewpoint, strange diseases, a dramatically diverse climate, and a primitive indigenous people haunted the shores and estuaries of New England, the Chesapeake Bay region, and the Carolinas. These early colonists arrived with no promise of royal protection from hostile indigenous peoples or encroaching armies of competing European powers. From the standpoint of the English Crown and Parliament, the colonists were on their own and would have to provide for their own defense. These circumstances gave colonists plenty of cause to be conscious of military matters. The warfare that developed in North America was not European in style or purpose, and it forced colonists to move away from military concepts of the Old World and open their minds to new but brutal ideas about warfare and military affairs that suited their unique situation.

The American Colonies and the British Military Tradition

It was only natural that English settlers would bring with them to the New World their ideas and traditions from home. This concept of transplanting one's customs, beliefs, and traditions is called cultural mimesis. To the American wilderness, English colonists brought their traditional notions on social order, localized representative government, fundamental rights, loyalty to the King, civic obligation, and military affairs. From the time of their initial settlement, English colonists became entangled in a paradoxical trinity of trade, alliance, and warfare that resulted in frequent conflict with Native Americans throughout the seventeenth century. In their adaptation to the unique circumstances of North America, English colonists developed their own attitudes toward military affairs and gradually created their own style of war. It was the beginning of what many argue became the American military tradition. This included an adapted English militia system that grew throughout the colonies and varied widely in form, regulation, and effectiveness compared to its counterpart back in England.

The English had developed two principal values concerning military affairs. First, the idea of a militia had become an English tradition in and of itself. Militia in England had been an institution with which all Anglo colonists would have been familiar. Each county in England was obligated to keep and train militia units, known as trainbands, under the leadership of a lord-lieutenant. Only about one-tenth of Englishmen participated in these local training units, whose discipline and ability varied widely. Rarely called to muster, few militiamen in England expected to be called into service because the very idea of defending England's shores from an invader seemed so remote despite the Spanish attempt to invade in 1588. Militia service and training also had become a sort of informal social control mechanism that helped regulate class relationships and bonded county to country. In times of war, militia units would not integrate as units with the English army. Instead, recruits who often had militia experience would augment already existing localized army units. Remember that England was principally a naval power, so it invested little of its defense budget into a large professional army.

This leads to the second value—the English looked upon a large professional army with grave suspicion, because many feared such an army might violate fundamental liberties that were guaranteed under Parliament and Crown. Standing armies also cost money, which England could ill afford, especially with so much of the national budget spent on naval power. Militia service in England was also a general obligation with centralized standards that applied equally to all county militia units. But this was on paper, and periodic drill was insufficient to lessen the contempt felt by professional army officers toward county militia.

In England, these values shifted during the 1600s. Numerous conflicts, notably the English Civil War and the Thirty Years' War, exposed the weaknesses of militia training and the shortcomings of temporary armies. Oliver Cromwell's New Model Army, officered mainly by Puritans, became a well-trained, well-disciplined force that soundly defeated the armies of Charles I in the English Civil War. Atypically, Cromwell's army also avoided needless casualties among noncombatants, and rarely employed terror as a tactic or strategy because Cromwell recognized the risks of alienating the population. The large, standing professional armies of the latter years of the devastating Thirty Years' War also gravitated toward more limited notions of warfare, employing discipline and training while avoiding terrorizing noncombatant populations.

Because of these and other destructive and costly conflicts, by the end of the seventeenth century the scale and risk of war on the imperial stage made a permanent well-maintained armed force a national necessity.

National political objectives in war had also become limited because of the expense and risk of state-on-state warfare. The colonies, however, did not reach such conclusions. Largely detached from European conflict and military advancements, the English colonists developed their own security system and concept of warfare based upon their developing traditions, geopolitical circumstances, and brutal attitudes toward indigenous populations.

The wilderness in which the settlers had planted themselves was untamed and felt hostile. The nascent settlements carved out of the forests of Massachusetts and the Chesapeake Bay region were in constant danger of Indian attack and within striking distance of rival French and Spanish colonies in Canada and Florida. For the English colonists, even the Dutch settlement at New Amsterdam was a possible threat. As the decades passed, the settlements grew in population and size, pushing more Native Americans off their lands.

This growth intensified imperial competition. Mercantilism became the path to imperial dominance, which required a strong navy to protect sea lanes between the mother country and colonies scattered literally around the world. French, Spanish, Portuguese, and Dutch fleets battled England's Royal Navy for maritime supremacy, pouring money into fleets while often neglecting armies at home. Only when war broke out on the European continent did these imperial powers attempt to modernize their armies. Colonies, however, were often left to their own devices, as few regular troops could be spared for colonial service. In North America, England had neither the means nor the money to provide regulars to defend English settlements, thus leaving the colonists to defend themselves for most of the seventeenth century.

Colonial Militia and Military Organization

The colonists proved quick learners and adapted to their surroundings with violent alacrity. They had not come to America wholly unprepared. Quite to the contrary, settlers in Virginia and Puritan colonists in Massachusetts brought with them their preconceived attitudes toward war and defense as well as weapons of war. The Virginia Company hired the English soldier, explorer, and adventurer Captain John Smith to shape a mostly defenseless Jamestown into a militarized outpost and train a militia company for its defense. Miles Standish and John Underhill were among the men with military background and experience who accompanied the Puritan Separatists to Massachusetts, helping them build defensive perimeters and organize militia. This was typical among the early colonizers—to establish a defensive fortification of some sort and organize militia based upon the English tradition while adapting both to the unique circumstances of colonial America.

Early colonial fortifications were rather simple; most consisted of either a stockade fence or a central blockhouse as a defense against Indian raids.

In an emergency, a general alarm would gather colonists from surrounding farms into the settlement's stronghold. Once inside, militiamen and other colonists would take up positions on ramparts and behind loopholes to fend off attackers. This strategy often worked well against small Indian raids, but anything more substantial in size and more prolonged put the settlers at a disadvantage. Scarce arms and valuable supplies had to be centralized at the stronghold. Food and water ran out quickly under any sort of siege, leaving the besieged colonists in dire straits unless relief arrived post-haste. Fortunately, the nature of Indian warfare allowed for few organized, lengthy assaults, much less for any sort of siege. Fleeing to the relative safety of the stronghold, colonists left homes and other property unprotected. Indians contented themselves with ignoring the settlers in the blockhouse to loot and burn homesteads and farms, having little patience or incentive for an organized siege.

Lines of small forts along the frontier did not fare much better. Fortifications were expensive, often making up the largest single expense in a colony's budget. Construction was costly, especially for the ring of forts that Virginia built along its frontier in the 1600s. Maintenance cost even more, as wood rotted and cannon rusted. Moreover, the men assigned to these outposts faced incredible boredom and idleness, which often led to breakdowns in discipline and poor morale. Forts on the frontier rarely proved useful, as Indians quickly passed between the forts, which were tens of miles apart in many spots and non-existent in most others. Pure chance, more often than not, brought indigenous raiding parties in contact with ranger patrols from the forts. Most of the time, raiding parties avoided the patrols through superior reconnaissance, or both groups simply missed each other unawares. Over time, blockhouses and garrisons in more established settlements fell into disuse and disrepair as the Indian threat moved further inland.

In theory, a well-trained and organized militia would have made this defensive system work against supposedly primitive Indians, but such was not usually the case. In scattered settlements and even more scattered farms across the countryside, gathering militia to respond to a sudden raid or attack was inefficient at best. Nevertheless, the militia was an integral part of early colonial society, though its form and regulation varied from colony to colony. It served three primary purposes: to defend settlements, to act as a police force, and to provide a trained pool from which a colony could draw soldiers for extended campaigns and wars.

Militia units became centralized agents of social cohesion in many settlements, much like the local church or congregation. In fact, in many places, particularly in New England, the two often were tied together. Normally, colonial law obligated all able-bodied males to serve. Age limits varied, usually from 16 or 18 to 45, or even up to 60. Virginia's militia system required that all members provide their own weapons, which had to be clean and in good working condition. All males in Virginia from age

16 to 60 were required to serve, participate in drill, and, when not in service, protect the property of neighbors who were fulfilling their militia obligation. This system operated under the auspices of the Virginia Company administration in the colony and continued when Virginia became a royal colony. By 1634, due to Virginia's growth, its militia was organized by county instead of settlement. Although the militia was under the direct control of the royal governor, it also could be called out by local commanders in emergencies. As the colony grew in size and population and the Indian threat lessened, the militia became smaller. Indentured servants were no longer required to serve. Slaves, of course, were exempted. The colony also began to pay militiamen when on active duty. Appointed by the governor, officers came almost exclusively from the gentry class.

Militia in New England was organized along similar lines but had the significant added dimension of religion. Like Virginia, Massachusetts and other New England colonies organized militia at the county level; thus, each county regiment was made up of smaller units from villages and hamlets in the county. All males fulfilled their militia obligation or faced a small fine. Of course, the wealthy could afford the fine and often did not serve. Unlike other English colonies in America, in New England substitutes were illegal. All men, including servants, had to provide for their own weapon, and each village had to keep a store of powder and shot. Each trainband unit consisted of members of the local congregation. Because the local militia unit was so closely tied with the local church, pressure within the congregation to serve and to serve well was indeed great. One did not want to let friends and neighbors, and pastor, down. New England militia developed a deep sense of martial spirit that was often enhanced by inspiring sermons from church ministers. The social contract established by the Mayflower Compact applied equally to militia service in Puritan New England. Such a system was consistent with Puritan ideology. Although Puritan social strictures were often rigid, Puritans valued democratic processes and participation in the congregation at all levels. Since ministers, sheriffs, magistrates, and the like were elected, it should come as no surprise that militia officers were also popularly chosen. Though militia officers were elected locally, a colony's general court or assembly usually reserved final approval of militia commissions.

This integrated system resulted in a militia with tight local bonds built around religion, choice, and deference, so much so that military organization and social structure were basically one and the same. Such a system valued decentralization and instilled a reluctant attitude toward centralized control. Under such arrangements, then, militias functioned as both an initial reaction force and a social stabilizer. Militia service provided a sense of security, established and maintained social parameters, and satisfied the expectations of civic duty.

Much overshadowed by its defensive purpose was the effective job militia performed as police, functioning as an overseer of internal order in a colony. Troubled times frequently brought riots and, as in the case of Virginia in 1676, occasional rebellion. Theft and violent crime plagued port cities. Economically displaced vagrants passed through towns and villages, rousing the suspicion of residents. Some drifters were actually impressed into militia service. To protect themselves from these threats, many communities recruited small numbers of militia to serve as watch patrols. Like militia, the colonial watch had its origins in England and was also transported to America by English colonists.

In the southern colonies, militias and the watch evolved into slave patrols, which roamed the countryside on the lookout for runaway slaves and signs of slave insurrection, much as the old ranger patrols had done against the Indian threat. Even in New York City, militia helped put down a slave revolt in 1741. In essence, militia came to serve more as a 'hue and cry' response force. Occasionally, militia could not be used to quell disorder because militiamen themselves made up much of the disturbing party. Such was the case in the Carolinas when roving militia patrols known as regulators grew into a law unto themselves and had to be reined in by legitimate legal authority. Indeed, the militia came to epitomize the precarious balance between civil order and the abuse of military authority.

Militia also served as a training mechanism and manpower reservoir for colonial expeditionary forces. Training was essential for several reasons, but in the broad context its most important function was to provide a ready pool of citizen-soldiers to fill county quotas for more sizable armies. Because militia units could not serve outside their home colony, colonial governments organized expeditionary forces to fight more serious conflicts, such as Indian wars and wars against other European colonial powers. Under such a system in the 1630s, Virginia could muster about 2,000 decently equipped men for a military expedition while leaving a bare minimum of militia in reserve to defend more populated settlements. In 1690, Massachusetts was able to put together a force of over 700 militiamen under the leadership of the daring Sir William Phips to overwhelm the under-defended French garrison at Port Royal.

Plucking men from local militia units to form a colonial expeditionary force was, however, not a straightforward process. Politics at both the local and colonial levels had to be considered. Additionally, all of the English colonies in America had economically diverse settlements. Port cities often had robust economies and larger populations, while frontier regions were sparsely populated and less economically advanced. Merchants tended to dominate coastal politics while gentlemen farmers exercised greater influence inland. Whenever a colonial governor or assembly needed to organize a military force, these diverse relationships had to be considered.

Moreover, such expeditions were costly. Outfitting expeditions with weapons, powder and shot, and other necessary supplies strained colonial coffers and forced assemblies and governors to raise taxes or risk crippling deficits. These circumstances were not unique to colonial America by any means, but the governmental process of preparing a military force helped establish long-standing principles such as civilian control of the military and power-sharing in American political culture. For example, a colonial governor often acted as commander-in-chief of all militia and military forces of the colony while the assembly exercised exclusive fiscal control over funding these enterprises. As such, the principle of power sharing in military affairs was set long before the Constitution outlined a similar civil–military balance.

Under the expeditionary model, local militia deferred to expeditionary commanders appointed by the governor and assembly. Individual militiamen were singled out or volunteered to serve in an expeditionary force. Rarely was an entire unit compelled into service, because that would leave that unit's homes and loved ones unprotected, causing low morale and discontent among the drafted troops. Such discontent could not only reduce the unit's effectiveness but could also put the local assemblyman in a precarious political situation. Thus, it was in the interest of the assembly and the governor to be certain of the need for an expedition and, if so, to ensure its proper supply and command to avoid jeopardizing their political positions.

The politics of colonial civil–military affairs impeded efforts toward intra-colonial military cooperation because it was difficult to muster support for expeditions that would take men away from their homes, leave their families unprotected, and put their own lives in jeopardy in faraway places for what appeared to be little direct benefit for one's home colony. Moreover, getting a colony to surrender control of its force to another colony infringed upon its sovereignty. Arguments over sovereignty plagued leaders during the American War for Independence, but it was a frequent concern as far back as the 1660s. As in most politics, colonial military affairs were, in the end, often personal and decided by political expediency.

Although the militia concept suited colonial security needs for the first few decades of settlement in the New World, in the long run, militias outlived their practical usefulness. Their experience as amateur citizen-soldiers in the Indian Wars of the 1600s left militiamen ill-prepared for the broader imperial conflicts of the 1700s. While the militia concept worked well for local security needs, the changing geopolitical conditions of North America required more comprehensive military institutions and redefined relationships in civil–military affairs at the intra-colonial as well as the imperial level.

A Clash of Cultures

Much has been written about the clash of cultures that was initiated when Europeans first stepped upon North American shores. Economy, religion,

worldview, technology, and other facets of cultural differentiation represented significant obstacles to finding common ground for common
existence. A critical difference between the Europeans, English settlers in
particular, and the indigenous peoples they encountered involved
approaches and attitudes toward warfare. The military culture of Native
Americans was vastly different from that of Europeans. Through violent
encounters, including several near-catastrophic wars, English colonists and
Native Americans were forced to alter their understanding and methods of
warfare. These changes allowed the Europeans to seize land and secure
settlements on the east coast of North America. For the indigenous
peoples, the changes so drastically altered cultural norms that life for
Native Americans would never be the same again. Because European
colonists understood war's intent as annihilation of the enemy, some
indigenous peoples eventually faced outright extinction.

English colonists brought to the New World their own ideas about
military service, purpose, and practice. A well-trained and equipped militia
based upon the English model provided protection from whatever dangers
were lurking in the dense forests of North America. Classic European
battlefield practices at first ruled the colonial warring style. Partly because
of tradition, but also in part because of financial limitations, many militiamen were armed with inexpensive pikes with which they maneuvered in
tight, lined formations. Matchlock and later flintlock muskets were used in
the same fashion—lines of troops, maneuvering to the commands of
officers usually on horseback. These single-shot, muzzle-loading muskets
required intensive training to fire properly and quickly, not to mention
accurately. Smooth-bore muskets weighed over 15 pounds and could be
as long as four and a half feet, not including the added length of a sizable
bayonet.

The vast majority of colonists had never handled a weapon before
coming to America. Whatever militia training they had in England most
likely had been accomplished with long wooden pikes rather than the
more expensive and complicated muskets. With its wooden shaft or pole
plus a large steel or iron tip, a pike could be as long as 15 feet. In the
thickly wooded hills of English North America, such weapons and line
formations quickly proved ineffective against Indian tactics. In Europe,
pikes were often used to defend against cavalry attacks but could also be
used in formation to attack infantry. Native Americans in colonial North
America, however, had neither cavalry nor lines of infantry, preferring
instead to ambush and use other stealthy tactics that left many a colonial
force frustrated by their inability to draw indigenous warriors into
a European-style decisive battle.

Native Americans' tactics reflected their strategic objectives. Unlike
Europeans, many Indians had little attachment to material goods or territorial conquest. Taking and holding territory was truly a foreign concept to
them. For indigenous peoples, warfare was more an individual or kin-group

activity than an act that involved whole societies, and it usually entailed righting perceived wrongs or forcing small tributes from weaker tribes. Contemporary Europeans frequently attested to the few casualties and lack of destruction in battles pitting indigenous peoples against each other. The indigenous population preferred quick, tactical raids rather than pitched battles in open fields, and war parties often dwindled as individuals reconsidered their commitment to hostilities. Spilling blood over largely symbolic matters did not make much sense in indigenous societies. Bows and arrows, tomahawks, and deadly looking knives made the Native American warrior seem fierce indeed, but these weapons rarely inflicted large numbers of horrific casualties in Native American battles.

Native American codes of honor on the battlefield were, in some respects, remarkably similar to those of Europeans. In indigenous warfare, women and children rarely suffered at the hands of an enemy, although they were often taken as captives. Declarations of war were used to formally commence hostilities. Torture, however, was another matter. While Europeans eschewed the practice in warfare but seemed to delight in it in jurisprudence, it was not uncommon for Native Americans along the eastern coast of North America to ritually torture and kill male prisoners of war. Torture served two purposes. First, it allowed for an emotional release that probably made restraint in combat possible. Second, in tribal society tortured captives gained stature and esteem with their captors by courageously accepting their horrifying fate. Colonists, who began to see Native Americans as less noble and more barbarous, as savages, easily misconstrued this notion of torture. Often, captives were adopted into the victorious tribe, a practice that became more common as European diseases decimated indigenous groups. The Iroquois, in particular, practiced this custom to replenish growing losses among their own tribes from disease and battle with European settlers.

Virginia and the Powhatan

Colonists' increasing conflict with indigenous peoples had more to do with their rejection of the view that Native Americans were noble savages than anything the indigenous peoples actually did. Jamestown settlers had the first extended encounters with Native Americans, and the rapidity with which settlers changed their strategic approach toward warfare with indigenous peoples was indeed extraordinary. Context is essential in this case, as the Jamestown colony suffered tremendously during its first two decades of existence. From 1607 through the early 1620s, only around 20 percent of the colonists who came to Jamestown from England survived. The vast majority died from starvation and disease, while only a comparative few died in skirmishes with Native Americans.

At first, these conflicts centered on food. Native Americans typically had only enough for themselves but nonetheless had generously given any meager but valuable surplus to starving colonists, who had primarily expected the local Indians to feed them in the first place. If the Native Americans did not offer foodstuffs, hungry colonists raided nearby villages and stole food. When Native Americans resisted, the colonists responded with astonishing brutality, as in 1610, when Captain George Percy led a small group of men against a Paspahegh village up the James River. The attack was, for the Paspahegh, a brutal introduction to what became the colonial style of warfare. Percy laid waste to the village, burning homes and destroying crops. His men killed more than 65 men, women, and children, and took the village chieftain's wife and children captive. As the colonists traveled by boat back to the settlement, Percy allowed the men to throw the children overboard and shoot them for sport. When Percy presented the chieftain's wife to the governor as a prize, the governor was offended, not because of the massacre, but because Percy had not also killed the woman. She was executed immediately. The strategic objective of the entire operation had not been to destroy the Paspahegh in particular; it was, instead, to send a clear signal to the other villages in the region that the same fate awaited them if they did not supply food for Jamestown.

Figure 1.1 Map of Virginia, discovered and as described by Captain John Smith, 1606; engraved by William Hole. Note the image of the Powhatan chief in the top left corner.

Source: Library of Congress.

To the surprise of Jamestown's leaders, more than a few men abandoned the settlement to live with the comparatively better off Indians, who welcomed them if the desperate colonists brought guns, powder, knives, and anything else of value that the Native Americans could not produce themselves. Violating the strict ban on selling arms and munitions to Native Americans resulted in harsh punishments for offenders, usually death.

Thus, the stage was set for more than 60 years of on-and-off warfare between the English colonists of Virginia and their Indian neighbors. The most serious of these conflicts were the Angle-Powhatan Wars, also known as the Tidewater Wars. The first war occurred in 1622, after several years of minor skirmishes and individual acts of vengeance committed by both sides. The catalyst, in this case, was a group of indentured servants seeking revenge for the apparent death of their master, a man named Morgan, who had disappeared on an inland trek to trade with area tribes. His men blamed a Powhatan named Nemattanow, whom they found and summarily killed.

Opechancanough, chief of the confederacy of Algonquin tribes that the colonists collectively called the Powhatans, boisterously vowed to avenge the murder. But equally belligerent colonists threatened to punish the Powhatans if they made the attempt, resulting in what appeared to be a stalemate. However, on March 22, 1622, after personally serving as a friendly guide for a group of Virginia planters only two days before, Opechancanough unleashed a string of well-coordinated attacks on Virginia settlements and farms, catching colonists and their militia entirely off guard. Three hundred and forty-seven colonists, almost a third of the Anglo population, were dead by the end of the day.

For the next ten years, the Powhatan and Virginia colonists warred on each other, with both sides committing ghastly atrocities. At one point, the governor invited Opechancanough and his warriors to a peace conference and then poisoned 200 of them by serving them poisonous drinks. Most of the desperately ill Powhatan warriors were slaughtered, but Opechancanough somehow managed to escape.

At the beginning of the Powhatan Wars, the Virginia militia was disorganized because of neglect, sickness, and inadequate arms, but it recovered enough to mount a nominal defense and to carry out several haphazard campaigns against Powhatan villages. Adopting a European tactic, the Powhatan at first attempted to lay siege against the handful of Virginian strongholds. Effective at first, these sieges fell apart as militiamen broke out to attack Powhatan villages, burning them to the ground while seizing stores of food. Neither side could gain advantage. Exhaustion on both sides brought the first Powhatan War to an end in 1632, as neither the Powhatan nor the colonists could continue the fight after years of neglected crops and economic degradation.

Twelve years of uneasy peace followed, allowing Virginia to recover and grow in population as, despite indigenous troubles, hundreds of colonists arrived to take their chances in what appeared to be a land of unparalleled opportunity. Feeling the pressure of Virginia's population growth and the colonists' thirst for land, Opechancanough, now nearly 100 years old, ordered another campaign against the Virginians. In coordinated assaults along the James River, warriors again attacked with stealthy surprise. This time 500 colonists were killed in the first hours of the attack, but their counterattack was much quicker and better organized. Virginia militia staged several attacks on Powhatan villages, again destroying crops and homes. Sensing the colony was now simply too big for them to fight, the Powhatan capitulated in 1646. What was once a grand alliance of Algonquin tribes, numbering some 10,000 people, was now a shell of its former self. Only around 4,000 Powhatan remained. For the Native Americans, political disorganization, the incapacity to produce powder, and the inability to maintain sustained military campaigns doomed any long-term effort against the Virginia colonists.

For the colonists, a way of war had developed that struck at the heart of the enemy—his homes, villages, crops, and families. It was brutal, but the colonists convinced themselves that fighting savages demanded barbarous strategies. Moreover, the apparent success at arms had come via the citizen-soldier, the militia. This convinced many in the colony that the militia system worked and could repel attack without the assistance of regular, professional troops. It was a false lesson.

New England's Pequot War

Aware of what was happening in Virginia, the New England colonies hoped to avoid bloody conflict with their indigenous neighbors. The colonies of Plymouth, Massachusetts Bay, and Connecticut all shared borders with a variety of tribal groups, including the Narragansett, Mohegan, and Pequot. As in Virginia, conflict exploded after years of territorial pressure, population decline, and cultural misunderstanding. The Pequot War of 1636–1637 and King Philip's War (also known as Metacom's War) of 1675–1678, the two major conflicts that occurred in this region, are illustrative of the New England experience with Native American warfare.

The death of two traders in January 1675 set in motion what would erupt into the Pequot War. A powerful tribe that occupied much of the land along the Thames River in southeastern Connecticut, the Pequot reigned over several tributary tribes that traded with Dutch and English settlers. The murders were committed by a Pequot tributary tribe, the Niantic, and the rival Narragansett. Authorities in Massachusetts Bay and Connecticut, however, ignored what seemed only semantics and went on the offensive against the Pequot.

Both colonies disputed rights to the Connecticut Valley, and whichever colony defeated or concluded peace with the Pequot would have the inside edge in securing the territory. In August 1636, Massachusetts Bay sent Captain John Endicott and a small militia expeditionary force to Block Island, where they hoped to draw the Pequot into a decisive engagement. The Pequot warriors, however, would not be baited and withdrew into the swamps. Endicott tried another attack from natives Harbor and again failed to bring the Pequot to battle. Frustrated, he let loose his militia upon the countryside to destroy Pequot homes and crops. The colonists then withdrew to Fort Saybrook at the mouth of the Connecticut River, where the Pequot promptly attempted a siege. Keeping the colonists penned down at Fort Saybrook, Pequot reinforcements raided Wethersfield, killing several colonists.

In May 1637, the Connecticut militia entered the fray with their new Narragansett allies. Attempts to stage a cooperative effort with Massachusetts Bay had stumbled, but circumstances would bring militia from both colonies together. Under the command of John Mason, the Connecticut militia and their Narragansett comrades fell upon a sleeping Pequot camp on the Mystic River. Mason's original orders had been to attack the fortified camp of the Pequot leader Sassacus, but upon hearing that hundreds of Pequot were concentrated at the Mystic River camp, Mason turned his force toward that new objective. Mason and his men may have deliberately moved on Mystic to massacre women and children in the hope of bringing the warriors under control.

Along with Captain John Underhill, Mason struck the sleeping Mystic encampment early on the morning of May 26. After encircling the sleeping Indians, the colonists set fire to the primitive fortifications and camp, shooting those who tried to escape, a tactic that colonists used against indigenous peoples time and time again into the nineteenth century. Within an hour, more than 700 Pequot had perished. Only seven escaped, while another seven were taken captive.

Massachusetts militia under the command of Daniel Patrick and Israel Stoughton united with the Connecticut expedition in June to deliver the final blow to the Pequot. Narragansett warriors played the villainous role of protector, bringing the Pequot out of hiding. Pequot warriors then found themselves surrounded by the combined militia force. Another slaughter ensued; hundreds of Native Americans died. In July, the few remaining Pequot were rounded up near New Haven, where they signed a treaty. Colonists' aggressive and gun-powder fueled tactics had very nearly exterminated a people. The Pequot nation ceased to exist, and the surviving members were given away as slaves to indigenous allies. Neighboring tribes captured those who had tried to escape, returning their severed heads as a sign of tribute to the colonists.

The Pequot War had been expensive and ruthless, but for the colonists of both Massachusetts and Connecticut, it had been worthwhile. At the cost of fewer than 50 colonists, the Pequot had been literally wiped out and their tribal lands opened to exploitation. The colonists were fine-tuning a way of war that used death and destruction to bring an enemy to bear. The Pequot were slow on the uptake and, in the eyes of the colonists, had wasted opportunities. In truth, however, what the colonists perceived as the Pequot being poor tacticians was really a demonstration of indigenous inhabitants' customary restraint in war. Across the ensuing decades Native Americans adopted and adapted the settlers' tactics, inflicting heavy casualties upon their white enemy. While colonists could not initially force indigenous fighters to engage *en masse* as was the practice in Europe, like their European counterparts in the Thirty Years' War they brought death and destruction upon noncombatant populations. Europe would move away from such devastation; the English colonists in North America would not, as their next conflict with indigenous peoples made the Pequot War seem like a series of small skirmishes.

King Philip's War

King Philip's War engulfed New England beginning in spring 1675, and before the conflict's conclusion brought the New England colonies together militarily and solidified the colonial way of war. King Philip's War began with the murder of a Native American, supposedly by three Wampanoag. Ordinarily, such a death would not matter much to the Puritan colonists of New England, but this particular man was a resident of one of the missionary prayer towns and, more importantly, was an informer for colonial authorities. Colonial authorities caught the three offenders and promptly executed them. The executions unexpectedly sparked an Indian uprising, led at first by young Wampanoag warriors who attacked isolated farms and homesteads. The war soon devolved into a civil war as colonists united with Indian allies against Indians and other Indian allies in a conflict that very nearly destroyed the unique mesh of colonial and indigenous societies in New England.

The Puritans conducted reprisal attacks against several tribes that were completely innocent in the matter, thus alienating potential Native American allies. Even the Narragansett, the region's largest tribe after the demise of the Pequot, found themselves on the receiving end of Puritan raids. The Puritans blamed the Wampanoag leader Metacomet, whom they had earlier dubbed King Philip as a sign of honor, for instigating his and other area tribes to rebel against the colonists. Metacomet was the son of the beloved Massasoit, who had helped keep an uneasy peace with the Puritans for several decades. Metacomet, however, felt the ever-encroaching colonists were a more significant threat than did his father. Metacomet never became involved in the level of conspiracy that the colonists assumed, but he nonetheless became, for the colonists, the symbolic leader of the revolt.

King Philip's War serves as an excellent example of the results of decades of acculturation through economic, religious, and military contact while continuing the tradition of misunderstanding. Illegal arms trading lessened the technological disadvantage Indians suffered in the Pequot War. They had now mastered the flintlock musket and had plenty of them. Many of the indigenous casualties in the war came from colonial attacks on the friendly Indians who were easily located—those in the several Puritan-established prayer towns that dotted Massachusetts. When they first arrived in America, the Puritans did not attempt to convert the

Figure 1.2 Brookfield, Massachusetts, attacked and burned by Nipmuck forces during King Philip's War, August 1675. From a nineteenth-century engraving, artist unknown.

Source: California State Library, San Francisco State University.

Native Americans, but, beginning in the 1640s, they turned to missionary work as a means to pacify local tribes and avoid repeating the terrible slaughter of the Pequot War. The great irony, of course, was that this effort now provided the colonists with an accessible killing ground.

Fearing annihilation, the Native Americans adopted colonial military methods. They burned settlements, attacking 52 of 90 settlements in 1675 alone, completely destroying 12. Entire families were massacred, and churches burned to the ground. So great was the indigenous success at the beginning of the war that the Narragansett boldly proclaimed that the English god had abandoned the Puritans and was now with them. By the end of 1675, the Puritan colonists were in severe trouble. Frontier settlements lay empty as the population fled to the relative safety of more densely populated coastal areas. The flood of refugees squeezed food supplies because few farmers were willing to risk their lives to bring in the crops needed to feed the burgeoning population. New England was in a state of shock and denial—could God really have forsaken the Puritans, and was he punishing them for failing in their dedication? It appeared so. The question now was how to regain control of the crisis and reclaim God's favor. Militant revenge with God's blessing was the answer.

Unable to bring the raiding Indians to battle, colonists turned instead on the peaceful Native Americans in the prayer towns and noncombatants in indigenous villages. An intra-colonial force of soldiers massacred more than 500 Narragansett, mostly women and children, in what the colonists called the Great Swamp Fight of December 1675. After formally declaring war on Metacomet the previous September, colonists in Plymouth, Massachusetts, Rhode Island, and Connecticut came together in November to establish the Army of the United Colonies. Under the command of Plymouth governor Josiah Winslow, this force of 1,000 slogged its way through a severe snowstorm to attack a Narragansett fort and encampment in a frozen swamp near Kingston, Rhode Island. On December 19, the Army of the United Colonies attacked in bitter cold across a landscape covered with deep snow. Winslow's men set fire to wigwams and then waited to shoot down helpless men, women, and children as they tried to escape the flames. As many as 600 of the estimated 3,000–4,000 Indians were killed that cold day, while Winslow's force lost a not inconsequential 80 men, including 14 company commanders. Winslow ordered a withdrawal to allow the now disorganized Army of the Unified Colonies, low on supplies and suffering from cold, a month's recovery from its 'victory.'

By the spring of 1676, the Native Americans were out of food, low on powder, and unable to repair broken muskets. In exchange for a multitude of gifts, the Mohawk gladly attacked Algonquian villages in New England, further pushing New England's indigenous enemies toward complete collapse. A second but much smaller Army of the United Colonies, this time commanded by the able Benjamin Church, finally tracked down

Metacomet after several skirmishes in summer 1676. Metacomet was killed in battle on August 12, effectively ending the war. His head was severed and taken to Plymouth, where it was prominently displayed for years.

Considering the ratio of casualties to population, it had been a costly, bloody war. Indeed, it was among the deadliest in the history of North America. More than 1,000 colonists lost their lives in the conflict, as did more than 3,000 Native Americans. Once again, however, the colonists could recover while the Native Americans could not. Several chiefs and their families were executed as traitors, as were some colonists who had taken indigenous wives. Many Native Americans, including Metacomet's nine-year-old son, were sold into slavery in the Caribbean or to New England tribes that had fought alongside the colonists, while the remaining survivors either escaped to New France or eked out a meager existence surrounded by growing colonial settlements.

Having lost more than a third of their population in the war, and with another third having fled the region or been forced into foreign slavery, the indigenous peoples of New England could not recover from such attrition. In 1670, Native Americans accounted for 25 percent of the population of New England; by 1680, they made up only 10 percent. The colonial population increased from 52,000 to 68,000 during the same ten-year period. Contemporary estimates placed the war's cost at £100,000, an amount comparable to £10 million in 2019. Colonists suffered property losses over £150,000—an enormous amount for the period. Even though the colonists came out better in the end, the victory had a Pyrrhic touch, as it would take New England years to financially recover and rebuild what had been destroyed in less than three years of war.

Though costly in blood and treasure, the New England victory in King Philip's War was perhaps the most significant of all the colonial wars with Native Americans. The colonies unified in common purpose and never lost governmental control of the war. Militia provided ample sufficiently trained recruits to fill quotas for colonial regiments. Troops, arms, and ammunition were plentiful throughout the conflict. The social strength of the Puritan community often acted as a centralizing force for militia training and filling quotas. The local meeting house and its congregation provided more than a headquarters for building morale and encouraging the troops; it also served as a barracks, an advanced base in some cases, and offered a mostly reliable support system that often fed troops passing through the region.

The colonists benefited from what could be called a civil war among the region's Native Americans and were able to take advantage of their own efforts at intra-colonial cooperation in prosecuting the war. New England forces also willingly adapted indigenous tactics to the colonial strategy of total war, and they realized that threats to colonial security could not be handled by one colony alone—cooperation and unity were now critical to security and military success. While King Philip's War was not the only factor that forced England to reorganize its imperial administration, it indeed removed whatever obstacles there were to creating the Dominion of New England. Still, the New England colonies were in shambles despite the victory, and they had driven many surviving tribes into the open and waiting arms of England's enemies, the French.

There were, of course, dozens of other wars and hundreds of skirmishes pitting colonists against Native Americans, all the way up to the American War for Independence. The Algonquian fought the Dutch from 1643 to 1645 in Kieft's War and again in 1655 in the Peach War. The Iroquois and French squared off intermittently from 1642 to 1696, while colonists in Maryland warred on the Susquehannock from 1643 to 1652. Colonists in northwest New England fought the Abnaki in 1675–1678, 1702–1712, and again in 1722–1727. Virginia found itself simultaneously in conflict with Native Americans and 1676. North Carolina defeated the Tuscarora in 1712, while South Carolina warred on the Yamasee from 1715 to 1716.

Women in the Indian Wars

Women, indigenous and colonist alike, and slaves also participated in and were subject to the violence of war. For the most part, these groups engaged in violence only when they had to, but they were always part of the landscape of war.

Despite the militias' intent, they could not prevent or immediately react to every threat. One striking instance is the Abenaki people's 1697 raid on Haverhill, Massachusetts, during King William's War. Hannah Duston, her newborn child, and others of her town were captured; many others were killed. After several weeks passed and her baby was murdered, Duston led a successful revolt against her captors. In the process she killed and scalped several of the Abenaki who imprisoned her. When she and her fellow captives returned to Haverhill, she was lauded for her bravery. Although women colonists were not allowed to serve in the militia, they often had the skills, strength, and fortitude required to fight the enemy. Hannah Duston is remembered for those soldier-like qualities.

Conclusion

Native Americans slowly recognized that war with colonists meant war to the death. To have a chance at survival, they too had to burn and destroy as the colonists did. Colonists came to believe that militia worked, that the expeditionary model could defeat indigenous uprisings, and that cooperation with other colonies was necessary to fight Native Americans whose lands and tribal allies did not recognize colonial political boundaries. Moreover, colonial governments realized that exploiting indigenous political fissures to form alliances with rival tribes could tip the balance in these wars. New England certainly would have had a much more

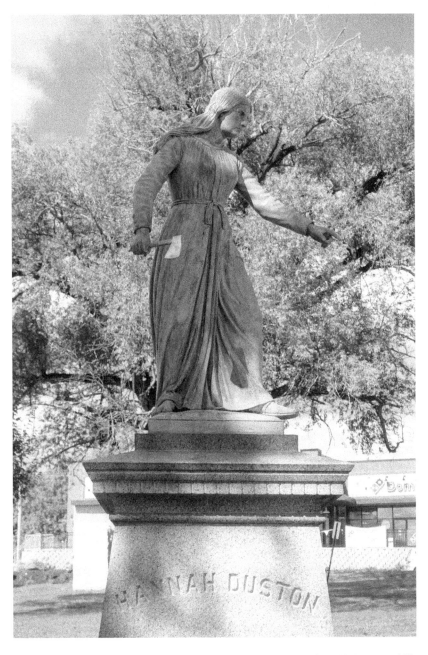

Figure 1.3 Hannah Duston Monument, by Calvin H. Weeks, 1879, Haverhill, Massachusetts.

Source: Wiki-Commons.

difficult fight on its hands had it not formed alliances with other tribes against Philip Metacomet and the Narragansett.

The American military experience in the New World began with violence. For the American colonists, the wars of the 1600s had transformed their European concepts of warfare into an American way of fighting that emphasized destruction of property and the annihilation of noncombatants as well as combatants. Success in these wars also gave the colonists an overblown sense of their own military capabilities, convincing them that their notion of the citizen-soldier was much more militarily effective and less threatening to personal liberties than were large standing armies. War in North America was about to broaden, however, to encompass more than conflict with Native Americans. Now that the various colonies of North America had matured and become more profitable, integral cogs in the imperial machines of England and France, they would be drawn into—and in some cases be the cause of—the wars of empire.

Further Reading

Ahearn, Marie L. *The Rhetoric of War: Training Day, the Militia, and the Military Sermon.* Westport, CT: Greenwood Press, 1989.

Cave, Alfred A. *The Pequot War.* Amherst, MA: University of Massachusetts Press, 1996.

Chet, Guy. *Conquering the American Wilderness: The Triumph of European Warfare in the Colonial Northeast.* Amherst, MA: University of Massachusetts Press, 2003.

Drake, James D. *King Philip's War: Civil War in New England, 1675–1676.* Amherst, MA: University of Massachusetts Press, 1999.

Ferling, John E. *A Wilderness of Miseries: War and Warriors in Early America.* Westport, CT: Greenwood Press, 1980.

Grenier, John. *The First Way of War: American War Making on the Frontier, 1607–1814.* Cambridge: Cambridge University Press, 2005.

Kupperman, Karen Ordahl. *Indians and English: Facing Off in Early America.* Ithaca, NY: Cornell University Press, 2000.

Lee, Wayne E., ed. *Empires and Indigenes: Intercultural Alliance, Imperial Expansion, and Warfare in the Early Modern World.* New York: New York University Press, 2011.

Lepore, Jill. *The Name of War: King Philip's War and the Origins of American Identity.* New York: Vintage Books, 1999.

Starkey, Armstrong. *European and Native American Warfare, 1675–1815.* Norman, OK: University of Oklahoma Press, 1998.

Steele, Ian K. *Warpaths: Invasions of North America.* New York: Oxford University Press, 1995.

Zelner, Kyle F. *A Rabble in Arms: Massachusetts Towns and Militiamen during King Philip's War.* New York: New York University Press, 2010.

2 The Colonies and Wars for Empire

Introduction

The colonial wars that culminated in the Great War for Empire had a profound effect on the American colonies, shaping colonial attitudes toward civil–military relations, civil liberties, intra-colonial cooperation, and even unity. Colonial wars also influenced already maturing concepts of colonial warfare, relations with Native Americans, and American exceptionalism. These wars were unique, as the strategic objectives of the warring powers in the Old World often did not match those of English ('British' after the 1707 Acts of Union), French, and Spanish colonists in the New World. In essence, although they were often fighting the same war, their reasons for doing so just as often differed.

The Colonies: Strategic Contours

As far-flung settlements became permanently settled colonies, their role in imperial trade and security systems became invaluable to their respective home countries. Throughout the seventeenth and eighteenth centuries, imperial competition between Great Britain and France, and to a lesser extent Spain, for control of North American trade created fluid alliances with Native Americans, who had become dependent upon trade with colonists for manufactured goods and gunpowder. By the beginning of the eighteenth century, the North American colonies were, indeed, worth fighting for. For Britain and France in particular, such substantial investments in the North American settlements represented the importance of these colonies to their imperial systems. Fishing, the fur trade, and timber, pitch, and tar for shipbuilding made the New England and middle colonies lucrative imperial possessions. In the Chesapeake and southern colonies, tobacco, indigo, rice, and other labor-intensive crops created an equally profitable credit-based trade system between the colonies and the mother country. For the colonies, such a situation required military organization, support, and participation, all of which evolved with violent effect throughout the colonial period in American history.

For the French in Canada and British colonists in the frontier regions of New England and western New York, the fur trade was king, and it was the fur trade that caused more mischief in the colonies than any other factor. Key to the fur trade were various Native American tribes, in particular the Algonquian, who traded with the French, and the Iroquois, who often traded with the British. In exchange for valuable pelts, British and French traders quickly addicted the Indians to metal utensils, steel knives, axes, mirrors, muskets, powder, lead for bullets, and a host of other goods with which Native Americans were unfamiliar before European contact. With the Native Americans dependent on European goods and the British and French just as dependent on profits from the fur trade, the stakes for controlling the trade skyrocketed.

It is essential to realize that for the British and French this situation took place within broader empires that incorporated possessions in the Caribbean, Africa, and southern Asia. Trade among these possessions created an elaborate financial network that required centralized regulation to balance regional deficits as well as increasingly costly navies and land forces to defend critical ports and far-flung colonies. The prevailing notion of imperial competition held that the only way to increase one's imperial might was to do so at the expense of one's imperial competitors. In other words, the imperial pie was finite; growing one's share of the pie meant taking slices from somebody else's empire.

In colonial North America, geography played a crucial role in the imperial game. The St. Lawrence River provided the only waterway to the French settlements at Quebec and Montreal, the Great Lakes, and the Canadian interior. Guarding the entrance to the St. Lawrence River was the impressive French fortress at Louisbourg on Cape Breton Island. Whoever controlled Louisbourg easily controlled the river. Of more direct importance for the colonists of New England and New York was the Hudson River Valley, its northern lakes, and the Richelieu River, which connected the British colonies to French Canada. To the west lay the Appalachian Mountains, through which only a precious few gaps, the main one along the Mohawk River, allowed armies to pass.

Consequently, the wars fought between the British and French, and their Native American allies, tended to concentrate around these natural invasion routes. For the French, an invasion through the Appalachian Mountains or down Lake Champlain could split New England from New York—a classic example of divide and conquer. For the British, controlling the St. Lawrence River would sever New France from its Atlantic lifeline. Geography lent itself to a strategy of conquest, and for both British and French colonists, the urge to expand territory and control trade proved too great to resist. The Spanish, increasingly pretenders in the imperial contest, found themselves subject to similar British restlessness in the Carolinas, Georgia, and the Caribbean.

King William's War

The first major colonial conflict coincided with the Glorious Revolution of 1688–1689 in England. What became King William's War began in 1688 in North America with French-supported Abnaki (a French corruption of the Algonquian name Wabanaki) raids on English settlements in Maine. New England governor Edmund Andros had ordered an expeditionary force of 1,000 volunteers and draftees to drive the Abnaki back into French Canada. The expedition, however, fell victim to winter, and Andros fell victim to the Protestant revolt against the Catholic King James II. The accession of Mary II and William III of Orange to the throne of England as a result of the Glorious Revolution of 1688 and the expansionist tendencies of Louis XIV of France initiated war in Europe and intensified the colonial conflict between Protestant England and Catholic France in North America.

France hoped to capitalize on what it assumed was administrative chaos in English North America because of the Glorious Revolution and the war in Europe. With Andros gone, France dispatched the aged but ambitious Count de Frontenac to Canada to oversee the conquest of New York. Frontenac had served as governor of New France once before and was familiar with colonial political and physical geography. His plan was straightforward—to attack New York via Lake Champlain and take Albany, and hope that the Iroquois would, as a result, abandon their English friends and side with the victorious French. From that point, the French assumed the entire colony of New York would collapse as a matter of course.

As is typical, the plans looked grand on paper but lost their appeal when actually implemented. When Frontenac finally reached the French capital at Quebec in late 1689, he found a colony in disarray. As was often the case for European possessions in the New World, there was a rather wide gap between what European imperial ministries supposed and what actually existed in the colonies. The French Canadians were in no condition to wage offensive campaigns against the English colonies.

Instead, Frontenac mounted several raiding expeditions using small units on multiple fronts to harass and terrorize the English. His so-called *la petite guerre* was soon commonly known as guerrilla warfare. In the winter of 1690, Frontenac sent a force of 160 Canadians along with more than 100 indigenous allies on a three-prong attack against New England. From Montreal, the combined force would hit New York, New Hampshire, and Maine. As had become the custom in colonial warfare, the French and their indigenous allies slaughtered their enemies. At Schenectady, they killed more than 60 men, women, and children. Similar fates befell English colonists at Salmon Falls, New Hampshire, and Falmouth, Maine, where more than 100 people were killed after having been granted safe passage.

On May 1, 1690, representatives from the now-defunct Dominion of New England met in Albany to organize a joint campaign to invade Canada in response to Frontenac's attacks. Two land forces, from New York and New England, would simultaneously invade Canada. A naval force would support these attacks by driving down the St. Lawrence River. Once again, great plans had disappointing results. The assault on Port Royal led by William Phips was the highlight, but his march on Quebec met not only French resistance but also smallpox. Neither side could marry its strategically ambitious objectives to its extremely limited resources. Phips lost Port Royal, and for the next five years, both sides resorted to guerrilla war, staging raids and counter-raids that further exhausted both sides. Colonists lived in constant fear of sudden attack by indigenous raiding parties that burned their farms and often took captives. Upon return to their families, captives, such as those taken at Deerfield and Haverhill in Massachusetts, often, but not always, told of horrific ordeals and brutal atrocities. To encourage terror, all of the English colonies paid bounties for scalps.

The war in Europe and North America ended in September 1697 with the Treaty of Ryswick, through which all gains reverted to *status quo ante bellum*. In North America, casualties were relatively light compared to those in earlier conflicts with Native Americans. Approximately 300 French were killed, along with 100 of their indigenous allies. The English colonists suffered around 650 dead from battle, disease, or captivity, while their Iroquois allies sacrificed more than 1,300 to combat and disease. Fighting along the frontier continued sporadically for the next few years, mainly between the indigenous allies of the French and the Iroquois nations. In the end, the Iroquois were severely mauled and significantly weakened, while the English colonies took years to recover.

Massive debt and a realization that individual colonies could no longer act unilaterally in military matters against the French, defensive or otherwise, forced the English colonies to reassess their strategic situation. Intra-colonial cooperation proved necessary for any future military adventure. With so much at stake in the imperial game, the colonies also realized that they needed more financial and military help from their mother country. Additionally, imperial growth and more permanent territorial security required that the French be removed from the North American scene, forcibly if necessary.

The English colonies had learned a hard lesson. Despite their loyalty to the king, they could not count on the Crown to protect them. Only a small handful of troops from England made their way to English North America. Their contribution was negligible. The colonists believed that the stakes were high in North America, and their new monarch had let them down. The colonists had to defend themselves, and whatever offensive campaigns they deigned to attempt had to come from colonial rather than Crown resources. In London, members of the Board of Trade saw the situation in precisely the same way, except for the critical difference that the board viewed the colonists as English subjects who were duty-bound to take care of themselves. From the standpoint of observers in London, excessive and irritating bickering among the colonies had stifled attempts to take Canada. Concerning colonial warfare, Frontenac's concept of *la petite guerre* and the value of Native American allies grew in strategic importance, even though such strategies would prove time and again to be fundamentally flawed. They would soon again be put to the test.

Queen Anne's War

Known in North America as Queen Anne's War, the conflict that broke out in the colonies in September 1702 was again part of a broader European conflict known as the War of the Spanish Succession. In North America, the French also again indirectly initiated hostilities. The French pursued a strategy of encirclement, hoping to strangle the English colonies along the Atlantic seaboard. Geographically, France was well on its way to achieving this objective de facto. From Port Royal near the mouth of the St. Lawrence River, around the Great Lakes to Fort Michilimackinac, and southward to the Gulf of Mexico at Biloxi and Mobile Bay, New France surrounded the British colonies and cut off Spanish Florida from New Spain (Mexico).

With Spain and France allied against England, the South Carolina legislature formed an expedition to seize St. Augustine, Florida, in September 1702. The expedition failed to take the formidable fortress there but contented itself with burning and destructive looting in the town, then withdrew. For the next few years, various expeditions from South Carolina, along with Chickasaw allies, raided with sporadic success along the Florida panhandle, threatening French Louisiana. These raids tended to avoid Spanish and French strongholds and concentrated instead on weakly defended Catholic missions. The French, however, had reliable indigenous allies of their own, including the Choctaw and Creek, who prevented a force led by South Carolina Governor James Moore from invading Louisiana in July 1704.

A combined Spanish–French force attempted to take Charleston in 1706, but was beaten back by South Carolina militia in strong fortifications. South Carolina's attempts to take Spanish Pensacola met with failure in 1707, as did forays into Alabama to engage the French garrison at Mobile. Logistical requirements limited whatever chance of success these expeditions had, and without the full support of local Native Americans, they really had no chance at all.

New York managed to stay out of harm's way in this war, concluding an uneasy peace with the Iroquois Confederation. New England was not so fortunate and, as was becoming customary, suffered the brunt of conflict because of its geographic position. Stirred by Puritan sermons, New Englanders lashed out at the local indigenous population, often disregarding attempts to discern friend from foe. Leadership failed early. Massachusetts Governor Joseph Dudley, for example, alienated the remaining local tribes and made little effort to find peace with the dangerous Abnaki. A conference in June 1703 promised peace, but English contempt toward Native Americans drove them again into the waiting arms of the French.

Dudley's attempts to recruit a strong militia force met with equal ineptitude, as only a few hundred were willing to leave their homes and communities unprotected to serve in an expeditionary force. All along the New England frontier, the French and their Native American allies attacked with vicious ferocity. Despite improvements in fortification, Deerfield was once again hit hard in February 1704 by a combined French–Abnaki force of more than 300, killing 50 colonists and taking more than 100 captives.

Benjamin Church, a veteran of many a conflict with Native Americans, was commissioned again in 1704 to raise a force of 550 to pursue the Abnaki and also take Port Royal. Typical of colonial warfare, Church's

Figure 2.1 An engraving of the fortifications at Port Royal, Acadia, attributed to Jean de Labat, 1702.

Source: Archives Canada-France.

army fell into predictable patterns of guerrilla war, raiding here and there as it made its way toward Port Royal. Church failed to take Port Royal, however, and was forced to return to Massachusetts at the end of the summer with little to show for the effort.

Dudley was undeterred and doggedly pushed for another expedition to Port Royal. He petitioned England for troops to take the strategically important fort but was denied. England remained convinced that colonial enterprises were just that—colonial. In 1707, Dudley gained permission from the Massachusetts General Court to try for Port Royal one more time. Under the command of Colonel John March, an intra-colonial expedition of 60 men from New Hampshire, 80 from Rhode Island, and two regiments from Massachusetts departed on May 13. The force of nearly 1,100 men approached Port Royal in two groups, forcing the French into the confines of the fortress. A well-coordinated siege appeared the obvious tactic, but the inexperienced and impatient colonial commanders badly bungled things, so much so that the militiamen lost all sense of discipline. They were not, after all, professional soldiers. They had not come all this way to sit and wait for victory through a lengthy siege.

With no plunder, no action, and little to occupy the troops' idle time, conditions quickly deteriorated. March decided to abandon the siege, but Dudley commanded him to return and engage the French. With an additional 100 men from Maine and a frigate, the expedition attacked Port Royal in August. The French had also received reinforcements and were able to hold off the New Englanders' disorganized attacks. March withdrew again. Officers on the expedition blamed one another for the adventure's failure. It was not a model intra–colonial effort by any means.

It took until 1709 for Dudley and Lord Lovelace, the new governor of New York (which had finally decided to enter the fray), to convince the Board of Trade that the only chance for success against Canada was a combined colonial–regular campaign. It was the first time the Crown would send regular troops in force to British North America. Two battalions of regulars along with six warships would join 1,500 volunteers from New York, New Jersey, and (for the first time) Pennsylvania. New England promised to send a 1,000-man force. The plan was for a two-prong attack on Canada: the first prong, which included the 1,500 troops from New York, New Jersey, and Pennsylvania under the command of former governor of Virginia Colonel Francis Nicholson, would leave from Albany and attack Montreal; the other prong, made up of New Englanders, would embark from Boston to join the British regulars against Quebec.

What looked so grand on paper quickly fell apart in the field. The Pennsylvania men never showed up. The British fleet carrying the regulars failed to appear. Nicholson departed Albany in May, slowly cutting a road to Lake Champlain. By September, with no sign of the promised British troops, Nicholson was ordered to stand down and demobilize. In

October, word reached the colonies that the decision had been made in England in late May to abandon the expedition; thus, no British troops would be sent to the colonies. Had the colonies kept an agent or representative in London, they would undoubtedly have received this incredibly important news much sooner. They would not make this mistake again.

The colonies tried again, this time meeting in Rhode Island. New York did not take part, but representatives from Massachusetts, New Hampshire, Connecticut, and Rhode Island agreed to petition for an attack on Port Royal. They wanted to move immediately to take advantage of the presence of a few Royal Navy ships nearby, but the captains of these vessels refused to help without orders from Nicholson's superiors. Instead, the colonies sent Nicholson to London to ask again for help.

In 1710, Nicholson was ordered to command colonial forces and 500 British Marines to take Port Royal. Finally, this time, the expedition was successful. The French had downsized the garrison at Port Royal, and as a consequence they surrendered in October. A British regiment was sent to garrison the critical fortress. The colonies, elated with their success, wanted more. Canada seemingly lay before them. Nicholson returned to London to push the old Montreal–Quebec plan and was armed further with an offer from the colonial governors that the colonies would pay for British regulars. Nicholson would command the colonials against Montreal, and the British regulars would attack Quebec. London agreed.

For the first time, then, Britain finally landed regulars in force in the North American colonies. Sixty ships with 5,000 regulars arrived in Boston in June 1711. The colonists were overjoyed at the sight; the British commanders, Admiral Sir Hovenden Walker and General John Hill, seemed less enthusiastic. They departed for the St. Lawrence River at the end of July. Then disaster struck. The fleet sailed into a deadly storm at the mouth of the St. Lawrence River and foundered. As many as 1,600 troops and sailors lost their lives as the ships crashed aground. General Hill wanted to continue toward Quebec, but the Royal Navy overruled him. The surviving vessels sailed for home, bypassing a return to Boston. Nicholson, by this time again at Lake Champlain, could hardly believe his ears upon receiving the devastating news. Once again, the two-prong attack had to be abandoned. Two expeditions had failed—two significant investments of scarce colonial resources and money lost. A third attempt was out of the question.

Events in Europe outweighed those in America. Peace came by treaty in 1713, although the fighting on both continents had halted by a truce in August 1712. This time *status quo ante bellum* did not rule the day, which gave the colonists some cause to rejoice. Great Britain gained Hudson Bay, Acadia (Port Royal), Newfoundland in North America, and St. Kitts and Nevis in the Caribbean, as well as strategically imperative Gibraltar from Spain. The Peace of Utrecht also preserved the Protestant throne in

Great Britain, permanently separated the French and Spanish Crowns, and gave Great Britain the massive monopoly on the slave trade, known as the *Asiento*, for 30 years. The balance of power in the New World now favored Great Britain, but only slightly. Without their knowledge or approval, the Iroquois became subjects of the British Crown. France still held Cape Breton Island and its fortress at Louisbourg. Ironically, casualties for the British colonials were extremely light, while the British Navy and Army suffered significant losses, mostly on the St. Lawrence River.

For the British colonies, initial euphoria gave way to a more mixed reaction to this apparent victory. Indeed, the colonies had shown they could cooperate, though unevenly. Their militia-trained expeditions had successfully defended the region against the French and, combined with British regulars, had provided significant and able forces. Yet, they again felt let down, even betrayed, by their home government. The perceived folly of British participation in the colonial war left the colonies with a feeling of disillusionment. Their strategic interests seemed to be growing apart from that of Great Britain, which held to a strategy of the balance of power in Europe combined with a conservative approach to colonial affairs. The colonies, on the other hand, wanted to eliminate France and Spain from North America. Canada was the grand prize. After two wars, France seemed just as entrenched as ever before in Canada, the Great Lakes, and Louisiana. The colonists would get another chance to gain at the expense of Britain's imperial rivals.

King George's War

King George's War, named for King George II of Great Britain, was an extension of what was known as the War of Jenkins' Ear (1739–1748) between England and Spain and the War of the Austrian Succession (1740–1748) pitting Great Britain and Austria against France, Prussia, and Spain. To kick off this convoluted conflict in America, Georgia's ambitious founder James Oglethorpe led an invasion of Florida in 1740. Indigenous allies, as was the norm, played a significant role, as Chickasaw, Creek, and Cherokee attacked Spanish missions and settlements in western Florida while Oglethorpe's force attempted to take St. Augustine. The plan resulted in a stalemate. For three years, raids and counter-raids resulted in little progress for the Georgians. South Carolina offered no help. Oglethorpe withdrew his force from near St. Augustine in 1743 when a Spanish fleet threatened his long and tenuous line of communication back to his Georgia colony.

Also, as part of this conflict with Spain, there occurred one of the worst disasters involving American arms. The Royal Navy developed an elaborate plan to take the Spanish port at Cartagena with a fleet of Royal Navy warships and a large force of colonials to supplement ground operations. The call for volunteers went out in 1740, with most colonies offering bounties and promises of pirate-like loot. Eleven colonies sent 36 companies of 100 men each, making up what was called the American Regiment, commanded by Virginia Governor William Gooch. Because most of the officers were also American colonists, military relations between the colonists and British professionals were taking an unprecedented approach. The regiment met the fleet, commanded by Admiral Edward Vernon, and British Army units, commanded by General Thomas Wentworth, in Jamaica. Their combined forces totaled more than 9,000 men.

The British professionals treated their American comrades in arms with unabashed contempt, assigning them the worst duties, poorest quarters, and most putrid rations. The campaign was a complete and utter disaster, encountering not only fierce Spanish opposition but also spring rains. Soldiers who survived the assaults against Spanish positions met an even stiffer foe in yellow fever, which killed hundreds. In mid-April, the expedition left Cartagena and foolishly tried to attack Cuba. By the time the American Regiment returned home, only 600 men were alive. Bitter resentment deepened as colonial governments blamed British incompetence for the disaster, which left the colonies much weakened against Spanish or French encroachments and made protection against raids by Native Americans that much more difficult. In yet another irony of the colonial wars, Captain Lawrence Washington survived only barely to return to his plantation along the Potomac River in Virginia in poor health. He renamed his farm Mount Vernon, honoring the admiral who so incompetently led the ill-fated expedition.

These events took place amidst yet another European conflict over royal succession, this time over the Austrian throne. It did not take much for this conflict to spill over into North America. Once again, Great Britain was pitted against Spain and France, and for the British colonies, Canada remained the strategic objective. For the most part, King George's War was a guerrilla war that inflicted only light casualties, conducted mildly destructive raids, and mounted small but failed campaigns. Ever-unlucky Deerfield, Massachusetts, was again on the receiving end of an assault. The strategic contours were similar to those in previous wars, including a British desire to conquer Canada, a French wish to divide and weaken the British colonies, and the desire of both to exploit Native American alliances against the other.

The major conflict of the war, not surprisingly, centered on the entrance to the St. Lawrence River. The French failed in an attempted assault on Port Royal, which the British had renamed Annapolis Royal in late 1744. In 1745, the British set their sights on Louisbourg, the principal thorn in their side that had long ensured the survival of French Canada. At the behest of Governor William Shirley, Massachusetts organized a huge —by colonial standards—expedition to take Louisbourg. Under the command of William Pepperell, 3,000 Massachusetts, 500 Connecticut, and 450 New Hampshire militia, along with cannon from New York, a ship from Rhode Island, and provisions from Pennsylvania and New Jersey, made up the most significant intra-colonial expeditionary force to date. The Royal Navy provided one 60-gun warship and three 40-gun warships. Their target was the fortress at Louisbourg, which was now a well-built, formidable Vauban fortification that some called the 'Gibraltar of the New World.' Its 30-foot-high walls were lined with more than 250 cannon. Intelligence reports, however, noted weaknesses, namely that only 100 of the guns were actually in place.

Moreover, poor food, tedious duty, and homesickness infected the garrison's morale. The high hills to the west of the town provided an unhindered line of fire down onto the fortress. Despite its reputation and impressive fortifications, Louisbourg was vulnerable to attack, especially siege.

Pepperell's force laid siege to Louisbourg for 49 days. The French apparently never suspected an attack from the landward side of the fort; thus, they had faced their guns out to sea to defend against naval bombardment and protect the entrance to the bay and river. The New Englanders captured the Grand Battery, exploiting two unrepaired breaches in the battery's otherwise well-defended wall. With cannon they peppered the town and fort. In mid-June, Pepperell and his Royal Navy counterpart Commodore Peter Warren planned a joint land–sea assault to take the fortress, but the French preempted these plans by surrendering on June 17. Low on supplies and food, the garrison could carry on no more. Louisbourg was in British hands at last.

It was a great victory, to be sure, but one tainted by events that reinforced the stereotypes that colonial militia and British professional military men held regarding each other. On at least two occasions, land assaults had to be redirected or terminated because large numbers of militiamen were drunk. In another instance, militia successfully stormed an island battery without drawing artillery fire from the fort, but their drunken cheers awoke the French cannon. Sixty militiamen were killed and 119 captured in the French counterattack. From the standpoint of the Royal Navy, such behavior was preposterous and typical of the poorly trained and poorly led colonial rabble.

The Royal Navy, however, also let down the colonials. After taking the fort, Commodore Warren insisted on leaving the French flag flying at Louisbourg to trick French ships into entering the harbor. It worked. Prizes quickly totaled more than £1 million, half of which went to the English Crown and the other to the Royal Navy's officers and crews that captured the ships. None trickled down to the colonials who helped win the fort and make such loot possible. Thus, while taking Louisbourg was a significant feat of arms and a long-awaited dream of the colonials, it did little to improve relations and perceptions between colonials and British regulars. Casualties were relatively light. The French lost 53 regulars killed out of a force of 600. How many of the 1,300 civilians in Louisbourg who lost their lives is unknown. The colonials lost approximately 140 men during the entire campaign, plus another 30 or so to disease, which is remarkable considering that at one point more than 1,500 men were prostrated with dysentery and other camp diseases.

For the British, the war began to go badly despite the victory at Louisbourg. Colonial legislatures failed to regularly pay their militias, causing some to mutiny in protest. The Iroquois joined the fight against the French in the west, but received little meaningful support from their British allies, leaving them feeling ill-regard toward their British 'Father.' The French took and destroyed the British fort at Saratoga. The Royal Navy showed its complete lack of colonial understanding by sending press gangs into Boston in November 1747. Governor Shirley suddenly had a violent mob on his hands, one that actually accosted and held as prisoners several naval officers. Shirley and the mob made an exchange— the officers for those who had been impressed, and then the Royal Navy rather hastily left Boston. No one seemed happy with this war.

In addition to conventional military operations, privateering was another vital part of strategy in King George's War. The lure of windfall profits from capturing enemy transports and supply ships made it very easy to bring daring sailors and ship owners on board for the war effort. Such practice had a long tradition in the colonial game. The mysterious English settlement at Roanoke (1585–1590), never intended to be permanent, was actually a base to support operations of British privateers—also generally engaged in slavery—against Spanish shipping. Hundreds of colonial, British, French, and Spanish ships prowled the Caribbean and other waters in search of prey. Investors poured money into what they believed would offer an easy return. In fact, a single prize could bring an average return of 130 percent on the original investment. Ports such as New York and Charleston financially benefited from privateering efforts during the war. For the British, the success and popularity of privateering was a double-edged sword.

On the one hand, privateering hurt the enemy and brought riches into increasingly strained colonial coffers. On the other, this same success and popularity took able seamen out of the available pool of sailors serving the Crown; for the Royal Navy, privateering meant increasing difficulty in finding experienced, worthy seamen to crew His Majesty's vessels. In the long term, the tradition of privateering helped give birth to an American navy during the War for Independence, and privateering's objective of individual gain for individual effort fit neatly into the independent attitude growing among many colonials.

The Treaty of Aix-la-Chapelle ended hostilities in October 1748, which for North America meant early spring 1749 because of communication delays. To the shock and disappointment of the colonists, Great Britain traded Louisbourg and Cape Breton Island to France to regain Madras in India. The one thing that seemed to secure the inevitable end of French Canada, control of the St. Lawrence River, had been lost in some faraway negotiation. New Englanders felt betrayed, to put it mildly. They had, after all, taken the fort without the help of the British Army and in their minds with only nominal support from the British Navy. For the home government simply to return the fort as if it were of little consequence only reinforced among colonists already deep suspicions about their mother country.

Despite this setback, events had inflated the colonists' sense of their own military prowess and deepened the contempt in which they held professional armies. The colonists also now firmly understood that the strategic contours of colonial wars demanded control of the St. Lawrence River. They knew they would have to fight to retake Louisbourg. Another 1,600 colonials, 3,000 French, and untold hundreds of Spanish and Indians had died from battle and disease in yet another colonial war that had given none of the three powers a clear advantage in North America.

The drain on imperial treasuries from these wars took longer and longer to recover, leading some among the British and French governments to urge a lasting military resolution to the imperial game. Believing the continuation of these colonial wars too costly in the long term, what was needed, they argued, was a final war for all of the pie rather than another fight for a mere slice.

The Great War for Empire (1756–1763)

The Great War for Empire was the first worldwide war involving the imperial powers, and it began in North America. While fought for the same strategic reasons as the previous colonial conflicts, this war—known as the French and Indian War in America and as the Seven Years War in Europe—would be fought in an entirely different way while confirming old assumptions and prejudices. For Great Britain, nothing less than the complete decapitation of the French empire in North America would suffice. Whereas in the previous wars, the colonies provided the bulk of manpower, materiel, financial support, and leadership, professional regulars from Great Britain would take the lead in this new conflict. While the earlier conflicts in North America were mainly a sideshow for continental operations, North America was the primary theater of operations in this war.

Consequently, the scale of the French and Indian War dwarfed all previous conflicts in North America. While colonial forces would continue their tradition of guerrilla war, the European professional armies warred in European style at places such as the Plains of Abraham, Fort William Henry, and Montreal. And finally, unlike previous wars, this conflict produced a clear and triumphant victor. The long-term repercussions of this major war could not have been told at its end, but in little more than a decade later, the colonials rose up in rebellion against mother Britain.

The conflict began in North America in 1754, well before the general war broke out in Europe and elsewhere between Britain and France. King George's War had left Britain in tenuous control of the lucrative and fertile Ohio Valley, using its sovereignty over the Iroquois as a pretext to lay claim to the extravagant colonial charters that asserted ownership of territory all the way across the continent. France, of course, laid claim to these same lands. With few troops and fewer outposts, both played a game centered on who could establish and hold a fort deeper into the other's claimed territory. In British North America, this time the Chesapeake colonies, Pennsylvania, and New York played the role of antagonists instead of New England. Speculators from these colonies began exploring in earnest into the Ohio Valley, forcing the French, who clung to the strategy of encirclement, to establish forts to stem British intrusion and lure the Indians caught in between into the French camp.

The French built a series of forts, erecting each one progressively southward from Lake Erie. Fort Presque Isle, Fort Le Boeuf, and Fort Machault followed French Creek to the Allegheny River. Virginians built a small stockade where the Allegheny and Monongahela rivers meet to form the Ohio River. The French could not let such a strategic post stand; they promptly ousted the Virginians and built Fort Duquesne. Virginia's Robert Dinwiddie took great umbrage at this insulting show of bravado and with the blessing of the British government, sent a young militia officer named George Washington and a regiment of Virginia militia to force the French to withdraw. The expedition was ultimately defeated by the French after a brief battle at a crudely constructed Fort Necessity in a clearing known as the Great Meadows in southwestern Pennsylvania. Surrounded, soaked by heavy rains, and with many wounded, Washington surrendered. Washington's not-so-glorious introduction to military command helped set in motion a series of events that started a war.

In response to French advances along the Ohio frontier, the representatives from the various colonies met at Albany in 1754 to discuss military unification and the establishment of a centralized indigenous affairs bureau to coordinate pushing the French out of the Ohio Valley. The Albany Plan of Union outlined such a collaborative effort, including the raising of regiments and commissioning of officers, but failed to receive the blessing of any of the colonial assemblies. Like previous efforts, this try at unification also failed.

The French would not withdraw, forcing Dinwiddie and the British government to take the initiative in 1755. This time London would not leave the matter to the colonials, sending Major General Edward Braddock and two under-strength Irish regiments to Virginia to take Fort Duquesne. According to the plan, volunteers drawn in part from Virginia militia would augment the weak regiments. Ultimately, a force of 2,500—

including three independent companies of regulars, the two Irish regiments, units of Virginia, Maryland, and North Carolina militia, and some indigenous allies—slowly set off from Fort Cumberland, Maryland, in June 1755 for Fort Duquesne.

The experienced Braddock came to North America with preconceived notions of colonials, their military prowess, and how to deal with the French and Native Americans. He considered his colonial colleagues as amateur adventurers who had no clue as to how to organize and command a military campaign. Not surprisingly, Braddock got off on the wrong foot with colonial administrations when they refused to provide a common defense fund to cover Braddock's military expenses despite their offer to do so at the Albany conference in 1754. Pennsylvania provided no money at all, while the others offered disproportionate amounts at irregular intervals. Not without some justification, Braddock and his officers found the colonial expeditionary units lazy, poorly trained, and undisciplined—a rabble that slowed his progress and would lose the baggage were it not for the presence of the seasoned professional British Army officers. The British also did not like their colonial counterparts refusing to accept colonial militia and volunteer officers as equals. Clearly, ill feelings worked both ways, as egos got in the way of good sense. Indeed, George Washington, now a colonel in the Virginia militia, refused a temporary captain's commission from Braddock because he was, after all, a colonel. Still hoping for a more fitting commission in the British army, Washington served with Braddock as a civilian volunteer, hoping to earn the British general's good graces and be rewarded with the coveted officer's commission. Braddock, however, held no high opinion of colonial military capabilities, particularly those of militia officers, and loathed having to come out to the wilderness to clean up what he considered the colonists' mess.

It took weeks for Braddock's force and its long baggage train to cut a path through the thick forests. After slogging his way through miles of densely wooded hills—on its own a significant feat of logistics—Braddock ordered and accompanied part of his force forward to cross the Monongahela above Fort Duquesne. Poor reconnaissance allowed this advance force to walk right into an advance party of French regulars, Canadian militia, and their Native Americans allies. The British, in a tight but lengthy marching formation, were completely surprised by the smaller French force that had enveloped them. Because of the narrow path, the British rear bunched up against the forward position, causing panic and confusion. Braddock fell, mortally wounded. With many British officers killed or wounded, George Washington stepped in to coolly help much of the British force get out of the debacle and make its retreat.

Braddock's defeat was a thorough disaster for the British, who lost 63 officers and 914 men killed or wounded against French losses of 23 dead and a handful of wounded. The French and their indigenous allies stayed hidden in the thick brush, firing into the British mass with deadly effectiveness. As they had been trained to do, the British regulars stood and fought but many of the Americans fled. This was an inauspicious beginning to a war that for any hope of success would require cooperation between the British regulars and the colonials. After hastily burning most of the wagons and supplies, the British and American survivors retreated to Fort Cumberland, leaving Braddock's newly cut path wide open to the French, and Washington sorely disappointed.

Braddock's failed approach to Fort Duquesne was part of a three-pronged British strategy to push the French back into Canada. By taking Fort Duquesne in the Ohio Valley, Fort Niagara and Fort St. Frederic in New York, and Fort Beauséjour off the Bay of Fundy in Nova Scotia, the British hoped to put the French on the defensive and open their offensive campaign to finally take Canada. The British navy would harass French troopships bound for Canada, which had already received 78 companies of French reinforcements.

While Braddock met disaster at Fort Duquesne, a Massachusetts force of 2,000 militia under John Winslow and some British regulars under the command of Brigadier General Robert Monckton set sail in May 1755 for Nova Scotia to secure Fort Beauséjour. The force landed at Fort Lawrence, on the British side of the vague boundary that separated British Nova Scotia from French Acadia. When Winslow and Monckton arrived at Fort Beauséjour, they found the fort ready to give up. A British agent provocateur named Thomas Pinchon had convinced the French garrison that resistance was futile. After a brief and mostly phony siege of four days, the French capitulated. On June 17, the British quickly took nearby Fort Gaspereau. The British now controlled Nova Scotia, except for the perennial thorn that was Louisbourg.

What followed in Nova Scotia eerily resembled ethnic cleansing efforts of the more recent past. Many French Acadians refused to take a loyalty oath to the British Crown. The British governor of Nova Scotia, Charles Lawrence, distrusted Acadians who did accept allegiance and ordered the entire population deported. Close to 7,000 were eventually dispersed among other colonies and Louisiana. They were allowed to take only what they could carry, sometimes nothing at all. The British destroyed their homes and the dikes they had built to contain the saltwater tides, and then attacked the Micmac tribe who had been friendly to the French. Many issues motivated the expulsion of the Acadians, including thinning out Catholic influence amongst the British Protestant majority and opening Acadia to new British colonization. Nevertheless, removing an entire civilian population was an unprecedented act by one European colonial power against another.

Papers found in the smoldering remains of Braddock's baggage train near Fort Duquesne revealed to the French the nature of his plan to attack French Canada. As a result, the French reinforced Fort Niagara and Fort St. Frederic and made plans to move on Fort Oswego on Lake Ontario. The Native

Figure 2.2 Painting of Lt. Col. Washington on horseback during the Battle of the Monongahela, *Régnier*, 1834.

Source: Library of Congress.

American allies that Braddock had counted on to rally to the British never materialized because word spread of his death and defeat. Instead, they joined the French and raided up and down the Virginia, Maryland, and Pennsylvania frontiers, killing more than 700 settlers. Pennsylvania again failed to organize militia and opted to pay settlers in the far reaches to defend themselves. Things looked bleak, indeed. Other than the success in Nova Scotia, reverse after reverse hit the colonies and the British Army.

Governor Shirley, who took over as commander-in-chief after Braddock's death, failed to attack Fort Niagara. Under temporary major general and superintendent of indigenous affairs for the northern colonies William Johnson, a force of 1,200 that was supposed to take Fort St. Frederic narrowly escaped a Braddock-like disaster at the southern end of Lake George in September 1755 to earn a minor victory in the Battle of Lake George. Rather than following up to destroy the French opposition and take his objective, however, Johnson regrouped and began building Fort William Henry. He quickly lost control of his ill-disciplined colonial troops, who wanted higher pay and to return home, costing Shirley opportunity and initiative.

Governor Shirley then tried to reinforce Fort Oswego in early March 1756. The first attempt to get much-needed supplies and men to the fort was met by a French–Native Americans ambush and the destruction of Fort Bull, whose inhabitants were put to the sword by the French. Lieutenant Colonel John Bradstreet led another expedition to Fort Oswego, reaching the beleaguered post in late May to deliver desperately needed food and ammunition. On his return, however, Bradstreet and his relief expedition were ambushed but managed to recover and inflict heavy casualties on their French attackers. This engagement proved only a flickering bright spot for the British, for Bradstreet's commander, Governor Shirley, was relieved in late March and replaced by a new commander-in-chief, Lord Loudoun, who had little sympathy for colonial concerns. Major General James Abercromby, a British regular, took command of all colonial forces. Abercromby promptly ignored all counsel from his colonial officers and the colonial governors, creating more antagonism between the colonies and Great Britain.

The French also received a new commander that May. The Marquis de Montcalm arrived in Canada to take over French regular and colonial forces just as England formally declared war on France. Like Frontenac years before, Montcalm was appalled at what he found in Canada—corruption in the colonial administration, incompetence at all levels, and no strategic direction for the hostilities in North America. Montcalm's hands would always be tied, however, because he was subordinate to Canada's corrupt and ambitious governor, the Marquis de Vaudreuil.

Ignoring Bradstreet's warning that Oswego was highly vulnerable, Abercromby was slow in sending Major General Daniel Webb to reinforce the garrison. Montcalm took the initiative and captured Oswego in August 1756 with little resistance. Indigenous allies of the French ambushed the British survivors who had been promised safe passage back to Albany. All of Lake Ontario was now under French control, as was the line of communication down to Fort Duquesne.

Despite alienating the colonials, Lord Loudoun demanded more colonial regiments, more substantial material support, and more money from the colonies he had been sent to defend. The situation had long since reached the crisis point, yet to his great frustration the colonies failed to cooperate. Colonial experience held that militia stayed close to home to defend their own frontiers. British authorities had confused local militia units with colonial expeditionary units and thus could not grasp why the colonies would not provide more men. The answer was simple—militiamen defended frontier settlements; expeditionary units were drafted from militia, but only under the proviso that enough men remained to defend the home colony.

Virginia and Pennsylvania spent their money in building defensive forts along their frontiers to defend against French–Native Americans raids. These forts, which were expensive to build, garrison, and maintain, left little money to contribute to the overall effort. New York and New England were ordered to use their own militia for defense and to fill large quotas for

Figure 2.3 The French and Indian War.

expeditionary forces. Only New York managed to fulfill the quota, and even then superficially because men deserted or quit service as soon as their brief enlistments expired. Officers had their problems, too—even the highest-ranking colonial officer had to answer to captains in the British army. Nonetheless, overall command of colonial forces remained with Lord Loudoun, even after he violated colonial enlistment regulations by trying to disband colonial units and enlist the individuals into regular British units.

Amidst these troubles, Webb dawdled, never making it to Fort Oswego, and in fact, blatantly avoided its defense. Loudoun ordered General Edward Winslow and his colonials to abandon an attack on Fort Ticonderoga on Lake George and return to defend Albany from an enemy that, in reality, was nowhere near. Loudoun then relieved Winslow and left the colonials behind, deciding that only regular British forces could win this war in North America. Manpower shortages, however, forced Loudoun to have a change of heart. He personally led an American detachment from New York to link with British regulars at Halifax in preparation for an assault against the grand prize, Fort Louisbourg. The expedition failed horribly, never managing to assault the fort, and losing almost 300 men to disease in the process. By August 1757, Loudoun abandoned the plan and returned to New York.

Montcalm hoped to finally realize a principal French strategic aim of the colonial wars—to control the waterways from the St. Lawrence, down the Richelieu River, Lake Champlain, Lake George, on to the southern end of the Hudson River, which would put French forces in the heart of New York. The ineptness of British commanders almost made this hope a reality. In early 1757, Webb went back out with 4,000 men and encamped at Fort William Henry, sitting idly by as Montcalm built up his French and Indian forces at nearby Fort Ticonderoga. When he finally decided to move, he went down the road to Fort Edward, leaving Lieutenant Colonel George Monro with 2,400 men to face Montcalm's 9,000 regulars and Indian allies. On August 9, Monro had little choice save capitulation, as his men were wracked with disease and without food. Webb made no effort to trek the ten miles to save Monro. Once again, warriors ignored the guarantee of safe passage and attacked Monro's men as they left Fort William Henry. The exact number of massacred soldiers, families, and camp followers is unknown, but estimates range from 200 to 1,500. The French stood by and did nothing to stop the murder. They may, in fact, have encouraged it, using the Native Americans to spread terror in the northern British colonies.

Incredibly, more than 4,000 hastily mobilized New England militia, requested in panic by Webb, suddenly arrived at Fort Edward just after Fort William Henry fell. In deciding not to move, Webb had little extra to feed and house this militia force, compelling him to send the militia home. For New England, mustering this massive force was yet another wasteful expense of money and manpower and only deepened the fissures between the British Army and the colonies. It was the low point of the British war in North America.

Meanwhile, in England, Lord Cumberland's government collapsed, enabling the very able and energetic William Pitt to take power and dramatically change British imperial strategy. Until that time, England took a Europe-first approach to imperial conflict. Pitt, however, had other ideas. Beginning in December 1756, when he came to power, and carrying through until late 1757, Pitt worked to change the strategic outlook of Great Britain's war plan despite strong opposition in Parliament (Pitt actually lost power in April 1757 before regaining control in June of that year). The result was a complete turnaround in the way Great Britain prosecuted the war. Pitt recognized that North America, rather than the European continent, was the key to the war if not the entire British imperial system. Holding France where it was strongest—on the European continent—would allow Great Britain to shift its might to strike France where it was weakest—Canada.

The Royal Navy would have to take firm control of the Atlantic and thereby strangle French supply lines to North America. Additionally, the British Army would have to be reinforced in North America. Moreover, Great Britain would have to rely much more heavily than ever before on the cooperation of volunteer colonial forces in joint campaigns aimed at conquering French Canada. By attacking the sources of French wealth—Canada, French colonies in Africa, India, and the West Indies—Pitt saw a way to bring France to its knees. Victory over France would leave Great Britain as lord and master of the world's imperial system.

To achieve his strategic aims, Pitt first had to repair the damaged relationship between Great Britain and its North American colonies. Knowing that the colonies had been regarded as unruly and undisciplined subordinates, Pitt began to treat them as valued allies in a common cause. He rescinded military authority over colonial governors and assemblies, restoring the traditional administrative chain of command that came from the British secretary of state for colonial affairs down to the governors and assemblies. In addition to acquiring financial subsidies from the colonies to support the colonial war effort instead of forcing the colonies to contribute levies, Pitt hoped that restoring a degree of autonomy to the colonies would induce rather than compel colonial cooperation and, indeed, patriotism. In 1758, he went even further to address poor relations between colonial forces and the British army by decreeing that all colonial officers would be treated as equals to their British regular equivalents rather than as subordinates. This was a significant change for the colonists, and Pitt's recognition of the problem went a long way toward rebuilding colonial trust and confidence in his plan for victory over France.

The colonists certainly desired a change in the Crown's attitude toward them after the failed attempt on Louisbourg and the loss of Fort William Henry in 1757. Pitt recalled Loudoun in December 1757, replacing him with General Abercromby. Massachusetts Governor Thomas Pownall praised Pitt's new approach to colonial affairs and, with the enthusiastic support of the Massachusetts Assembly, authorized a new army of 7,000 volunteers. New campaigns signaled renewed offensives against French Canada in 1758. General Geoffrey Amherst carried Pitt's banner to take Louisbourg, while Brigadier General John Forbes was entrusted with an attack on Fort Duquesne. Abercromby led a force of 16,000 in July 1758 to invest Fort Ticonderoga. Abercromby split his army, failed to wait for his artillery, and showed little imagination in his repeated frontal assaults against Montcalm's well-entrenched and well-reinforced French fort. What appeared to be assured defeat for the French—they were prepared to beat a hasty retreat to Fort St. Frederic—turned out to be a stunning victory. Abercromby turned tail and retreated to Albany.

Amherst's campaign against Louisbourg, however, brought the British effort out of what must have seemed its lowest point. While Abercromby was meeting with self-inflicted disaster at Ticonderoga, Amherst, and a force of 9,000 regulars and 500 colonials, ferried by a fleet of 40 vessels, began a textbook siege on Louisbourg. Starting June 8, British troops under James Wolfe began digging the trenches that signaled the beginning of a siege. Louisbourg could be overcome—according to the military architect Vauban, who originated the fort's style—by the principles of siege warfare. With no relief from the outside, a besieged fortress could not hold out against a well-supplied siege.

Siege warfare required the attacker to patiently dig a series of alternating parallel and approach trenches, slowly moving to within cannon range of the fortress walls. Once within range, siege cannon pounded the fortress walls, creating numerous breaches. The perfect siege, however, would not require a dangerous infantry attack into these breaches, for the besieged fortress would surrender, realizing that breached walls made defense futile. Typically, however, defenders did whatever they could to delay the unavoidable; musket and artillery fire and small harassing raids on the 'sappers' could only temporarily stop the digging. Vauban had concluded that a properly invested siege would bring a fortress to its knees in 40 days. Louisbourg took six weeks. By July 26, Louisbourg had fallen. Amherst and Wolfe had conducted one of the more effective Vauban sieges in history.

With Fort William Henry in fresh memory, however, Amherst and Wolfe refused the honors of war to the Louisbourg defenders. Wanting to avoid revenge for those slaughtered after the fall of Fort William Henry, Amherst closed Louisbourg to plunder. Also, although Amherst deported Louisbourg's residents to France—a fate similar to the Acadians' in 1755—he allowed them to keep their possessions. French soldiers were made prisoners and sent to England to sit out the rest of the war. Pitt wanted Louisbourg as much as any other prize in North America. He had every intention of keeping the fort in postwar treaty negotiations, a much easier task with the fortress in British hands. Pitt also wanted to end French harassment of British shipping and open the Grand Banks to the British fishing industry. With Louisbourg under British control, the Prime Minister could achieve all of these objectives.

Not wanting to incur Pitt's wrath for his failure at Ticonderoga, Abercromby sensibly gave Bradstreet the go-ahead to lead an oddly mixed force of fewer than 135 regular troops with substantially more than 2,000 colonials and 70 Iroquois warriors for an attack on Fort Frontenac on Lake Ontario. Bradstreet was no genius; nevertheless, he understood speed and logistics. Badly outnumbered and poorly supplied, the French had no chance against Bradstreet's force. Warned of the impending British approach, the French capitulated. Taking Fort Frontenac helped soften the disaster at Fort Ticonderoga, for without Fort

Frontenac, the French supply line to Fort Niagara and Fort Duquesne was cut. For the first time, the British controlled Lake Ontario.

The fall of Fort Duquesne topped off the remarkable British turnaround in 1758. The French garrison at Fort Duquesne, under the command of Francois-Marie le Marchand de Lignery, was small, poorly supplied, and under strained relations with its indigenous allies. Brigadier General John Forbes had been charged to lead the British expedition to Fort Duquesne. Forbes had to overcome many obstacles just to get the expedition on its way. Basing the campaign in Pennsylvania, Forbes and the Pennsylvania assembly butted heads over logistical and manpower matters. They finally reached a compromise that opened the colony's store of arms and ammunition to the British and required Pennsylvania to raise a regiment of 2,700 volunteers for the campaign. Native American troubles also hampered British preparations because well-intentioned, Quaker-supported peace initiatives muddied Forbes's negotiations with the Iroquois, Cherokee, and Catawba intended to convince the tribes to join the campaign. In the end, the Treaty of Easton settled few issues except to ease relations among the rival Indians and secure their allegiance to the British Crown.

To add to his troubles, Forbes fell desperately ill and had to be carried by litter to Carlisle. There, he found confusion: the supply train was in disarray; colonial 'volunteers' from Pennsylvania and Virginia were the most ragged lot Forbes had ever seen. An emboldened Colonel George Washington of Virginia pleaded with Forbes to use Braddock's Road to approach Fort Duquesne. Instead, Forbes decided to cut his own road through western Pennsylvania.

Once again, the colonials failed to endear themselves to the British army. In addition to the ragged Pennsylvanians and Virginians, North Carolina sent an ill-equipped group of 300 men, while South Carolina and Maryland, seeing no advantage to participating in such an expedition, sent none. Once again, the colonies presented independent self-interest that highlighted their disunity in the face of crisis. Taxation, manpower, and regional security limited broader colonial vision, leaving the British army, and Forbes in particular, with a reinforced prejudice against colonial provincialism.

Under these circumstances, Forbes forged ahead, as his men painstakingly cut a road toward the French outpost. Rain, mud, desertions, and supply problems harried Forbes and his men throughout the campaign. The French were in equally bad straits but found brief success on the battlefield by defeating a British reconnoitering party of 800 men, which was surprised that the French attacked instead of remaining inside the fort. Still, French commander Lignery had to take excessive risks to defend the post. He tried a preemptive raid on Forbes' advance column on October 12, but the assault failed and lost Lignery his Native American allies, who saw little point in the endeavor. Fewer than 1,000 French soldiers remained to face the 5,000 British. Low on supplies and morale, the

French decided to withdraw on November 24, burning Fort Duquesne to the ground before moving to Fort Machault.

Forbes occupied the ruins on November 25, thankful that an assault against the formidable fortress had not been required. He rebuilt the fort, renaming it Fort Pitt, and he named the new settlement Pittsburgh—both in honor of the headstrong British prime minister. Taking Fort Duquesne was an achievement of immense importance for Pitt's strategic plan and further served to soften Braddock's defeat in 1755. However, not all was serene. Forbes' army of colonials rapidly disintegrated through desertion and expired enlistments. At the end of December 1758, fewer than 200 men garrisoned Fort Pitt. Fortunately, trade goods arrived in January 1759, to help improve relations with area indigenous peoples, and Forbes's replacement, Brigadier General John Stanwix, eventually brought more than 3,000 troops to keep the Ohio Valley free of the French.

With success won, Pitt had vital political support for the final conquest of Canada. He proposed a tidy plan to isolate western Canada from the St. Lawrence River by taking Fort Niagara and reinforcing Fort Oswego. British and colonial forces would simultaneously drive into the St. Lawrence Valley via Lake Champlain, a movement that would place the British at the gates of Quebec. By July 1759, British forces under Brigadier General John Prideaux were laying siege to the French garrison at Fort Niagara. In June, an army of more than 9,000 under the command of British General James Wolfe approached Quebec from the north shore of the St. Lawrence River, probing for weaknesses in the city's defenses. Montcalm, in command at Quebec, began a long and tedious game of cat and mouse with Wolfe, trying to outwit and outlast his British opponent. Wolfe initiated a siege that lasted until September.

Meanwhile, at Fort Niagara, an impatient Lieutenant Colonel Eyre Massey, in command following the untimely death of Prideaux, ordered a hasty but successful assault. Participation by young Joseph Brant and several hundred warriors from the Iroquois Confederacy played a significant role in Massey's victory. The fort surrendered on July 23. Western Canada had now been cut from the St. Lawrence River. On the Lake Champlain front, the French abandoned Fort Ticonderoga and Fort St. Frederic to General Amherst in late July and retreated toward Quebec. By late summer, only Quebec remained, a symbolic heart keeping French Canada alive.

Quebec was the decisive theater for the war in North America, and the battle there placed Wolfe and Montcalm at the forefront of the pantheon of great generals of Anglo-French conflict. Both died during the climactic, European-style battle on the Plains of Abraham outside the city. Wolfe used stealth and amphibious operations to land a large force above Quebec, completely surprising Montcalm, who assumed the British would assault the town proper. On the Plains of Abraham, Montcalm hastily organized his French soldiers into line to meet the

British head-on. Montcalm ordered a charge that was received by a well-disciplined British line that held its fire until the very last moment. The effect was devastating. Montcalm's attack was repelled within 15 minutes. Out of an initial force of 4,500, 200 French and French colonial troops lay dead, while another 1,200 were wounded. The British lost 60 killed with another 60 wounded. Quebec formally surrendered on September 18. More than 80 years of colonial warfare for control of North America had culminated in a European battle lasting little more than a quarter of an hour. France was finished in North America.

While a few more battles occurred—namely, along Lake Champlain and, incredibly, a failed French siege of Quebec—the British were content to consolidate their hard-won gains during the winter of 1759–1760. Amherst assaulted Montreal in September 1760, forcing Governor Vaudreuil to surrender the whole of Canada. Detroit fell to Major Robert Roger's famous Roger's Rangers that same month, solidifying Britain's hold on the French province and swiftly gaining the allegiance of Native Americans who had forsaken the French.

Not all of the indigenous peoples remained pacified, however. In the somewhat misnamed Pontiac's Rebellion, Ottawa, Seneca, Delaware, Iroquois, and Shawnee violently attacked the new British outposts in the west to take advantage of the French defeat. Before finally being put down, these loosely connected attacks killed more than 2,000 civilians as well as 400 British and colonial troops, and cost Native Americans untold losses from battle and disease.

The Treaty of Paris (1763) formally ended the Great War for Empire. The French imperial system was neutered, losing all its possessions in North America. Great Britain was now the unquestioned ruler of the high seas and an imperial superpower. Spain's late entry into the war against France was rewarded with French Louisiana. But the initial euphoria of victory soon wore thin for the Crown's loyal subjects in both Britain and the colonies. Taxes had reached unprecedented levels, yet the British treasury lay barren. His Majesty's army and navy now had to defend an empire twice as vast as it had been in 1754.

For the colonies, Parliament's new interest in colonial matters began to intrude on what had been a tradition of salutary neglect. Postwar depression hit the colonial economy hard. A policy of taxation from the Crown caused colonial rumblings of reform if not independence. Victory in a war that had been fought to solidify and strengthen the British imperial system now threatened the system it was intended to preserve. As an example of these difficulties, Pontiac's Rebellion caused Parliament to pass the Proclamation Line of 1763, prohibiting settlement west of the Appalachian Mountains. The arbitrary move infuriated colonists, who felt they had fought and sacrificed for the right to capitalize on these vast and fertile lands. Parliament was trying to prevent future conflict in North America, but the colonists wanted to claim what they considered their just reward for the victory they helped achieve. Parliament and the colonies seemed to be headed in opposite directions.

In colonial and military matters, the war had profound and lasting results. Pitt's attempt at reconciliation with the colonial administrations failed in part because the colonial assemblies took advantage of Pitt's generosity to further their own independence in military affairs. Colonial assemblies argued with Parliament over money, control, and prerogative concerning British regulars, whom they considered under their jurisdiction. This was especially the case concerning quartering troops, an issue on which the assemblies gradually took the lead. Since British regulars had rarely visited the American colonies before this conflict, few barracks existed. As a result, British commanders occasionally forced colonists to quarter troops in their homes. Quartering troops in private homes without the owner's consent violated the spirit of English law and tradition, and colonists would not soon forget the presence of British soldiers on their property. When Parliament attempted to impose quartering, the assemblies resisted.

The presence of large numbers of British troops, particularly in New England and the middle colonies, brought colonists unaccustomed to a military presence into close contact with regular British forces. The British army relied heavily upon recruiting colonials into regular regiments, but questionable recruiting methods made service distasteful to many colonists and caused petty but long-lasting rifts between British authorities and the communities from which they recruited. Indentured servants were a prime target of recruiters, a fact that aggravated colonists who considered indentures to be legally binding contracts. The British army, in essence, was undermining a contractual obligation and a long-standing, although dwindling, source of labor.

Moreover, the continuing conflict between British military authorities and colonial assemblies over enlistment quotas, money, materiel, and objectives left a bitter taste on both sides. Colonial assemblies felt threatened by what they perceived as an overt military threat to their governing prerogative, while British commanders such as Loudoun and Amherst were insulted by the impudent if not treasonous lack of deference to their command and judgment. British regulars stereotyped colonial volunteers as disorganized, undisciplined, and cowardly militia. Such a characterization completely misunderstood the American colonial militia system and its purpose of local defense.

In attempting to fulfill their enlistment obligations, many colonies resorted to impressing vagabonds, thieves, and other undesirables to clear out their towns and cities of an unwanted population. While many volunteers served with distinction, the bad apples at the bottom of the barrel polluted the entire lot in the eyes of the British regulars. From the viewpoint of the colonials, the British regular army mistreated them in almost every military arena—colonists tended to get the most undesirable duty, most inferior equipment, most cramped quarters, most rotten food, and perhaps most significantly the harshest end of military justice.

Despite the victory, the British perception of the colonists as unruly, ungrateful, and ill-mannered children hardened, while the colonists grew to see Britain as an overbearing, threatening, and unsympathetic parent who failed to appreciate the value of traditional liberties in the colonies. Although victory had come and benefited both Britain and colonies, the aftermath left discord festering in the British imperial house.

Slaves and Free Men

Just as during the earlier Indian wars, African American men were prohibited from joining the militia. Or, at least, African-American men were unwelcomed until the colonies could not recruit enough white men to protect the colonial frontier. At that point, authorities turned a blind eye to the legal exclusions and enlisted whoever was available and willing, regardless of race. Initially, slaves were taken into the ranks, most of their wages and any death indemnity going to their owners. Official records offer very little information about such men, sometimes only a single name or the name of their master.

A growing population of free African-Americans also enrolled in the militias, most often because they needed the pay or white neighbors who did not want to risk their own lives pressured them into service. As with enslaved African American men, there is little detail about the free men who fought unless, like Benjamin Gire from Grafton, Massachusetts, they received war-related disability payments.

Conclusion

These perceptions were all but confirmed for the colonists during the colonial wars, in which colonists proved their mettle against French and Spanish regulars, demonstrated an ability to think strategically, and established concrete notions of civil–military relations under colonial conditions. Their extraordinary but disappointing experience fighting alongside their British brethren left the colonies with lingering resentment. Selective memory held the citizen-soldier in much higher esteem than the professional regular. Still, the American colonists generally never fully appreciated that the security interests of the British Empire extended beyond the colonies' own immediate security needs.

It is indeed ironic that the colonies came away from the Great War for Empire believing that their way of war had stood the test when it was, in fact, the British professional regulars who had organized an effective strategy, commanded the campaigns, and fought most of the battles. The victory that so greatly benefited the colonies had, in truth, been won by

British know-how and experience. In fact, this same British army ultimately served as the model for the new American army that was born in 1775.

Further Reading

Anderson, Fred. *Crucible of War: The Seven Years' War and the Fate of Empire in British North America, 1754–1766*. New York: Knopf, 2000.

Barr, Daniel P. *Unconquered: The Iroquois League at War in Colonial America*. Westport, CT: Greenwood Press, 2006.

Boscawen, Hugh. *The Capture of Louisbourg, 1758*. Norman, OK: University of Oklahoma Press, 2013.

Brumwell, Stephen. *Redcoats: The British Soldier and War in the Americas, 1755–1763*. Cambridge: Cambridge University Press, 2002.

Dowd, Gregory Evans. *War Under Heaven: Pontiac, the Indian Nations, and the British Empire*. Baltimore, MD: Johns Hopkins University Press, 2002.

Ferling, John. *Struggle for a Continent: The Wars of Early America*. Arlington Heights, IL: Harlan Davidson, 1993.

Fowler, William. *Empires at War: The French and Indian War and the Struggle for North America, 1754–1763*. New York: Walker & Company, 2005.

Kidd, Thomas S. *American Colonial History: Clashing Cultures and Faiths*. New Haven, CT: Yale University Press, 2016.

Laramie, Michael. *King William's War: The First Contest for North America, 1689–1697*. Yardley, PA: Westholme Publishing, 2017.

Leach, Douglas Edward. *Roots of Conflict: British Armed Forces and Colonial Americans, 1677–1763*. Chapel Hill, NC: University of North Carolina Press, 1986.

Preston, David L. *Braddock's Defeat: The Battle of the Monongahela and the Road to Revolution*. New York: Oxford University Press, 2015.

3 Independence and the Birth of a National Military

Introduction

While the Great War for Empire had left Great Britain the primary global imperial power, the cost of the war and of now defending a more enormous empire placed even higher demands on a nearly empty British treasury. To raise revenue, station British regulars permanently in the American colonies, and restrict colonial settlement west of the Appalachian Mountains, Parliament inadvertently sparked a revolution that would cost the British Crown 13 of its North American colonies.

Born of this revolution, the United States of America and its fledgling military successfully fought a war for independence and then experienced postwar economic and political problems that forced the new nation to reconfigure its governing administration and its military establishment. Achieving this was difficult because the colonial traditions of loathing centralized authority, abhorring a standing military, and regarding militia highly survived the revolution and greatly influenced the way the new nation approached military affairs and national security.

Toward a Break with Great Britain

Despite the victory over the French in the Great War for Empire, Great Britain faced severe financial and strategic problems. The need for revenue to pay for the war and to sustain a permanent military presence in North America led Parliament to pass a series of revenue acts aimed at the colonists, who until then had rarely paid taxes directly to Great Britain. Having managed their own affairs for several decades, the colonists took for granted that Parliament's salutary neglect would continue. Beginning in 1763, however, this lax attitude toward the colonies came to an abrupt halt. A preemptive measure, the Proclamation Line of 1763, prohibiting colonial settlement west of the Appalachians, aimed to prevent further conflict with Native Americans. The colonists, believing western settlement a spoil of victory over the French, thought the Line an arbitrary restriction of their right to pursue their happiness.

Parliament then embarked upon a series of similar restrictive measures and revenue acts, each causing varying degrees of reaction from the colonies. The hundreds of thousands of pounds expended annually to maintain several thousand British troops in the colonies, Parliament asserted, was a cost that should be absorbed by the colonists themselves. Clinging to their militia tradition and distrust of standing armies, the colonists believed that the presence of British regulars was unnecessary and intrusive.

As revenue generators, the Sugar Act of 1764 and the Stamp Act of 1765 elicited fervent protests among some segments of the colonial populace. With a stagnant postwar economy and resentment against Parliamentary intrusion into what had been the purview of colonial legislatures, colonial resistance to these taxes erupted in a string of riots and attacks against tax collectors. A Stamp Act Congress of representatives from across the colonies met to formally protest the hated Stamp Tax. Parliament repealed both acts more because the taxes did not raise the intended revenue than because of colonial protest, but also reminded the colonies of Parliament's supremacy over the colonies through the Declaratory Act of 1766.

With tax revenue still far short of the amounts needed to relieve the debt and pay for British troops in America, Parliament tried again to tax the colonies through the so-called Townshend Duties. The colonists responded with nonimportation and boycotts of British goods. Outside the Boston customs house in 1770, British soldiers guarding the building squared off against an angry mob. Shots were fired, killing five Bostonians and wounding several others. Defended by the able John Adams, the British soldiers involved in the incident were mostly exonerated of any wrongdoing or malicious misconduct. This, however, did not stop the Sons of Liberty from turning this minor incident into the infamous Boston Massacre. Heightened tensions in Boston and severe losses for British businesses because of the nonimportation movement convinced Parliament to repeal the Townshend Duties in 1770.

The passage of the 1773 Tea Act placed the American colonies squarely on the path toward independence. Previous parliamentary measures and the colonial reaction to them had been relatively contained, but the Tea Act sparked more passionate widespread protest. In December 1773, the Sons of Liberty led a mob in dumping hundreds of pounds of the East India Tea Company's tea overboard from company ships anchored in Boston Harbor. Faced with wanton destruction of private property and angry stockholders, Parliament now had to respond with a firm hand.

The following year Parliament passed a series of punitive measures that the colonists collectively called the Coercive Acts. These included closing the port of Boston, limiting freedom of assembly across Massachusetts, and moving trials involving British officials and soldiers out of the colony. Moreover, the new Quartering Act allowed Great Britain to force colonists in Massachusetts to do what British subjects in England had been doing for decades—housing British troops in their own homes.

Boston already had a large garrison of British regulars, but now hundreds more poured into New England's main port. Finally, Boston was placed under martial law. While Parliament considered the rebellious colonists of Massachusetts primarily a localized problem, across the colonies many wondered how far Parliament would go to regain control not only of Massachusetts but of all the colonies.

The answer came in 1775. For over a year, the Sons of Liberty and Committees of Correspondence had been working feverishly to build colonial support for armed resistance against British intrusion into colonial affairs. The First Continental Congress met in Philadelphia to alleviate the crisis with the mother country and hesitantly began to prepare for the worst while hoping to find a peaceful resolution. Militias trained, gathered and stored arms, and listened to impassioned sermons and read political tracts urging the colonists to stand firm in defense of their rights as subjects of the British Crown.

In 1775, King George III declared Massachusetts to be in a state of rebellion and ordered the colony's militia to stand down. It did not, forcing the British military governor of Massachusetts, General Thomas Gage, into a showdown with the militia. In April, Gage sent 700 regulars to secure stores of arms held by militia near Concord. At Lexington, along the route to Concord, an advance party of British regulars found several dozen militiamen with muskets primed and at the ready awaiting them on the village green. The British ordered the colonials to disperse, after which shots rang out. It is not known who fired the first shot, but volleys were exchanged, killing ten Massachusetts militiamen. The British wisely withdrew from Lexington and doggedly fought their way to Concord, where they found several hundred militia also at the ready. After a fierce skirmish, the British withdrew—in orderly fashion at first, then falling into mass panic as militiamen took potshots at the retreating force all the way back to Boston. The British suffered at least 20 percent casualties among their total strength of more than 1,500.

In a matter of days, more than 20,000 militiamen besieged Gage and his garrison of regulars in Boston. The Second Continental Congress (1775–1776) formally reorganized the ragtag force surrounding Boston as a national or 'continental' army. On June 14, 1775, it created the Continental Army. The 'shot heard round the world' had now pushed the colonies past the point of no return. The first phase of the American Revolution had ended, as the national political institutions that had evolved since 1765 were now in place to conduct a war for independence. The second phase of the Revolution, the war itself, had now begun.

The War for Independence

It is extraordinary that the colonies ultimately managed to sufficiently unify themselves in common cause to build an army, attract the support of France, and defeat the most powerful military in the world. At first, the

Figure 3.1 A view of the town of Concord, April 18, 1775, engraving by Ralph Earl.
Source: The Miriam and Ira D. Wallach Division of Art, Prints and Photographs: Print Collection, The New York Public Library.

Continental Congress simply wanted Parliament to restore the rights of the colonies, but as this objective became less attainable, Congress decided upon independence as the only alternative. With no professional army, no navy, no money, no support from an outside power, a divided populace (many of whom did not want independence), and many poorly learned lessons in their collective military past, the colonies warred against the most powerful nation in the world.

In 1775, the colonies had a population of about 2.5 million, including almost half a million slaves. Great Britain, on the other hand, could boast a population several times that of the colonies as well as a professionally trained army of at least 50,000 men and a navy second to none in quantity and quality. Bookmakers would undoubtedly have placed the British as heavy favorites in this apparent mismatch.

The advantages and disadvantages for each side, however, did not stop at the mere number of population and troops. Consider that the American revolutionaries (or rebels from the British point of view) had the benefit of knowing the land, waterways, and the political mood of people across the colonies. This localism was a distinct advantage over the British, who often did not have as good a grasp of local conditions. The Americans also had the benefit of fighting a defensive war. In essence, they did not necessarily have to win—all they had to do was avoid losing. They fought for liberty, freedom, and rights that they had always assumed as British subjects. Still, they were not professional soldiers, had little money, and did not enjoy total popular support. Moreover, the colonies were united only in the cause for independence; beyond that they bickered amongst themselves over resources, men, and money throughout the conflict.

Despite their overwhelming military might, the British found themselves in a delicate spot. On the one hand, Parliament certainly had to preserve its control over the American colonies and could not let these rebels set the dangerous precedent of getting away with flouting the mother country's authority over the empire. On the other hand, the economic and philosophical arguments supporting the rebellion rang with some truth for many in Great Britain. How far should the British go to crush a rebellion of subjects of the British Crown? And once broken, then what?

Moreover, the sheer logistical requirements of a military campaign in North America were well known to the British. A war against American rebels could be an extremely costly war. Parliament never adequately addressed these problems, nor did it form a cohesive strategy in North America.

Both sides nonetheless attempted to develop strategies that played to their strengths and took advantage of the other side's weaknesses. For the Americans, forming an army that could stand against the British juggernaut was paramount. Since there was no center of gravity in the American colonies, such as a central city that if captured would cause the entire movement to collapse, such an army could move about the colonies and stay alive. It was imperative that the new army avoid a decisive battle with British forces. The Americans also needed the support of a foreign power. France was the obvious candidate. Having lost its North American possessions in the last war, France was eager to get back into the imperial game and break up the British mercantile system in North America.

At first, the British followed a strategy of containment. By containing the rebel cancer in and around Boston, the British army hoped to excise it before it spread to other parts of the colonies. After this strategy failed, the British then tried to lure the American army into a traditional set-piece battle in which the rebel force could be totally destroyed; such a decisive victory would end the rebellion. The problem was in determining exactly how to do this. Logistical needs tied the British to a base of operations, which in this case would have to be a deep-water port. Conducting operations away from such a crucial base was risky, as supply lines would get strung out and become vulnerable to rebel attack. With few roads and uncertain knowledge of the land, the British could not afford long campaigns deep into the American interior.

Of equal importance for both the British and the American revolutionaries was winning the support of unaligned colonists. Traditionally, historians have estimated that approximately one-third of the population supported independence, another third remained loyal to the Crown, and the remaining third did not lean either way. Convincing these unaligned people to join the cause for independence or stay loyal greatly influenced the way both sides fought the war.

The Northern Phase (1775–1777)

As more colonial militia descended upon the outskirts of Boston to contain British forces, the Continental Congress made its most monumental decision of the war. Even though there would be an army, each state demanded to retain its respective militia. Having a coexistent army and militia unintentionally created a dual army tradition in the new nation. An army was necessary, requiring not only soldiers to fill its ranks but someone to lead them. The Continental Congress simultaneously had to build the army while using it to fight the British. Moreover, Congress also had to find a commanding general to both form the militias into a usable force and lead the new army. Few in the colonies had that sort of military experience, and fewer still were willing to place their lives on the line for the cause.

George Washington, however, wanted the job and Congress gave it to him. He had been a delegate to both Continental Congresses and wore his Virginia militia uniform while Congress was in session. He was capable, had a commanding presence, had limited but valuable military experience, and served a broader political purpose for Congress, which needed to shape the rebellion into more of a 'continental' movement. As a Virginian, Washington was not part of the radical Massachusetts revolutionary crowd. But some feared that as a Virginian Washington would defend only Virginia's interests in the conflict. Washington promised that he would do what was best for the colonies as a whole, favoring no region or particular interest. He kept his word.

Washington's first task was to go to Boston and take control of colonial forces. Militia enlistments were expiring, and many men simply returned home. Washington had to recruit a new army in the field and keep the British contained in Boston at the same time. Washington's first big break came in early 1776 when a force under the command of Henry Knox brought 50 cannon from recently captured Fort Ticonderoga—a Herculean task considering the snow-covered terrain of the 300 miles to Boston. Washington had the guns placed on Dorchester Heights, where the barrels looked down upon the city, putting the British in an untenable situation. The new British commander, Major General William Howe, decided to withdraw from Boston in March 1776 to the safe confines of Nova Scotia, where he planned his next move.

In Nova Scotia, Howe decided to relocate his primary base of operations to New York City in August 1776. The previous month the colonies had unanimously declared their independence from Great Britain, making an official and hopefully permanent break with the mother country. Sensing that strong loyalist sentiment among New Yorkers would provide better accommodations for his growing force than would the uninviting citizens of Boston, Howe sent more than 30,000 men—supported by a large Royal Navy fleet commanded by Howe's brother Vice Admiral Richard Howe—to invest Manhattan Island. A smaller force of British regulars made their way down Lake Champlain from Canada to recapture Fort Ticonderoga and link with Howe in New York City.

In the meantime, Washington struggled to form an army and recover from Benedict Arnold's ambitious but unsuccessful invasion of Canada, undertaken in the vain hope of enlisting Britain's northernmost colony's support for the revolution. Taking a two-pronged pincer-like approach, one wing managed to take Montreal; but Arnold's men suffered tremendously from cold and exposure before reaching Quebec in December 1775. An assault on the fortified city failed, not least because of miserable weather and Arnold being severely wounded. The rebels laid siege to Quebec until the spring of 1776 when the arrival of British reinforcements forced them to withdraw. Battered and exhausted, Arnold's force withdrew southward, ending the gamble to make Canada part of the revolution.

Between his Continentals and militia Washington now had almost 20,000 troops. He took them to New York to defend the city against Howe's invasion. Recruiting men for the new Continental Army had been, and remained, extremely difficult. Fear of a standing army was the least of Washington's recruiting problems. Militia service carried more prestige, short enlistments, and, often, better supplies. Service in the new army, on the other hand, offered sustained privation, inadequate supplies, and little else. Still, despite a host of deferments and different ways to avoid serving, many men chose to serve in Washington's army. The Continental Army never reached more than half its authorized strength, and while men from all segments of American society served as soldiers, most came from the lower rungs of the colonial social ladder.

With his motley force of Continentals and militia, Washington set up to defend New York City by splitting his forces between Long Island and Brooklyn Heights. Howe coolly teased the rebels with the real threat of annihilation while offering amnesty for those who returned to the loyalist fold before the British launched the assault. In late August, Howe attacked and very nearly wiped out the Continentals on Long Island. Washington's forces on Brooklyn Heights barely escaped destruction by retreating to Manhattan. Howe may have allowed Washington to slip away in a fruitless effort to convince the Americans to give up the fight before the Continental Army was physically destroyed. Additional battles occurred in New York City, Forts Washington and Lee, and White Plains. Despite heavy losses due to combat, capture, and desertion, Washington managed to get a small portion of his original force out of New York and into New Jersey. He now had less than 3,000 men. It was, perhaps, the low point of the war for the Americans.

Although Arnold had managed to stop the British approach down Lake Champlain, Howe comfortably occupied New York City. Washington laid low in New Jersey throughout the fall and winter of 1776–1777 so that he could rebuild his fading army. Making no progress in his efforts to get the rebels to surrender, Howe reluctantly sent the able General Lord Charles Cornwallis into New Jersey in pursuit of Washington. In a bitter

Figure 3.2 The War in the North, 1775–1777.

winter campaign, during which the Americans more frequently employed guerrilla tactics than they fought a conventional war, Cornwallis and Washington dueled across the New Jersey countryside, fighting for food and forage and inflicting as much damage upon the other's force as possible. In Congress, some delegates argued that Washington should be sacked for incompetence. This was not the last time that Congress and Washington were at odds; fickle delegates repeatedly demanded that Washington be replaced. In turn, Washington refused to hide his frustration with Congress for failing to adequately supply the army.

Washington needed a success, no matter how trivial, to boost morale in Congress, the army, and the 13 now-independent states. He found it at Trenton on Christmas night, 1776. Facing expiring enlistments, bitter cold, and a professional army of Hessian mercenaries brought into the fight by King George III, Washington hatched a daring if not reckless plan to attack the Hessian garrison at Trenton. Making a tedious and dangerous crossing of the Delaware River at night, Washington's men managed not so much to surprise the Hessians but rather to overwhelm them. It was a small but stunning victory for a victory-less army. It was the shot in the arm that Washington and his men so desperately needed. Washington followed this success in January 1777 with an attack on Princeton that ultimately forced Cornwallis and Howe to reconsider their strategy in New York and New Jersey.

When the 1777 campaign season got underway, Howe ordered the dashing and ambitious General John Burgoyne to attempt another push from Canada to split New England and New York. Burgoyne knew little of the American wilderness and insisted on a long and heavy supply train. His army of about 8,000 regulars and loyalists hacked their way through the thick forests, literally building a road as they advanced, sometimes covering only yards in a day. American Major General Horatio Gates, a former British army officer who had served with Braddock in the previous war, harassed Burgoyne with his small Continental force and large number of militia until finally baiting the British to attack strong American defensive positions around Saratoga in the fall of 1777. In a series of battles during September and October, Gates maintained the initiative. With supplies running out and no hope of reinforcement, Burgoyne had to surrender. The victory over the British at Saratoga became the turning point of the war for the American cause, as France considered the success a definite sign that the Americans might indeed have a chance of winning, and, thus, decided to support the Americans with money, arms, and ultimately troops.

Washington huddled his meager force at Valley Forge in Pennsylvania during the winter of 1777–1778. Lacking adequate shelter, provisions, and clothing, the Continentals suffered tremendous hardship from freezing temperatures and harsh winter storms. Washington badgered Congress for help. Congress was doing all it could, but this was rarely enough. With

Philadelphia occupied by the British, merely finding a place to meet in safety was often the priority. In the meantime, troops deserted, died, and talked of mutiny. But the men who stayed, and survived, became an army that the British would not recognize when compared to their own. Whereas the British soldier was often forced into service, the Continental soldier often volunteered for little more reason than peer pressure and a desire to not let down comrades in arms. Bounties and the promise of pay no doubt encouraged many to enlist as well. With the help of a former Prussian officer, Baron Friedrich Wilhelm von Steuben, Washington slowly turned the bedraggled men into soldiers. In Congress, Robert Morris used creative financing to better supply the army. From what should have been the demise of Washington's army grew a stronger, better-trained force, bonded in common cause and suffering.

This revitalized force had its baptism by fire at the Battle of Monmouth in New Jersey in June 1778. General Henry Clinton, who had replaced Howe as British commander in North America, withdrew most British forces in the North to New York City to consolidate and reorganize. Along the way, Washington, with a combined force of Continentals and militia, hit Clinton's flank near Monmouth Courthouse. Just as General Charles Lee's assault on the British began to fall apart, Washington arrived to rally the men. Monmouth was a European-style battle, line army versus line army, in which Washington's army could not have engaged the year before. Darkness halted the action, and Clinton withdrew during the night. From this point, Clinton had to change the British strategic approach to the war. As the Americans and British warily eyed each

Figure 3.3 Baron Friedrich Wilhelm von Steuben at Valley Forge, 1777, photograph of oil painting by Augustus G. Heaton (1844–1930).

Source: National Archives and Records Administration.

other in New York, the British regrouped, intending to take advantage of loyalist support in the southern colonies.

The Southern Phase (1778–1781)

Failing to destroy the rebellion at its heart in Massachusetts, and missing more than a few opportunities to wipe out Washington's small but determined army in New York and New Jersey, the British tried another tack. The face of the war had changed dramatically in 1778 when France entered the fray as both ally of the American rebels and worldwide belligerent against Great Britain. Holland and Spain also joined the war, which now had become a world war with combat operations in India, the Mediterranean, the South Atlantic, and elsewhere. North America, in some respects, became a secondary theater. Now, in addition to fighting a war in North America and coping with its increasing cost, Great Britain had to consider its own security against French attack. More members of Parliament began to question the war in America, and British public opinion seemed to be swinging against this expensive and lengthy war.

Some fighting had already occurred in the Carolinas, mostly to the advantage of the British. Without strategic guidance in the south, however, the British failed to take full advantage of these small successes. Clinton believed that loyalists in the southern colonies would rally to the Crown, and he thought that the prominence of slavery in the southern colonies could be used to British advantage. All this talk of freedom might place slavery in jeopardy, and thus, the reasoning went, more Southerners might stick with the British in the long run. Clinton also hoped that regiments of volunteer loyalists would augment his shrinking army in North America. Battle and disease were taking their toll on the British just as they had on the Americans, and with a broader war, fewer reinforcements would be coming to America.

Moreover, with an increased French naval presence in the Caribbean the British needed a base of operations south of New York to augment naval stations in the West Indies. Charleston on the coast of South Carolina was perfect. From there, Clinton planned to gain control of the Carolinas and then move up to Virginia.

Clinton made his move in December 1778. He secured Savannah with rapidity and ease, a fact that makes his year-long sojourn there before moving on Charleston seem remarkable. This delay allowed the Americans to form a southern Continental army and recruit militia and irregular forces in the Carolinas. Clinton laid siege to Charleston, taking the port city along with Major General Benjamin Lincoln's force of more than 5,000 Continentals a month later. It was indeed a disaster for the Americans, perhaps the greatest of the war.

In June, British Lieutenant Colonel Banastre Tarleton and his Loyalist British Legion defeated a force of Virginia militia at the Waxhaws near

Lancaster, South Carolina. Known for his ruthlessness and hatred of those he considered traitors against the Crown, Tarleton apparently gave no quarter, killing more than 100 Virginians despite them throwing down their muskets in surrender. The way the war was being fought began to matter. Washington had already mandated that all surrendering British troops be treated as prisoners of war in the European tradition of warfare—with the utmost respect and best possible care. The British, on the other hand, treated American prisoners as well as non-combatants inconsistently and often brutally.

Assuming that the southern colonies were under British control, Clinton departed for New York, leaving mopping-up operations to General Cornwallis. Meanwhile, in Morristown, New Jersey, Washington and his army endured an even worse winter than they had at Valley Forge. Mutinies, desertion, sickness, and death once again threatened to defeat the cause, for if Washington's army disintegrated, so too would the rebellion.

Without Washington's consent, Congress authorized a new Continental army in the south, giving it to the hero of Saratoga, General Horatio Gates. Gates was arrogant, overconfident, and careless, and quickly met with disaster. In August 1780, Gates's 1,500 Continentals and several hundred militiamen collided with Cornwallis at Camden, South Carolina. Entrusting his left flank to the undisciplined militia, Gates kept his trained Continentals together on the right. Recognizing this unwise division of force, Cornwallis hit the militia hard. They fled in panic, leaving Gates and his Continentals outnumbered and exposed. Gates and the regulars were all but destroyed.

With Gates in the south with virtually no army, Benedict Arnold plotting treason at West Point in the North, and Washington's army barely managing to keep Clinton entrenched in New York, prospects indeed looked bleak for the American cause. The situation, however, began to turn in the Americans' favor. Significant help from France finally arrived. The first French troops to join the fight landed in Newport, Rhode Island, in July 1778, under the command of the Comte de Rochambeau. Washington convinced Congress to relieve the incompetent Gates, replacing him with Nathaniel Greene, a courageous commander but one whose battlefield success came at considerable risk. In the south, loyalist support for the British eroded as Cornwallis either allowed or ignored the brutality of his troops against noncombatants. British troops pillaged, raped, and managed to alienate many among the nonaligned colonists, as well as some loyalists.

The turning point for the Americans in the south came at the Battle of the Cowpens in South Carolina in January 1781. Brigadier General Daniel Morgan, a veteran of the French and Indian War, and his joint force of Continentals and militia, capitalized on the increased discipline of his regulars and superior tactical use of terrain to draw Tarleton's overconfident British into a costly defeat. Despite this enormous loss, Cornwallis pursued Greene and Morgan deeper into the North Carolina wilderness, stretching the British supply line to Charleston dangerously thin.

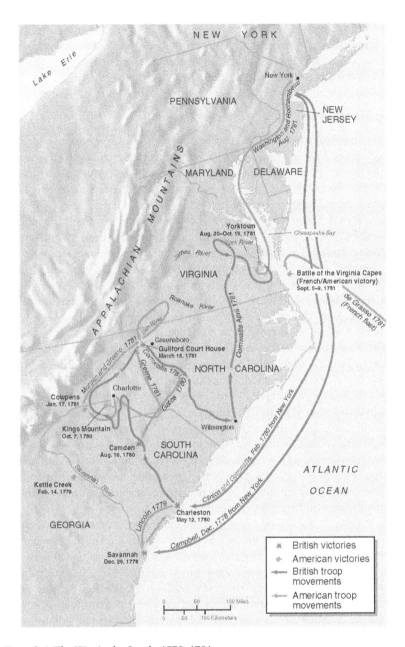

Figure 3.4 The War in the South, 1778–1781.

At Guilford Courthouse in March, Greene and Cornwallis clashed in a substantial but disorganized battle that left both sides badly battered. Even though the British commanded the field, they had again suffered debilitating casualties. Greene escaped with the remnants of his army, and Cornwallis, short of men and supplies, decided to move into Virginia in the hope of getting help from Clinton in New York. With French land and naval assistance finally available, Washington seemed to have the edge as the war entered its climactic moment.

The Naval War

Naval operations during the American War for Independence are often overshadowed by the land war. Facing the mightiest navy in the world, the American rebels had woefully little with which to meet the British at sea. Still, the small American navy, formally created in October 1775, played a crucial role in the war.

The Royal Navy blockaded much of the Atlantic seaboard throughout the war but kept its own shipping lanes open to allow limited trade and to enable resupply. To combat this situation, Congress created a navy and also granted letters of marque to privateers. During the colonial wars, American seamen had learned that privateering was often lucrative and thus many seamen forwent service in the new navy to instead pursue privateering. By the end of the war, American privateers (more than 1,500 of them) had captured more than 600 British ships.

The Continental Navy, on the other hand, was pitiably small and on paper hopelessly outgunned and inexperienced when compared to the Royal Navy. At its height during the war, the Navy had fewer than 60 ships, including 13 frigates, ten of which were either destroyed or captured by the British. To support the Navy, Congress established a Naval Committee under the leadership of Robert Morris and ordered the states to recruit men for naval service. None of the states reached their recruitment goals, in part because many seamen opted for serving aboard a privateer. All of the states, save New Jersey and Delaware, formed navies of their own, made up mostly of small ships to defend coastlines and ports; all of the states authorized privateering.

As mighty as the Royal Navy was, it, too, had challenges to overcome. Many of the great ships of the line built during the 1756–1763 war needed refurbishing due to poor maintenance or mothballing at the end of that war. Unlike the previous war, in this one the Royal Navy had to maintain its main logistical line back to Portsmouth in England. American naval stores, pitch and tar, and most importantly timber for masts and spars were no longer available, forcing the British to seek these vital supplies else-where and often in inferior form. And unlike the American navy, crewed by volunteers, the Royal Navy still relied on impressments to crew its fleet. Personal motivation for service, be it greed, liberty, or both, simply did not resonate in the Royal Navy as it did among the American navy and privateers.

Not yet mature enough to engage in fleet actions against the Royal Navy, the Americans followed their privateering tradition and went after defenseless merchantmen on the high seas. This strategy actually proved useful, forcing the Royal Navy to take valuable ships away from blockade duty—and, later, from fighting the French navy—and reassign them to convoy duty to protect British merchantmen from American raiders. In the young Continental Navy, bold captains, such as Nicholas Biddle and John Paul Jones, had better success in harassing British trade than in engaging ships of the line. Jones even operated near the British coast. So effective was this strategy that the British suffered tremendous commercial losses during the war, which greatly displeased business interests in Parliament. Throughout the war, American privateers and the Continental Navy accounted for more than $60 million in losses for the British merchant fleets.

The many actions fought by the Navy during the war included an assault on Nassau by Esek Hopkins. Inexperienced and rash, Hopkins disobeyed orders to patrol the Chesapeake Bay area and instead attempted to capture the British port at Nassau in the Bahamas. While the raid was partly successful, HMS *Glasgow* found Hopkins and his 24-gun frigate USS *Alfred* off the coast of Connecticut making its way back to port. Hopkins lost his ship and was subsequently court-martialed for disobeying orders.

The Continental Navy used the first submarine in a combat operation in 1776. The *Turtle*, a single-man underwater craft operated by Ezra Lee, unsuccessfully attempted to attach an underwater mine to HMS *Eagle*, the flagship of the British fleet at New York. Western navies would continue to experiment with underwater craft throughout the nineteenth century before perfecting their use during the two world wars of the twentieth century.

Britannia ruled the seas until France entered the war in 1778. Now, with the French navy harassing the Royal Navy in the Caribbean and elsewhere, the American navy and privateers had more considerable latitude in commercial raiding. Because such a significant French naval presence now operated in American waters, it was easier for Washington to keep Clinton in New York. Clinton could ill afford to sail with his army out of New York to reinforce Cornwallis in the south lest he be caught on the open seas by the French fleet.

The Final Campaign

With Cornwallis in southern Virginia, Clinton still bottled up in New York, and the French Caribbean fleet willing to sail northward to escape hurricane season in the Caribbean, Washington finally had an opportunity to deliver a decisive blow to the British. Effectively abandoning Georgia and the Carolinas, Cornwallis left only token forces to hold strategic centers in the south. Nathaniel Greene was able to reclaim the southernmost states for the rebel cause, even though he did not command a single victorious battle. As Cornwallis's forces gathered at Yorktown in Virginia, Washington ordered an American force under the Marquis de Lafayette to trap them there. Following his army and the Comte de Rochambeau's 7,000 French troops, Washington abandoned his original hope to converge his land force and the French fleet of the Comte de Grasse on the British at New York. Now, with de Grasse sailing toward the Chesapeake and Cornwallis on the Yorktown peninsula, Washington decided instead to bag Cornwallis.

Cornwallis understandably found Yorktown a strategically advantageous location. It afforded access to the sea for resupply or rescue, but because it lay on a peninsula, Yorktown could also be quickly cut off. Sea access disappeared in early September, however, when de Grasse and his French fleet, in the Battle of the Chesapeake, forced the British fleet to withdraw to New York.

With siege equipment thoughtfully included in the French expeditionary arsenal, Washington and his French allies dug in and began pounding Cornwallis in late September. Washington had 6,000 Continentals and more than 3,000 militia, combined with de Rochambeau's 7,000 French, to Cornwallis's 8,000 men who were under siege at Yorktown. For three weeks, the Americans and French hammered away at Cornwallis, who now had no hope of rescue or resupply. He formally surrendered on October 19, 1781.

First Saratoga, and then Yorktown—the British could not tolerate such losses. The British people were already divided on the war, and Parliament had been split over how to pursue the conflict after Burgoyne's surrender and French entry into the conflict. Lord North's ministry fell on March 20, 1782. Now, after Yorktown and still facing an increasingly stronger French enemy and determined rebel army, the British made the difficult decision to let the colonies in America go their separate way.

Great Britain had underestimated the problems posed by the American interior with its deep forests, hills, valleys, rivers, and rugged landscape. Logistical challenges plagued the British effort to end the rebellion, as did the lack of a coherent strategy and poor generalship. Perhaps their most critical mistake was in failing to convince the nonaligned American colonists to join the loyalist cause, as well as a failure to effectively use the one-third who were indeed loyal; instead, bumbling policies and inept commanders managed to alienate both groups. Carrying on a war in such a place and in such a manner for six years to an inglorious conclusion would shake any nation to its core, as it did Great Britain during the American War for Independence.

For the Americans, the war had been a bloody affair, one of the deadliest as a percentage of casualties in proportion to population in American history. More than 25,000 soldiers lost their lives, mostly from disease and privation; the death toll amounted to just less than 1 percent of the population (the Civil War, by comparison, cost the lives of slightly more than 1.6 percent of the population). Victory had been hard-won. Indeed, the Americans took advantage of localism and of their familiarity with the terrain, and they fought the war in a way that did not alienate the bulk of the population. Despite bickering among the states and Congress, and Washington's seemingly insurmountable problems of supply, enlistment, mutiny, and the overall poor condition of the Continental Army, America prevailed.

Victory could not have been achieved without France, which played the odd role of a monarchy helping to create a republic with not only no king but without hereditary titles of any sort. France had much to gain from seeing the American rebellion succeed: revenge for the total defeat in the previous conflict, delivering a severe blow to the British mercantile system through the loss of its colonies in America, and establishing a primary trade relationship with the new United States. All of these achievements would benefit France and its power on the European continent and abroad.

Important as France was to the American victory, so too was the role of George Washington as commander-in-chief of the Continental Army. Washington proved himself adaptive, flexible, and a skilled strategist who kept the army, and thus the revolution, alive. He channeled the varied motives of his volunteers into creating a European-style army that could ultimately face the British army on its own terms. As commander-in-chief, he managed to find subordinate commanders, such as Henry Knox and Nathaniel Greene, who could lead men in battle and maintain a broad strategic view of the war. Washington overcame discontent, hardship, and even mutiny among his troops and some of his officers to persevere against a weak and often ineffective Congress and uncooperative states. While he did not overcome his disdain for the militia, he learned how best to employ them on the battlefield.

Finally, and perhaps most importantly, Washington came to embody the ideals of the revolution. He was an elitist who expected deference, but he also genuinely practiced public virtue. While it would have been easy for him to abandon the rebel cause and defend the interests of his native Virginia, he did not. Even at the expense of Virginia's security, throughout the conflict Washington managed to retain perspective and see the revolution as a national movement.

Women

Women were part of the war in a variety of ways. They wrote pamphlets, plays, and poems in favor of the revolution, worked as camp followers, spied, and sometimes fought. Mercy Otis Warren's pamphlets and plays were openly patriotic. *Sentiments of an American Woman*, by Esther De Berdt Reed, encouraged women to work together to boost the morale of American soldiers, leading to the establishment of a nationwide fundraising effort to provide soldiers with much-needed clothing and other necessities.

Camp followers traveled with the army, providing needed services such as cooking, sewing, laundry, and nursing. They were also instrumental in scavenging to supplement short rations. Some provided sex work, but that was not a camp follower's primary function. In fact, camp followers typically 'joined' the army because it was a way to earn wages, to gain protection from the enemy, or because their husbands were in the ranks.

Patriot women spied on the British as well as Loyalists, generally as the opportunity arose rather than through organized effort. Because they were women, they were less suspect than men, and soldiers were more reluctant to question their motives or search them. As a result, women such as Lydia Darragh and Emily Geiger were able to use their household duties and their biological sex to avoid being discovered. Darragh's information allowed Washington's troops at White Marsh, Pennsylvania, to prepare for an impending attack by the British. Because the British were unwilling to search Geiger, she had time to memorize and destroy a written message from General Nathanial Green to General Thomas Sumter. Upon her release she delivered Greene's request for Sumter's aid in time for Sumter to reinforce Greene's effort.

Margaret Cochran Corbin, or Captain Molly, was seriously wounded during an artillery exchange while fighting alongside her husband during the Battle of Fort Washington. Congress awarded her a disability pension. Later she became one of the Corps of Invalids at West Point and is buried at the United States Military Academy. Other women masqueraded as men to join the fight. Historians will never know precisely how many women chose to do this, but there are a few for whom there are clear records. Deborah Sampson first enlisted as Timothy Thayer in 1782. When she was discovered, she enlisted in another regiment as Robert Shurtleff. When she fell ill with fever the doctor who treated her protected her secret but sent her to see George Washington, who gave her an honorable discharge. Massachusetts later granted Sampson a pension for her service.

Slaves and Free Men

Black men fought for American independence throughout the revolutionary years, but their presence in the ranks was often disputed. Racism and fear of a slave revolt dogged African American men, free or slave, throughout the Revolution.

The earliest engagements of the American Revolution, the Battles of Lexington and Concord in April 1775, and the Battle of Breed's Hill (Bunker Hill) two months later, included African American men who fought well and became a permanent part of the independence story.

Another former slave, Salem Poor, received credit for killing the commander of British forces at Breed's Hill. Poor's regiment awarded him a gallantry commendation for his actions that day.

During the early months of the Continental Army, significant numbers of African American men enlisted and received praise for their conduct regardless of whether on fatigue duty or under fire. Before long, however, objections arose to their enlistment. In October 1775, George Washington and Congress agreed that the army would no longer accept slaves, and even most free African American men, as soldiers. State militias held to the same policy. The new policy excluded even those African American patriots who had acquitted themselves well at places like Lexington and Breed's Hill. There were no official objections, however, to using African American men as laborers. As the war lengthened, and enthusiasm for service waned, however, the white-only policy became less important than filling enlistment quotas.

By December 1775, Washington was encouraging recruiters to give special consideration to African American veterans who wanted to reenlist. Congress approved reenlisting such men, but still prohibited enlistment of other African American volunteers. With permission to reenlist, the gallant Salem Poor stayed with the Continental Army until his discharge in 1780. During his years of service, he fought at White Plains, New York, and endured the Valley Forge winter of 1777–1778. In 1975, the United States Postal Service issued a stamp in his honor as part of the Contributors to the Cause Series.

Service in the Continental Navy was always open to African American men. Life at sea lacked all ordinary comforts, required months or even years of separation from family, and the work was especially difficult and dangerous. At sea, African American men typically faced none of the restrictions imposed in the army. All duties—caulking, handling sails—and risks—manning guns and fighting in boarding parties—were obligations of all sailors.

Although proscriptions against enlisting free men or slaves remained in effect throughout the Revolution, governing authorities learned to turn a blind eye to the color of recruits in favor of the revolutionary cause.

The End of the Continental Army

Following the victory at Yorktown, Washington and his army nervously kept watch over the remaining British troops that continued to occupy New York and Charleston as peace negotiations commenced in Paris. Washington by no means took it for granted that the war was actually over, for much of the British army in America and Canada remained undefeated. French attempts to influence the new United States stalled the peace talks until, finally, the American negotiators abandoned the French and made a deal directly with the British. Among other things, the Treaty of Paris, ratified by Congress in 1783, guaranteed American independence, established American control of all territory westward to the Mississippi River, and promised British withdrawal from posts west of the Appalachian Mountains.

With his charge from Congress accomplished, Washington sought nothing more than to retire from public life and return to his wife Martha and his beloved Mount Vernon. But as word came of the Treaty of Paris, Washington's officers were in the midst of what could have been a most shameful ending to a most honorable achievement. Having fought a long and costly war, Washington's men awaited promised wages from Congress for their service to the new nation. In 1780, Congress had passed legislation that promised officers of the Continental Army a pension of half pay for life that was consistent with pensions granted by European states to their armies. Impatient and prone to ambitious talk, Washington's officers anxiously awaited word at their winter camp in Newburgh, New York, that this promise would be carried out before Congress disbanded the army.

At issue among these officers was more than just back pay and promised pensions, however. Many nationalist officers and like-minded members of Congress wished to increase the power of Congress to strengthen the central government over the growing influence of the individual states, which had plagued national governance during the war. General Alexander McDougall presented a petition to Congress from these officers that demanded the pension in one lump-sum payment. Despite strong support among nationalists in Congress and implied threats that the army might not obey a congressional order to disband, Congress refused the petition. The old fear of a standing army still held prominence despite the Continental Army's vital role in achieving independence; it had fulfilled its duty and was no longer needed. At Newburgh, gossip and idle talk escalated; various circulars were passed around the officer corps in camp, including one that called for a meeting to respond to Congress's refusal to meet their demands and another that outright threatened mutiny against congressional authority.

Washington sympathized with the officers' frustrations but did not support their threats against Congress. To Washington, civil–military relations were paramount to the survival of the young American nation. He had already made plans to return his commission to Congress and had ideas about the establishment of a permanent military structure to defend the security of the new nation. But such talk of mutiny and defiance of civilian authority could gravely taint not only Washington's reputation, which he indeed held most dear, but also that of the United States as a new country.

When Washington got wind of a pending meeting where the discontented officers were to air their grievances and plan what they would do about Congress's failure to act, he called a preemptive meeting. In the officers' barracks in Newburgh, Washington reminded them of their service and obligation to their country. He appealed to their sense of duty and patriotism, then promised to ensure that their sacrifice would not go unrewarded by Congress. When pleading his case before them, Washington took from his pocket a letter suggesting that Congress would address their concerns. He began to read it but then stopped, putting on a pair of eyeglasses. His men had never seen him wear glasses. Washington told them he had not only grown gray in their service but that he was now growing blind. He left the building, leaving some officers in tears. They passed a resolution pledging their support of Congress. The so-called Newburgh Conspiracy had collapsed, affirming civilian control of the first national army in American history and setting the precedent of military noninterference in government affairs. Although Washington had prevented what would have been a disastrous movement, less than a month later Pennsylvania troops in the Continental Army marched against Congress, meeting in the Pennsylvania state house in Philadelphia, demanding discharge and back pay. Congress refused their demands and the crisis abated, but as Washington feared, such action fueled doubts that a republic could long survive a standing army.

With the navy all but dissolved, Congress debated what to do with the army it had created back in 1775. To avoid more mutinies and disaffection among the officer corps, Robert Morris, a financial wizard, worked out a way to pay the troops as Congress slowly furloughed and then discharged them. By 1784, only a handful of soldiers remained, most at Continental Army headquarters at West Point along the Hudson River in New York. The Continental Army that had won American independence ceased to exist. Although its tradition remained steadfast as an organization, the Continental Army was only a temporary structure created to fight the British in a war. It was never meant to be a permanent fixture of American security.

With independence won, many in Congress saw no need for a permanent military establishment. State militias could ably defend the United States against foreign enemies, as they had done in the past. Congress, however, seriously considered the problem and appointed a committee—chaired by one of Washington's staff officers, Alexander Hamilton of New York—to study the issue of a permanent standing army. Hamilton and other New Yorkers had earlier balked provisions in the Articles of Confederation that had governed the states since 1781 prohibiting individual states from creating permanent armies. With the British still occupying forts in predominantly indigenous lands west of the Appalachian Mountains, New York wanted to use its contingent of Continentals to relieve the British and keep watch over Native Americans and settlers along the frontier. Other states had similar concerns, and many in Congress came to accept that the westward growth of the new nation, combined with its unique security needs, required some sort of permanent military establishment.

Hamilton's committee solicited the opinion of Washington, who, in turn, asked his senior generals, including Knox and von Steuben, to weigh in on the matter. All supported creating a national army to police the western frontier, establishing a navy, building coastal fortifications and arsenals to equip this force, and founding military schools to promote the study of the military arts. All agreed that militia was inadequate for these functions.

The problem was, however, to create such an establishment without arousing traditional fears of a standing army, without creating an elite military class, and without giving the new government the power to tax. To make the concept more appealing to the states, Washington and his colleagues proposed reforming the traditional militia system by making it uniform from state to state, improving training, and improving the quality of the militia officer corps. With such improvements, a standing national army of militia numbering perhaps around 25,000 could be at the ready to defend the nation from any outside attack.

In his final report to Hamilton, Washington recommended these proposals and additionally suggested that active-duty militia should serve as a real national army to discourage foreign attack and defend the western frontier. Four infantry regiments and one artillery regiment, some 2,600 officers and men, could protect New England against an attack from Canada, defend the Great Lakes region, patrol the Ohio River Valley, and protect the Georgia and Carolina frontier. Arsenals, a military staff, and even a military academy to train artillerists and engineers rounded out Washington's plan for a national military establishment.

Hamilton liked the proposals, not least because they suited his nationalist political leanings. He accepted Washington's ideas in principle but went further to centralize the new military in the national government rather than in the states, as had been the militia tradition. Hamilton proposed that Congress, rather than the states, appoint officers, recruit and pay the troops, and supply the army. He also wanted to make the national army the core for an expansible army during a national emergency. Finally, the committee recommended that the new national army be an army of citizen volunteers rather than made up of state militia.

While both Washington's and Hamilton's proposals made sense as a means to provide security for the new nation, convincing a Congress with little money and a people who held fast to a deeply held anti-standing army tradition to accept these ideas was another matter. Although Hamilton's report to Congress coincided with the Pennsylvania mutiny, Congress still approached these radical ideas with extreme caution if not hesitancy. Worse again for Hamilton and his committee was that under the Articles of Confederation, Congress could not raise an army during peacetime. Politically, too many in Congress continued to think regionally. They abhorred centralized government at the expense of state power and convinced themselves of plots by nationalists, ambitious military men, and others to use a national army to seize control of Congress. While many of Hamilton's proposals ultimately found their way into the nation's military establishment in the early nineteenth century, doing so just after the end of the War for Independence made Congress unenthusiastic about meddling with what they perceived as a sound military policy that had brought success in the war.

The national government did not yet have the legal structure or the political will to create a permanent military structure. As it stood in 1784, the best Congress could do was to raise a temporary force of 700 state militia to defend the frontier against Indian attack. The next year, Congress transformed this hodgepodge creation into a regular army unit called the 1st American Regiment. Under the command of Pennsylvanian Josiah Harmar, the 1st American Regiment never had the strength or the support to effectively deal with either Native Americans or the British on the frontier.

A New Constitution and a New Military

In September 1786, a mob of angry farmers in western Massachusetts descended upon Springfield to protest requirements that property taxes be paid in specie rather than with paper currency. A struggling postwar economy, high taxes, restrictive requirements for voting and office holding, foreclosures, and the threat of debtors' prison made life difficult for many in rural Massachusetts. It seemed that the divide between the political and financial power of Boston versus the poor economic conditions of the Massachusetts hinterland had reached a breaking point. Instigated by Samuel Ely and Luke Day, what became known as Shays' Rebellion started as a farmer's protest but turned into an armed rebellion.

The event's namesake, Daniel Shays, was a veteran of the War for Independence. After fighting at Bunker Hill, Saratoga, and Stony Point, Shays fell on hard times upon returning to his farm in Pelham, Massachusetts. Shays had attended several town meetings to air farmers' grievances, and when the Massachusetts legislature adjourned in the summer of 1786 without addressing these concerns, the farmers decided to shut down court proceedings in Northampton and Worcester. With his military experience, Shays was chosen to lead the 'army' of farmers against the militia that Massachusetts governor James Bowdoin sent to quell the uprising. Shays led his band of rebels to Springfield in January 1787 to capture the arsenal there but were turned back by Bowdoin's militia, under the command of Benjamin Lincoln and Rufus Putnam. Lincoln chased Shays and his army of about 1,200 to Petersham, where he defeated the rebels and ended the rebellion. Shays escaped. Newly elected governor John Hancock addressed many of the farmers' concerns and pardoned all of the rebels except for Shays and other leaders of the uprising. Shays was tried and convicted in absentia for treason and sentenced to death but was later pardoned.

Congress attempted to send a force of more than 2,000 men under General Henry Knox to defend the arsenal at Springfield and stop the rebellion, but raised only a token force and was thus left powerless to do much of anything. The Articles of Confederation made Congress impotent to deal with such domestic crises. Shays' Rebellion alerted many, including Washington, to the weaknesses of the Confederation. If Congress could not put down an uprising of Massachusetts farmers, how could it defend the country against a foreign attack? Although it was just one of the many reasons that political leaders from across the states agreed to attend a convention that would reconsider the Articles of Confederation, Shays' Rebellion underscored the need to address the absence of adequate military power at the national level.

As what became the Constitutional Convention convened in Philadelphia during the summer of 1787, few of those present doubted that the principal purpose of a national government was to provide for the security of the nation and its citizens. Exactly how to provide that security without also creating a potentially oppressive centralized government that could endanger the rights of those same citizens was a question that occupied much of the ensuing debate that long hot summer. One of the first decisions made by the delegates reflected the importance of military matters in reforming the national government. Convinced to come out of retirement to return to public life as a delegate from Virginia, George Washington was chosen to preside over the convention. Who else but the man who epitomized civic virtue despite having exercised supreme military power could symbolically assure the American people that the secret meetings in the Pennsylvania state house were for the public good?

Deciding to scrap the old Articles of Confederation, the delegates created a new government structure based upon balance and separation of powers to provide for the security of the new nation while at the same time protecting the power of the states and individual rights from burdensome government intrusion. It was a delicate process that required compromise and forethought, for the nation would surely change and grow with coming generations.

In military matters, the new Constitution provided for the creation of a national military establishment, the power over which was shared between the new Congress and the chief executive, or president. Article 1 authorized Congress to establish an army and navy and collect taxes to provide for the maintenance of both. It could also regulate and provide for militia and use state militia in national service. Funding for the army was limited to two years so that Congress could determine whether to continue the existence of a standing army via new budgetary appropriations.

While Congress had the supreme power and authority to declare war in the new Constitution, Article 2 made the president the commander-in-chief of national military forces and gave him authority to commission officers with the consent of the upper house of Congress, the Senate. Authority for military affairs was shared, then, between Congress and the executive branch, both civilian bodies. Such power-sharing was designed to prevent despotic abuse of whatever national military power might be created.

The states reserved the right to maintain their own militias, which would serve as a check against the national standing army. But they lost all other sovereign uses of military power. They could not declare war, enter into alliances, or maintain an army or navy in peacetime. States appointed their own militia officers, but training, procurement, and organization were mandated by Congress to assure uniformity and effectiveness.

Great debate surrounded the new document. The ratification process stirred nationalist and anti-nationalist emotions alike. Those against a strong national government created by the Constitution argued that the document gave excessive military power to the federal government and the president in particular. Nationalists countered that checks and balances made it extremely unlikely that any government body or individual would be able to undertake such an abuse of power. In the end, the Constitution was ratified by the summer of 1788, putting a new government in place in 1789.

As part of the compromise to attain ratification, however, the first Congress that met in 1789 was obliged to enumerate rights not listed in the Constitution. These amendments to the Constitution collectively became known as the Bill of Rights and included important protections against abuses by a standing military. The Second Amendment ensured that citizens had the right to own firearms in case there was a need for a well-regulated militia. Mindful of the uproar caused by the Quartering Act, the Third Amendment prohibited the quartering of troops in people's homes.

Conclusion

The War for Independence made the American Revolution possible, a revolution that was realized in the drafting and ratification of the Constitution in 1787–1789. The United States had been born through the force of arms. A dual citizen army made up of both militia and volunteers made it possible to break the link binding the colonies with Great Britain, but the hardships of that process did not go unnoticed when the framers of the Constitution considered how to provide for the security of the United States. Civilian control over the military was maintained throughout the process of securing independence and establishing a national government. No hereditary military class grew out of this experience, as many had feared might occur.

With an ocean discouraging European intervention into the affairs of the new republic, security seemed assured. But such was not the case; the United States faced threats from within and abroad, threats that forced the nation to continue to consider its military establishment and use of military power in a democracy.

Further Reading

Allen, Thomas B. *Tories: Fighting for the King in America's First Civil War*. New York: Harper, 2010.

Atkinson, Rick. *The British Are Coming: The War for America, Lexington to Princeton, 1775–1777*. New York: Holt, 2019.

Berkin, Carol. *Revolutionary Mothers: Women and the Struggle for America's Independence*. New York: Alfred A. Knopf, 2005.

Egerton, Douglas. *Death or Liberty: African Americans and Revolutionary America*. New York: Oxford University Press, 2011.

Ferling, John. *Almost a Miracle: The American Victory in the War of Independence*. New York: Oxford, 2009.

Fischer, David Hackett. *Washington's Crossing*. New York: Oxford University Press, 2004.

Hibbert, Christopher. *Redcoats and Rebels: The American Revolution through British Eyes*. New York: W.W. Norton, 2002.

Lengel, Edward G. *General George Washington: A Military Life*. New York: Random House, 2007.

Mayer, Holly A. *Belonging to the Army: Camp Followers and Community during the American Revolution*. Columbia, SC: University of South Carolina Press, 1996.

Middlekauff, Robert. *The Glorious Cause: The American Revolution, 1763–1789*. Revised. Expanded. New York: Oxford University Press, 2005.

O'Shaughnessy, Andrew Jackson. *The Men Who Lost America: British Leadership, the American Revolution, and the Fate of the Empire*. New Haven, CT: Yale University Press, 2014.

Patterson, Benton Rain. *Washington and Cornwallis: The Battle for America, 1775–1783*. New York: Taylor, 2004.

Richards, Leonard L. *Shays's Rebellion: The American Revolution's Final Battle*. Philadelphia, PA: University of Pennsylvania Press, 2003.

Royster, Charles. *A Revolutionary People at War: The Continental Army and American Character, 1775–1783*. New York: W.W. Norton, 1975.

4 Challenges for a New Nation

Introduction

Despite the significant improvement of the new Constitution over the ineffective Articles of Confederation, the new nation remained nonetheless weak and vulnerable. The idealism of the anti-Federalists, or Republicans, held that the new nation could defend itself by rallying citizen militia that would patriotically answer the call to arms in a crisis. The Federalists, on the other hand, had taken a much more realistic view, maintaining that nothing short of a regular army and a strong navy could adequately defend the new nation against foreign designs.

Threats to the young United States were indeed real. Great Britain retained control of Canada. Various confederations of Native American tribes held sway along much of the frontier. Spain held Florida, and republican France had regained the vast Louisiana Territory. Despite the ocean separating the United States from the European continent, events in Europe would have a significant impact on the new nation. Great Britain and Napoleonic France would war on each other during much of this period for the United States. Sound military policy was essential, but competing partisan visions of the new nation's future made creating such a plan difficult. Instead, the United States took a compromising and reactionary course that placed its very existence in jeopardy as it fended off a variety of threats to survive its fledgling years.

The Quasi-War with France, troubles with the tribes of the Northwest Territory, Barbary pirates, and a new war with Great Britain forced the United States to defend its desire for economic growth and territorial expansion.

Building an Army

The traditional fear of a standing army and support for a citizen militia blocked President George Washington's efforts to establish a viable regular army at almost every turn. The various states jealously guarded their long-standing militias and control over them. The federal government had little money to support state militias, much less for a national army. Few Americans wanted to serve in the regular army anyway, preferring instead the prestige associated with many local militia units that had come to resemble social clubs more than effective military forces. Washington's vision of a national militia or reserve force was infeasible in the climate of the new Republic. Instead, the states clung tenaciously to their militia traditions.

Congress only reluctantly passed legislation regulating state militias. The Calling Forth Act of 1792 authorized the president as commander-in-chief to exercise his constitutional prerogative to mobilize the militia to enforce the law or suppress rebellion, but only if a federal judge had certified that local authorities no longer exercised civil control. It said nothing about using the militia to stop an invasion by a foreign power. The Uniform Militia Act, passed the same year by Congress, required all able-bodied men from the ages of 18 to 45 to enroll in local militia units and provide their own weapons and equipment. No militiaman would be expected to serve more than three months in a 12-month period. Washington wanted a standardized, well-regulated militia across the nation, well-trained and equipped to meet a national emergency. Instead, he got a law that failed to punish states for noncompliance. Many states simply ignored the law and continued to organize militia along regionalized models just as they had as colonies. Officers continued to be appointed locally, training remained inconsistent, and politics infested militia issues at every level.

Still, Congress could not ignore the potential threats to American security. A standing army, no matter how distasteful, was necessary. In 1790, the United States Army consisted of the 1st American Regiment and an artillery battalion to total just over 1,200 men. In response to Indian trouble in the Ohio River Valley and Kentucky, Congress authorized the formation of the Legion of the United States in 1792. The creation of Secretary of War Henry Knox, the Legion of the United States was a mixed force of infantry, cavalry, and artillery, allowing for flexibility in balance and organization. Perhaps more important politically, Congress liked the idea of a 'legion' because it did not suggest unpleasant visions of a standing army. Four sub-legions of 1,800 troops each comprised the Legion of the United States. Congress reorganized the Legion into the 1st, 2nd, 3rd, and 4th Regiments of Infantry and a Corps of Artillerists and Engineers. In 1798 the cavalry was reconfigured into the Regiment of Light Dragoons, and in 1808 a light artillery regiment was created along with a regiment of riflemen.

Fighting Indians and Insurrection

Much of the reorganization occurred while the Army was in the field engaged against Native American tribes in the Old Northwest Territory. Often at British instigation but indeed prompted by threats to their own autonomy and territorial integrity, the tribes of the lower Great Lakes and the Ohio River Valley determined to stand against the incoming tide of settlers from east of the Appalachians. The Delaware, Miami, Ottawa, Cherokee, Shawnee, Chippewa, and others intimidated, raided, and killed settlers who ventured into what Native Americans considered as their lands and the settlers regarded as American territory. Resolving these conflicts could happen in one of two ways—by treaty or by force. Often, settlers failed to respect the provisions of treaties, thus virtually guaranteeing the use of force to reach a lasting solution.

Initial efforts to deal with Native Americans in the Old Northwest Territory offered little promise and said much about the poor organization and leadership of the Army and a lack of national direction for policy. Responding to raids that President Washington and Secretary of War Knox thought had been staged by renegade bands of Shawnee and Cherokee, Washington ordered territorial governor Arthur St. Clair and General Josiah Harmar, commander of the 1st Regiment, to organize a punitive expedition to deal with what was then considered a nuisance. Washington's instructions seemed clear—punish the renegade raiders, respect legitimate tribal authority, and offer peace whenever possible. St. Clair and Harmar had other ideas; both wanted an intense campaign to end the problem once and for all.

Early peace efforts made no progress, leading St. Clair to call for militia from Kentucky to join the 1st Regiment at Fort Washington (Cincinnati) for a campaign against Wabash and Miami villages in Indiana and Ohio. President Washington ordered levies of 2,000 volunteers to augment the regulars and militia in part to gain federal control at the expense of state militias. Levies were not militia; thus, the administration did not have to worry about the political consequences of calling state militias to serve outside their home areas on a lengthy and dangerous campaign.

St. Clair planned a two-prong campaign that would divide his force to raid the villages, then establish a post on the Maumee River to ensure the security of the region. Washington, Knox, and General Harmar approved the plan less the establishment of the Maumee post. It possibly never occurred to Washington or Knox, or St. Clair, that the expedition might meet defeat and start a larger war, perhaps even involving the British.

Harmar took his force toward the Maumee River in October. Militia and regulars did not get along, discipline suffered, and a long, cumbersome baggage train slowed the expedition's pace to about ten miles a day. Although the force destroyed several Native American villages, when it faced Native Americans in battle it endured embarrassing defeats. Harmar insisted on splitting his army and further allowed his subordinate commanders to divide their forces in a strategy that played into the Native Americans' hands by allowing them to engage smaller American units rather than being drawn into a sizable set-piece battle. By the end of October, Harmar turned back, having lost 200 men. One

Figure 4.1 Indian Resistance 1790–1816.

hundred and fifty years of warfare with the Indians had taught the Americans very little, it seemed. Harmar and St. Clair tried their best to put a positive spin on a near-disastrous campaign, but Washington and Knox were not fooled.

St. Clair organized another effort for 1791. The War Department approved his plan for a force of 3,000 men, including a new regiment of regulars, volunteer cavalry, and another levy to serve for four months. However, such shortcuts did not guarantee better troops, as the levies often lacked training and discipline, and suffered low morale. Nothing went right. Logistics broke down, leaving many soldiers without adequate clothing and ammunition. The levies often had only a few muskets with which to train, much less fight. Discipline among the levies became a severe problem, which soon also infected the regulars. Smallpox also ravaged the camps. St. Clair absented himself from the preparations to run frivolous errands to Fort Washington or Kentucky. His lack of leadership fed dissent among his officer corps. The expedition finally set off in early October with less than 1,500 troops and traveled only about five miles a day. Because of the delays in getting started, the enlistments for many of the levies began to expire. They understandably wanted to go home.

The ultimate disaster hit St. Clair's force on November 4. St. Clair knew his army was not prepared to face a large force of Indian warriors, a fact the Indians knew as well from their own scouts and American deserters. As the expedition camped under full alert along the Wabash River the night of November 3, over 1,000 Miami and allied warriors, including a young Shawnee named Tecumseh, prepared to attack under the able generalship of Little Turtle. Early in the morning of November 4, just as many of the soldiers and levies assumed that the height of danger had passed, the warriors made their move to overrun the camp. The levies and militia broke, then ran for their lives but were cut down by Native American warriors as they fled. Regulars formed a line and held out for nearly three hours before breaking through to flee southward. Over 600 Americans were killed and another 300 wounded in the attack. It was an unmitigated disaster for St. Clair, who was, nevertheless, cleared of responsibility, as Washington and Knox could not politically afford to admit they had placed the wrong general in command.

St. Clair's Defeat, as it is known, brought down a rain of criticism upon Washington's administration. Many in the eastern United States claimed that land-hungry settlers and frontiersmen had initiated the conflict by violating already-established treaties with the Indians. Others worried that the costly campaigns were destroying what little remained of the Army and pushing the young nation toward financial ruin. Still others voiced concerns that such intense focus on the Native American problem ignored threatening developments in Europe.

With suspicion of standing armies still entrenched in the United States, Washington's plan to enlarge the Army and not use levies or militia in the coming campaign was politically, if not militarily, risky. To command this newly expanded force, Washington chose aggressive and courageous General 'Mad' Anthony Wayne. Diplomatic efforts gave Wayne almost two full years to train and equip his new army. But Wayne was also eager, and the two-year wait frustrated him despite his recognition that having the extra time had given him a much better army than he would have had if the campaign had begun in 1792. When talks stalled in the fall of 1793, Knox ordered Wayne to move out. The force did not get far before disease, expiring enlistments, and lack of supplies forced a discouraged Wayne to abort the campaign. He stopped in October to winter at newly built Fort Greenville. Native American warriors raided and sniped at his posts, knowing that Wayne could do little in retaliation while talks continued.

Meanwhile, it became clear to Washington and others that the British supported and encouraged Indian attacks. Long suspected, the proof came when Chief Joseph Brant publicly claimed that British Indian agents in the west were paying Native Americans to make attacks on American settlements and outposts. This was further confirmed when the British built Fort Miamis on the north bank of the Maumee River just above the rapids from Lake Erie.

The tribal alliance, however, had begun to crumble despite the able leadership of Chiefs Little Turtle and Blue Jacket. Knox ordered Wayne to destroy the tribal alliance and eject the British from American territory. In July 1794, Wayne's force reached the confluence of the Auglaize and Maumee Rivers to establish Fort Defiance. His movements thus far had been peaceful as several tribes bowed to his superiority in numbers and strength. Little Turtle nevertheless refused to surrender.

In August Wayne moved his force closer to the British fort where Little Turtle also was encamped. Early in the morning on August 20, Wayne's scouts ran into a line of Native American warriors and British-Canadian militia in an area of fallen trees and undergrowth. In what became known as the Battle of Fallen Timbers, Wayne slowly pushed the Indians back toward Fort Miamis. The Native Americans finally broke and ran for the fort only to find the gate shut and barred. The British faced a choice—support their Native American allies and risk war with the United States or abandon their friends and avoid a broader conflict. They chose the latter. Little Turtle's force disintegrated. For several days Wayne and his troops razed Native American villages, storehouses, and crops near the fort. The British did not reply despite Wayne's overtly aggressive attempts to goad them into battle.

In 1795, Wayne concluded the Treaty of Greenville with the tribal confederation to give the United States complete control of the region and pave the way for the Jay Treaty with Great Britain that finally removed the British presence from American territory. Wayne's triumph erased four years of misguided, poorly implemented, and strategically failed military and political policies to achieve peace in the Northwest Territory.

The Whiskey Rebellion

While Wayne advanced up the Maumee River toward Fort Miamis to deal with the Native American problem in the Northwest Territory, another threat to the stability of the new nation erupted in western Pennsylvania. The Whiskey Rebellion was the most serious internal challenge the young country had faced to that time. Farmers in west Pennsylvania responded violently to the new federal excise tax on whiskey passed by Congress as part of Secretary of the Treasury Alexander Hamilton's plan to reduce the national debt. Farmers often used home-made whiskey as a medium of exchange in rural areas; thus, the tax hit these farmers hardest.

Figure 4.2 The Whiskey Rebellion, attributed to Frederick Kemmelmeyer, circa 1795, depicting President George Washington and troops near Ft. Cumberland, Maryland, before their march to suppress the Whiskey Rebellion in western Pennsylvania.

Source: Metropolitan Museum of Art.

As in the early days of the Revolution, citizens resisted government attempts to collect a legally authorized tax. Mobs of farmers attacked tax collectors and interfered with other government business. In much of western Pennsylvania, the government ceased to function. Supreme Court Justice James Wilson certified that the courts in the region no longer operated, thus allowing President Washington to declare a state of emergency and send troops and militia into the area to restore order.

Because of Wayne's campaign in the Northwest, Washington had little military force available and was left with only militia. He was hesitant to use the Army in any case since doing so would make it easy for Republicans to contend that the 'true nature' of the Federalist army had been revealed—could this be a Federalist plot?

Washington put out the call for militia, to which Pennsylvania, New Jersey, Virginia, and Maryland responded with 13,000 troops. Washington commanded the force for a few weeks before turning it over to Henry Lee and Hamilton. As it marched on Pittsburgh, which the rebels had threatened to burn to the ground, the rebellion collapsed. Only a handful of rebels were arrested; only two were tried for treason. Both were subsequently pardoned.

Using force against the Indians of the Northwest Territory and the rebels in western Pennsylvania were decisions crucial to the development of the new Republic. Washington made it clear that the national government would use executive power to enforce the laws of the land and protect Americans on the frontier. After the 'successes' of Wayne's campaign and putting down the Whiskey Rebellion, Federalists could argue with some ease that the nation needed a permanent standing army to garrison frontier posts and guard against internal rebellion. Republicans countered that such an army could just as easily be used against the people of the United States in an abuse of power that could destroy the Republic. Besides, now that the British finally had agreed to quit their posts on the American frontier, a large army no longer seemed necessary. Republicans argued that settlers on western lands could defend themselves with the militia.

In 1796, Congress disbanded the Legion of the United States, leaving only four infantry regiments and some dragoons. It was a clear signal that standing armies were still viewed with suspicion. Yet, the fact remained that there was a standing, though very small, army that could be expanded during a crisis to meet threats against the Republic. This would remain the model for American military organization for the next 100 years.

An Academy at West Point

Of equal symbolic importance in the political conflict between Federalists and Republicans over the establishment of a permanent military was the founding of the United States Military Academy at West Point. As headquarters for the Corps of Artillerists and Engineers, the old fort on the Hudson River had been the site of an earlier attempt to formalize officer training under the tutelage of foreign officers in the 1790s.

Washington had called for a military academy to train new officers during peacetime. By 1800 the various models for such an academy under consideration did not include what the Corps of Artillerists and Engineers had attempted. Alexander Hamilton pushed one model in 1799 that included an academy of five schools, beginning with a common school for all cadets followed by schools for specific branches of service as well as for naval service. The plan went to Congress but was defeated by Republicans, who saw it as a plot to further Federalist domination of the small officer corps. Many Federalists voted against the proposal because of its association with the controversial Hamilton.

In 1800, Secretary of War Samuel Dexter reintroduced the idea of a military academy for artillerists and engineers. Dexter presented his plan as organizationally efficient and proposed combining training for artillerists and engineers in a single location. Because these regiments already existed, Congressional approval was not needed save for an appropriation. It was a good idea to circumvent the bitter politics of Congress, but the timing fell flat as President John Adams' term ended before the school could be formally established. Thomas Jefferson—long an opponent of a military academy, claiming that such an institution was not provided for in the Constitution—entered office in 1801 and quickly established just such an institution. After barely a month in office, Jefferson and his Secretary of War, Henry Dearborn, hired a mathematics teacher to conduct classes for artillerists and engineers at West Point, an established post and a well-maintained fortification. Through the Peace Establishment Act of 1802, Congress formally established the academy.

The Peace Establishment Act not only gave congressional approval for a military academy but it also dramatically reshaped the Army. It authorized Jefferson as Commander-in-Chief to discharge many Federalist officers and replace them with Republicans. The academy provided a convenient means to introduce Republican officers to the lower ranks. Some historians suggest that Jefferson wanted a top-notch school of science and mathematics to train engineers for civil use, but the engineering curriculum was mediocre at best, comprising little beyond basic instruction and a few courses on military fortifications. Others more convincingly argue that establishing the academy was part of Jefferson's attempt to bring the Army and the government into closer harmony with Republican ideology and partisan goals.

Federalists had governed the nation since its founding; now it was the Republicans' turn, and Jefferson used his power as president to make sweeping social and political changes in all areas of government. Intent to add more Republicans to the officer corps, his appointments to the academy clearly showed favoritism toward the sons of loyal party supporters. What should have been an attempt to depoliticize the officer corps served only to further politicize it.

Building a Navy

From the ratification of the Constitution to the end of the War of 1812, two competing naval policies characterized American maritime security strategy. Expanding American maritime trade demanded a deep-water fleet, while defending American shores from seaborne threats required a naval presence beyond coastal fortifications. Politics, of course, weighed in on these strategic issues, as Federalists supported a more outward-looking national security policy, while Republicans looked inward to avoid provoking the European powers.

The Constitution authorized the creation and maintenance of a navy, and events at sea in the late 1780s warranted such an authorization. American merchant ships in the Mediterranean fell victim to the well-organized extortion racket of the Barbary pirate states of North Africa. Tensions between Great Britain and France brought on by the French

Revolution also endangered American merchant ships since Americans traded with both belligerents. At the end of the War for Independence the United States Navy had been demobilized, and by 1785 it had all but ceased to exist. For over 100 years American merchants had depended upon and expected the protection of the Royal Navy. Now, as the newly independent nation had no navy, American seagoing trade had become dangerously vulnerable.

Such circumstances made the U.S. government a ripe target for the North African pirate states of Morocco, Tripoli, Algiers, and Tunis. Each demanded and received ransom from the United States in exchange for the release of hostages and tribute in return for leaving American ships unmolested. Paying bribes also encouraged France and Britain to blatantly ignore the sovereign maritime rights of the new United States. The American flag on the high seas commanded little respect from either pirates or other seafaring nations.

Without a navy to protect its shipping and 'fly the flag,' the young nation quickly found itself entangled in the conflict between its helpful ally France and its recent enemy Great Britain. Tensions between the two countries erupted in open warfare in 1793, which further exacerbated the American shipping situation. The United States maintained that as a sovereign neutral nation it could trade with either belligerent while accepting that both countries had every right to confiscate war contraband. Through Orders in Council, Great Britain added more and more goods to its contraband list with each passing month. The Royal Navy blockaded the French coast and declared that any trade goods bound for France were subject to seizure—neutrality be damned.

France grew embittered toward its former ally because the United States allowed trade with Great Britain. Still, French and British warships stopped and boarded American merchant ships to impress sailors who could not prove their citizenship. More than 300 impounded American merchant ships sat idle in British ports and hundreds of impressed Americans crewed Royal Navy ships. The United States government seemed powerless to do anything but offer the mildest protest.

A navy, however, might bring respect for the flag, and Congress began debating authorization for a fleet of first-rate warships. The debate was intense as critics condemned the establishment of a permanent navy and increased taxation to pay for the new ships. The current crisis, however, lent weight to the argument for a navy, and in March 1794 Congress authorized the creation of a six-frigate navy. The frigates were to be first-rate ships, a bold signal to Great Britain and France that the United States meant business.

Congress appropriated close to $700,000 to pay for ship construction and eagerly recognized the political benefit of building the new vessels, as contracts were handed out from New Hampshire to Virginia. Portsmouth, New Hampshire, built the 38-gun USS *Congress*; in Philadelphia, Joshua

Humphreys designed and constructed the 44-gun *United States*; the famous 44-gun *Constitution* was built in Boston; Forman Cheesman constructed USS *President* with its 44 guns in New York; Baltimore laid the 38-gun *Constellation*; and the Norfolk shipyard produced the *Chesapeake* with its 38 guns. These were genuinely American ships—slaves cut down huge pines, cedars, and oaks along the Gulf Coast for framing, masts, and timbers, and Paul Revere made the brass work for the *Constitution*.

To resolve outstanding issues with Great Britain remaining from the War for Independence, Washington sent Supreme Court Chief Justice John Jay to London to negotiate a treaty. As Jay left for London, the Republican faction in Congress managed to pass an embargo on American trade to British ports. This congressional effort to impress the British fell flat as Jay had no intention of being so firm with the British. In the end, Great Britain agreed to evacuate its forts in the American Northwest—which it was supposed to have done under the Treaty of Paris of 1783—and open trade in India to American merchant ships. Additionally, the British gained navigation rights on the Mississippi River, a concession that had direct strategic consequences for the United States. Southern states complained bitterly that Jay had not secured financial compensation for slaves taken by the British in the War for Independence.

Jay's efforts achieved little. The British continued the practice of impressment, refused to recognize American neutrality in the war with France, and, in keeping with its rejection of American neutrality, Parliament also refused to let American ships pass through the Royal Navy's blockade of the French coast. Although the treaty sneaked through the Senate in 1795, Jay's work pleased no one. Protesters burned Jay in effigy, and the House of Representatives threatened to delay appropriations to enforce the treaty's provisions.

The Quasi-War

France was incensed by the Jay Treaty and severed diplomatic relations with the United States in 1796. President Washington urged continuing the naval building program to increase the size of the Navy. Upon assuming the presidency in 1797, John Adams echoed his great predecessor but noted that the strength and size of the navy the United States required could not be built to meet the present crisis—it would be a long and laborious process that might take decades.

In April 1798 Congress established a Navy Department separate from the War Department and in July formally established the Marine Corps. Also in July, Congress appropriated money for 24 warships in addition to the six frigates already under construction. Tensions with France dramatically increased that same summer when the infamous XYZ Affair exposed French attempts to bribe American negotiators to begin talks on a new treaty with France. With President Adams' blessing, Congress nullified all existing agreements with France. The break with France appeared complete.

Thus began what became known as the Quasi-War with France that lasted until late 1800. Neither side formally declared war nor were land forces ever used, although Federalists took the opportunity to enlarge the Army just in case. The Quasi-War was a naval war fought mainly by privateers and in scattered ship-to-ship actions, taking place primarily in the West Indies. The United States Navy, however, was now much stronger than it had been in the War for Independence. Officers had some experience, and the new frigates were first-rate, fast, well-armed ships. Perhaps more importantly, American strategy had also matured. With much of its fleet trapped by the British blockade in harbors around the coast of France, the French navy could not mass a large force against the American navy. With the French fleet bottled up in home ports, the United States chose to hit France in the West Indies, the location of some of the most valuable French imperial possessions. Patrolling in four small squadrons across the Caribbean, the U.S. Navy achieved some spectacular successes.

Two of these involved the Navy's most promising officer, Thomas Truxtun. He not only captained the *Constellation* but had also overseen its construction. Truxtun was unusual among officers in the American navy. He wrote on naval tactics and practices and insisted that his subordinate officers study them. Truxtun was a consummate officer who viewed his naval service as a profession. In February 1799, Truxtun brought *Constellation* southeast of Nevis and engaged the French Frigate *L'Insurgente*, which surrendered in less than an hour. Truxtun and the *Constellation* faced off against a more massive French warship, the *Vengeance*, in February 1800, which disengaged after a four-hour intense fight only to run aground, never to sail again. Despite losing the prize, Truxtun firmly established himself as one of the best American naval commanders.

Diplomacy ultimately ended the Quasi-War. France accepted that it was no longer the principal ally of the United States and that the Jay Treaty between the United States and Great Britain was legal and binding. The United States was finally free of all obligations to France. Although at a great political cost, Adams had kept the United States out of a full-scale war. Federalists and Republicans had become deeply divided over the Quasi-War, a division that carried forward into the Jefferson administration. The fact remained, however, that the United States had gone toe-to-toe with France, a world power, and had emerged arguably in a better position.

Jefferson's Gunboats

Many in Congress agreed that coastal defense was a primary concern for the young United States, but opinion was sharply divided on how the coast should be defended. Taking office in 1801, Jefferson came to support a blue-water fleet as an essential part of the overall American defensive strategy, but he doubted such a fleet's ability to defend the American coast and its all-important ports.

To address the gap in the coastal defense system, Jefferson proposed a fleet of shallow-draft gunboats. These small craft, not more than 80 feet long and 20 feet across with one or two masts, seven feet of draft, and armed with a couple of 24- or 32-pounders, could move through coastal waters with relative ease. As part of Jefferson's broader coastal defense strategy, these gunboats complemented floating artillery platforms and coastal fortifications. Gunboats were cheap, which pleased both Jefferson and Secretary of the Treasury, Albert Gallatin. With his gunboats, Jefferson attempted to beef up the coastal defense system while decreasing the public debt and tax burden.

Gunboats were not a new idea. Most coastal European nations employed them for coastal defense, many with good success, and they had been used in the American War for Independence. Wherever gunboats had been used they had served as a complement to an overall naval strategy rather than as a replacement for seagoing vessels or permanent coastal fortifications. Cost savings were substantial as well. Not only did a $12,000 gunboat fall well below the cost of a new $300,000 frigate, but a gunboat also required only a small crew. Jefferson planned to recruit from the naval militias that staffed fortifications at American ports and harbors. These citizen-sailors would operate a few gunboats during times of peace and would also crew the many boats that could be brought out of mothballs during a war. Maneuverable, versatile, economical, and, for the Republican Jefferson, egalitarian—on paper the gunboats seemed to have it all for a president of distinct political philosophy faced with complicated defense challenges.

As with the construction of the frigates, the development of the gunboat fleet offered an appropriations boom for several congressional districts. Jefferson wisely dispersed the contracts for individual boats around the nation to increase popular support for Republican policies other than the gunboat program and national security in Republican states and perhaps inspire modest gains in Federalist strongholds. From 1804 through 1808, contracts for 257 gunboats, of which 177 were built, were issued to contractors in 11 of the 17 states. Many of the contracts went to shipbuilders in New York, Massachusetts, Connecticut, South Carolina, and Virginia, while several were also awarded to builders along the Ohio River in Ohio and Kentucky as well as Lake Champlain and Lake Ontario. Some of these contracts went directly to congressmen and senators themselves—arms procurement and congressional politics have a long history.

Gunboats were sent to New Orleans to patrol the mouth of the Mississippi River during the Burr conspiracy and afterward to scare privateers away from American shipping into and out of New Orleans. The 1807 Embargo Act brought gunboats to the fore of a failed national policy as the small craft served as the primary though ill-fitted tool for enforcing the embargo. Smugglers always used the fastest ships they could lay their hands on, and they easily outran the lethargic gunboats, which were built for neither speed nor the open sea. In 1810, gunboats around Charleston vainly tried to put a dent in the now-illegal slave trade.

During the War of 1812, gunboats were used primarily for their original purpose—coastal defense. Their actual record, however, was mixed. Gunboats often discouraged British warships from entering harbors, but they could do nothing to prevent British fleet operations up the Chesapeake. Far more significant was their contribution to the war effort in other ways—as transports, convoy escorts, and hospital and prison ships, as well to gather intelligence and boost local morale. Only during the naval actions preliminary to the Battle of New Orleans did Jefferson's gunboats fulfill their intended mission. By 1825, most of the gunboats had been retired with only a few surviving as tenders.

The gunboats' record is indeed mixed. They certainly served a practical purpose in defending a nation with hundreds of miles of coastline and navigable inland waterways, and they also fit Jeffersonian politics. As naval vessels, however, they handled poorly and were often cheaply constructed. Jefferson's idealized view of the citizen-sailors who would crew these craft never really took hold. Naval officers shunned service on gunboats, preferring the much more high-profile billets aboard frigates and other warships, and the naval militia remained small and stagnant. Critics charged that the boats stood idle much of the time, promoting vice and poor discipline among both crew and officers. Still, the gunboats are an excellent example of how arms procurement, national security, and national politics blend to address a national security challenge.

The Tripolitan War

The Tripolitan War began after years of tension between the United States and the Barbary kingdoms of Morocco, Tripoli, Tunis, and Algiers. After the British Royal Navy ceased protecting American shipping in the Mediterranean in 1783, the United States had little choice but to pay the bribes demanded by the Barbary States in exchange for not harassing American merchant ships. Paying tribute, however, undermined the United States as a sovereign nation that desperately needed respect abroad. As presidents, both Washington and Adams swallowed their pride and paid tribute through negotiated agreements that freed captured sailors in exchange for an annual payment. Jefferson, a member of both administrations, contradicted his long-held insular views and urged building a large fleet and using force to subdue the Barbary pirate states. Jefferson remained a voice in the wilderness until he was elected president in 1800. By then the Barbary States' rulers had played into Jefferson's hands.

By 1800, Tripoli demanded more substantial tribute from the United States, which could not afford to pay, prompting Tripoli to announce that it would commence war against the United States in six months if the new tribute was not forthcoming. Five months later, the United States learned of this brazen announcement, leaving little time to respond. Jefferson had anticipated this breakdown in relations and upon taking office ordered a small squadron under the command of Commodore Richard Dale to the Mediterranean. In the meantime, Tripoli captured more American ships and held several crews hostage. Dale tried to blockade Tripoli with limited success for six months, then gave up. In 1802, Commodore Richard Morris arrived with a squadron of six ships, but like Dale had trouble enforcing a blockade and, along with several other misadventures, also returned to the United States having achieved very little.

Enter here the very able Commodore Edward Preble. An already successful and highly regarded naval officer with combat experience in the War for Independence and the Quasi-War, Preble was finally the right commander for the situation. A man of action and intellect, Preble became the first in a 'who's who' of Navy officers who served in the Mediterranean during the first half of the nineteenth century. Stephen Decatur, William Bainbridge, and Isaac Hull are some of the more notable officers who succeeded Preble. With seven ships under his command, including the venerable *Constitution*, Preble made his way west to east across the coasts of the Barbary States. He captured two Moroccan vessels, including one towing an American prize behind it. In Tangier, Preble staged a serious show of force that included three frigates. Convinced of American naval might, the Moroccan regency quickly agreed to renew the 1786 treaty with the United States and dropped the demand for more tribute. Preble's tour had started with a bang.

With things well in hand at Tangiers, Preble ordered Bainbridge to take *Philadelphia* and *Vixen* to Tripoli. In late October disaster struck when the *Philadelphia* grounded on an uncharted reef while pursuing a corsair into Tripoli's harbor. Bainbridge could not get the frigate free of the reef and owing to the position of the stranded ship he could not effectively use most of the *Philadelphia*'s guns. He was forced to surrender his ship and crew of 300, a shocking loss for the young U.S. Navy. The pasha demanded $3 million for ransom and a new treaty, which Preble rejected without hesitation. In February 1804 a daring and audacious attack by Stephen Decatur and the *Intrepid*, a refitted captured Tripolitan ketch, used deception and stealth to approach the insecurely guarded *Philadelphia*. After boarding and quickly subduing the handful of guards on the moored frigate, Decatur had the *Philadelphia* put to the torch, then promptly made his escape from Tripoli Harbor. It was the high point of the war for the Americans, and Decatur became a household hero back in the United States.

The loss of the *Philadelphia* convinced Preble that only shallow-draft boats could make an effective attack on Tripoli Harbor. Acquiring six

Figure 4.3 Painting by Michele Felice Cornè, depicting Commodore Edward Preble's
       squadron engaging the Tripolitan gunboats and fortifications during the
       afternoon of August 3, 1804.

Source: United States Naval History and Heritage Command.

gunboats and a couple of bomb vessels from nearby Sicily, Preble gathered
the largest American fleet to date and attacked Tripoli in August 1804.
Over the next four weeks, he launched five attacks but made little
progress. His patience running out, Preble took the drastic measure of
using a fire ship to attack the harbor. Loading the *Intrepid* full of powder
and explosives, a volunteer crew took the ship into the port on the night
of September 4. At about 10:00 p.m. the vessel prematurely ignited in
a tremendous explosion that killed the volunteer crew on board. It is not
clear if the blast was accidental or if the crew ignited the ship after being
boarded. Regardless, the *Intrepid* did little damage to the harbor. Preble's
desperate gamble had failed, and now he too was finished in the
Mediterranean.

Tobias Lear, the former personal secretary to George Washington now
turned diplomat, was the one who finally concluded an agreement with
Tripoli. Lear understood the complexities of Barbary politics and knew
that the pasha would never surrender the crew of the *Philadelphia* without
payment of some sort. Captain John Rodgers had now established a firm
blockade and was eager to shell the city as Preble had months earlier. Lear
believed that the pasha was close to surrender and interested in making
a deal. The pasha first asked for $200,000, then $130,000. Rodgers,
unimpressed, rejected both offers. Lear countered with $60,000 and
a promise that the United States would also withdraw from Derna. If the
pasha rejected this offer, Lear promised that Rodgers would be let loose to
shell the city. The pasha realized his precarious position and accepted the

new treaty to end the war but left the question of future payments unresolved.

Tunis remained a problem for a short time, but it too found common ground with the Americans after the threat of bombardment. Once again, Rodgers yielded to Lear, who found a peaceful resolution to the stand-off. The treaty, however, ran into stiff resistance in the Senate. The United States had both paid off the pasha and failed to use its military resources in defense of national honor, so went the arguments against the treaty. The fact remained, however, that what had been done was done. Lear had paid off the Pasha and freed the *Philadelphia* prisoners, who now returned home as heroes. The Mediterranean Squadron also returned home while Barbary pirates continued to harass American shipping through the 1810s, although at nowhere near the levels of intensity that they had between the 1780s and 1805.

The Tripolitan War had been a convoluted affair—inconsistent leadership, lack of strategy, and a confused political objective hampered American effectiveness. Still, Jefferson had made a bold statement to the rest of the world—the United States would fight a war not only for practical economic reasons, but it would also fight for an ideal, in this case, the principle of unhindered sovereign trade. Moreover, the young United States had stood up to extortion and terror, thus sending what should have been a clear signal to Britain and France that America would also resist interference from them. Militarily the United States had fought its first war on foreign soil, used allies and mercenaries, and established overseas bases. The war provided the Navy with invaluable experience. America soon faced a much more serious and deadly threat to shipping on the high seas, and the Navy would need every bit of experience it could muster to meet the challenge.

The *Chesapeake–Leopard* Affair

On June 22, 1807, the 40-gun USS *Chesapeake* commanded by Commodore James Barron sailed from Hampton Roads, Virginia, to take up station in the Mediterranean. Waiting off the Chesapeake Bay was HMS *Leopard*, a 50-gunner with orders to stop and board the *Chesapeake* to search for deserters from the Royal Navy. Based in Halifax, the Royal Navy's North American squadron patrolled up and down the Atlantic seaboard in the hope of catching French prizes trading in American ports. The Royal Navy suspected that deserters from British ships could be found in most major American ports. With gun ports open, the *Leopard* stopped the *Chesapeake* and sent aboard a dispatch demanding that any Royal Navy deserters be returned to the *Leopard*. Completely surprised by the encounter, Barron steadfastly denied he had any deserters among his crew and refused to allow the British to board his ship.

At this point, things went terribly wrong for Barron and the *Chesapeake*. Surprised by the British boldness at stopping an American naval vessel just off the Virginia coast, Barron had not cleared for action. Angered by the American refusal of what the Royal Navy considered just demands, the *Leopard* opened fire, raking the *Chesapeake* with three horrific broadsides. Barron managed one rather pathetic shot before surrendering. Four crew members were taken from the *Chesapeake*, one of whom was later executed for desertion. Barron was subsequently court-martialed for failure in the face of the enemy and permanently relieved of command—an outcome that caused division among the Navy's officers.

The young 'Hawks' in Congress demanded a declaration of war against Great Britain to avenge what they considered an egregious affront to American sovereignty. Jefferson would not be goaded into a war against the supreme naval power in the world that his country was not politically, economically, or militarily prepared to fight. The encounter between the two ships was the near-inevitable culmination of numerous meetings on the high seas between Royal Navy ships and American merchant and naval vessels since hostilities had broken out between Great Britain and France in the 1790s. The Royal Navy contended that it had the right to 'impress' British sailors into service aboard Royal Navy vessels regardless of the flag of their ship. The United States maintained that as a sovereign nation, as well as a neutral nation in the conflict between Great Britain and France, impressing sailors who served on American-flagged ships was a violation of its sovereignty and neutrality. American sea captains, however, openly and regularly recruited British deserters to crew American ships. Yet the Jefferson administration did next to nothing to stop either the British or the American practice. That is, until the *Chesapeake–Leopard* encounter.

Jefferson could not agree to war, but he could vigorously protest to the British government. He demanded that Great Britain renounce impressment and rescind Orders in Council, a demand that the British found impossible to accept. As if the British Orders in Council were not bad enough, Napoleon put in place his continental system, which also restricted American shipping and challenged American neutrality. Jefferson, followed by his successor James Madison, implemented controversial and ill-advised embargoes, including the Embargo Act of 1807, the Non-Intercourse Act of 1809, and Macon's Bill No. 2, none of which proved effective at changing British, or for that matter French, policy. Both Britain and France stopped American vessels on the high seas, searched them, and seized cargo they considered war contraband. As the principal belligerents in an increasingly costly and widening war, Great Britain and France appeared to be forcing the United States to choose one side or the other.

Going to war in 1807 or 1808, however, was out of the question. The Army was still small, although Congress approved a modest expansion in response to the *Chesapeake* crisis. The Navy was also equally minute, having just one gun to every Royal Navy ship. Although British military and naval resources were engaged across the world, they could still rally plenty of force against the American nuisance. As Congress debated whether to pour money into coastal fortifications or more of Jefferson's gunboats, the diplomatic situation stalemated, for both sides had made demands that the other could never accept.

The *Chesapeake–Leopard* affair itself did not directly lead to the War of 1812, but the incident was among several that point to the poor state of American military preparedness, lack of national strategy and clear policy objectives, and the overall disrespect that the major powers exhibited toward the young United States. For five long years, Great Britain and France played what they thought was a relatively low-stakes game of poker, using American trade, sovereignty, and neutrality as cheap chips.

The Hunger for Expansion

While American merchantmen and naval vessels struggled on the high seas, the growing population west of the Appalachians found itself embroiled in related troubles. In the west prices on everyday goods increased because of the embargoes on the coast. While the price increases had some legitimate foundation, westerners could not help thinking that some eastern price gouging was at play. A firm response against Great Britain, they claimed, would stop the nonsense on the high seas and restore standard pricing. Moreover, more people were heading across the Appalachians, creating what they perceived as a need for more land. Settlers wanting the fertile soils of Ohio and Indiana ignored the Treaty of Greenville before the ink had dried, once again giving tribes cause to band together.

Tecumseh and his brother the Prophet brought together another federation of Native Americans to fight white encroachment. At a new settlement along the Tippecanoe River called Prophet's Town, Tecumseh gathered over 1,000 warriors. William Henry Harrison, whom Jefferson appointed as governor of the new Indiana Territory in 1801, feared Tecumseh's movement would get in the way of his ability to uphold the Treaty of Greenville and his own ambitious land schemes. At Harrison's behest, in 1809 Little Turtle agreed to sell more than three million acres of land in northern Indiana to the United States. Harrison wanted statehood for Indiana, but Native American territory stood in the way. Tecumseh met with Harrison at Vincennes in the spring of 1810 to discuss the unfavorable land sale that Harrison had negotiated. The two leaders found themselves at an impasse. Tecumseh left to visit southern tribes to invite them to join his confederation while Harrison remained at Vincennes to plan a punitive expedition for the following year.

Harrison had been a young lieutenant on 'Mad' Anthony Wayne's staff at the Battle of Fallen Timbers. He had experience in 'punitive' expeditions and probably planned all along to war against Tecumseh. During the winter of 1810–1811 President Madison approved Harrison's campaign plans. By the summer of 1811 Indiana militiamen, the 4th U.S. Infantry Regiment, and Governor Harrison were ready to hunt down the Prophet. Once again, the regulars were well trained and, although lacking combat experience, were mostly disciplined, while the militia was undisciplined but eager to clear away Native American resistance to open northern Indiana to settlement.

Harrison's force of 900 militia and regulars left Vincennes on September 26, 1811, heading up the Wabash River to an abandoned Wea village to build an outpost that Harrison unabashedly named Fort Harrison. By early November they were only a few miles from Prophet's Town. A delegation of chiefs met with Harrison to arrange a parley and offered Harrison and his army a place to make camp, which Harrison suspiciously accepted. Tecumseh was away, still in the south visiting the more powerful tribes on his recruiting tour. Without Tecumseh's superior military leadership on the other side, Harrison knew he had the advantage. The Prophet, himself no military genius, conjured up visions and spells to take Harrison's encampment by surprise. He also promised his warriors that the American bullets would harmlessly bounce off them. The Prophet's mysticism seemed to almost work, but then while attempting to encircle the camp under cover of darkness, a sentry saw movement and fired. The Prophet's warriors charged the camp as weary soldiers pulled themselves out of their bedrolls and into line. On the northwest side of the encampment, the fighting was hand to hand. By daybreak, the Native Americans had reorganized on the left and right flanks of Harrison's bloodied line. Major Samuel Wells led a reckless but effective charge on the north flank to drive the Prophet's warriors back in disarray. The southern side broke as well, reeling back into a swampy wood to shield itself from a punishing charge of cavalry.

Despite the Prophet's assurances, hundreds of warriors had been killed and wounded by the supposedly harmless American bullets. The day after the battle, November 7, Harrison found Prophet's Town deserted. The tribes abandoned the Prophet and Tecumseh to return to their villages. His victory was stupendous in effect, breaking the confederation and opening the Old Northwest Territory to settlement. Harrison talked of annexing part of Canada to the United States and blamed British agents for the Native American troubles, although in this exceptional case they were innocent in the matter. Such bold talk came at a great price— Harrison had lost over 180 killed and wounded in the Battle of Tippecanoe, but the cost was overlooked as congressmen and settlers west of the Alleghenies applauded Harrison's ambition and cheered for war against Great Britain to expand American territory.

Conclusion

Security concerns over both the West and the Atlantic had forced the new Republic to reconsider its defense needs, often at the expense of previously held high ideals about standing armies and centralized author-ity. Molding effective defense policy out of domestic political disputes, regional interests, republican ideals, and military capabilities proved extre-mely difficult; yet, as evidenced by Jefferson's gunboat program, the United States was willing to at least try radical ideas to address its unique security needs. It is ironic that the conflict with Native Americans along the frontier, British harassment of American shipping on the Atlantic, and the American thirst for expansion would come together in 1812 in a general war with Great Britain. The new nation was ill-prepared for such a conflict, one that would be a second war for its independence.

Further Reading

Gaff, Alan. *Bayonets in the Wilderness: Anthony Wayne's Legion in the Old Northwest.* Norman, OK: University of Oklahoma Press, 2004.

Galloway, Colin G. *The Victory with No Name: The Native American Defeat of the First American Army.* New York: Oxford University Press, 2015.

Hoagland, William. *The Whiskey Rebellion: George Washington, Alexander Hamilton, and the Frontier Rebels Who Challenged America's Newfound Sovereignty.* New York: Scribner, 2006.

Jortner, Adam. *The Gods of Prophetstown: The Battle of Tippecanoe and the Holy War for the American Frontier.* New York: Oxford University Press, 2011.

Kilmeade, Brian, and Don Yaeger. *Thomas Jefferson and the Tripoli Pirates: The Forgotten War That Changed American History.* New York: Sentinel Books, 2015.

Kohn, Richard H. *Eagle and Sword: Federalists and the Creation of the Military Establishment in America, 1783–1802.* New York: The Free Press, 1975.

Toll, Ian. *Six Frigates: The Epic History of the Founding of the U.S. Navy.* New York: Norton, 2006.

Tucker, Spencer C. *The Jeffersonian Gunboat Navy.* Charleston, SC: University of South Carolina Press, 1993.

Unger, Harlow Giles. *The French War Against America: How a Trusted Ally Betrayed Washington and the Founding Fathers.* Hoboken, NJ: John Wiley and Sons, 2005.

5 The Second War of Independence

Introduction

The War of 1812 was both a war of expansion and a second war of independence for the young United States. American economic and strategic desires in Canada and Spanish Florida were widely known and even popular among the American people. Indeed, the United States had embarked on a policy of expansion long before the War with Mexico in 1846. On the high seas, American merchant vessels and naval ships ran into far more trouble with the British and French navies than they had ever met against the Barbary pirates. With Napoleon's domination of Europe in the balance, the United States found itself caught in an untenable situation that threatened its sovereignty and notions of neutrality. Bumbling and inexperience showed in ineffective American diplomacy and inadequate military preparedness, both of which made the War of 1812 a perilous conflict for the young nation. Yet the threats to the United States by Great Britain demanded defense of the nation's honor, if not its liberty.

A Declaration of War

On June 1, 1812, President James Madison delivered a message to Congress declaring that a state of war existed between the United States and Great Britain. The impressment of American citizens into the Royal Navy; the unlawful search and seizure of American ships, sometimes just off the coast of the United States; the Orders in Council; and the assumed British agitation of Native American tribes in the west made for a wide-ranging list of reasons that Madison believed war necessary to defend American sovereignty.

Congress approved the declaration on June 18 by a vote of 79–49 in the House of Representatives and 19–13 in the Senate. Opposition came from representatives of New England, New York, and New Jersey, while strong support for war came from those representing western and southern states, led by 'War Hawks' Henry Clay and John C. Calhoun. While geographic splits in the vote were apparent, so too were partisan lines, with Federalists holding most seats in New England and Republicans dominating the West and South. Mr. Madison's War, as it was known, was for many Americans precisely that.

While war fever ran high, financial support for the war was limited. Congress initially offered no appropriation for expanding the Navy and allowed the Army to increase from around 10,000 to only 35,000. Madison could call out volunteers, up to 100,000 for six months, to supplement the small regular force. In 1812 the War Department had a Secretary, William Eustis, and 11 clerks. Many senior officers were aged and owed their appointments to politics rather than merit. While many had served in the War for Independence and the conflicts with Native Americans in the 1790s, they had since grown soft intellectually—and in some cases physically—from inactivity. Younger officers had little, if any, experience. Among the troops, desertion and poor discipline were common. Pay was poor, and because of equally poor administration, it was also rare—sometimes as much as six months behind. Volunteers were enticed to enlist with bounties of up to $124 and 320 acres of land. Enlistees, however, did not equate to an effective fighting force. Militia units were in worse condition. Jeffersonians had always resisted a large standing army in the expectation that in crisis the militia would rally to the nation's defense.

Now, the crisis was at hand, and the militia was almost universally in complete confusion. The Uniform Militia Act of 1792 had not worked, mainly because of neglect rather than flawed policy. On the eve of the War of 1812, Congress hoped to use state militias as an inexpensive auxiliary force to fill out the small regular Army, but the poor condition and initial performance of the militia quickly convinced commanders and Congress alike that a national volunteer system was a better option. Congress responded with a call for 50,000 volunteers to serve primarily as a national militia, while the Army was increased by 25,000 men.

American political objectives far outstretched American military capacity and capability. With a weak navy, the United States did not dare to punish Great Britain for the litany of offenses committed against America on the high seas. As an alternative means of inflicting some harm against Great Britain, the United States turned its sights on Great Britain's most vulnerable point in North America—Canada. To connect an appropriate military strategy to American political objectives, an offensive plan seemed the only alternative. Yet American political leadership failed to make the war's objectives clear to its military leadership, resulting in a muddled military strategy. In a war that was apparently about maritime rights and foreign support of Native American tribes, the United States chose to invade Canada as its first military move. Even with Great Britain embroiled in the struggle against Napoleon on the European continent, the American strategy was bold indeed, considering the young nation's economic and military limitations.

The logistical, natural, and strategic problems that had plagued the colonial wars in North America and the War for Independence resurfaced in the War of 1812. The British would have to ship men and supplies across the Atlantic—a rough and often uncertain journey of six to eight weeks. Draft animals were always in short supply. Moreover, the Americans had only one arsenal at Springfield. The geography offered limited and mostly poor roads, so rivers and other waterways would once again play a pivotal role in the strategy of both armies. The St. Lawrence River, Lake Champlain and the Richelieu River, Lakes Ontario and Erie, the Mississippi River, and Chesapeake Bay each played leading roles in this war just as they had in the past. Moreover, the clear lesson of the previous wars showed that the key to breaking Canada was control of the St. Lawrence River. Achieving that objective required naval superiority.

Two days before Congress voted to approve the declaration of war, the British government withdrew its Orders in Council to nullify many American grievances. But Great Britain failed to publicize its increasingly ad hoc policy changes, and since the United States had no ranking diplomat in London at the time, it remained mostly in the dark as to British intentions. By the time news reached Washington that the British had changed their tack, it was too late. Yet the United States remained deeply divided on war, so much so that violent riots broke out in Baltimore between Republican proponents and Federalist opponents of the war. Because the Republicans received most of the blame for starting the riots, Federalists were able to sweep the November congressional elections, leaving Madison with a Congress strongly opposed to his war.

First Moves—Western Canada

For the divided United States, little strategy existed beyond an invasion of Canada via Montreal in the hope of splitting western Canada from the more populous and accessible eastern half. Once western Canada fell to American forces, so the thinking went, the remainder of Canada also would collapse.

Major General William Hull attacked Canada from his base at Detroit. Hull's campaign excited war supporters in the West, but the effort proved disastrous as Hull's army was forced back into American territory before the year was out. Hull crossed the river from Detroit into Canada in July with about 1,200 regulars and militia. General Isaac Brock knew that Hull was coming—Hull's papers had been found aboard a captured transport on Lake Erie just days before he crossed into Canada. With his own assorted lot of regulars and militia, Brock moved to counter the invasion.

Brock and Tecumseh approached the fort at Detroit, using deception to convince Hull that he faced a considerable force of British regulars and hundreds of Indians when Brock's force outnumbered Hull's by about two to one. Based on the captured letters, Brock gambled that Hull had lost his nerve—he was right. After an early morning cannonade into Fort Detroit and a brazen show of force outside its thin walls, Brock got what he wanted: Hull surrendered without firing a shot. Fort Dearborn, near modern Chicago, promptly followed suit. With Detroit and Fort Dearborn in their hands, the British easily advanced as far south as the Maumee River. Hull faced a court-martial and was convicted of cowardice before the enemy and sentenced to death. Taking into consideration Hull's service in the War for Independence, President Madison pardoned him.

William Henry Harrison replaced Hull and tried to correct the western disasters. Hoping to retake Detroit and avenge Fort Dearborn, Harrison left Fort Wayne with a large force of regulars and militia in September 1812. In January 1813 Harrison lost part of his army in a very one-sided affair at Frenchtown on the River Raisin near modern-day Monroe, Michigan.

By this time the weather and expired enlistments forced Harrison to halt his campaign. Near the site where Anthony Wayne had defeated Tecumseh at the Battle of Fallen Timbers almost 20 years before, Harrison established Fort Meigs on the Maumee River as a base of operations. Other than personnel, logistics proved his greatest challenge, as supplies had to be wheeled by wagon across hundreds of miles of poor roads, many of which were nothing more than trails. Because the British controlled Lake Erie, supply from ships was spotty at best. Harrison's resolution of this problem turned the corner for his western campaign.

Like Hull, Harrison believed that the only way to defeat the British in the west was to control Lake Erie. While Harrison fretted at Fort Meigs, Commodore (Captain) Oliver Hazard Perry put in motion a plan to make Lake Erie an American lake. A professional sailor, Perry read every naval and military work he could find. He had commanded a small squadron of gunboats at Rhode Island and feared he might miss the war. When the campaign went sour in the west, Perry offered to command a squadron to gain control of Lake Erie. At Erie, Pennsylvania, in February 1813, Perry arrived to find work already started on two brigs and plans laid out for gunboats.

Commander Robert H. Barclay commanded the British squadron that dominated Lake Erie and kept British forces in Michigan well supplied. Although he could not mount an amphibious assault on the American shipyard at Erie, Barclay could try to bottle up whatever the Americans were building. By July, Perry's small fleet was ready to sail, but he lacked the skilled sailors to handle the tricky waters of Lake Erie. Finally, hurriedly assembling skeleton crews for the vessels, Perry took advantage of Barclay's unexplained absence on August 1 to sneak out onto Lake Erie in force. Barclay suddenly found himself outnumbered. With Perry on the water, control of the lake was up for grabs. The British could no longer assume the proper supply of Forts Malden and Detroit.

Figure 5.1 The War of 1812.

Perry and Harrison held a council of war and came up with a daring plan. Perry first had to destroy Barclay's squadron to give his own squadron and Harrison's men the ability to maneuver freely, which would allow Perry to ferry Harrison's force across the lake to attack Fort Malden. Barclay came out to challenge Perry, who had stationed his squadron near Bass Island, on September 10. Barclay had six ships with 63 guns against Perry's nine vessels and 54 guns. The British ships were armed with long-range cannon, while Perry had mostly short-range carronades.

Aboard his flagship *Lawrence*, Perry hoisted a blue ensign decorated with 'Don't Give Up the Ship.' Just before noon, Perry led the *Lawrence* and four other ships straight at the British. British and American ships exchanged intense fire that eventually forced Perry to abandon the

Lawrence and take command of the *Niagara*. When Barclay fell wounded, the British *Detroit* surrendered, followed by most of the British squadron.

Meanwhile, Harrison crossed his army to the Canadian side of the lake. British commander Henry Proctor studied the strategic situation and declared it hopeless, allowing Harrison to take both Fort Detroit and Fort Malden unopposed. Tecumseh and his large band of Shawnee warriors and their families found themselves virtually abandoned by the British, just as they had at Fallen Timbers. At Moraviantown near the Thames River, Harrison engaged Tecumseh and what remained of Proctor's army. Proctor fled in panic, leaving his men with no option other than surrender. Tecumseh was killed while making a last stand with his 600 warriors, who, like their British counterparts, found themselves leaderless. The Battle of the Thames, over in less than an hour, permanently weakened the Native American tribes of the Northwest.

The Niagara Campaign

The Army turned its attention toward the Niagara River frontier and Lake Ontario. In October 1812, Major General Stephen Van Rensselaer planned to lead his mostly militia force across the Niagara River against Queenston. However, many militia units refused to cross the river and fight on foreign soil. The attack failed miserably and highlighted the lack of cooperation between militia and regular forces. Van Rensselaer's militia lacked even the most basic supplies, and regulars under the command of General Alexander Smyth failed to support the attack. British General Brock was killed defending the town.

Van Rensselaer resigned to leave Smyth to take overall command. Smyth failed to move, however, claiming that his army was not ready and that the militia was unreliable. Both regulars and militia deserted in droves. After two aborted campaigns, Smyth released the militia, an action that prompted accusations that he was a coward. The Niagara River frontier remained weakly defended on the American side, a great irony since it was the Americans who had initially intended to take offensive action there.

In 1813, new Secretary of War John Armstrong made plans for an ambitious campaign to sever Upper Canada from the eastern half. He wanted to separate Kingston from Montreal, forcing the British to withdraw from the western areas and concentrate at Montreal. In a two-part campaign, former Secretary of War and now Major General Henry Dearborn would take the excellent harbor and well-fortified town of Kingston on the north shore of Lake Ontario. After Kingston, Dearborn would subdue the capital of Upper Canada, York (Toronto). Last, he would secure the Canadian side of the Niagara River. Dearborn, however, failed to stage an earnest campaign on Montreal in late 1812. Poor recruitment, undisciplined militia, disease, and a confused command structure forced Dearborn to give up his campaign and retire to winter quarters.

Dearborn got started again in April once the ice had cleared and the weather had improved. Convinced that Kingston was too well defended, Dearborn instead concentrated on York and the Niagara River region. In a joint operation, Commodore Isaac Chauncey's Lake Ontario squadron escorted Brigadier General Zebulon Pike's attack force from Sackett's Harbor across the lake to York, which was surprisingly and easily captured on April 27. Pike, however, was killed when the British exploded the powder magazine. As York was put to the torch, Kingston was left unmolested.

Bad weather and disease forced the Americans to delay the next step in the campaign—an attack against Fort George on the Niagara Peninsula, which was taken on May 27. On paper, it was a stunning success, but Dearborn did not pursue the escaping British ranks. Colonel Winfield Scott, paroled from capture at Queenston, commanded the amphibious assault that captured the fort. But his pursuit of the fleeing British came to naught because he was ordered to halt. Although the fort had been taken, an excellent opportunity to destroy a British army had been lost. The failure to capture the British forces on the peninsula contributed to the low morale and worsening conditions among American troops at Fort George. In one of the few attempts to hunt down the British, two American generals were captured in a disorderly battle at Stony Creek in June. Another American force of 600 surrendered in an ambush at Beaver Dams. Many lower-ranking officers resigned their commissions in disgust over poor conditions and frustration with the War Department. Armstrong relieved Dearborn and sent him into retirement.

While Dearborn was making a mess of the Niagara campaign, the British staged an offensive of their own. In a daring amphibious operation, Sir George Prevost, the Governor General of Canada, took a force of 900 men across Lake Ontario from Kingston to attack Sackett's Harbor. Jacob Brown, a major general of militia, with his 400 regulars and nearly 800 militia, organized a spirited defense of Sackett's Harbor. After two hours of fighting, Prevost thought his force had achieved its mission. Burning barracks lit up the dawn sky as one of the naval stores exploded into an enormous ball of fire. Prevost prematurely ordered a withdrawal, thinking his work done but not wanting to engage American reinforcements he wrongly assumed were on the way. Prevost lost 26 percent of his landing force, including 48 killed and almost 200 wounded. Brown suffered 21 dead and 85 wounded in his successful defense of Sacketts Harbor.

For the Americans, the uninspiring year of 1813 closed with a failed campaign against Montreal. Major General James Wilkinson, a veteran of the War for Independence and Dearborn's replacement, planned a two-pronged advance against Montreal for November. With the British threat in the west apparently gone after the Battle of the Thames in October, Wilkinson believed that the time was right for such an attack. Wilkinson himself would lead the western advance of 8,000 regulars from Sackett's Harbor up the St. Lawrence River, while Major General Wade Hampton would lead his force of 5,000 from Plattsburg with the two wings converging on Montreal. Hampton and Wilkinson, however, despised each other—a sad fact that grossly affected their command.

Wilkinson's force ran into trouble just as it left Sacketts Harbor, hitting foul weather and driving sleet. The men were crammed into hundreds of small boats to cross the St. Lawrence, which swamped the tiny vessels with its turbulent waters. Over 50 sank, taking much of their human cargo with them to the bottom. To make matters worse, a British force of 800 shadowed the fleet from shore. At the Long Sault Rapids, Wilkinson disembarked his troops; he then ordered Jacob Brown and Winfield Scott with their respective brigades to occupy the village of Cornwall. Brigadier General John Boyd's brigade guarded the boats but abandoned them when Wilkinson learned that the British force was encamped at nearby Chrysler's Farm.

On the morning of November 11, Boyd attacked, sending wave after wave into repeated British repulses. Boyd's losses were high—over 100 killed, 230 wounded, and another 100 missing. The British lost only 22 dead and less than 150 wounded. The Battle of Chrysler's Farm convinced Wilkinson to abandon his part of the campaign. Hampton fared no better as his New York militia refused to cross the border into Canada. With only 4,000 troops remaining, Hampton pressed on, only to hit a smaller but determined force of British regulars in the Battle of the Chateauguay on October 26. After two hours of repeated assaults on the British entrenchment, Hampton gave up and went back to Plattsburg. The 1813 campaign for Montreal was over.

The year 1813 had exposed several critical weaknesses in the American effort. Militia had proven unreliable. Generalship lacked imagination and determination. Political maneuvering between Federalists and Republicans not only affected decision making on the national level but also infected the officer corps, particularly in the upper ranks.

The campaign of 1813 suffered from a near complete disconnect between political objectives and military objectives, and more so between political goals and military capabilities. Joint operations on the Great Lakes showed some promise, but the naval war on the high seas had not gone well. Heavily outnumbered, the American navy largely remained blockaded in ports up and down the Atlantic seaboard. The British blockade was also having its desired effect on prices in the United States, which began to climb dramatically.

While the British had also missed opportunities, by December 1813, they had retaken Fort George and captured Fort Niagara on the American side of the river. To top it all off, the Prussians and their allies scored a tremendous victory over Napoleon at Leipzig in October, thus forcing Napoleon to withdraw from Germany and allowing the British to free up forces for duty in North America. Despite the British having the initiative as 1814 began, the United States controlled Lake Erie and Tecumseh's confederation had been destroyed, developments that left the Americans with at least a few offensive options.

The Campaign of 1814

Following the failures of 1813, President Madison made significant command changes. After another disastrous defeat by a British force that he outnumbered eight to one at La Colle Mill in March 1814, Wilkinson was relieved of command. Hampton also resigned over what he considered incompetent prosecution of the war. Madison commissioned Jacob Brown as a brigadier general in the regular Army and gave him command of the Niagara frontier. Brown had Winfield Scott, also now a brigadier general, in command of one of his brigades. Major General George Izard took command in the Lake Champlain/Plattsburg area, along with Brigadier General Alexander Macomb as his subordinate.

Brown granted Scott's request for time to formally train the Left Division of Brown's army. Scott, a voracious reader on military affairs, did not disappoint Brown. For three months, Scott drilled and trained the Left Division, whipping it into fighting shape. With so few soldiers reenlisting, Scott had little choice but to train new recruits hard to replace the more experienced troops the army had lost. He ordered and personally conducted frequent inspections, instructed on proper drill, and read aloud to officers from various military texts—including Alexander Smyth's *Regulations for the Field Exercises, Maneuver, and Conduct of the Infantry*, a rather fundamental abridgment of the standard French regulations. Scott used strict discipline, drill, and motivation to teach his men how to operate in unit formations and convince them that doing so in strict obedience to their officers would likely save their lives. The standard-issue blue uniform of the regular Army was unavailable, so Scott commandeered gray and white cloth for uniforms. Impressively, Scott eradicated common camp diseases through proper sanitation and discipline.

Secretary of War Armstrong hoped to move on the Niagara frontier and gain control of Lake Ontario, thereby opening the door to attacking Kingston and Montreal. On the Niagara front, Brown crossed the Niagara River in yet another amphibious operation and took Fort Erie with little fighting. Two days later, as the army advanced toward the Chippewa River, American militia encountered British-supported Indians and attacked. Quickly, however, the small force hit a strong line of British regulars and broke and fled. Winfield Scott stepped into the breach with his 1,500 regulars. Well-disciplined and well-trained, the gray-clad regulars held their line as they advanced into withering British fire. British

General Phineas Riall, convinced that the gray soldiers must be militia, suddenly realized that indeed they were regulars. Scott boldly ordered a bayonet charge that broke the British right flank, forcing Riall to withdraw his entire force back across the Chippewa River.

At the Battle of Chippewa, Riall lost 500 killed, wounded, and missing to Scott's 325. Although the battle was strategically indecisive, Scott had notched his belt with yet another admirable example of combat command and gave Brown's army a substantial morale boost. In honor of Scott's 'Grays' success, the United States Military Academy at West Point adopted the gray tunic as its official uniform.

Just a few weeks later, the American army was engaged again, this time in a large affair near Niagara Falls at a spot called Lundy's Lane. With only 1,000 troops, Scott struck at a British force of 1,800. Reinforcements increased Scott's strength to 2,100 and the British numbers to over 3,000 by the end of the day. Fighting continued into the night. A battery at the British center was overrun by the Americans, who in turn had to repulse several bloody British assaults to retake the battery. Some veterans of earlier battles in the War of 1812 and the Napoleonic Wars claimed that this was the fiercest fight they had ever witnessed. Both Scott and Brown received severe wounds. As the fighting subsided out of sheer exhaustion, Brown ordered his men from the field and detailed wagons to collect the wounded. Hard-fought battles had come to naught; and now the initiative, which Brown and Scott had so brilliantly exercised, seemed to pass back to the British. Casualties amounted to over 800 for each side, but the Americans felt they had won the day by voluntarily withdrawing from the field in good order. The British, however, could equally claim victory in this, the bloodiest battle of the war.

Now the British took the offensive. In August a British force of 2,100 attacked Fort Erie. After a two-day artillery barrage, the British assaulted the fort with bayonets fixed at 2:00 a.m. on August 15. Hand-to-hand combat raged during a driving rainstorm. After two hours the affair was decided by an exploding magazine, which killed and wounded many more British than Americans. The British withdrew, leaving behind over 500 killed, wounded, and missing to the Americans' 130. The British did not give up. They placed three batteries some 500 yards from the fort and opened a continuous fire. Jacob Brown did not want to abandon Fort Erie, but neither could he allow his men to be shelled into submission. Brown ordered two brigades of New York militia to assault the batteries. On the night of September 17, the New Yorkers performed well, taking two of the three batteries in fierce fighting. The British withdrew. On November 5, so too did the Americans, destroying the fort as they evacuated. The bloody fight achieved little of strategic importance, but the Americans had clearly shown they could go toe-to-toe with the British army.

Figure 5.2 American Infantry attacks at the Battle of Lundy's Lane, July 25, 1814. The wounded officer at the center is Brigadier General Jacob Brown.

Source: Library of Congress.

While Fort Erie lay under siege, Prevost set his sights on taking control of Lake Champlain as part of a broad British strategy to attack into American territory from Canada as well as to hit strategic points along the American coast. Prevost hoped to put the Americans on the defensive and maintain initiative by destroying the American naval squadron on Lake Champlain and defeating land forces at Plattsburgh. His army of 8,000 crack British troops, many just arrived after defeating Napoleon, crossed into the United States on September 3. Brigadier General Alexander Macomb abandoned Plattsburgh to Prevost on September 6, withdrawing across the Saranac River to earthworks on the high ground opposite Plattsburgh. Prevost's attempts to cross the Saranac River via two bridges were repulsed by determined American regulars and militia.

Prevost then decided to let Captain George Downie's flotilla of 93 guns take care of Captain Thomas Macdonough's squadron of 86 guns formed for battle in Plattsburgh Bay. In a two-hour, bitterly fought battle that killed Downie, Macdonough prevailed by using difficult anchor maneuvers that allowed his ships to swing quicker and at a shorter distance and thus to outmaneuver the British vessels. The British hauled down their colors and surrendered.

While the British attempt to invade via Plattsburgh had failed, joint operations in the Chesapeake Bay region nearly achieved decisive success. British activity in the Chesapeake Bay had been limited to sparse but effective raids. Two thousand troops, mostly French prisoners of war known as the *Chasseurs Britannique*, quickly chased off 450 militiamen defending the town. British operations in the Chesapeake also affected slavery; as in the War for Independence, the British offered captured slaves the opportunity for freedom and resettlement in exchange for service in His Majesty's forces. An estimated 600 slaves enlisted.

In 1814, however, the British decided to make a more determined diversionary campaign in the Chesapeake region in the hope of forcing the Americans to redeploy forces from the Niagara front to the Chesapeake. Moreover, taking Washington, Baltimore, or Philadelphia would undoubtedly give the British a considerable advantage in peace negotiations. By July 1814, Madison had become increasingly alarmed that the British would indeed invade up the Chesapeake Bay and destroy the American capital, much as the Americans had razed York earlier in the war.

Remarkably, before July 1814, the United States had no established defense strategy for the Washington–Baltimore area. Madison made Brigadier General William Winder, a Federalist, commander of the new 10th Military District for the defense of Washington and Baltimore. Three thousand regulars and over 10,000 militia would do the job with the help of various natural obstacles, not the least of which was the dense undergrowth and swampy bogs of the Tidewater region. Secretary of War Armstrong, who disagreed with Madison's fear for Washington, neglected Winder's requests for staff, materiel, and ammunition. The governors of Maryland, Virginia, and Delaware, among other states, acted slowly to fulfill Madison's demands for more militia. The nation's capital was exceptionally vulnerable to attack.

British General Robert Ross eagerly took command of the British effort, knowing what taking the American capital would mean for British morale both in North America and at home. Admiral Alexander Cochrane shared Ross's enthusiasm for the campaign, hoping to cash in on prize money from the prosperous port of Baltimore. On August 20, Ross and Cochrane sailed up the Patuxent River and landed 4,500 troops at Benedict, Maryland. By August 22, the British had advanced to Upper Marlborough, Maryland, just 16 miles away from Washington. Pandemonium struck the capital city, and the Army command structure, never efficient to begin with, began to break down at the most critical moment.

Winder had about 7,000 troops of mostly hastily trained militia under his command. With his force formed in three lines between the British and the capital, Winder lost operational control. Secretary of State James Monroe, who had volunteered as a cavalry scout and was nominally acting

Secretary of War, personally ordered the second line to redeploy to a position where it could not support the front line. The third line had already been placed in a position where it could not support the second. General Tobias Stansbury, commander of Maryland militia in the second line, obeyed the order as if it had come from Winder. It had not—Monroe had no authority whatsoever.

On August 24, British troops easily crossed the Potomac River via a poorly defended bridge near Bladensburg. The first American line was quickly outflanked. Militia ran rearward, while the few regulars manning the defenses staged a mostly orderly retreat. The retreating militia ran pell-mell into the second line, causing widespread panic—the infamous Bladensburg Races were underway.

Holding the third and last line was Navy Captain Joshua Barney, who had commanded the gunboat flotilla on the Chesapeake Bay. With naval guns positioned on high ground, Barney hit the advancing British lines with devastating grapeshot. Still, the British managed to overrun Barney's militia-defended flank, putting the British in a strong position to overwhelm the guns. Although the British suffered over 250 casualties to the Americans' 70, they had won the Battle of Bladensburg. The road to Washington was now wide open for the British advance.

By 8:00 p.m. that same day, the British marched into Washington. Ross searched in vain for anyone with authority to arrange for the surrender of the city. The executive mansion, the capitol building, and the Treasury, War, and State Department offices were looted and burned. The American navy captain in command of the Washington Navy Yard followed his orders and set fire to the Navy's best-supplied shipyard and two frigates moored there. The sacking of Washington was a bitter pill indeed for the United States.

Baltimore lay next in the path of the seemingly unstoppable British onslaught. Ross left Washington on August 25. In Baltimore, the alarm had been sounded. Senator and Major General of Maryland militia Samuel Smith organized over 10,000 militia to defend the city from a land attack. Fourteen miles from Baltimore at North Point, Ross landed his 4,500 troops. There a force of 3,200 militia tried unsuccessfully to stop the British advance. Although the British prevailed in the Battle of North Point, the victory came at a high price—340 British casualties, including Ross, who was killed by a sharpshooter.

Lacking naval support, the British had to stop just short of Baltimore on September 13. To get to Baltimore, Ross first had to pass Fort McHenry, a Vauban-style fortification built as part of the coastal defense program. Admiral Cochrane's guns fired over 1,500 shells at the ramparts but did little damage. Fort McHenry held, an event immortalized by Georgetown lawyer and artillery volunteer Francis Scott Key in his poem 'The Star-Spangled Banner.'

September 1814 had been a good month for the American war effort, despite the sacking of the capital city. Victories at Plattsburgh, Lake Champlain, and now Baltimore should have given the Americans a sense of relief and newfound confidence. Baltimore had been successfully defended by militia and the local community—a fact that somehow masked the repeated failures of militia, most recently at Bladensburg. The British had been repulsed, and peace negotiations at Ghent seemed to be making headway.

Partisan politics in Congress and deep divisions in the Madison administration, however, overshadowed the short-lived sense of optimism. Congressional committees immediately began investigations into the loss of Washington. The secretaries of War, the Treasury, and the Navy resigned. James Monroe ambitiously, if not recklessly, tried to be Secretary of State and War at the same time. New Englanders began their controversial meetings in Hartford and openly talked of secession unless the war was ended. By November Ross's army had rendezvoused with the British fleet in Jamaica to refit for the next campaign. British plans for what had initially been another diversionary campaign turned into hopes for a decisive strike at arguably the most strategic, important American possessions—the Mississippi River and New Orleans.

The Battle of New Orleans

President Madison earlier approved of plans to ignite an uprising in Spanish Florida supported by American troops and naval forces. The United States had taken similar action in Spanish West Florida in 1810, and Congress had approved a secret act to occupy and acquire all Spanish Florida in 1811. By 1812 as the war with Britain got underway, American filibusters, or private adventurers, supported by Georgia militia and with the blessing of the Madison administration, secured Amelia Island just off the Florida coast and were preparing to lay siege against St. Augustine. Americans in Georgia and South Carolina strongly supported expansion into Florida, while New Englanders denounced the plan as Republican aggression. President Madison had to play an extremely delicate role by publicly denying the effort while privately cheering it on. Strategically Madison claimed that American aggression in East Florida was a pre-emptive move to counter British possession of the region. The so-called Patriot War failed in the end but cleared the path for the United States to acquire Florida through the Adams–Onís Treaty of 1819.

General Andrew Jackson had just triumphed in the Creek War. The great warrior chieftain Tecumseh visited the Creek in 1811 in a vain attempt to gather Creek support for his united front against Anglo encroachment upon Native American lands. Tecumseh was a long way from home and arguably had little influence on the Creek, who were in the nascent stages of their own civil war. But like Tecumseh, many Creeks found the idea of returning to their indigenous ways appealing as European customs seemed about to bury the old ways forever. The Red Sticks surfaced as leaders of this resistance movement. Conflict broke out among the Creek in 1813 after some Upper Creek warriors killed several white settlers. The Creek Council condemned the warriors to death, but Upper Creek and Red Sticks protested and raided several Lower Creek towns, killing several hundred men, women, and children, including over 500 in the massacre at Fort Mims in Alabama.

This complex intertribal conflict quickly erupted into a full-fledged war with the United States, which feared the Creek might be lured into an alliance to assist British operations in the South. The massacre at Fort Mims occurred amid these concerns and quickly persuaded the Madison administration to send Federal troops and militia from Tennessee, Georgia, and Mississippi to deal with the Creek. Among these was a significant force from Tennessee that was later reinforced to total some 5,000 troops led by the rugged Jackson. A harsh disciplinarian, Jackson kept his Army well trained and supplied, and it grew more disciplined as the campaign continued.

Jackson and the Red Sticks fought several engagements, with neither side gaining a sustainable advantage. Red Stick casualties in these battles were high, numbering in the hundreds in some instances. Finally, in March 1814, Jackson attacked a large Red Stick encampment at Horseshoe Bend along the Tallapoosa River in Alabama. The Creek had a well-entrenched position but were easily diverted by a small unit of Jackson's force. Jackson took advantage of the opportunity, and his forces overwhelmed the battlement. Few Red Sticks surrendered or had the chance to do so, resulting in almost 1,000 Creek deaths. Over 300 Creek men, women, and children were captured. Jackson lost fewer than 30 troops killed. It was a stunning and complete victory in what had become a very bloody small war within the War of 1812. Jackson was given a regular Army commission and promoted to major general, then ordered to New Orleans to take command of the 7th Military District. The Creeks were finished as a political–military force in the American South as the Treaty of Fort Jackson forced them to cede much of their 20 million acres of land to the United States.

After defeating the Creeks, Jackson had occupied Mobile and garrisoned Fort Boyer on the eastern shore of the mouth of Mobile Bay with a force of 160 men. In September 1814 a British force of 225 Royal Marines from Pensacola landed nine miles east of Fort Boyer, while a small British squadron of 78 guns approached the mouth of Mobile Bay. Major William Lawrence, commander of Fort Boyer, exchanged fire with the British ships and managed to shoot away the rigging of HMS *Hermes*, which had to be abandoned by the British. The weather favored the Americans, as calm winds made naval maneuver dangerously slow under the accurate fire of American artillery on the walls of Fort Boyer. Taking

Fort Boyer had been key to British plans for taking Mobile, which in turn was the key for mounting an invasion against Louisiana.

Instead of waiting for the British to return with a more substantial force, Jackson took the initiative against the British base of operations at Pensacola. Joining forces with General John Coffee's 2,000 cavalry from Tennessee, Jackson amassed an army of 4,000, including several hundred Indians and 1,000 regulars. Pensacola was still a Spanish possession, yet the Spanish had allowed the British to garrison Fort Barrancas. Two other forts, St. Rose and St. Michael, were weakly occupied by a few hundred Spanish soldiers. Jackson arrived at Pensacola and camped on the west side of the small village and the Spanish forts.

The Spanish rejected Jackson's terms for surrender; then, on November 7, Jackson attacked the town. A small demonstration on the west side of Pensacola fooled the Spanish as well as the British squadron in the bay into believing that the American attack would come from that direction. Instead, Jackson attacked with his main body from the east, quickly investing the town. The Spanish commander quickly surrendered the forts, but officers in the forts delayed giving up in the vain hope that the British ships would be able to reposition to support them. Furious, Jackson was forced to postpone his assault on the British at Fort Barrancas. Fortunately, he would not have to take Fort Barrancas by force as on the next day the British withdrew from the fort, destroying it in a tremendous explosion.

With the British gone, Jackson returned Pensacola to the Spanish and headed back to Mobile, arriving there on November 19. With the expeditionary force back from the Chesapeake and further reinforcements coming from Plymouth, the British made sail from Jamaica to take New Orleans. They were led by Lieutenant General Sir Edward Pakenham, a seasoned veteran of the Peninsula Wars. Jackson, still not wholly certain that New Orleans was the target, took the gamble and set out with 2,000 men for the Crescent City.

New Orleans possessed impressive natural defenses. The turbulent Mississippi River bordered its southern edge, while Lake Pontchartrain provided a formidable barrier north of the city. To the west and east as well as the north, hundreds of creeks, bayous, and swamps made New Orleans a daunting objective for an invading force. Man-made levees in and around the city itself added further protection. Two forts, St. Leon nearer the town and St. Philip 60 miles further south, guarded the southern approaches along the river. Pakenham concluded that the northern and eastern approaches would be the least defended.

Jackson found help in New Orleans, and more support was on the way from Tennessee. Militia and two battalions of free African Americans combined with 3,000 militia from Tennessee under General William Carol and Jackson's 2,000 men to give Jackson a force of almost 6,000 to defend against Pakenham's 14,000 troops. Even the slave-smuggling adventurer Jean Lafitte, whose men had for years been notorious for raiding ships near the mouth of the Mississippi River, contributed his services in exchange for Jackson's promise that the pirate and his men would be pardoned for their past deeds. On December 16 Jackson declared martial law in New Orleans, risking the support of Louisiana's state government and causing no end of legal problems for his command.

The British had already landed near Lake Borgne, where a Royal Navy squadron defeated the American gunboat fleet to clear the way for Pakenham's troops. A British advance force of 1,600 came within seven miles of the city on December 22. The next day, in a daring night attack, Jackson and 2,000 men managed to stall the advance. He then retreated three miles to the Rodriguez Canal, a defensible position with the Mississippi River on the west, the dense Cypress Swamp on the east, and a ten-foot-wide canal connecting the two. Three ditches also ran west to east in front of the Rodriguez Canal. Jackson's men feverishly dug to build a rampart along the canal but found another enemy in the wet Louisiana soil. Fences, slave cabins, cotton bales, and whatever else his men could tear down and transport to the canal were used to shore up the

Figure 5.3 The Battle of New Orleans, from an engraving of a painting by Jean Hyacinthe de Laclotte, eyewitness to the battle.

Source: Library of Congress.

breastworks. Pakenham assaulted this position on December 28, but deadly artillery fire from the American line and the *Louisiana* from the river forced him to withdraw.

Pakenham tried again on January 1, 1815, launching a massive artillery assault on the Rodriguez Canal. Jackson replied in kind. For over 90 minutes the two sides pounded each other, but the British failed to make a dent in Jackson's line. Pakenham then resolved to take the position by frontal assault. In the early hours of January 8, Pakenham sent a force of 600 across the river to the west bank to engage the force of 1,200 that Jackson had positioned there to prevent a British attempt to simply go around on the other side of the river. Jackson held his main force on the canal. Pakenham sent 3,500 men directly at Jackson's line at about 7:00 a.m. On their left lay the mighty Mississippi River; on their right was the Cypress Swamp. They had nowhere to go but forward into the well-entrenched American line. Jackson laid down a murderous wall of musket fire and canister shot that decimated the British ranks, most of whom were veterans of the Napoleonic wars. Pakenham fell dead. In just over an hour the British suffered almost 300 killed, 1,200 wounded, and 480 captured to Jackson's 13 dead and 39 wounded. The Battle of New Orleans was a stunning defeat for the British and an extraordinary victory for the Americans.

The War Ends

On February 8, 1815, a British force launched a final assault against Fort Boyer to renew the offensive to take Mobile. Fort Boyer fell, but just afterward news reached both sides that a peace treaty had been signed at Ghent on Christmas Eve, 1814. The war had been over for six weeks and for two weeks before the Battle of New Orleans. News of Jackson's victory reached Washington just before the word of the treaty. The Treaty of Ghent restored the geopolitical situation to *status quo ante bellum.* With the war against Napoleon finished, there was no longer any need to harass American shipping and impress American sailors. With Tecumseh's confederation broken in the Old Northwest Territory and the Creeks under control in the south, the Indian threat and British irritation had apparently vanished. Canada had not fallen to America, but neither had New England seceded from the Union. The United States had survived an apparent 'second war of independence' by fighting the world's foremost military power to what amounted to a draw.

The war had touched people across the young nation. Over 450,000 militia had been mustered, and tens of thousands of volunteers had been recruited. Over 50,000 served in the regular Army during the war, and another 20,000 had served in the Navy and Marines. According to official records, only 2,260 had been killed in battle with another 4,500 wounded, but perhaps as many as 17,000 men died from nonmilitary causes, mostly disease. The war had cost $158 million, including Army and Navy expenditures, interest on war loans, and veterans' benefits. The national debt had risen from $45 million in 1812 to over $127 million at war's end. The economy was slow to recover, hitting rock bottom in the Panic of 1819–1820.

Despite the euphoric celebrations at war's end, problems that had plagued American foreign and military policy since the founding of the Republic had become more serious. The war had exacerbated the spirit of factionalism and sectionalism to further divide the nation. The military faced a critical crossroads—would it remain small and weak, reliant upon the militia, or would it begin the long process of becoming a professional peacetime standing army? Would the naval successes in 1814 justify a larger, more powerful permanent fleet? For the United States to capitalize on its newfound respect abroad and continue its commercial and territorial growth, it would have to address these and many additional issues. As is often the case, the end of a war may resolve some problems but create others.

The Beginnings of a Professional Military

Efforts to assess the successes and failures of the military after the War of 1812 had already become clouded by selective memory and political purpose. Junior officers who had risen through the ranks, such as Scott, had been frustrated by incompetent generalship, glacial bureaucracy, nightmarish logistical shortcomings, and other maladies that had plagued an unprepared nation and its military during the war. Although they had not forgotten these problems, many junior officers chose to sugarcoat them because of the way they remembered, with great pride, the exaggerated success of the regular Army during the war. Lundy's Lane, Chippewa, and Plattsburgh, among others, highlighted for these officers the increasing professionalism of the regular Army and confirmed their doubts of the unmanageable militia. Granted, the militia had failed on numerous occasions, but so too had the regulars. Many officers had conveniently forgotten that it had been mostly militia that defeated Tecumseh and Brock in 1813 and gave Jackson victory at New Orleans. Career officers easily formulated an argument promoting their own military prowess and denigrating the shameful failures of the militia, quickly convincing themselves that the United States could no longer depend upon a citizen-led army. Only a large, disciplined army led by professional officers could save the nation from the total disintegration it nearly faced in 1812 and 1813.

Winfield Scott went immediately to work at the end of the war to rectify the gross shortcomings of the Army. He had learned that not only did field armies need organized staffs, so too did the generals in

Washington. Moreover, politically appointed officers had to be driven out in favor of an officer corps that saw military service as a career and a profession. The lack of recruiting, training, and operational standards had created a force that suffered from poor morale, inconsistent performance, and high rates of attrition. Many frustrated officers left service after only a few years due to the lack of opportunity for promotion, inferior quality of life, and general corruption that had seized the officer corps. Scott, Brown, and Macomb, among others, would lead this effort to reorganize the officer corps and make the best of an Army reduced from its authorized wartime strength of 65,000 to just 10,000. While much dead weight was cut away from the Army, demobilization caused thousands of men with few prospects to be put out on the streets. No pensions or bonuses were immediately available to ease the financial pain.

Scott and his compatriots faced a Congress and a nation that retained a fear of standing armies; once again, most people wanted to hastily dismantle the wartime military and return to a militia-based peacetime establishment. Officers who earnestly desired to make it a professional force believed that too much dismantling would risk the valuable experience that had been gained from the war.

Scott and others proposed instead to implement George Washington's original idea from 1783. Using a skeleton structure, the current regimental organization would be retained but at less strength. In a crisis, the skeleton could be filled out with volunteers or conscription rather than state militia. Scott and Secretary of War Monroe suggested a similar plan in 1815. Scott wanted an army of 65,000 troops, then, realizing the political climate of the time, he proposed 20,000. Through the Army Reduction Act of 1815, Congress allowed only 10,000. Over the next several years the skeleton or expansible army plan gained support in Congress.

Scott helped write a new uniform manual for tactical drill, based upon French models of the day. While criticized for being merely a translation of French drill manuals, slightly adapted for American conditions, Scott's manual was significant. For the first time, it provided uniformity and consistency for Army drill and infantry tactics. Several officers, including Scott, took advantage of leaves of absence and official assignments to visit Europe and discuss military matters with their British and French comrades in arms.

Although Congress reluctantly maintained a minimal professional force, it was less hesitant to pass legislation to better organize that force. In April 1816, Congress authorized the Army to adopt wartime staff organization in peacetime. In 1816, only three generals heading staff departments had headquarters in Washington—the Adjutant General, the Paymaster General, and the Chief of Ordnance. In 1818, Calhoun convinced Congress to authorize three additional positions—the Quartermaster General, Surgeon General, and Commissary General. In addition to the already existing chief of the Corps of Engineers, the new departments also had headquarters in Washington. On paper this staff organization looked effective; however, as an unintended consequence, this new structure created more conflict between staff and line officers, as well as a system increasingly bureaucratic and decentralized.

Moreover, the war provided motivation for expanding and enhancing the coastal defense system. Madison established a board of engineers to study the nation's sea-coast defenses. Their 1821 report found serious gaps and highlighted the need for significant additions that would better secure the United States from foreign attack. Congress had provided a paltry $800,000 in 1816 to repair aging fortifications, but more was needed. Since the Navy remained relatively small, coastal fortifications would have to serve as the actual first line of defense. The board suggested 50 sites for new fortifications, but recommendations and Congressional appropriations to fulfill those suggestions often proved to be two different things.

The Navy also received a much-needed boost from the war. Having performed well considering its size and the enemy it faced in battle, the expanded fleet of frigates had scored several brilliant one-on-one victories during the war. Organizationally, a Board of Navy Commissioners was created to advise the Navy Department. Made up of three captains, the first board included John Rodgers, David Porter, and Stephen Decatur. How well it worked over the next several decades depended upon the management style of the Secretary of the Navy and the makeup of the board. Often, as in the case of the first board, the advice was limited to logistical and administrative matters.

As for the fleet, Congress passed an act in 1816 that provided a generous $1 million per year for six years for naval construction, including 12 44-gun frigates and nine 74-gun ships-of-the-line. Congress had been convinced that a stronger peacetime navy was necessary for the postwar environment, especially with Great Britain still in command of the seas.

The debate continued about how best to employ the Navy. Sticking to traditional strategies, the Navy continued to use its frigates in squadrons that really amounted to a few ships acting independently under a commodore who exercised regional command. By 1821 the Navy, like the Army, came under the budgetary and ideological knife of politicians who wanted to severely limit the peacetime military establishment. The Navy's annual appropriation dropped from $3.7 million for the years 1817–1821 to $2.9 million for the years 1822–1825. Navy personnel also declined, from 5,500 in 1816 to 4,000 in 1821.

Conclusion

The young republic survived considerable challenges to its sovereignty, indeed its very existence. In military affairs, it had learned much but still had much to learn. Experience shaped the way the nation approached military matters and warfare, and it was changing the ideological landscape that governed the way the American military would be organized, comprised, and used. Experience also gradually better defined American national interests. Seaborne trade, territorial integrity and expansion, and defense of liberty at home evolved from basic concepts to real national strategic objectives.

The military strategy to achieve and maintain these objectives had also matured to include strong coastal defense, an established navy, a peacetime army of some size, and continued reliance upon militia to expand both the Army and Navy in times of danger. The nation had survived birth. It next had to face the growing pains of an ambitious and expanding population. The military would be at the forefront of such national movements as Manifest Destiny, the Market Revolution, the beginnings of industrialization, and the expansion of democracy in America.

Further Reading

Barbuto, Richard V. *Niagara 1814: America Invades Canada.* Lawrence, KS: University Press of Kansas, 2000.

Daughan, George. *1812: The Navy's War.* New York: Basic Books, 2011.

Hickey, Donald R. *The War of 1812: A Forgotten Conflict, Bicentennial Edition.* Urbana, IL: University of Illinois Press, 2012.

Laxer, James. *Tecumseh and Brock: The War of 1812.* Toronto: House of Anansi Press, 2012.

Pitch, Anthony S. *The Burning of Washington: The British Invasion of 1814.* Annapolis, MD: Naval Institute Press, 1998.

Randall, Willard Sterne. *Unshackling America: How the War of 1812 Truly Ended the American Revolution.* New York: St. Martin's Press, 2017.

Remini, Robert V. *The Battle of New Orleans.* New York: Viking, 1999.

Skaggs, David Curtis, ed. *The Battle of Lake Erie and Its Aftermath: A Reassessment.* Kent, Ohio: Kent State University Press, 2013.

Skeen, C. Edward. *Citizen Soldiers in the War of 1812.* Lexington, KY: University Press of Kentucky, 1999.

Taylor, Alan. *The Civil War of 1812: American Citizens, British Subjects, Irish Rebels, Indian Allies.* New York: Knopf, 2010.

6   Agents of Empire

Introduction

From the early 1800s through the Civil War, the United States experienced tremendous territorial, economic, and democratic growth. Settlers occupied lands that few had thought habitable as well as other lands already claimed by Native Americans. The Louisiana Territory, Texas, Oregon, and the Mexican Cession lands became organized territories and states. The Market Revolution broadened economic opportunity, just as political reforms expanded the electorate and egalitarianism shaped democratic values during the Age of Jackson. At the same time, the beginnings of an industrial revolution changed labor patterns and made material goods more widely available than ever before. New technology, such as the steam engine, revolutionized transportation, communication, and production. While stunning in scope and effect, such change and growth had disadvantages. Territorial expansion brought contact with other peoples, adding more territory to police and defend, offering difficult challenges to the young American military establishment.

The Military and a Changing Nation

Because the oceans continued to protect the growing nation from external threats, the American military remained small and technologically behind the times. Yet, during this period the Army performed many nonmilitary tasks for which it had no training and little experience while continuing in its primary purpose to defend the United States.

From the beginning of the nineteenth century through well after the Civil War, the Army and Navy used the experience gained from nonmilitary duties to improve military knowledge and skills. Officers found professional stimulation in exploration and science, and in studying the Napoleonic Wars that had engulfed the European continent from 1799 to 1815. Internal matters, such as Indian removal and frontier garrison duty, however, often interfered with the pursuit of professionalism because such duties required that the Army function more as a constabulary than as a military force preparing for war. Nonetheless, when war against Mexico came in 1846, the United States had an Army and Navy much better equipped and led than they had been in the War of 1812. Efforts toward professionalism paid off in a military that, although far from perfect, had successfully carried out difficult and distant campaigns against a formidable enemy.

With relative peace from the War of 1812 through the early 1840s, military officers eagerly volunteered for exploring expeditions on land and sea. These expeditions contributed valuable knowledge to various scientific fields, produced improved maps and navigational charts, and brought prestige and pride to both the military and the United States. Moreover, exploring gave the Army and Navy an opportunity to improve upon and learn new skills, practice large deployments, and develop a sense of purpose. A greater sense of professionalism accompanied the improvement in knowledge and skill level. As the only government entity with the organization, resources, and leadership skills to carry out such missions, the military became the 'pointy end' of American expansionism.

The Army and the West

On March 31, 1804, U.S. Army Captain Meriwether Lewis and Lieutenant of Artillery William Clark conducted a brief ceremony to formally enlist 22 soldiers into the 'Detachment destined for the Expedition through the interior of the *Continent* of North America.' Also known as the Corps of Discovery, the Lewis and Clark expedition to find a water route from the Missouri River to the Pacific Ocean and to explore the lands acquired through the Louisiana Purchase in 1803 was first and foremost a military operation. President Thomas Jefferson had little choice but to look to the Army to carry out this critical and dangerous assignment because no other department in the federal government had the organizational and logistical capability, the training and discipline, or the resources necessary to put together, equip, staff, and conduct an exploration of such extended length covering such enormous space.

Jefferson ordered captains Lewis and Clark (Lewis gave his good friend an informal brevet promotion to captain so that the two officers could co-command the expedition) to locate a water route to the Pacific and explore the newly acquired territory. The president also wanted the explorers to record the diverse flora and fauna found along the way, to make extensive notes on the indigenous peoples encountered, and to map rivers and possible trade routes. The expedition carried the latest scientific equipment to assist in drawing maps and recording and preserving the plants, animals, rocks, and minerals collected.

Despite failing to find a water route to the Pacific Ocean—because none existed—the Lewis and Clark expedition successfully reached the Pacific and returned to St. Louis two years later, with only one fatality among the forty members of the expedition's company. The Corps of Discovery maintained strict organization and discipline for the duration of the journey, and, when necessary, overawed many of the Native Americans it encountered by displaying its military prowess by demonstrating gunpowder weapons and wearing dress uniforms brought along in anticipation of just such events. Only rarely did the expedition members have to shift from scientist to soldier to defend themselves against potentially hostile Indians, often the Teton Sioux or the Blackfoot. The Native Americans of the northern Louisiana Purchase territory had been, for the most part, peacefully introduced to the United States government and the Army.

The wealth of scientific information in the form of specimens, maps, weather measurements, and other data proved more in both quantity and quality than Jefferson had dared hope. Moreover, the expedition sent a subtle but clear signal to the British and Russians, who had interests in the Pacific Northwest, and to the Spanish, who claimed the territory south and west of the Louisiana Purchase, that the United States not only held claim to this territory but also possessed it. Lewis and Clark, as well as Jefferson, understood that only a military presence could keep hostile Indians subdued, regulate the movements of traders and settlers, and check the intrigues of foreign powers. With that in mind, Clark recommended a chain of forts at strategic points along the Missouri River and other major rivers in the region, while Lewis suggested nonmilitary approaches to establishing order in the now explored but still untamed territory.

Even before Lewis and Clark emerged from the Missouri River country, Jefferson had organized more expeditions. Nationalism, security, diplomacy, and science motivated Jefferson's desire to know more about the expanded Republic. Again, he turned to the military, which had several ambitious young officers who considered themselves gentlemen scientists and were eager to make a name for themselves through exploration. Thus began a tradition of scientific and exploratory service in the American military that indirectly promoted both national security and professionalism.

Jefferson ordered exploration of the Red River and Arkansas River in 1804. The first expedition, led by civilian scientists under military escort, was forced to change course because of threats from nearby Spanish troops and Osage Indians. Congress authorized another attempt up the Red River in 1805 under civilian surveyor Thomas Freeman and botanist Dr. Peter Custis. The Freeman Expedition left Fort Adams, near Natchez, Mississippi, in April 1806, accompanied by a reinforced military escort in response to rumors of Spanish troops patrolling the Red River area. Indeed, after encountering a sizable Spanish patrol, Freeman's group returned to Fort Adams in July 1806. Although neither of the Red River expeditions was successful, the efforts are noteworthy in that they demonstrated that Jefferson and the War Department considered the military essential to exploration.

In 1805, General James Wilkinson, governor of the Louisiana Territory, sent Lieutenant Zebulon Pike up the Mississippi River to discover its source. Like Lewis and Clark, Pike had orders to note flora and fauna, record geographic features, map possible sites for settlement, collect weather data, and identify strategic locations for military posts. British traders still worked the upper reaches of the Mississippi, and Pike had to warn several that they were not welcome in what was now American territory. Ultimately, after a year in the field, Pike did not find the source of the Mississippi River, nor did he force British traders to scale back their activities on American soil. His expedition report described what is now called the Great Plains as unsuitable for agriculture and fit only for Native American tribes already living there.

Pike set out again in July 1806 on a more audacious expedition into the heart of the Spanish borderlands. Splitting his force of 20 men, Pike sent a small party to survey the Arkansas River while he took the rest of the company up the Red River into Colorado, where he and his men spent a severe winter. In February 1807, Spanish officials in New Mexico heard rumors of Pike's presence in Colorado and sent a patrol to locate the Americans. Upon finding Pike's group, the Spanish escorted them to the provincial capital at Chihuahua. The Spanish treated the Americans with courtesy and generosity but confiscated Pike's notes and journals. Finally, in July 1807, the Spanish delivered Pike and most of his men to the Texas border with the United States. While the Pike Expedition sorely tested American relations with Spain for little scientific gain, the publication of Pike's journal in 1810 stimulated widespread interest in the region. Pike did not live to see his legacy. During the War of 1812, he died as a brigadier general while leading an attack against a British force at the Battle of York.

The War of 1812 temporarily halted military exploration, but the surge of nationalism following the conflict sparked renewed effort. In the 1820s, Secretary of War John C. Calhoun developed a plan to link military posts along the Missouri River with those along the Mississippi to create a cohesive western defense system. Although Calhoun's defensive network of posts was never realized, his effort resulted in several expeditions.

Perhaps the more important of the Calhoun-sponsored enterprises was the Yellowstone Expedition, led by Major Stephen H. Long. In addition to Long and his fellow soldiers (including two military topographers), the company included a botanist, a geologist, a zoologist, and an artist. After spending the winter of 1818–1819 at Council Bluffs, Iowa, Long and his party headed west across the plains along the Platte River. Reaching the Rockies, the expedition discovered Long's Peak, ascended Pike's Peak, and descended what they believed was the Red River but was instead the Canadian River. After a grueling journey during which he and his comrades nearly starved, Long's group reunited with the rest of the Yellowstone Expedition at Fort Smith, Arkansas. Long's published report and maps supported the idea that the Great Plains region was unfit for farming, declaring it useful only as a barrier between American and Spanish territory. His expedition map identified the region as the 'Great Desert,' inspiring the term 'Great American Desert,' the name used to describe the Great Plains until the 1870s.

In the 1830s, Army expeditions mapped the Great Basin, an area that encompasses most of Nevada, large portions of Utah, and parts of California, Idaho, Oregon, and Wyoming. An Army expedition also mapped the Trans-Mississippi West for possible routes for a transcontinental railroad, a task that was possibly the most important cartographic achievement in the United States before the Civil War.

In 1838, the quality of exploration and mapping improved with the establishment of the Army Topographical Corps, and an enhanced engineering curriculum at West Point. Of the 72 officers who served as topographical engineers from 1838 to 1863, 64 graduated from West Point. The Military Academy's new curriculum provided future officers the skills compatible with the expanding nation's needs. Earlier Army explorers had to learn many of these skills on their own, but now the core curriculum at West Point was geared toward preparing young officers for exploration as well as war.

John C. Frémont was, perhaps, the most famous Army explorer. He did not attend West Point and owed his prominence to his father-in-law, Missouri Senator (and proponent of Manifest Destiny) Thomas Hart Benton. Through Benton's influence, Lieutenant Frémont commanded a secret reconnaissance to the Rocky Mountains in 1842. With several fur trappers and mountain men—including Kit Carson, who became Frémont's closest friend—Frémont led his party up the Platte River and west to the Rockies. He mapped South Pass in Wyoming, climbed the Wind River Mountains, and then turned for home. Along the way, he lost many of his personal notes and journals when his raft capsized in the Platte River. Enough remained, however, to complete a report providing latitude and longitude readings, meteorological information, geological descriptions, and a map of the area from Fort Laramie to the Wind River Mountains. These scientific observations paled, however, in comparison to the nationalistic sentiment his report inspired. Congress and people eager to settle Oregon country believed that Frémont's report showed a practical route to Oregon.

In 1843, Frémont received orders to lead another reconnaissance to find a pass across the central Rockies and then to Oregon. Science took a back seat to politics, as Benton and other Manifest Destiny proponents wanted to build on Frémont's first expedition to support various schemes to expand American territory westward. Frémont's 1843–1844 route took him from the central Rockies (where he found no pass), back north to South Pass, then to the Great Salt Lake, north to Fort Hall in Idaho, and then overland to Fort Vancouver in Washington. There, his official

Figure 6.1 Exploration of the West

mission ended; his orders dictated returning east via the Oregon Trail. Frémont had other plans, however, and he began an extraordinary journey from Fort Vancouver, south into eastern California, across the Sierra Nevada mountains through Carson Pass, and along the American River to Sutter's Fort in California. He then found the Old Spanish Trail to southern California and traveled back across the Great Basin, the Wasatch Range, and across the Continental Divide. He continued down the Arkansas River until he reached St. Louis. It had been a remarkable journey.

Frémont's report on the expedition was a sensation. He endorsed the mouth of the Columbia River as the best port for trade with Asia and claimed that the agricultural potential of Oregon could rival that of the eastern United States. Most importantly, he detailed the geography of the West. Emigrant trains along the Oregon Trail found Frémont's information indispensable. Now known as 'the Pathfinder,' Frémont was feted by Congress and President James K. Polk and was promoted to captain. Although much of the region he traveled had already been explored and, in some cases, well-traveled by others, and his maps contained errors (as most maps then did), the expedition's nationalist and expansionist effect was beyond measure. Frémont's report of his second expedition was the most comprehensive on the West at that time.

Frémont's third expedition in 1845 was controversial. With increasing interest in western settlement, expansionists' eyes on Texas and Mexican California, and growing tensions with Mexico, Frémont had little difficulty getting orders to make a third journey west. The War Department ordered Frémont to confirm river routes and drainages for rivers running east of the Rockies. Frémont himself planned to go back to California for what he claimed were scientific reasons, but in reality, he had commercial and expansionist ambitions. Frémont had stretched orders before, and with Senator Benton's protection, he would do so again. At Bent's Fort, Idaho, Frémont gathered his men, including several trappers, soldiers, scientists, and officers. Rather than surveying rivers east of the Rockies, Frémont headed across the Rockies and into the Great Basin and the southern shore of the Great Salt Lake. After spending some time resting the horses and gathering specimens, Frémont led his party across the desert toward California. Frémont's path across the desert would later be known as the Hastings Cutoff, the same trail that the ill-fated Donner Party would follow in 1846.

Frémont's presence in California alarmed and irritated Mexican authorities. Once in California, Frémont met with Mexican General Don José Castro at Monterrey, telling the general that his expedition hoped to further the cause of science and explore commercial opportunities. Frémont's well-armed force made it difficult for Castro to accept the Pathfinder's explanation. After resupplying at Sutter's Fort early in 1846, Frémont led his men into the Salinas Valley; there, Mexican authorities ordered his arrest. Frémont held out for several days in a hastily built fort and then retreated toward Oregon. On his way north in May, Frémont learned that war with Mexico was imminent. He then turned his men southward, now as an army of invasion. Frémont openly encouraged rebellion against Mexican rule and led a motley force of his own regulars and American settler volunteers against Mexican authorities. When the war ended, Commodore Robert F. Stockton appointed Frémont as governor of California. However, Frémont refused to relinquish the position when ordered to by Brigadier General Stephen W. Kearny and thus was court-martialed for inciting mutiny and dishonorably discharged. Although President Polk issued a partial pardon, Frémont resigned and returned to live in California.

Frémont's expedition was only one of three undertaken by the Army in 1845. Then-Colonel Kearny took a company of dragoons along the

Oregon Trail to South Pass and then down the east slope of the Rockies to Bent's Fort, Colorado. In addition to keeping Indians in line, Kearny surveyed and mapped the region and took the opportunity to experiment with dragoon movements on the open plains. Another smaller, expedition, traveled up the Canadian River into Comanche territory. Like Frémont's, both expeditions had a thinly veiled military purpose as war with Mexico broke out.

The 'high point' of Army expeditions came after the war with the transcontinental railroad route surveys, including one led by Frémont. Weighing options for the best route for a railroad to the Pacific, the Corps of Topographical Engineers produced a 13-volume report that included volumes on natural resources, topography, zoology, and botany. The report rivals any of those produced by the military during the nineteenth century. It was natural for the Army to lead this effort—only it had the organization, experience, and skill to conduct such an enormous undertaking. Moreover, the Army had a strategic stake in a transcontinental railroad.

Army exploration achieved many political, diplomatic, scientific, and military objectives. The Army had become a willing tool of proponents of expansionism, because expeditions of discovery established the territorial integrity of the western United States, although often at the cost of blatantly violating the borders of the northern Mexican frontier. Native American tribes had been contained or at least monitored. In the realm of science and discovery, the Army explorations contributed substantially to geographic, botanical, zoological, and meteorological knowledge. By far the most important contribution was the updated and more accurate maps of the vast expanse that became the American West. The Army had been on the 'pointy end' of expansion in many ways, and it gained a reputation as a professional force possessing the knowledge and skills to perform tasks that were nationally useful beyond maintaining the security of the United States.

The Naval Expeditions

Naval exploration grew out of the concerns and conflicts that plagued American sea trade from the beginning of the Republic. These included protecting the merchant fleets, securing access to ports in China and other lucrative locations, instilling respect for the flag, protecting American citizens, and promoting an American presence on the high seas. By the 1830s, the dramatic increase in American seaborne trade and the growth of the seal and whaling industries in the United States demanded a better navy.

Traders, whalers, and sealers increasingly journeyed to poorly charted or uncharted waters in the western and southern Pacific, the northwestern Pacific coast of North America, and the Antarctic (where it was rumored an entire continent might exist) in search of profit. For example, the whaling industry relied heavily on hunting in the Pacific, accounting for annual earnings of several million dollars per year with a fleet of whaling ships valued at over $225 million. Scientists also had interests in naval exploration and charting, including discovering new lands, mapping currents, and understanding weather patterns. The United States had clear strategic, economic, and scientific reasons to better understand the world's oceans.

Even before the Navy sponsored expeditions of discovery, American naval vessels had done some remarkable exploring. The *Vincennes* traveled to ports in the Pacific Islands and the Far East in 1829, sailed around the Cape of Good Hope in 1830, and became the first American naval ship to circumnavigate the globe. The *Potomac* accomplished the same feat between 1831–1834, making several stops in the East Indies, including the first American intervention in Asia at Sumatra. One member of that cruise, Jeremiah Reynolds, pushed for congressional support of an expedition to confirm the existence of the Antarctic continent, to map whaling and sealing routes, and to conduct general scientific observation. Through the efforts of Reynolds and others, Congress finally agreed to appropriate $300,000 for an expedition to the South Atlantic and southern Pacific, the United States Exploring Expedition of 1838–1842.

It is remarkable that the U.S. Navy was able to undertake this expedition. The Navy and Congress agreed that a peacetime navy's only task was to protect merchant shipping, and had thus shaped the Navy for that purpose. The Navy Board of Commissioners, with congressional approval, expanded the 'squadron' system in the early 1820s. Thus, the West Indian (1822), the Pacific (1822), the Brazilian (1826), the Mediterranean (1835), the Home (1841), the East Indian (1835), and the African (1843) Squadrons patrolled oceanic regions to protect American shipping and strategic interests. Depots at Key West and San Francisco (after 1848) in the United States, and abroad at places like Hong Kong and Rio de Janeiro, kept these small squadrons of ships supplied. The concept of fleet operations, however, had yet to fully develop and squadrons typically did not operate as fleets, but rather as individual ships patrolling an assigned area.

Senior naval officers and Congress seemed content with a sailing navy versus one powered by new steam technology. After brief flirtations with steam power, the United States doggedly stuck to sail, while the British and French navies continued experimenting with steam vessels. While Robert Fulton's steam-powered warship *Demologos* (1814) and David Porter's *Seagull* (1823) were put through trials, the Navy did not launch a steam-powered vessel for permanent sea duty until 1839. After intense lobbying from Captain Matthew C. Perry and Secretary of the Navy Abel P. Upshur, Congress funded two paddle-wheel steamers, USS *Mississippi* and USS *Missouri* (completed in 1842), and the first screw-propeller-powered warship in the world, USS *Princeton* (completed in 1841).

Tragically, Upshur (appointed Secretary of State by President John Tyler in 1844) and Secretary of the Navy Thomas W. Gilmer were killed when one of the *Princeton*'s new guns exploded during a demonstration firing. To design, build, maintain, and operate these steam vessels, the Navy established a Naval Corps of Engineers. Still, the Navy lagged behind Great Britain and France. By 1854, Britain had 141 steamships while the French had 68, compared to the U.S. Navy's 18.

The Navy and merchant marine also needed accurate charts and maps, better navigation instruments, and the ability to use both to compete with their British and European counterparts. The Navy established the Depot of Charts and Instruments in 1830 to bridge this gap, and in 1842, built the Naval Observatory to update astronomical data for navigation books. Young naval officers took short courses to learn how to use new instruments, translate new data to charts, and get up to date on the latest advancements in meteorology, oceanography, geography, biology, and other sciences. The Naval Observatory gained a reputation among young naval officers as a center for professional education, and among foreign navies as a center for maritime science. In 1849, the Navy established the Nautical Almanac Office to publish advancements in naval sciences and the latest astronomical, oceanographic, and meteorological data. Headquartered at Cambridge, Massachusetts, the Nautical Almanac Office employed some of the leading mathematicians and astronomers in the United States.

To better manage the Navy's mission, Secretary of the Navy Upshur abolished the Navy Board of Commissioners in 1842, replacing it with a bureau system like that of the Army. Although the Navy still lacked an academy like the one that the Army had at West Point, technology, science, and education had become vital to the Navy well before the outbreak of the Civil War.

Amidst these developments, the United States Exploring Expedition got underway in 1838. Lieutenant Charles Wilkes, typical of the Navy's junior officers in the high value he placed on science and education, and adventure, commanded the expedition. Wilkes, an accomplished navigator and chart maker, actively sought the command. Secretary of the Navy James Paulding ordered Wilkes to explore and chart the South Pacific and the Antarctic region, then return northward to chart shores in and around Puget Sound. Along the way, he and his contingent of scientists would make extensive studies of the oceans, weather, animal and plant life, geology, and astronomy. Wilkes set sail on August 22, 1838, with four ships: the sailed schooner *Seagull*, which sank off Cape Horn in 1839; the schooner, *Flying Fish*, sold in Singapore in 1842 too worn out for repair; the sloop *Peacock*, which had seen action in the War of 1812 and had to be abandoned off the coast of Oregon in 1841; and the brigantine *Porpoise*, the only vessel from the original squadron that completed the entire voyage. The *Vincennes*, which had already circumnavigated the globe, joined the expedition in Rio de Janeiro.

Wilkes's expedition was nothing short of extraordinary. The expedition explored the Society Islands, stopped briefly at Samoa, and then sailed on to Australia. Wilkes then sailed due south, where he charted over 1,000 miles of previously unmapped ice and coastline. This part of the journey tested Wilkes's command and his officers and crew. His strict discipline and questionable decisions left many officers doubting his ability, but none mutinied. During a four-month stay in the Fiji Islands, where Wilkes meticulously charted reefs and shoals, two of his officers were murdered by Fijians. Wilkes killed over 50 islanders in retribution. After wintering in Hawaii, Wilkes led his expedition to the American Northwest, where it surveyed the northern California and Oregon coastlines and Puget Sound. He then headed across the Pacific to the Philippines, on to Singapore, around the Cape of Good Hope, and home to New York in June 1842.

Wilkes returned a hero, but public charges against him by some of his officers clouded the expedition's achievements. The Navy cleared Wilkes of the serious charge of conduct unbecoming an officer but convicted him on 17 charges of illegal punishment. The Navy reprimanded Wilkes but had little choice but to hail him a great explorer.

Wilkes and his men had sailed over 85,000 miles and surveyed over 280 islands. The Antarctic coastline explored and mapped by the expedition is still known as Wilkes Land. Wilkes's brief public report on the expedition aided whalers, sealers, commercial shippers, and the Navy alike. The official report comprised over 20 volumes, some of which were not completed until after the Civil War, while others were never published. The United States government kept some parts of his final report secret, however, due to concern that his description of San Francisco Bay and his recommendation that the United States claim Oregon might cause increased tension with Great Britain and Spain.

Thousands of the new species and specimens collected by the expedition's scientists were haphazardly displayed in the National Gallery in the Patent Office, causing several of the scientists to resign in disgust. Wilkes ultimately reorganized the exhibition himself. Despite Wilkes's court-martial and the scientists' resignations, the first official exploring expedition of the U.S. Navy had been a stunning success. The Navy was still using Wilkes's meticulous charts and maps when war broke out with Japan 100 years later.

More expeditions followed as the Navy rode the wave of the Wilkes Expedition's success. From 1847 to 1849, Lieutenant William F. Lynch and the store ship USS *Supply* explored the River Jordan and the Dead Sea and even attempted sailing up the Euphrates. Lynch's primary task was gathering scientific information, but he also had orders to ascertain the commercial situation in the region. The Navy sponsored an expedition to the Amazon from Lima to the Brazilian coast in 1851–1852. With pack mules loaded with boxes of scientific instruments, notebooks, tents, weapons, and other necessities, the expedition departed Lima in

Figure 6.2 Lieutenant Charles Wilkes, portrait by Thomas Sully, 1840.
Source: United States Naval Academy Museum.

May 1851. In addition to the usual scientific tasks, the expedition was to explore which Brazilian waterways could be navigated, to note Brazilian trade goods, the economic condition of the people encountered, and any undeveloped commercial resources. The journey was arduous, with the explorers enduring bouts of jungle fever, close calls with South American indigenous tribes, and daunting river obstacles. Yet, the men survived, becoming the first Anglos to descend from the source of the Madeira River to the Amazon.

Expedition reports were detailed, offering insightful observations about economic, political, and social conditions. Unfortunately, the many specimens the men had collected sat unstudied in the Patent Office for several years before being transferred to the Smithsonian Institution.

Other naval expeditions established an observatory in Chile that operated from 1846 to 1852 to study the movement of Mars and Venus, and to make other astronomical observations; explored the Rio de la Plata and Rio Paraguay from 1853 to 1856; conducted a reconnaissance of Liberia in 1852; and explored the Bering Strait and China Sea from 1852 to 1863. Diplomatically and commercially, the most important of these expeditions was Commodore Matthew Perry's mission to Japan from 1852 to 1854. American commercial and naval vessels had contacted the isolationist Japanese Islands before Perry's mission in 1852. But, aside from rescuing stranded American whalers or foiled attempts to establish relations, the United States had made little headway in opening Japan to American commerce. Fearing that Great Britain, its main trading rival in the Asian market, would be first to get a trade agreement with the very cautious Japanese, the United States dispatched Perry to open relations with Japan.

Perry's mission was at once commercial, diplomatic, and scientific. He had just been named commander of the East India squadron and had conducted successful negotiations with Naples, Turkey, and Mexico. Much respected by his fellow naval officers, Perry had a reputation for hard work, fair leadership, and seemingly limitless physical endurance. In preparation for his mission, he read logs and reports from previous voyages to Japan, talked with officers from some of these voyages, and tried to learn as much as he could about Japanese history and culture. He knew that Japan had not wholly sealed off outside contact and that the Japanese were aware of Western medicine, military affairs, and technology. Perry organized a fleet of four ships—the *Susquehanna, Plymouth, Saratoga,* and the steamer *Mississippi,* arriving in Tokyo Bay in July 1853. In 1854, several other naval vessels joined Perry's fleet.

Perry understood the delicate diplomacy required to conclude an agreement with the shogunates of Japan. On March 31, 1854, Perry and the Japanese signed the Treaty of Kanagawa, which gave the United States access to the ports of Shimoda and Hakodate, arranged for future transfers of stranded American sailors, established an American consulate at Shimoda, and gave Japan most-favored-nation trade status. What should have been a significant moment for Japan, however, instead turned dark; over the next few years, deep division between Japanese open to Western contact and those committed to isolation erupted in a protracted civil war that lasted until 1868. For Perry, however, the treaty was a success; he returned to the United States a hero and Congress voted him a $20,000 bonus (equal to over $500,000 today) for his achievement.

Perry's ships had explored and charted the China Sea and much of the coastline of the Japanese Islands. Several volumes of the expedition's

Figure 6.3 Japanese print of American naval officers, including Commodore Matthew
Perry, center.
Source: Library of Congress.

findings were published, primarily sailing directions and harbor charts, but
also details of Japanese currents and wind directions. Perry issued
a personal narrative of the voyage, and several other officers and scientists
on the voyage also published memoirs of the journey. The many gifts
received from the Japanese, as well as specimens collected on the journey,
were given to the new Smithsonian Institution.

The pre-Civil War Navy had indeed shown a willingness to undertake
expeditions that delicately balanced commercial, scientific, military, and
diplomatic objectives. Naval officers proved enthusiastic and adept in
organizing, carrying out, and reporting the results of these expeditions,
acting in many ways like pro-consuls of ancient Rome. Although the
Navy undertook fewer such missions after the Civil War, leaving organizations such as the Smithsonian Institution and the National Geographic
Society to sponsor scientific expeditions, the Navy retained the capability
and eagerness required to do so when called upon. For officers, the
experience, knowledge, and overall growth gained from organizing and
participating in these expeditions contributed to a growing sense of naval
professionalism.

Frontier Constabulary and Indian Affairs

Frontier duty remained the Army's primary task after the War of 1812. Although this role was ill-fitted to the service's principal mission of defending the United States from foreign enemies, the Army was the natural agency for maintaining order along the frontier and regulating relations between settlers and Native Americans. Although civilian Indian agents commonly represented the federal government to Indian tribes, military officers often assumed the role of agent in the absence of the civilian official. Indian agents were often housed on Army posts on the frontier, and disputes between commanders and agents frequently erupted over the implementation of federal Indian policy. Agents, officers, settlers, and the Indians themselves made plenty of mistakes, both honest and otherwise, for there to be enough blame to go around for the tragedies of nineteenth-century relations with Native Americans.

Few officers subscribed to the noble-savage idea so prominent in antebellum American literature. Military officers, often, were realists in their approach to, and outlook on, Indians. Experience shaped their opinions. Words like 'treachery,' 'indolence,' and 'savage' frequent officers' writings about Indians. Yet, their writings also reflect grudging empathy for Native Americans due to their situation and military skill. Officers often did not attribute Indian behavior, as they observed it, to race, but instead to environmental determinism.

Army officers often saw the indigenous tribes of the Southeast as the most civilized and socially sophisticated. Of these, the Cherokees impressed them. The Plains Indians and the tribes of the Southwest ranked in the middle, as officers admired their warrior skills but found their tendency toward brutality uncivilized. Few officers saw much hope of assimilation for these mostly nomadic tribes. The Indians of the Rocky Mountains and California ranked at the bottom of the scale. Officers saw these peoples as nothing more than diggers and beggars; many officers compared them to animals due to their poor living conditions.

Despite having a generally negative attitude toward frontier constabulary duty, the officers' views moderated when the tribes were at peace. Because of their own sense of professionalism and their disdain for greedy settlers—and often, their sincere concern for the plight of indigenous peoples as human beings—officers frequently adopted a racially paternalistic attitude toward Native Americans. The United States, according to these officers, had a moral obligation to protect Indians. Many officers supported the assimilation policy, which up to the 1830s had some success. Many officers, including then Zachary Taylor, defended Native American rights and tried to enforce treaties. There was a sense among military men that the tribes had been taken advantage of, and that they were owed protection from further humiliation. Such ideas were indeed noble, but sympathetic officers found it increasingly difficult to transfer noble thoughts into practical reality.

Because of the constant reductions in the size of the military and the expansion of its duties during the 1820s through the 1850s, the Army never had enough troops on the frontier to adequately maintain order. As a result, conflict broke out with increasing frequency along the Trans-Mississippi frontier, in Georgia, Alabama, Mississippi, and Florida. Army posts had the problematic responsibilities of keeping white settlers from encroaching upon Indian lands and prohibiting the trade of illegal goods, such as whiskey and arms, to Native Americans. Soldiers generally held disdain for aggressive frontiersmen and overzealous traders. In the early 1830s, Captain William R. Jouett, commander of Fort Snelling on the upper Mississippi River in Wisconsin, frequently seized illegal liquor from Indian traders in his jurisdiction. In one instance, the American Fur Company even charged Jouett with unlawful trespass and assault but lost the case. Captain John Stuart, the commander at Fort Smith in Arkansas, tried in vain to stop the illicit liquor trade with Indians but did not have the men to police his vast jurisdiction.

Frontier officers often found themselves on the unpopular side of the law, as well as of local law enforcement. Fearing legal ramifications for what they considered to be carrying out the letter of the law, many officers were reluctant to act as law enforcement. The influential political power of the American Fur Company in Washington made the officers' and Indian agents' jobs harder to carry out. Many officers supported declaring martial law in Indian country to curb the power of the traders and their control of local courts. The War Department, however, proved unhelpful. Commanders at such posts as Fort Armstrong, Illinois, and Fort Des Moines, Iowa, found themselves helpless to control illegal trade with Indians and encroachment upon tribal lands.

The Black Hawk War

During the 1830s, frontier tensions erupted between the federal government and Native Americans over the government's Indian policy. As one example, the Black Hawk War of 1832 started as a series of misunderstandings that turned into a bloody conflict during which hundreds on both sides were killed.

Beginning in the 1820s, increasing numbers of white settlers in Illinois had pushed the Sauk and Fox Indians out of their territory and across the Mississippi River. In 1832, Chief Black Hawk led a large band back into Illinois. Governor John Reynolds called out more than 1,500 militia to confront Black Hawk and force his band of warriors back across the Mississippi. The first engagement took place along the Rock River where Black Hawk and 40 warriors attacked a force of 300 militiamen in retaliation for the murder of two tribal peace envoys. The undisciplined militia fled, forcing Governor Reynolds to call for help from the federal government. In June, dissatisfied with the progress of the war, President

Andrew Jackson ordered Brevet Major General Winfield Scott to take command and defeat Black Hawk's augmented force of Sauk, Fox, Potawatomi, and Winnebago warriors. Cholera, however, ran rampant throughout Scott's army, killing more than 200 of his men and preventing him from taking the field.

After raiding isolated settlements and killing over 200 settlers, Black Hawk decided to retreat back across the Mississippi River but was hit by regular forces under General James D. Henry in the Battle of Wisconsin Heights. Suffering heavy losses, Black Hawk continued to retreat. While the band was crossing the Mississippi at its confluence with the Bad Axe River on August 1, regular troops hit the Indians again and killed more than 300, half of whom were women and children. Black Hawk was captured on August 25 and taken hostage to ensure that his surviving followers met the terms of the Treaty of Fort Armstrong ending the war. The war had been a poorly managed affair. Nonetheless, none of the tribes involved ever again threatened the region. Wisconsin and Iowa were now open to settlement.

Indian Removal

During the Black Hawk War, the Jackson administration tasked the Army to carry out the Indian Removal Act of 1830. While tribes initially had been treated as independent nations within the borders of the United States, and thus the federal government had concluded treaties with them as nations, this interpretation of tribal status had changed by the late 1820s. Constitutional questions about national status within the boundaries of the United States persuaded the Supreme Court to nullify these arrangements, such as in *Cherokee Nation v. Georgia* (1831), wherein the Court ruled that tribal nations were dependent on rather than independent of the United States. Jackson, concerned for the welfare of the tribes in question and acquiescing to encroaching settlers and land speculators, could think of only one solution—remove the tribes to western lands where they would be safe and could live in peace. Such a policy had been discussed for decades, but now it became law. The only federal organization large enough and strong enough to carry out the task was the Army. The Army wanted no violence, hoping instead that careful organization would be sufficient to provide for and protect tribes as they migrated westward. Responsibility for the removal was placed with the Commissary General of Subsistence, with civilian superintendents overseeing the removal.

First to move were the Choctaws. They signed over all their lands east of the Mississippi River in 1830 and had three years to move out, but impatient settlers illegally squatted on Choctaw land. The Army provided escort for Choctaw officials to scout out possible settlement sites west of Arkansas in what became known as Indian Territory and posted troops along the migration route as well as in Indian Territory to help the Choctaw. The Army renovated Fort Smith to serve as a supply station,

Figure 6.4 Indian Removals, 1830s.

reestablished Fort Towson (in what is now Oklahoma) to keep settlers out of Indian Territory and helped locate water and livestock sources in the area designated for Choctaw settlement. While passing through Arkansas, white settlers preyed upon the Choctaw, charging them inflated prices for basic goods. Despite these and other hardships, by 1834 nearly 13,000 Choctaws had made the trek to Indian Territory.

At first, the Creek Indians peacefully resisted removal, but by 1831 squatters had begun to overrun Creek lands. Moreover, the government of Alabama began enforcing state laws over the Creeks. Because of this increased pressure, in March 1832, the Creeks signed over their lands to the United States government and agreed to move west. Although the agreement allowed individual Creeks to remain to farm a parcel of land for five years and at the end of that period receive title to it, the treaty nonetheless strongly encouraged the Creeks to move west. Moreover, the federal government failed to keep settlers out of Creek lands and prevent speculators from defrauding individual Creeks of their allotments. The emigrant agents assigned to remove the Creeks had been the same individuals who had earlier tried to swindle them. Many Creeks fled to Cherokee territory in Georgia and Alabama. As the federal investigation into the fraudulent dealings wallowed in a bureaucratic morass, the Creeks began to suffer from poor conditions brought on by economic stagnation. Georgia militia attacked Creek refugee camps, while bands of Creeks raided farms and settlements in retaliation.

Secretary of War Lewis Cass ordered the Army to remove the Creeks without delay. General Thomas S. Jesup first had to subdue the renegade bands and then organize the removal. Thus began the Creek War of 1836. Jesup placed Winfield Scott in overall command of the campaign. With more than 1,000 regulars augmented by more than 8,000 Georgia and Alabama volunteers, Scott divided his force in a bid to catch the Creeks from two directions. Scott delayed his movements, claiming he needed more time to get his army ready for the field. Fearing that the Creeks might flee to Florida and join the Seminoles, Jesup moved ahead without Scott, capturing the main Creek encampment along with 400 warriors and their leader, Eneah Micco. This rapid success impressed the Creeks so much that they lost their enthusiasm for further resistance. Jesup wrote to Scott that the Creeks had been pacified, but Scott insisted on capturing all Indians who had escaped Jesup's attack. After a few weeks, the Creeks had been rounded up and subdued.

Removal began in July 1836. Over 2,500 Creeks traveled by wagon to Montgomery, then by water to their designated lands. The journey took a month. Creek warriors were shackled together for the entire journey. The peaceful Creeks followed in August and September under military escort. Over 14,000 Creeks immigrated to Indian Territory in 1836. In 1837, the Chickasaw left their homeland in a comparatively uneventful removal. The Cherokee removal, however, remains the most infamous of the removal policy.

The Army played its most controversial role in the removal of the Cherokee. By far the most advanced of what was known as the 'civilized tribes,' the Cherokee stubbornly resisted removal despite the settlers already squatting on Cherokee lands. The discovery of gold there brought still more illegal settlement. By using legal challenges and stubborn negotiations, the Cherokee held out for almost eight years before signing a removal treaty in 1835. Even then, many Cherokee resisted. They had two years to move west to their new lands in Indian Territory, by which time Martin Van Buren had assumed the presidency.

Van Buren ordered the Cherokee to move. The Georgia militia, poorly led and poorly trained, forced Cherokee families from their homes at bayonet point. Scavengers ransacked their houses and farms. Hastily constructed stockades (in effect concentration camps) held 17,000 Cherokee while their removal west was organized. Horrid conditions in the camps killed more than 4,000 Cherokee while they were under the charge of Georgia militia. As the Army escorted the survivors of the camps along what came to be known as the Trail of Tears, more perished. Winfield Scott commanded the trek west, but he and his troops received little support from the government and even less from local citizens along the route. A horde of greedy agents, speculators, lawyers, and other profit-seekers cheated the Cherokee. The Army also conducted itself poorly; several soldiers disgraced themselves during the removal by robbing, abusing, and assaulting Cherokee. The Cherokee removal proved to be a dark stain on the Army's record of Indian affairs.

The Black Hawk War of 1832 and the long and bloody Second Seminole War of 1835–1842 cost hundreds of lives and forced removal of Native American tribes from their lands. Of the available options, all of which seemed inhumane, perhaps the least inhumane was removal. The Indians were the clear losers in this policy; more than 45,000 Native Americans were uprooted from their homes and crowded onto lands already inhabited by other indigenous peoples. In exchange, the U.S. government gained nearly 100 million acres of land at the cost of $68 million. Despite this poor record, Jackson maintained until his death that he had saved the tribes from extinction.

A Military Policy for the West

Even as Indian removal commenced, the U.S. government looked ahead, planning how it would protect both Indians and settlers in the West. Despite removal, Native Americans still lived near new settlements, which steadily pushed westward to the Mississippi River and beyond. British interests in Oregon and the upper Mississippi River region threatened to cause conflict, while the Spanish borderlands presented potential security problems that were, in turn, made more threatening by the 1836 Texas Revolution. The United States needed a frontier military policy to secure the dual objectives of regulating settlement and Indian relations new maintaining national security.

To meet these objectives, mounted dragoons patrolled a string of outposts occupied by infantry. Located along the frontier between new settlement and Indian lands, these small forts allowed the Army to strike quickly and served as a safe haven for settlers during Indian uprisings. These posts amounted to little more than tented settlements, from where the Army tried to regulate the movement of settlers in frontier areas. With limited troop numbers covering a cordon hundreds of miles long, dispersing units most efficiently became the primary goal of military planners.

In 1836, Jackson's Secretary of War Lewis Cass presented a plan for frontier military policy. Cass maintained that Native Americans had no concept of the military might of the United States and that they measured American military power solely by what they could see. Thus, Cass decided to station sufficient numbers of troops along the frontier to overawe the Indians. In case of an uprising or Indian attack on a settlement, the Army needed a way quickly to concentrate large forces in the area in question. For Cass, the answer was a military road that ran roughly south to north from Fort Towson on the Red River to Fort Snelling along the upper Mississippi River. Because the frontier had moved west, posts east of this line could be abandoned for cost savings and using troops more efficiently. Each post was garrisoned by a minimum number of soldiers and augmented by so-called 'disposable' forces that could move from post to post or respond to emergencies, using the road and waterways for transportation. The post and road system that Cass proposed was like, for example, the frontier defensive outpost system used by the ancient Romans on the German frontier.

Congress appropriated $100,000 for the road in 1836. Troops would build the road and the outposts. Just when the program got going, however, it changed direction. Benjamin Butler replaced Cass as Secretary of War, serving only briefly from 1836 to 1837. Where Cass had focused on the Native American threat against settlements, Butler saw the same danger in settlers threatening Indians and was worried about conflict between tribes caused by the Indian removal policy. He therefore added posts in interior areas, including Indian Territory. Butler's successor, Joel R. Poinsett, altogether rejected Cass's idea of a single north–south road. Lines of communication could be compromised easily. Thus, Poinsett recommended establishing two lines of posts. The first line, the exterior, would place advanced posts deep into Indian lands; the second line, the interior, would establish positions closer to settlements. A large force of troops would be held in reserve at Jefferson Barracks, Missouri and Baton Rouge, Louisiana.

Occupying these forts posed a challenge. The Army recommended 30,000 troops but had to settle for fewer than 10,000. Poinsett's plan got congressional backing, but Congress also insisted on completion of the road, a task that the Army finished in 1845. While the Army and successive secretaries of war discussed these ambitious strategies for frontier security, the actual implementation of these schemes moved piecemeal. The establishment of outposts and the strength of garrisons had more to do with local conditions than any plan. Increased emigrant traffic on the Oregon Trail and war with Mexico demanded unique strategies no matter which national policy was in vogue at any given time.

Conclusion

During the first half of the nineteenth century, the American military was the only federal entity adequately organized and disciplined, and sufficiently funded to support America's expansionist impulse. The Army and the Navy explored and mapped tens of thousands of miles, adding to scientific knowledge, opening doors for American trade, and building a sense of prestige and professionalism within the American military. Not all was grand and glorious, however, for the Army was saddled with frontier constabulary duties and the unpleasant task of implementing the Indian removal policy. Nonetheless, a precedent was set. The American military could, and would, be used by the federal government to carry out tasks beyond providing for the security of the United States. This precedent continues, remaining a hallmark of the flexibility of American military forces.

Further Reading

Chaffin, Tom. *Pathfinder: John Charles Frémont and the Course of American Empire.* New York: Hill and Wang, 2002.

Jung, Patrick J. *The Black Hawk War of 1832.* Norman, OK: University of Oklahoma Press, 2007.

Orsi, Jared. *Citizen Explorer: The Life of Zebulon Pike.* New York: Oxford University Press, 2014.

Philbrick, Nathaniel. *Sea of Glory: America's Voyage of Discovery, The U.S. Exploring Expedition, 1838–1842.* New York: Viking, 2003.

Remini, Robert. *Andrew Jackson and His Indian Wars.* New York: Viking, 2001.

Ronda, James P. *Finding the West: Explorations with Lewis and Clark.* Albuquerque, NM: University of New Mexico Press, 2001.

Tate, Michael L. *The Frontier Army in the Settlement of the West.* Norman, OK: University of Oklahoma Press, 1999.

Van DeVelder, Paul. *Savages and Scoundrels: The Untold Story of America's Road to Empire through Indian Territory.* New Haven, CT: Yale University Press, 2009.

Watson, Samuel J. *Jackson's Sword: The Army Officer Corps on the American Frontier, 1810–1821.* Lawrence, KS: University Press of Kansas, 2012.

Wiley, Peter Booth. *Yankees in the Land of the Gods: Commodore Perry and the Opening of Japan.* New York: Viking, 1990.

7 Toward a Professional Military

Introduction

The impact of the Napoleonic Wars, the experience of the War of 1812, and the changing roles of the American military moved many in the officer corps to view their craft not merely as a job, but as a profession and a career. Education and the study of the art of warfare became essential to the officer corps not only in the Army but also in the Navy. Officers came to see the principal role of the military as the defense of the United States. To fulfill this role, the officer corps believed the military had to prepare itself, and the nation, for war.

The War with Mexico gave the military, especially the Army, the chance to exhibit this initial move toward professionalization. Ironically, many of the officers who fought against Mexico would, just more than a decade later, fight each other in one of the bloodiest wars in American history, the Civil War.

Napoleon and Military Thought

The Wars of the French Revolution and Napoleonic Wars (1792–1815) caused a revolution in military affairs, one that continues to influence the practice of warfare and the way many nations approach military organization and purpose. The establishment of the French Republic in 1792 reflected and encouraged an intense nationalism among the French people. The French government obligated all male citizens to serve in the military, allowing France to form huge armies with which Napoleon conquered neighboring countries, established republican governments in those subjugated states, and tried to make a republican empire out of the European continent. The monarchies that had escaped France's initial conquest, however, developed their own sense of nationalist energy that they could channel toward a massive effort to contain the French state. If victory came with breaking the enemy's will to fight, then nationalism made that objective more difficult for both sides by the time of the Napoleonic Wars. Warfare became an unprecedented year-round endeavor that harnessed the total resources of the state. These resources included conscription, which gave states an almost inexhaustible pool of manpower to maintain such large armies. With seemingly unlimited numbers of soldiers, generals became bolder in their battle plans and more willing to accept considerable casualties in pursuit of victory.

Napoleon Bonaparte became the master practitioner of this new style of warfare. Napoleon took control of the French Republic, declaring himself emperor in 1804, and accelerated French expansion during the first years of the nineteenth century. His hallmark strategy involved seeking a climactic battle that would destroy the enemy's army. Employing overwhelming force and swift maneuver, Napoleon inflicted huge casualties and extracted a devastating psychological toll on the enemy.

With such large national armies facing him, however, Napoleon's strategy required him to sacrifice substantial casualties of his own, which he willingly did. Tactically, more mobile artillery allowed him to employ cannon at close range without increasing the risk of losing them to enemy fire. Case shot at close range fired by mobile artillery batteries made Napoleonic battles a holocaust of gunfire. Moreover, Napoleon's organization and placement of divisions before and during battle gave him both operational initiative and strategic advantage. Even in the United States, military officers took note of this intensified way of war.

Napoleon's way of war gave birth to modern military thought. A new generation of military thinkers examined Napoleon's successes and failures and wrote about this new approach to warfare. Antoine-Henri Jomini, a French officer born in Switzerland, and the Prussian Karl von Clausewitz were the most prominent of these thinkers. Their writings helped solidify Napoleon's influence on modern warfare.

Jomini had the most immediate effect on American military thought. He was a major general in Napoleon's army and later served in the Russian army of Alexander I. During the Napoleonic Wars, Jomini held staff positions that permitted him to carefully observe Napoleon's methods. His post also gave him experience in logistics and troop movements during battles, but he never personally commanded troops in combat. Following the wars, Jomini wrote prolifically, publishing 27 books on Napoleonic warfare. His most influential work was his 1838 *Précis de l'art de la guerre* (Summary of the Art of War). Jomini was influenced by Enlightenment thought and found the human and financial cost of Napoleonic battle disturbing. As a result, Jomini found perfection in the less costly tactics and strategy of Frederick the Great, who ruled Prussia from 1740 until 1772. Still, Jomini admired the brilliance of Napoleon's offensive capabilities and sought to interpret them for professional military study. Jomini argued that warfare had universal fundamental principles that military strategists should understand and could apply.

Jomini suggested four primary rules for battle: maneuver one's forces to bear upon the enemy's most important points and disrupt his communications without placing one's own forces in a vulnerable position; concentrate one's forces on only part of the enemy's army rather than bringing them to bear on all of the enemy's force; determine the decisive point of the battlefield and the enemy's army to maneuver one's strength against it; and when concentrating mass upon decisive points, do so swiftly and in a well-timed and coordinated maneuver. To conduct these moves required forethought and planning. The strategically intelligent general could plan and carry out such a campaign to bring his mass against the decisive point of the enemy's force in a climactic battle, thus achieving military victory.

Key to Jominian thought was the idea of maintaining the initiative. The general who had control of his forces and who, therefore, could force his opponent to react to his wishes had the strategic initiative. Ideally, according to Jomini, when a general dominated the battlefield through superior maneuver, the enemy would capitulate without a battle of annihilation. Departing from Napoleon, Jomini contended that gaining territory, not annihilating the enemy's force, would achieve the overall political objectives of the war. In the 1830s, Jomini's ideas became central to the curriculum at the United States Military Academy at West Point. His principles influenced Army thinking well into the twentieth century.

Although Clausewitz did not enjoy much influence in the United States until the middle of the twentieth century, like Jomini, he also sought to discover universal principles of warfare from the Napoleonic experience. Clausewitz served in both the Russian and Prussian armies during the Napoleonic Wars. He served as superintendent of the Prussian *Kriegsakademie* until 1830, when he briefly returned to field service as Chief of Staff of the Prussian Army. He died shortly afterward. Clausewitz's single great work was *Vom Krieg* (On War), an enormous and complex posthumously published tome that outlined his concepts of the universal principles of war. Unlike Jomini, Clausewitz understood war as a violent act that was not subject to a set of strategic principles. Instead, factors beyond human control—what he termed 'fog' and 'friction'—determined the course of war. For Clausewitz, war was a 'continuation' of diplomacy, a tool used to force an adversary to concede to your demands. Much like Napoleon, Clausewitz argued that such coercion worked by destroying the opposing military force and the enemy's will to use military force, rather than by taking territory. War, according to Clausewitz, was not an end but rather a means to an end. Perhaps his most important concept is what students of military theory call the 'Trinity'—the interaction of three forces that determine war's development: primordial violence, chance, and reason. Clausewitz did not gain widespread popularity among American military professionals until well into the twentieth century.

Clearly, Jomini was the source of theoretical discussion among pre-Civil War American officers. Even before Jomini's *Précis* was published, however, American officers had begun to explore the significance of the

Napoleonic Wars, with the U.S. Military Academy at West Point serving as the center of that study. West Point-educated officers increasingly dominated the officer corps. In 1817, West Point accounted for 15 percent of Army officers. By 1830, 64 percent of Army officers graduated from the military academy, and by 1860, West Point produced 76 percent of Army officers. The appointment formula for West Point broadened significantly by the 1830s, giving each congressional and territorial district one selection and providing for additional at-large appointments. In addition to making each class geographically diverse, the formula gave Congress a political interest in the academy, which helped soothe Jacksonian Era complaints about the non-egalitarian nature of a professional military. From this system, the American officer corps shared a common educational foundation and military ethos.

American Military Thought

West Point Superintendent Colonel Sylvanus Thayer, an 1808 graduate of West Point, began the process of making strategic theory part of the curriculum after the War of 1812. His travels in Europe after the war exposed him to the new literature on military thought, convincing him that Europe was indeed leading the new field of military studies. Thayer strove to establish an integrated military strategy for the United States, bringing together the maritime defense tradition with the contemporary strategic thought on land war. Although he added strategic theory to the academy curriculum, several factors limited Thayer's progress and kept West Point primarily a school of engineering, including the traditional fear of a standing army, a reduction in the Army's size, a lack of funds, the subsequent small number of cadets, and, not surprisingly, peace.

President Andrew Jackson's harsh criticism and high-handed interference with the academy prompted Thayer to resign as superintendent in 1833, returning to the Corps of Engineers for the remainder of his Army career. Upon Thayer's resignation, his protégé, Dennis Hart Mahan, became the leading proponent of Jominian thought at West Point. Mahan, an 1824 graduate of the academy who finished top of his class, studied in France before joining the faculty. As Professor of Civil and Military Engineering, Mahan taught at West Point for over 40 years, influencing dozens of West Point graduates. He taught warfare as both science and art, focusing on strategy, fortification, logistics, and tactics, as well as on the role of warfare as a tool of statecraft. Mahan used S. F. Gay de Vernon's *Treatise on the Science of War and Fortification* as his textbook. Gay de Vernon's work focused on engineering and fortification but included a chapter on Jomini's ideas.

One of Mahan's students, Lieutenant Henry W. Halleck, became the first American military officer to write a book on military thought and strategy. Published in 1846, just as the war with Mexico began, Halleck's

Elements of Military Art and Science applied Jominian thought to the American strategic situation. On the surface, Halleck promoted the Jominian principle of offensive warfare and concentration of mass on decisive points. The book, however, gradually strays from this bold approach to a more cautious one. In applying these precepts to the United States, Halleck backed away even further from offensive war, focusing instead on the necessarily defensive nature of American military policy. Despite its territorial and commercial growth, the United States, according to Halleck, had no need for an aggressive military policy because of its unique geostrategic situation. In his mind, the primary role of the American military was to defend the nation against foreign attack and to protect American resources in the continental United States.

Halleck strongly supported the traditional policy of fixed coastal fortifications intended to help repel foreign invasion; major ports and cities must be denied to the enemy, and the threatened cities' populations protected. Yet, Halleck cautioned against becoming too dependent on such a static fortification system. Offensive warfare still had a role, although Halleck never seemed comfortable in fully endorsing it. In the end, Halleck's prescription was largely Jominian in that he supported the defense of places rather than the Napoleonic preference for the destruction of enemy forces.

In 1847, Mahan published *An Elementary Treatise on Advanced-Guard, Out-Post, and Detachment Service of Troops, and the manner of Posting and Handling Them in Presence of an Enemy. With a Historical Sketch of the Rise and Progress of Tactics, &c., &c.*—more simply referred to as *Out-Post*. Mahan believed that Napoleon had discovered all there was to know about the art of war; thus, by studying Napoleon and his campaigns, one could learn the art of war. Nevertheless, like Halleck, Mahan was cautious in his discussion of the movement of forces and the security of defensive positions. As for the offensive, Mahan, like Halleck, cautioned against recklessness, instead suggesting that the best attack is the one that gains position through deception and maneuver at the least cost to one's own forces. This was not, however, an endorsement of a Napoleonic willingness to accept tremendous losses to destroy the enemy's forces. And, again like Halleck, Mahan believed in strong defensive fortifications as the best long-term military policy for the United States.

Neither soldier-scholar attempted to apply the principles of Napoleonic warfare to frontier constabulary duties or to the Indian problem. In trying to apply Napoleonic ideas to the United States, both men had to compromise those ideas to make them fit the American strategic situation. Both Halleck and Mahan seemed to confirm a preference for George Washington's defensive strategy in the War for American Independence or Winfield Scott's strategy of limited territorial gain to achieve political objectives in the War with Mexico, both of which are more Jominian in principle than Napoleonic.

It is essential to understand the strategic context that influenced these men. The United States did not have serious concerns about a foreign invasion from the 1820s through the Civil War. Nor did American military officers spend much time studying Jomini, Halleck, and Mahan. The strategy course at West Point represented only a small portion of the overall curriculum, which remained dedicated to engineering and mathematics. As educated military men, officers thus had only a rudimentary understanding of Napoleonic warfare—mainly that a climactic battle to annihilate the enemy's force would bring victory.

Military Professionalism

Studying strategic thought was an important step toward professionalism. Throughout the pre-Civil War decades, a growing number of officers wrote books, articles, and reports on a wide range of mostly military subjects. They had undoubtedly been influenced by similar trends in Europe. While the tradition of using European military officers as expert teachers in the United States slowed after the War of 1812, American officers increasingly traveled to Europe to learn European military strategy, education, and training techniques. Despite some resistance to European military ideas among some senior officers, scores of junior officers spent time abroad to learn. They witnessed military exercises; visited military schools, fortresses, and ports; brought back hundreds of books and treatises; and examined what they could of the latest European military technological developments.

Lieutenant Daniel Tyler, for example, visited France in 1828–1829 and somehow gained access to new weapon designs and observed field maneuvers of French artillery. Tyler translated the plans into English and produced a report that profoundly influenced American artillery development before the Civil War. Many officers translated other French, Austrian, and Prussian infantry, cavalry, and artillery studies and manuals into English for American study. In 1840, a group of ordnance officers toured munitions factories, arsenals, and proving grounds across Europe, gaining invaluable knowledge about European munitions production and capabilities. Several officers spent as long as two years in Europe touring the continent and meeting with their European counterparts. Even Thayer made a return trip in 1844 for a two-year tour of fortifications and schools, bringing back books, knowledge, and experience to the Corps of Engineers. Some American officers attended European military schools. For example, six cavalry officers attended the French cavalry school in 1839, while some artillerists participated at the French artillery school at Metz.

Another trend in American military professionalism involved assigning American officers as observers with European armies in training or on actual operations in the field. Many officers who visited European armies, their schools, and installations noted the camaraderie and the common sense of purpose and dedication among officers, especially in the Prussian and Austrian officer corps. As a lieutenant, Philip Kearny observed and even participated in French military operations in Algeria. Lieutenant Colonel Edwin V. Summer observed British and French cavalry maneuvers in 1854. During the 1859 War of Italian Unification, several American officers observed combat operations.

The Crimean War of 1855–1856 presented the most significant opportunity to see modern European military forces in action. Secretary of War Jefferson Davis, a veteran of the War with Mexico, sent Major Richard Delafield of the Corps of Engineers, Major Alfred Mordecai of the Ordnance Department, and Captain George B. McClellan of the 1st Cavalry Regiment to observe operations. Arriving too late to witness the major battles, the officers nevertheless conducted extensive studies of battlefields, logistics, and transportation. Their reports offered valuable information on the organization of field armies, forts, arms design and manufacture, necessary field equipment, and field hospitals.

Early professionalization also involved standardization of training, ordnance, and equipment. Secretary of War John C. Calhoun established the Artillery School of Practice at Fort Monroe in Virginia in 1824 and an Infantry School of Practice at Jefferson Barracks in St. Louis in 1826. Using the French 'schools of practice' concept, units rotated through these schools to receive standardized training and drill. During the Jackson administration, egalitarianism and a need for troops during the Second Seminole War forced the closure of both schools. In the early 1840s, however, the War Department established four schools of practice at regimental posts across the country. In 1858, the artillery school reopened at Fort Monroe with an expanded mission to study the theories behind the use of artillery. A cavalry school of practice informally operated at Jefferson Barracks before being formally established at Carlisle Barracks in Pennsylvania in 1855. At West Point, Mahan created a two-year postgraduate course for engineers. The schools of practice improved the Army's use of light artillery and infantry tactical maneuver and, although the Civil War placed many of these schools on hiatus, the movement toward specialized, advanced military education gained even more momentum after the Civil War.

Standardizing fortification and ordnance also received much attention during the 1840s and 1850s. The Corps of Engineers proposed hundreds of projects to strengthen and diversify fixed fortifications. Among the ideas put forward were floating batteries powered by steam (a favorite of Secretary of War Lewis Cass), and fortress design and placement that used railroads for logistics and troop movement. Individual engineers debated the merits and flaws in the coastal fortification system. At the same time, the Ordnance Department standardized munitions and equipment. Artillery design, the percussion rifle, breech-loading weapons, and other equipment and weapons received the Board of Ordnance stamp of approval. The board also considered proposals for new technologies from both military officers and civilian inventors. Its method of testing and approving new weapons and equipment for standardized use by the Army made the Board of Ordnance the Army's first real research and development program.

Finally, any profession needs a means of sharing information, raising questions and discussing issues that affect the ability of that profession to fulfill its purpose. Before the Civil War, the American military already had developed such a process. Through various revisions of field manuals for artillery, infantry, and cavalry, officers discussed not only different methods and tactics for defense against foreign invasion, but also how best to deal with the Indian problem, maintain frontier security, and incorporate new technology. Journals, such as the *Army and Navy Chronicle* and the *Military and Naval Magazine of the United States*, became de facto professional publications in which officers could express concerns, raise issues, and share ideas. Some officers even wrote military history. Congress published a wide range of military reports on topics from military pay and infantry tactics, to the diplomatic implications of exploratory expeditions and sanitation. Pre-Civil War era officers had a variety of publications available to promote discussion about their profession at arms.

While steeped in tradition, the Navy lagged behind the Army's embrace of professionalism. The establishment of the Depot for Charts and Instruments, the Naval Observatory, and the Nautical Almanac Office initiated some standardization, but resistance to new technology, especially steam, remained entrenched among senior officers. Naval education was inconsistent and mostly relied on the traditional midshipmen apprentice system. As a challenge to this system, Matthew Perry established what he called the Naval Lyceum at the Brooklyn Navy Yard in 1833, but there was no formalized curriculum, only loosely directed independent study. A Naval School had also been established at Philadelphia for midshipmen, but it hardly qualified as a military academy.

Secretary of the Navy (and historian) George Bancroft finally formalized midshipmen education in 1845 and moved the Naval School from Philadelphia to Annapolis, Maryland. Congress, which had been in recess when Bancroft made the switch, turned a blind eye once it learned that Bancroft had saved money by moving the school. Congress approved the move and appropriated funds for its operation, thus officially creating the U.S. Naval Academy.

Nevertheless, the Navy faced difficult challenges. Inconsistency in quality of command resulted in even more disparity in the administration of discipline. Questionable hangings for mutiny on the *Somers* in 1842, and other dubious executions and floggings brought naval justice and officership into public question. It took decades before these and other issues were addressed adequately.

For the Army, at least, education, thought, and standardization in the pre-Civil War era put the American military on the path to professionalism. Army officers came to see themselves as part of a unique subculture with a sense of purpose and mission. The concept of the educated, well-mannered, and courageous officer who was intellectually involved in the development of his craft gradually became the norm rather than the exception.

War with Mexico

American expansion encroached upon Mexican lands primarily via expeditions and illegal settlement. The exception to this pattern was the permission that Spanish authorities gave to Americans to settle in Texas in 1821. Shortly after that, Mexico gained independence from Spain, and disagreements between Texians, as they called themselves, and the Mexican government quickly ensued. When Mexico outlawed slavery in 1835, the Texians rebelled. The Texas Revolution ended in April 1836 with a treaty granting independence from Mexico and recognizing the Rio Grande River as the southern border of the new republic. When the United States annexed Texas in 1845, Mexico severed diplomatic relations with the United States. Historically, Mexico considered the Nueces River as Texas's southern boundary and saw the American annexation of Texas as a grab at Mexican territory. The Mexican government also worried that the United States wanted California. In fact, President James K. Polk intended to annex California and offered to buy the territory from Mexico as well as settle the dispute over the Texas–Mexico boundary. Territorial expansion was not the only impetus for war; the expansion of slavery also fed war fever, particularly among Southerners.

Polk anticipated a Mexican invasion of Texas and, perhaps, hoped that negotiations would break down. In preparation, the president ordered Brevet Brigadier General Zachary Taylor to position 1,500 troops along the Nueces River in July 1845. In February 1846, negotiations with Mexico collapsed. Polk ordered Taylor to move his force to the Rio Grande. Supplied by sea at Point Isabel, Taylor established Fort Texas, near modern-day Brownsville, as a defensive stronghold to repel a Mexican attack, which he assumed would come from Matamoras, directly across the border from Brownsville.

On April 23, an American detachment sent to intercept a force of Mexican cavalry crossing the Rio Grande was ambushed by a Mexican patrol. Of the 60 American dragoons, 11 were killed and the rest captured. Taylor informed President Polk of the hostile action. The American press proclaimed that 'American blood had been shed on American soil.' Polk asked for a declaration of war, which Congress overwhelmingly approved on May 11, 1846. Taylor called on the state of Texas to provide four regiments of volunteers rather than state militia. The militia could not leave American territory, but volunteers could.

Even before Congress formally declared war, Taylor fought the Mexicans at Palo Alto, north of the Rio Grande River, on May 8. Lieutenants Ulysses S. Grant and George Meade saw their first combat there. After suffering more than 300 killed and 300 more wounded, the Mexicans retreated to a dry riverbed called Resaca de la Palma, where they dug in to await Taylor's advance. On May 9, Taylor again prevailed over the Mexicans in a fierce hand-to-hand contest. By the next day, the remaining Mexican forces had retreated across the Rio Grande. Without supplies, however, Taylor was unable to move his army across the river in pursuit until weeks later.

Polk had a clear objective in going to war with Mexico. He wanted Mexican territory north of the Rio Grande and west to the Pacific, including California. Polk and Major General Winfield Scott developed a three-pronged strategy to achieve this objective. Taylor, now a brevet major general and in command of all armies in Mexico, would drive west from Matamoras to Monterrey, then south toward Mexico City. From San Antonio, Brigadier General John Wool would move south into Mexico toward Saltillo. From Fort Leavenworth, in present-day Kansas, Colonel Stephen W. Kearny would move southwest to take Santa Fe and then San Diego. By occupying these places, Polk would have the advantage in negotiating an expansionist peace with Mexico.

Both Polk and Congress hoped for a quick war. Congress appropriated $10 million for what like 'Mr. Madison's War' in 1812 was now known as 'Mr. Polk's War' of 1846. The authorized strength of the Army grew to 15,540 troops by filling out 64-man companies to 100 with new recruits. Congress also approved 50,000 volunteers with a term of one year. Militia units were not called. Instead, the idea of an expansible army prevailed as volunteers augmented many existing units.

West Point graduates played their greatest role yet in an American war. Jefferson Davis, Robert E. Lee, Ulysses S. Grant, George B. McClellan, and Thomas J. Jackson, among many others, learned a great deal from their Mexican War experience that influenced their leadership in the Civil War just over a decade later. The Mexican War, however, was commanded by generals who had not graduated from West Point, and who held to pre-Napoleonic concepts of warfare. And, despite the growing influence of West Point in depoliticizing the officer corps, political disputes among senior officers influenced the conduct of the war. Polk disliked both Taylor and Scott because each had made no secret of their presidential aspirations. Seeing Scott as the more significant political threat, Polk gave Taylor overall command. Polk could not keep Scott out of action for long, however, because his successes in northern Mexico had made him very popular. Maneuvering by prominent political figures such as expansionist Senator Thomas Hart Benton, who wanted Polk to appoint him a general, and Polk's direct interference in command issues further complicated relations among the leadership.

Figure 7.1a General Zachary Taylor, portrait by Joseph Henry Bush, circa 1848.

Source: White House Historical Association.

Figure 7.1b General Winfield Scott at Veracruz, lithograph by Nathaniel Currier, 1847.

Source: National Archives.

Taylor and Northern Mexico

Taylor began his advance on a Monterrey in June 1846, with over 3,000 regulars and 3,000 more volunteers after several weeks of preparation, during which disease and desertion ravaged his army. At Monterrey, a well-armed force of 7,000 Mexican troops awaited Taylor's army in well-fortified positions. On September 20, Taylor sent a force of regulars and Texas Rangers to secure the Saltillo road to the west. Batteries of American howitzers shelled the Monterrey citadel and other fortifications in and around the city. On September 23, the Americans converged on the town from east and west in fierce house-to-house fighting. By the next day, the Mexicans were trapped around the central plaza and forced to surrender. Taylor, hoping to show his generosity and sway the Mexican government toward peace negotiations, allowed the Mexican army at Monterrey to withdraw under an eight-week armistice.

Polk, however, canceled the armistice and acquiesced to Scott's audacious plan to invest Mexico City through the port of Veracruz. The president hoped that capturing the enemy capitol would raise sagging popular support for the war and force the Mexican government into peace negotiations. General Scott commanded the forces destined for

Veracruz. In preparation for the invasion, Scott ordered Taylor to remain on the defensive at Monterrey and to send a large portion of his regulars to support the Veracruz campaign. Scott wanted regulars; he had a long memory of dealing with troublesome volunteers in the War of 1812. Angry at what he perceived as Scott's attempt to undermine his political ambitions, Taylor advanced his remaining 6,000 troops south to an indefensible position at Agua Nueva. Meanwhile, former Mexican dictator General Antonio de Santa Anna had returned from exile and accepted command of a large army at San Luis Potosí that was intended to repel the American invaders. Learning of Taylor's weak position and small force of mostly volunteers, Santa Anna advanced north, hoping to smash Taylor's army.

In February, Taylor's lead force of 5,000 troops met Santa Anna's army of now more than 20,000 soldiers just outside Saltillo at Buena Vista. Santa Anna quickly gained the initiative through superior artillery placement, but his cavalry was almost useless in the rugged terrain. Still, a regiment of Indiana volunteers broke and ran, leaving the field open to the Mexicans. Taylor then arrived with Jefferson Davis's Mississippi

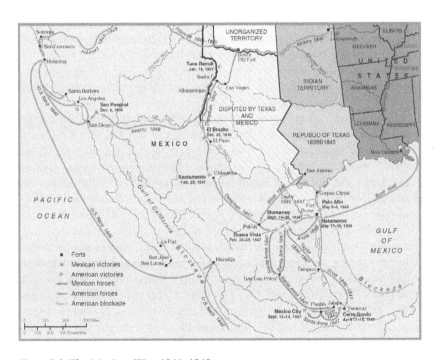

Figure 7.2 The Mexican War, 1846–1848.

Dragoons, headed off a Mexican cavalry assault, and ordered American artillery into the fight. This turned the tide of the battle, and Santa Anna, having lost nearly 2,000 killed and wounded, fell back to San Louis Potosí under cover of darkness on September 23. Taylor had suffered 264 dead and about 450 wounded, but he could have lost many more. The terrain, weather, and deadly use of artillery made the Battle of Buena Vista one of the fiercest fights of the war. Santa Anna had to abandon the north to the Americans. Taylor, motivated by political ambition, had with great battlefield courage led his men well. But now the focus shifted toward Kearny's advance in the west and Scott's drive to Mexico City.

The War in the West

From Fort Leavenworth, Kearny set out for Santa Fe with 300 Army dragoons and 1,000 Missouri volunteer mounted infantry. Arriving near Bent's Fort in July 1846, Kearny's men had suffered tremendous deprivation on their journey. The heat, lack of potable water, sunburn, and vicious mosquitoes plagued them. Kearny lost several men to sun-induced madness and dozens of horses to the heat. Despite these losses, in late August Kearny occupied Santa Fe, where the Mexican territorial governor had fled before the Americans' arrival. Kearny encountered no resistance among the local population, which included several American traders. He then set up a provincial government, writing a new constitution that combined American and local Hispanic governing organization, which came to be known as the Kearny Code.

Having taken Santa Fe without firing a shot, Kearny then set out for San Diego—a long, grueling journey. Along the way, he met Kit Carson from whom he learned that the Navy and John Frémont had all but secured much of northern California. He suffered a setback against a force of Californios (the Spanish-speaking settlers of California) at the Battle of San Pascual; his army was saved only by a contingent of sailors and Marines sent by Commodore Robert Stockton, who unbeknownst to Kearny had already taken San Diego. In 1847, Stockton's and Kearny's combined force defeated a small Californio army near Los Angeles, taking the town on January 10. Frémont's California Battalion, made up mostly of Americans from Sutter's Fort, arrived days later. At this point, Frémont signed the Treaty of Cahuenga with the defeated army, granting terms that Stockton had earlier refused. Stockton, angry, but eager to conclude affairs, approved the treaty on January 13. California was now in American hands. The California campaign had benefited from the poor state of Mexican and Californio forces but was almost derailed by inter- as well as intra-service bickering between Kearny, Stockton, and Frémont.

Scott's Campaign against Mexico City

With California and northern Mexico under American control, all that remained for Polk was to force the Mexican government to the peace table. With the defiant Santa Anna in command, however, the prospect seemed unlikely. Scott had to proceed with his campaign against Mexico City. On March 9, 1847, Scott landed 10,000 troops just three miles south of Veracruz in the first major amphibious landing in American military history; specially built surfboats ferried troops and supplies to the beach. Facing a Mexican force of over 4,000 behind Veracruz's formidable walls, Scott took his time preparing artillery positions for siege guns to bombard the city. On March 22, ten-inch mortars began firing on Veracruz from just half a mile away. Commodore Matthew C. Perry, in command of the naval force off Veracruz, loaned Scott several naval guns, which had an even greater effect in shelling the city. Veracruz surrendered on March 27. Scott occupied the city, declaring martial law, which applied to his own troops as much as it did to the civilian population. He had a soldier hanged for rape, making it clear that no depredations would be tolerated.

Scott now faced the long and challenging 200 miles from the coast up through the mountains to Mexico City. Poor transportation plagued his effort from the beginning, as there were never enough wagons or draft animals to keep his army moving as a single unit. Still, he needed to get his army off the coast before malarial fevers destroyed it and before the Mexicans could organize defenses.

Santa Anna had lost almost half of his army in fights with Taylor and his forced marches back to Mexico City to thwart an attempted coup. He now moved east along the National Highway to stop Scott. Santa Anna positioned his small army in a series of cliffs just outside Cerro Gordo to block Scott's advance, down the National Highway. While Scott did come that way, a daring reconnaissance by Captain Robert E. Lee found a route around the cliffs to even higher ground that, with artillery, commanded Santa Anna's positions. After the Herculean effort of moving artillery up and down steep ravines and cliffs, Scott opened fire on the morning of April 18, forcing the Mexicans into a chaotic retreat and leaving Scott to deal with over 3,000 prisoners of war.

Now it seemed that the highway to Mexico City was wide open. Scott's good fortune, however, was soon overshadowed by new challenges. At Puebla, Scott had to rest his men and await resupply and reinforcements. Over 2,000 of his men were sick, and to make matters worse, 3,000 volunteers returned to Veracruz to await transport home when their enlistments expired in May. It took over 600 wagons to carry the sick, the former volunteers, and their equipment back to Veracruz, forcing Scott to make the risky decision to cut his supply line and live off the land.

To further complicate Scott's situation, Polk's appointed negotiator, Nicholas Trist, arrived while Scott was at Veracruz. Trist did not like Scott, and Scott had no need for Trist or his mission. The two men got off on the wrong foot, but Scott's concern for Trist, who became very ill in Vercruz, helped bridge the gap between these two enormous egos. Polk ordered Trist to negotiate an end to the fighting and to offer the Mexican government $1 million for a treaty. Trist failed to make any headway in negotiating with the Mexican government, notably because Santa Anna had forced the Mexican Congress to pass a law making it illegal to negotiate with the United States. Consequently, Scott made his final plans for assaulting Mexico City.

By August 10, Scott's isolated force had advanced within 14 miles of Mexico City. Santa Anna had occupied several well-fortified positions to the east of the city, forcing Scott to approach from the west. The route was narrow, confined by lakes, mountains, and apparently impassable lava fields known as the Pedregal. The Pedregal did indeed seem impassable to everyone—except Robert E. Lee. Lee found a path through the challenging terrain that could be widened to a road. Supporting Brevet Major General Gideon J. Pillow's road crews, Brigadier General David E. Twiggs's division and light artillery served as a covering force. Before long, both Twiggs and Pillow had a fight on their hands against well-placed Mexican howitzers near Contreras. The next day, reinforced American units sneaked through a path in the Pedregal to hit the Mexican rear. The Battle of Contreras was brief but deadly for the Mexicans, who lost over 700 killed and 800 captured to the Americans' 60 killed and wounded. Scott, however, did not rest.

Scott ordered his forces to pursue Santa Anna, chasing the Mexican forces through San Angel and then to Churubusco. The battle went back and forth all afternoon but subsided as the Mexicans ran low on ammunition. Santa Anna had lost another 4,000 killed and wounded while Scott suffered 1,000 casualties. A unit of over 200 American deserters—mostly Irish Catholic immigrants who sided with the Mexican Catholics—had fought against the Americans since the Battle of Monterrey. Many among this unit, known as the San Patricios, were captured at Churubusco; now, their fate lay in Scott's hands. Just as American forces raised the flag over Chapultepec Castle, Scott ordered the execution of 35 of these deserters, an incident that fit too well the nativist anti-Irish, anti-Catholic attitudes in the United States.

Both sides were exhausted and agreed to a brief armistice for negotiations. Trist and the Mexican government, however, could not find common ground. Santa Anna used the break to rebuild his beleaguered forces. Scott, knowing that time only made the Mexicans stronger, terminated the armistice and prepared to make a final assault on the city.

Two strong positions threatened to stop Scott's assault—Chapultepec Castle, and El Molino del Rey. Recognizing their significance, Santa Anna personally oversaw deployment of troops to those strongholds. Located high on a bluff, the castle served as the Mexican equivalent to West Point. Chapultepec blocked Scott's approach to the city. Below, the castle's causeways and steep slopes made for a difficult approach. When intelligence suggested the Mexican Army was casting cannon at El Molino del Rey, Scott determined to attack it. Curiously, Scott anticipated little resistance. To his surprise, the Battle of Molino del Rey (September 8, 1847) was a violent, bloody affair, one of the bloodiest of the war. It cost Scott 700 casualties, while the Mexicans suffered 2,000. After taking El Molino del Rey, Scott's forces discovered only a few cannons. Scott launched his attack against Chapultepec on September 13. After a horrific few hours of fighting the castle fell, but the work was not done for the Americans. Scott kept the momentum going, pushing deep into the city. After enduring a day of house-to-house fighting, the Mexicans surrendered their capitol. Santa Anna fled with what little was left of his army, leaving Scott to occupy Mexico City and declare martial law.

Figure 7.3 The attack on Chapultepec, September 13, 1847, lithograph by E. B. & E. C. Kellogg, New York and Hartford, Connecticut.

Source: Library of Congress.

Trist and Scott pursued negotiations with the defeated government, which concluded in February 1848. Interestingly, Trist had been recalled by an angry President Polk in October 1847, having learned of the recall in November but at Scott's counsel had ignored it. By the time Washington learned of the current situation in Mexico City, Trist had reasoned, the war might be over, and the treaty signed. After several weeks of negotiations, the Mexican government finally agreed to terms. The Treaty of Guadalupe Hidalgo gave the United States modern-day New Mexico, Arizona, Nevada, Utah, and California, and parts of Wyoming and Colorado. Both sides agreed to the Rio Grande as the southern boundary of Texas. The United States assumed American claims against Mexico and gave Mexico $15 million. The American occupation force left Mexico in August 1848.

Despite the victorious hoopla around the United States, the Mexican War of 1846–1848 had not been a very glorious affair. For the Americans, disease and hardship took many more lives than did battle. Of the 13,780 American dead, only one in eight died as the result of combat. Over 2,000 regulars and 3,000 volunteers had deserted during the war. The war also had a high financial cost—close to $100 million.

Despite the human and financial cost, the United States military had prevailed in a difficult war. Leadership was key to the American victory. Both Taylor and Scott, despite their personal and political rivalry, exhibited strategic creativity and daring. Scott's decision to cut his supply line from Veracruz remains studied to this day. Cooperation between Navy and Army commanders continued to improve, as it had in the War of 1812. The war had been a proving ground for the professional military education provided at West Point, whose graduates dominated junior-officer ranks in the regular army.

Yet, the very public postwar bickering among Army commanders—particularly Scott (who had to face a court of inquiry after the war), Frémont, and Stephen Kearny—over alleged affronts and charges of incompetence tarnished the military's achievement in carrying out a limited war in support of clear national objectives. Ironically, these very national objectives caused other problems. The addition of such a vast territory to the United States irritated the festering wound of slavery and territorial expansion, ultimately leading to civil war. Mexico, arguably, never recovered from the 1846–1848 war.

Conclusion

By the 1850s, the American military had made great strides in professionalism, training, and, to a lesser extent, technology. Both the Army and Navy had developed a sense of *esprit de corps* among their officers, especially the junior grades, as well as a sense of professional ethics and an understanding of the military as a career. More officers stayed in service for several years, even decades. The military had also found a purpose beyond defending the territory of the United States. The War with Mexico had given it wartime experience, though there were still lessons to learn. At an operational level, the Army and Navy had worked well together at Veracruz. More broadly, war remained a romantic and glorious affair for many officers, who openly promoted a new, heroic tradition of American military prowess. While the war had been a great success for American combat arms, officers could not help but compare the achievement to Napoleonic conflicts earlier in the century.

The American military had improved dramatically since the War of 1812. Despite success in the War with Mexico, serious issues remained. Civil–military relations continued to be tense. The Indian dilemma left a bitter taste among Army officers. Significantly, sectionalism began to divide the officer corps. The regional crisis over slavery and expansion that erupted in civil war provided the supreme test for the American military, one that would force it to come of age.

Further Reading

Dugard, Martin. *The Training Ground: Grant, Lee, Sherman and Davis in the Mexican War, 1846–1848*. New York: Little Brown and Company, 2008.

Eisenhower, John S. D. *Agent of Destiny: The Life and Times of General Winfield Scott*. Norman, OK: University of Oklahoma Press, 1997.

Foos, Paul. *'A Short, Offhand, Killing Affair': Soldiers and Social Conflict during the Mexican-American War*. Chapel Hill, NC: University of North Carolina Press, 2002.

Greenberg, Amy S. *A Wicked War: Polk, Clay, Lincoln, and the 1846 U.S. Invasion of Mexico*. New York: Knopf, 2012.

Guardino, Peter. *The Dead March: A History of the Mexican-American War*. Cambridge, MA: Harvard University Press, 2017.

Henderson, Timothy J. *A Glorious Defeat: Mexico and its War with the United States*. New York: Hill and Wang, 2008.

Johnson, Timothy D. *A Gallant Little Army: The Mexico City Campaign*. Lawrence, KS: University Press of Kansas, 2007.

Lewis, Felice Flanery. *Trailing Clouds of Glory: Zachary Taylor's Mexican War Campaign and his Emerging Civil War Leaders*. Tuscaloosa, AL: University of Alabama Press, 2010.

Peskin, Allan. *Winfield Scott and the Profession of Arms*. Kent, MI: Kent State University Press, 2003.

Skelton, William B. *An American Profession at Arms: The Army Officer Corps, 1784–1861*. Lawrence, KS: University Press of Kansas, 1992.

van Wagenen, Michael. *Remembering the Forgotten War: The Enduring Legacies of the U.S.-Mexican War*. Amherst, MA: University of Massachusetts Press, 2012.

Winders, Richard Bruce. *Mr. Polk's Army: The American Military Experience in the Mexican War*. College Station, TX: Texas A&M University Press, 1997.

8 Civil War and Reconstruction

Introduction

As America's bloodiest conflict, the Civil War is integral to not only American history but also the American cultural tradition. Divided North and South, the nation warred on itself for four years, with each side bringing a near-total commitment of not only military forces but also of government and the whole of American society to the fight. The delicate issue of slavery was at the conflict's core. What began for the North as a war to restore the Union also became a war to finally end slavery. In the southern Confederacy, the war was perceived as akin to the War for Independence in some respects. From the viewpoint of many Southerners, an oppressive government was close to taking away fundamental rights, among which was the right to own other human beings as property. Only by having their own country, Southerners reasoned, could they continue to maintain slavery as the primary labor system to support the South's economy and its unique society.

Militarily, the Civil War was a Jominian conflict in part because West Point graduates versed in Jomini's writings commanded the most massive armies ever seen in North America. Throughout the war, however, a new way of war evolved—one with its roots in the colonial conflicts of the seventeenth century. This total war concept not only included making relentless war upon armies but also involved mobilizing and attacking industry, agriculture, transportation, and other war-making capacities. The goal of total war was to destroy the will of both military forces and the noncombatant population to carry on the fight by depriving both of military supplies, food, and other necessities.

The Civil War remains a topic of the most intensive study among historians. The war's significance to American military history emerges through studying the strategies of the Union and Confederacy, reviewing the main theaters of operations and significant battles, and examining the effects of the war on the future development of the American military.

Billy Yank and Johnny Reb

Regionalism, in this case, a sense of allegiance to either the North or the South, developed because of westward territorial expansion and the War with Mexico, the growth of Northern manufacturing, and the expansion of the South's cotton economy. By the 1850s, regionalism had manifested itself most intensely in the debate over slavery. Since 1820, successive compromises had failed to resolve the issue to either side's satisfaction, and with the election of Republican Abraham Lincoln in 1860 Southerners were convinced that slavery and the white society founded upon it were about to be destroyed by Northern abolitionists in Congress. Successive Southern states subsequently seceded from the United States to form the Confederate States of America. The United States that remained, the Union, faced few alternatives: either let the Southern states go or bring them back into the Union by force, if necessary.

When hostilities broke out in April 1861, the Union had a population of more than 20 million people to the Confederacy's nine million. Almost half of the Confederate population was slaves who were never allowed to serve as soldiers in the Confederate army. In the North more than one million people worked in more than 100,000 factories, while in the South fewer than 110,000 people worked in about 20,000 factories. The total industrial output of the Confederacy equaled that of the state of New York alone. The Northern rail network had more than 31,000 miles of track—more than 70 percent of the railroads in the United States. Among other industrial resources, the North dominated steel production and coal mining. The South had comparatively little with which to fuel and supply its handful of factories. Based on these facts alone, oddsmakers would have heavily favored the North in any armed conflict against its southern neighbor.

Union victory in the Civil War, nevertheless, was not assured. Like the patriots in the War for Independence, the Confederates did not have to win; instead, they had to only continue fighting long enough for the Union to lose the will to continue the war. The South could fight a defensive war, hope for foreign intervention, and, perhaps, achieve a decisive victory that would force the Union to negotiate a settlement preserving Southern independence. The Union, on the other hand, barring a decisive victory against the Confederacy, would have to fight an offensive war without the benefit of interior lines of communication. Such a war would require large armies, extraordinarily long and complicated logistical lines, and immense industrial output. The Confederacy might be able to hold on just long enough to break the will of the Northerners to fight such a protracted and costly war.

It is ironic that Lincoln, a man with little military experience—he had served 36 days of militia duty in the Black Hawk War (1832)—was a better war president than Jefferson Davis, who was a graduate of West

Point, a veteran of the War with Mexico, and former Secretary of War. Both men served as commanders-in-chief of their respective nations during the Civil War. Davis was at a disadvantage from the beginning of the war because the Confederate constitution limited his presidential powers. Also, as in the old Articles of Confederation, states retained power over a relatively weak central government. Lincoln had much more leeway as commander-in-chief, and used his constitutional authority in unprecedented ways, permanently expanding the power of the president. He caused a continuing argument about presidential power when he suspended habeas corpus in 1863. Although rarely noted, Article I, Section 9, clause 2 of the Constitution allows the government to suspend that right during times of insurrection. Despite a constitutional framework that better supported war-making, Lincoln had to contend with more partisan bickering throughout the war than did Davis, as both Democrats and Republicans constantly criticized, questioned, and interfered with Lincoln's war effort.

Strategic and Technological Contours

Civil War grand strategy mainly revolved around two ideas. First, many believed that capturing the opponent's capital city would end the fighting and force a peace settlement. Such an approach clearly required defending one's own capital from capture. Second, Napoleonic tradition held that destroying the enemy's armies could achieve the same goal. With so many West Point graduates among the Confederate and Union officer corps, all having studied in depth the Napoleonic Wars and Jomini, and in many instances having served in the War with Mexico, it is not surprising that these ideas held so much prominence in Civil War strategy.

When the war began, Lieutenant General Winfield Scott, the experienced and aged head of the Union Army, proposed a tight naval blockade against Southern ports that was intended to deny the rebels support from abroad. Meanwhile, Union armies would seize control of the Mississippi River with simultaneous approaches along the Ohio River from the north and from New Orleans in the south. Scott then planned to let the Confederacy slowly suffocate. His so-called Anaconda Plan, however, did not satisfy public demands in the North that the rebellion be put down quickly. Thus, the Union attempted to capture Richmond as well as destroy Confederate armies—initially through attempts to fight decisive battles, but later through a strategy of attrition. This strategy guided Union strategic thinking throughout the war. Confederate strategy remained simply to fight a defensive war until the Union tired of the conflict, or a foreign power intervened to help guarantee Confederate independence.

Neither Union nor Confederate strategy changed much until the spring of 1864. In March of that year, Lincoln appointed Lieutenant General Ulysses S. Grant as commander of all Union forces. Under Grant, the strategic landscape changed. Grant held strategic notions that went far beyond the decisive battle and slow strangulation. He expanded the strategy of attrition into total war. By fighting a total war, Grant aimed to utterly destroy the Confederacy's war-making capacity. He hoped to erode the political will of the people of the Confederacy by ruining its ability to either protect or succor its people.

Additionally, Grant relentlessly pursued Confederate armies in the field, notably the Army of Northern Virginia, forcing its commander General Robert E. Lee into a war of attrition that the Confederacy could not win. As an experienced commander, Lee also coveted the decisive battle, even though it arguably did not fit with the overall Confederate strategy or resources. Lee strategically and tactically took the defensive while looking for the critical decisive victory, which often required taking costly offensives instead. The Confederacy was indeed caught in a strategic dilemma —it had to outlast the Union, but could it last that long while sustaining substantial losses in men and materiel?

Civil War armies began the fight expecting to use Napoleonic practices, but they were forced to adjust tactics because of technological advancements in shoulder arms. During the War with Mexico, the U.S. Army had largely replaced smoothbore muskets with more accurate and deadly percussion-lock rifled muskets that used a conical bullet. The French Army officer Claude Etienne Minié in the 1840s designed a new bullet with a conical-shaped nose and a hollow base to replace the traditional round ball. When fired from Minié's new rifled musket, the base expanded into the rifling of the barrel, causing the bullet to spin horizontally and driving it outward faster, farther, and more accurately. Minié's new cartridge made reloading quicker, which meant that each soldier could fire more often and expect the bullet to strike the enemy at greater distances. Although these technical advances were not as significant as historians initially argued, new military technology still ushered in essential changes to the character of war.

More rapid, accurate fire made possible by the new rifles and the new bullet meant that the traditional tight attack formations and massed fires had to give way to less dense battle lines of soldiers, firing at the enemy from greater distances. Larger intervals between men created lines sometimes three-fourths of a mile long, if not longer. Also, armies increased the gaps between them when they met for battle. As a result, combat actions tended to last much longer, and the much sought-after decisive battle became more elusive. Rifled muskets and conical bullets also shifted the advantage from the attack to defense. Increased firepower spurred defending soldiers to seek shelter behind quickly constructed earthworks, a development that also eased distribution of ammunition. Thus, attacking soldiers were forced to advance across expanses of open ground against punishing rifle fire delivered by relatively well-protected enemy soldiers.

Assaulting forces also faced deadly fire from opposing artillery batteries. The smoothbore Napoleon 12-pound cannon was a mainstay for both armies, and it could fire canister, shrapnel, or case shot, depending on what the battlefield situation warranted. Napoleon guns had an effective range of about 1,200 yards. The advent of rifled artillery, however, dramatically changed the battlefield as had rifled musketry. With a range of over 2,500 yards, rifled artillery provided greater accuracy at a greater distance. New and improved percussion fuses also made artillery more lethal.

Advances in technology across the spectrum added to the changing landscape of war. Extensive rail networks gave the railroad a pivotal transportation role for moving armies and supplying them in the field. Steam-powered riverboats allowed for greater mobility along inland waterways. The telegraph also played a prominent role, for now commanders could be in almost instant communication on the battlefield as well as with political leaders in Richmond and Washington.

Civil War Armies

Army organization was mostly the same for both the Union and Confederate armies, with each comprising the three combat arms: infantry, artillery, and cavalry. The regiment was the basic unit in Civil War armies. Infantry, long the 'queen of battle,' was the centerpiece of both Union and Confederate forces. Brigades were composed of four to six regiments, with three to four brigades making up a division, of which three to four would make up a corps. When fully manned, the ten companies in an infantry regiment totaled 1,000 men, but as the war dragged on unit rolls listed fewer and fewer troops. By 1863, as men died, enlistments expired and recruiting lagged, regiments typically carried fewer than 350 soldiers. Despite their reduced size, these units assaulted enemy positions in successive waves while in line formation, in the face of deadly artillery and rifle fire.

Cavalry troops (a troop of cavalry was the same as a regiment) had 12 companies, with the same command structure as infantry. Improved firepower made traditional cavalry charges too costly, so most cavalrymen functioned as scouting or screening parties. In combat, cavalry more often than not performed as dragoons, riding to the battlefield to fight while dismounted. Due primarily to this development, cavalry largely discarded the romantic but impractical saber early in the war in favor of the Spencer repeating rifle and generally became highly effective fighters.

Similarly, artillery batteries were about the size of an infantry company and were attached to units from infantry corps down through to brigades. Artillery was used mostly in defensive positions, and once dug in, artillery emplacements became formidable obstacles. Artillery could, however, function in a more mobile manner. Lighter cannon with smaller horse-drawn caissons could quickly run into place and fire, then just as quickly, move to a new location.

To build these massive armies, both the Union and Confederacy used a variety of mobilization methods. The Union did not rely upon state militia, instead once again using volunteers in the expansible army concept. Each state was obligated to fulfill a quota of volunteers to be formed into units from that particular state. By 1863, however, volunteerism waned as the war dragged on and Union troop demands increased. Congress passed the Enrollment Act, which put in place conscription or, as it was known, a draft. This unprecedented expansion of federal authority and the several legal ways to avoid the draft caused riots in protest of the law, the most infamous of which occurred in New York City during July 1863. The Confederacy earlier instituted a draft in April 1862. In both the Union and Confederacy, a myriad of exemptions and replacement provisions allowed many who were financially able to escape the draft, thus leaving the more impoverished adult male population available for conscription. Still, the threat of being drafted and the social stigma attached to it motivated many to volunteer for service. In 1865, the Federal government amended the Enrollment Act making draft evaders subject to having their citizenship revoked. Even though conscription was controversial and drew a great deal of attention, it was not the primary means to raise forces.

The Eastern Theater

When the war began, Lincoln ordered most federal posts abandoned except for a small few, including Fort Sumter in Charleston harbor. Confederate General P. G. T. Beauregard began bombarding the fort on April 12, 1861, but Major Robert Anderson and his small garrison of men could offer little in reply. The following day a barracks caught fire, prompting Anderson to concede. Although hardly a great military victory, Anderson's surrender, along with Lincoln's call for volunteers to suppress the rebellion, was enough to rally rebel spirits spur Arkansas, North Carolina, Tennessee, and Virginia to join the Confederacy, thereby providing the new Confederacy with much-needed resources and more troops.

Most importantly, Virginia's entry into the Confederacy convinced Lee to resign his U.S. Army commission for loyalty to his home state. Fort Sumter's capitulation also united the North in support for war against the rebels. Now that the Confederacy had fired the first shot, state governments in the Union responded enthusiastically to Lincoln's April 15 call for 75,000 90-day volunteers to put down the rebellion.

Lincoln believed that the rebellion could be crushed by taking the Confederate capital at Richmond, some 100 miles to the south of Washington. From Washington, Union forces under Brigadier General

Irvin McDowell headed toward Richmond in July 1861. At a vital railroad junction at Manassas along Bull Run Creek, McDowell's army encountered Confederate forces in the first major battle of the war. Poorly trained and not well-led, McDowell's force of some 30,000, mostly volunteers, set out from Alexandria on July 16. They took four days to reach Manassas, where Beauregard's force of 22,000 rebels awaited them. Reinforced by Brigadier General Joseph E. Johnston's 11,000 Confederates brought by railroad from the Shenandoah Valley, Beauregard now had a numerical advantage.

McDowell hoped to flank the Confederate battle line, then destroy the Confederate force in total. As prominent Northern politicians and other Washingtonians watched the action from what they thought was a safe distance, the Union attack began to falter. The long march, the July heat, and a courageous stand made by Brigadier General Thomas J. Jackson—which earned him the nickname 'Stonewall'—caused the Union line to waiver, and then break into a chaotic retreat all the way back to Washington. What was supposed to have been an easy Union rout of rebel forces had turned into a Union disaster. Fortunately for McDowell, the Confederates were too elated with victory, or perhaps too exhausted, to maintain the initiative and give chase to the fleeing Union troops. The Battle of First Bull Run cost the Union 3,000 casualties and the Confederacy almost 2,000. Such a decisive Confederate victory shocked the North while bringing great hope for a swift victory across the South.

Lincoln promptly relieved McDowell and named Major General George B. McClellan to command the new Army of the Potomac. 'Little Mac,' as his troops affectionately called him, refused to take his men into battle until he thought they were absolutely trained and ready. It took months, but the cautious McClellan managed to build a disciplined army exceeding 150,000 men. Having shaped this excellent army, however, McClellan proved reluctant to use it.

Meanwhile, Confederate General Johnston and his rapidly growing army of 50,000 men stood between the Army of the Potomac and Richmond. Finally, in early 1862, Lincoln ordered McClellan to move on Richmond. McClellan moved his army at a glacial pace, landing on the Virginia Peninsula to approach Richmond from the east. Always fearing that the Confederate army was more substantial than it really was and angry that Lincoln had forced him to keep 40,000 of his men near Washington to protect the capital from Jackson's small but mobile Confederate force, McClellan hesitated, giving Johnston time to reinforce and plan for the defense of Richmond. Finally, on May 31, the two armies met in a battle at Seven Pines near Richmond, where Johnston was severely wounded. To replace Johnston, President Davis chose General Robert E. Lee to command what became known as the Army of Northern Virginia.

Lee attacked the Army of the Potomac's right flank in the Battles of the Seven Days, between June 25 and July 1, 1862. Despite poor coordination of attacks at places like Mechanicsville and Gaines Mill, Lee managed to drive McClellan away from Richmond. Now, with high confidence, Lee attempted to stage the decisive battle at Malvern Hill. Well-entrenched and fortified, the Army of the Potomac repulsed wave after wave of assaulting Confederates. Of Lee's 20,000 casualties during the Seven Days, more than 5,000 occurred at Malvern Hill.

Impatient at McClellan's lack of progress, Lincoln decided to make yet another change. The president had learned, however, that he could not personally direct the war. Although a gifted organizer, McClellan was too timid in the field, and Lincoln needed a fighting general. Henry W. Halleck replaced McClellan as General-in-Chief of the Union Army, with McClellan retaining command of the Army of the Potomac. Major General John Pope took command of the new Army of Virginia, which was scattered about the Shenandoah Valley. Although Halleck also proved a disappointment in coordinating field armies, he did provide a useful conduit between the field armies and Lincoln.

McClellan and Pope converged their armies at Fredericksburg in northern Virginia. Fearful that the combined armies might be too much for his Army of Northern Virginia, Lee struck Pope as the Army of Virginia slowly made its way toward Fredericksburg. With McClellan nowhere near Fredericksburg, Pope was left to fight Lee on his own. In the Second Battle of Bull Run, Lee and Pope clashed where Confederate and Union armies had battled the previous year. Lee distracted Pope by bringing Jackson's force behind the Army of Virginia. Jackson's troops then led Pope's army right into Lee's hands on August 29–30, 1862. Pope suffered casualties exceeding 16,000, while Lee's force lost 9,000 men.

Infuriated at the failure to trap the Army of Northern Virginia, Lincoln fired Pope and incorporated the Army of Virginia into the Army of the Potomac to restore McClellan to overall field command. The bold Lee again chose to seek a decisive battle by invading Maryland with the hope of drawing the Army of the Potomac into the open where he could destroy it. Doing so would leave Washington, Baltimore, even Philadelphia, open to Confederate attack. With Major General J. E. B. Stuart's cavalry screening his right flank, Lee crossed his army into Maryland to march into Hagerstown.

What happened next was one of those odd twists of luck that often occur in wars. Union troops investigating an abandoned Confederate camp found several cigars, one of them wrapped in a copy of Lee's orders for the march into Maryland. McClellan now knew precisely where the Army of Northern Virginia was headed and where it would converge. McClellan, however, squandered the opportunity by hesitating again—this time, he delayed longer than half a day. He could have attacked Lee's forces before they had converged. Instead, the delay and

Lee's discovery that Union soldiers had found his plan prevented such a move. Lee abandoned the invasion and gathered his army at Sharpsburg near Antietam Creek. With little room to maneuver, but with the advantage of interior lines, Lee made his stand in the Battle of Antietam, the bloodiest day in American history, and a turning point in the war.

On September 17, Lee's army of 40,000 faced off against McClellan's 70,000 near Sharpsburg. McClellan believed he had the chance to wipe out the Army of Northern Virginia and gain a Napoleonic-style decisive victory. Throughout the day at places like the Cornfield, Bloody Lane, and Burnside's Bridge, the two massive armies clashed. Neither one could gain the advantage. McClellan failed to put in his reserve corps when doing so might have won the day for the Union. Battered and bloodied, the two armies warily eyed each other throughout the following day, then Lee withdrew into Virginia. Between the two armies, almost 5,000 men were killed with another 21,000 wounded or missing. Neither side could continue to sustain such casualties. McClellan did not pursue Lee. Arguably, his force was so bloodied that it simply could not do so. Still, the Army of the Potomac held the field in what had been a tactical draw, and Lincoln was able to put enough political spin on the Battle of Antietam to renew Northerners' hopes for victory.

Lincoln replaced McClellan with Major General Ambrose E. Burnside on November 7, 1862. Burnside had shown promise as a combat commander, serving with distinction at Antietam and other battles. Lincoln wanted Richmond, and Burnside sought to give it to him. Burnside marched his Army of the Potomac, now exceeding 120,000 men, southward from Washington to get between Lee and Richmond before Lee could block him. Burnside attempted to cross the Rappahannock River at Fredericksburg, but before he could do so, Lee arrived with the Army of Northern Virginia's now 70,000 troops to occupy the high ground on the south side of the river. Burnside still managed to cross to attempt a series of futile frontal assaults on Lee's entrenched lines. The idea of hitting weak points in the enemy's line with overwhelming mass still guided battlefield tactics.

The Battle of Fredericksburg began in earnest on December 13, 1862. Along Marye's Heights, Major General James Longstreet's Confederates unleashed devastating rifle fire from behind a stone wall as Union troops attempted to cross a mile of open ground to assault Longstreet's position. As at Antietam, the casualties were horrendous. Burnside lost more than 12,000 killed and wounded, while Lee lost a not-insignificant 5,300. Although he had initially planned a second attack on December 18, Burnside reconsidered and withdrew the Army of the Potomac across the Rappahannock.

As 1862 drew to a close in the east, the massive armies had bloodied each other badly but made no strategic progress. A stalemate seemed to be the best way to characterize the situation. Lincoln fired Burnside, whose subordinates had lobbied for his removal. Burnside's replacement was

Major General Joseph Hooker, yet another proven combat leader given a chance to guide the Army of the Potomac to Richmond.

Lincoln also determined the time was right to strike the Confederacy where it hurt most. Slavery remained at the foundation of Southern culture and the Confederate economy and distracted many Southerners from the main fight. African Americans, Southerners believed, were going to exact bloody revenge on their white masters. It was a brilliant political stroke that changed not only the Union's war aims but opened the way for imposing total war upon the South.

Lincoln issued the Emancipation Proclamation on January 1, 1863, freeing slaves only in states that were in rebellion against the United States. Border states still in the Union could retain their slaves, but Lincoln's announcement served as notice that slavery, even in those states, would soon end. Although Lincoln was opposed to slavery, the Emancipation Proclamation practical wartime measure aimed at weakening the South's war effort economically and diplomatically. The Confederacy did not enlist slaves into its ranks but did rely heavily on slaves for military as well as civilian labor. By freeing slaves in areas controlled by Union forces, the Proclamation hit hard at the Southern economy. Also, freed slaves were welcomed into the Union Army, thus providing more manpower for the Federal war effort. As word of emancipation spread, thousands of slaves abandoned their owners to seek Union lines and freedom.

Diplomatically, Lincoln's proclamation ended the Confederacy's hope for foreign assistance. Both Great Britain and France were considering supporting the South. Although Great Britain had abolished slavery in 1833, the United States' growing economic power seemed a threat to European economic hegemony. If the Confederacy won, that threat was eliminated. However, when Lincoln expanded Union war aims to include ending slavery, Great Britain's already waning interest in aiding the South fell away.

Hooker used the winter to improve discipline and training and to restore morale. Toward the latter goal, he began what remains an important American military tradition. Each corps received its own distinctive insignia to help build unit identity through each corps' history. As the weather improved, however, Hooker still faced Lee's army firmly entrenched at Fredericksburg. Learning from Burnside's mistakes, Hooker planned a double envelopment to dislodge Lee from Fredericksburg and divided his force of 130,000 to hit the right and left flanks of the Army of Northern Virginia.

Realizing what was happening, Lee divided his force, leaving part on Marye's Heights and withdrawing the rest to nearby Chancellorsville. The Battle of Chancellorsville is often considered the finest example of Lee's combat command ability. During this engagement, Lee utilized economy of force, surprise, offensive maneuver, and daring to again defeat the Army of the Potomac. The first contact was made in a wooded area of thick

Figure 8.1 From Fredericksburg to Gettysburg.

undergrowth called the Wilderness. Having hacked its way through this dense forest, on May 1 Hooker's army was surprised by Stonewall Jackson's smaller force. Hooker withdrew through the Wilderness to Chancellorsville.

Lee again divided his force, using protective screens and rapid, long, marches to surprise Hooker. On May 2, just outside Chancellorsville, Union Major General Oliver O. Howard mistook Confederate movements for a retreat and ordered his men forward just before dusk. The trap set by Jackson very nearly destroyed Howard's force. Later that same night, the Confederate general was mistakenly shot by one of his own sentries as he returned from a reconnaissance of Union lines. He died a long eight days later. Lee's army never fully recovered from the loss of Jackson's talent.

On May 3, Lee struck Chancellorsville and drove Hooker out of the city. Meanwhile, in Fredericksburg, Major General John Sedgwick broke through the Confederate lines to reach Chancellorsville. On May 4, Lee again divided his force to stop Sedgwick's advance. Near Salem Church, Lee and Sedgwick clashed in a fierce fight. Hooker refused to send reinforcements to help Sedgwick. Incredibly, over one-third of the Army of the Potomac had yet to be engaged. With Sedgwick thwarted and Hooker uncertain, Lee had another opportunity to destroy the Army of the Potomac. Before he could pull it off, however, Hooker withdrew across the Rappahannock. Hooker's grand plan to take Richmond had miscarried, resulting in more than 17,000 Union casualties to Lee's 13,000. In addition to sustaining such a significant number of casualties, Lee had also failed to crush the Army of the Potomac, despite his brilliant tactical movements during the battle.

Lee then planned his boldest campaign—an invasion deep into Northern territory, perhaps as far as Philadelphia. Among his many objectives, Lee hoped to relieve Richmond by forcing the Army of the Potomac out of Virginia and destroying it, much as he had tried to do in 1862.

By June 30, 1863, Lee had his three corps across the Potomac and into Maryland. Using the Shenandoah Valley and the hills of western Maryland to screen his movements, Lee was able to move his 75,000 men deep into Union territory before the Army of the Potomac realized what was happening. Hooker proposed hitting Richmond while Lee was absent. Lincoln rejected the idea, wanting instead to protect Washington and Baltimore and destroy Lee's army. One problem was that for several days neither side seemed to know exactly where the other was. Lee's cavalry, under the command of J. E. B. Stuart, failed in its mission to act as Lee's eyes and ears. Stuart lost contact with Lee, instead of engaging in raids that were otherwise of little use in Lee's strategy. Hooker headed north, keeping the Army of the Potomac between Lee and Washington.

Knowing that Hooker was on the move, Lee ordered his far-flung corps to regroup in southern Pennsylvania near Gettysburg. On the same day, June 28, Lincoln replaced Hooker with Major General George Meade. Gettysburg was a crossroads, as several roads from almost every direction came together there like the hub of a spoked wheel. It was there that the most massive battle in the history of North America and arguably the most crucial battle of the Civil War took place—the Battle of Gettysburg.

Advance units of Union cavalry under the command of Brigadier General John Buford literally ran into advance units of Confederate infantry belonging to Lieutenant General A. P. Hill's Confederate corps to the west of Gettysburg on July 1. Major General John Reynolds and his more than 20,000 Union troops arrived to support Buford. By late afternoon both Hill's and Lieutenant General Richard Ewell's Confederate corps were engaged, pushing Reynolds's men back through Gettysburg to Culp's Hill and Cemetery Hill southeast of the town. Reynolds preferred the defensive advantage of the hills; thus, from his viewpoint, being pushed through Gettysburg was not catastrophic. Before Reynolds could move to the hills, however, he was killed. Meade replaced him with the very able Major General Winfield Scott Hancock. Lee ordered Ewell to take Cemetery Hill lest the Union troops establish a formidable defensive position, but Ewell's advance failed. Throughout the night, the main bodies of the two armies converged on Gettysburg, with Meade placing his men on the hills as well as along a slight ridge to the south called Cemetery Ridge.

On July 2, Lee tried to flank the Union units. Longstreet's advance division did not arrive until early afternoon, thus delaying Lee's plan to launch a coordinated attack on both flanks while attacking the center of the Union line. The Confederates held a long exterior line along Seminary Ridge to the south and west of Gettysburg. It took Longstreet until late afternoon to get his men in position to make the attack on the Union's left flank. The immediate objective was an unoccupied rocky hill known as Little Round Top, from which the Confederates could flank the entire Union line on Cemetery Ridge. Noticing the Confederate movement, Brigadier General Gouverneur Warren managed to get two brigades on the hill just before the assault began. By this point, the coordination of the Confederate flanking attacks had failed, so each attack occurred in relative isolation from the other. Ewell's assaults on Culp's Hill were unsuccessful, as were the Confederate attacks on the Union center. At Little Round Top Longstreet's repeated assaults also failed. At the end of the second day's fighting, Lee was convinced that although he had not pushed Meade's men off the high ground, the flanks must be weak from the repeated assaults. He assumed that Meade would have to weaken his center line to reinforce the flanks on the hills anchoring the northern and southern ends of the battlefield.

Figure 8.2 This oval-shaped map depicts Gettysburg Battlefield during July 1, 2 and 3, 1863. Prepared by Theodore Ditterline and published by P. S. Duval & Son in Philadelphia in 1863, the map reveals the troop and artillery positions and movements, relief by hachures, drainage, roads, railroads, and houses with the names of residents at the time of the Battle of Gettysburg.

Source: Library of Congress Geography and Maps Division.

July 2 was an extraordinary and horrific day of battle at Gettysburg. Colonel Joshua Lawrence Chamberlain's 20th Maine managed to hold the extreme left end of the Union line at Little Round Top despite repeated Confederate charges and running desperately low on ammunition. Fierce fighting immortalized places on the expansive battlefield such as the Peach Orchard, the Wheat Field, and Devil's Den. Casualties were enormous on both sides. High temperatures and the stress of battle sapped the soldiers' strength. Meade did not think Lee would attack the following day.

On July 3, Lee did attack. This time, Lee launched a coordinated attack that feinted at both Union flanks, followed by a sharp strike against the Union center. Lee believed that a massive infantry assault supported by an artillery bombardment would split the Army of the Potomac in two, but his timing failed. Units took too long to get into position, and Ewell renewed his attack on Culp's Hill too early. These movements alerted Union lines to the plan of attack, allowing them to prepare for the assault on their center, and the Confederate artillery barrage proved ineffective despite its scale and ferocity. Lee sent Major General George Pickett's division along with brigades from other divisions to make the frontal assault on the Union center—across a mile of open field and up a slight rise—where Union forces waited, firmly dug in.

The engagement at Little Round Top is among the best-known moments in American military history. Chamberlain's regiment endured a long, intense bombardment by Confederate artillery in preparation for the assault. Despite the heavy fire, the regiment took little damage and stood ready to receive the 13,000 Confederates as they marched out of the woods along Seminary Ridge toward the Union line on Cemetery Ridge. Union artillery began punching large holes in the Confederate lines with canister shot. As the Confederates crossed the Emmitsburg Road just in front of the Union line, Yankee musketry unleashed a deadly barrage of fire that mowed the Confederates down by the hundreds. Only a handful of Confederates actually reached the Union line, where they were promptly killed or captured.

Pickett's men fell back to Seminary Ridge, where a horrified Lee met them, telling them that the attack had been his idea, his decision, and therefore his fault. He waited for Meade to counterattack, but Meade did not—and arguably could not. Both armies were low on supplies and ammunition, and they were simply worn out. Almost half of the Confederates who made the charge against the Union center were killed or wounded. During the three days of fighting at Gettysburg, casualties totaled 51,000 men killed, wounded, or listed as missing. The Army of the Potomac suffered more than 3,000 killed, 14,000 wounded, and 5,000 taken prisoner or missing. Lee's Army of Northern Virginia lost almost 4,300 killed, more than 18,500 wounded, with at least 5,400 missing or taken prisoner.

Lee retreated through Maryland and across the Potomac into Virginia. Much to Lincoln's irritation, Meade, his army tired and bloodied, chose not to pursue the retreating Confederates. Although Lee and his army survived, the Confederacy simply did not have the reserve to replace such huge losses. Lee had failed, catastrophically.

The Western Theater (1861–1863)

For the Union's grand strategy, the western theater of operations (encompassing the region extending from west of the Appalachians to west of the Mississippi River) was just as crucial as the eastern theater. Control of the Mississippi River had been a vital objective for the North, and extensive combat operations were directed toward that end. From a Union perspective, one of the more unique aspects of the campaigns to gain control of the Mississippi was joint operations involving both Army and Navy units.

In addition to controlling the Mississippi River, the Union had to retain control of as much of Kansas, Missouri, and Kentucky as possible. Existing posts, supplies, and telegraph communications made it doubly important to keep the Confederacy out of this region. Union troops kept an uneasy eye out for Confederate activity along the Ohio River, eastern Kansas, and Missouri. One of the earliest significant engagements occurred in August 1861 at Wilson's Creek in Missouri, resulting in a nominal Confederate victory that gave the South control of southern Missouri. Soon after, Union commander Major General John C. Frémont was relieved as head of the Department of the Missouri and replaced by Henry Halleck. Under Halleck were Brigadier General Ulysses S. Grant and Major General Samuel Curtis, commanding corps of 20,000 and 30,000, respectively. The Department of the Ohio, under the command of Brigadier General Don Carlos Buell, had only 45,000 troops. The Confederate commander was Major General Albert Sydney Johnston, who had a force of more than 40,000.

Much of 1861 and early 1862 were consumed with occupying strategic locations. Grant occupied Paducah and Smithland, Kentucky, at the confluence of the Tennessee and Cumberland rivers, while other Union forces under Buell occupied Louisville. Johnston took Bowling Green and Columbus. To protect his interior lines of communication, Johnston established Fort Henry on the Tennessee River and Fort Donelson on the Cumberland River. Because of organizational issues, Buell and Halleck had a difficult time coordinating efforts in the region, especially since practicality called for operations that would violate arbitrary borders established between the Departments of the Missouri and the Ohio. Buell tried to secure eastern Tennessee, while Halleck focused on taking the new Confederate forts on the Tennessee and Cumberland rivers.

Halleck sent Grant with 15,000 troops supported by Navy river-gunboats under Flag Officer Andrew H. Foote to take Fort Henry. Grant quickly took Fort Henry on February 6, 1862, and then set his sights on nearby Fort Donelson. Johnston reinforced Fort Donelson with 12,000 troops as Foote arrived to begin a naval bombardment of the heavily fortified Confederate position on February 14. Confederate gunners forced Foote to withdraw, but not before Grant was able to stage an assault on Fort Donelson. Inside the fort, a divided command argued about what to do next. Sensing that the fort was untenable, Brigadier General John B. Floyd and Major General Gideon J. Pillow sneaked away in the night with their forces, leaving Brigadier General Simon Bolivar Buckner to deal with Grant. Buckner surrendered unconditionally to Grant on February 15. Grant and Foote had now secured the Cumberland and Tennessee rivers, and with the fall of Nashville just days later to Buell's army, western Tennessee was under Union control.

Lincoln then unified these disparate departments into a single western command under Halleck. Halleck sent Grant and Buell down the Tennessee River to secure Corinth in northern Mississippi. The two generals and their armies planned to meet at Pittsburgh Landing in southern Tennessee near Shiloh Church. Meanwhile, Johnston tried to get his force up past Corinth to hit Grant before Buell joined him. On April 6, Johnston attacked a surprised Grant at Shiloh.

Johnston nearly pushed Grant's force back into the Tennessee River, but the Confederate commander was mortally wounded at the moment when victory seemed at hand. Grant rallied the next morning, reinforced by some of Buell's advance units. The Confederates, now under the command of P. G. T. Beauregard, fell back in disarray all the way to Corinth. Out of 63,000 Union troops engaged, more than 13,000 were casualties. The Confederates suffered 11,000 killed, wounded, and missing. Halleck did not pursue Beauregard. It was not until the end of April that Halleck occupied Corinth. Still, the Union now controlled the Mississippi River southward to Memphis, where Foote and John Pope had captured Island No. 10. With the occupation of New Orleans by Major General Benjamin Butler and Navy Captain David G. Farragut, all that remained was to link the two port cities.

Union forces thwarted Confederate counteroffensives in 1862. The Battle of Pea Ridge secured Missouri for the Union, and Union victories at Perryville and Stone's River ended Confederate attempts to invade Kentucky. A half-hearted effort to regain Corinth was also unsuccessful. Vicksburg, Mississippi, an important river port, was key to Union control of the river. Grant made four attempts from December 1862 to March 1863 to take Vicksburg, but the well-fortified bluffs and swampy approaches made assaulting the Gibraltar of the Mississippi River extremely difficult and costly.

Finally, in late March, Grant gathered his three corps, marching them past Vicksburg on the west side of the river on a swampy road they had to cut. Appropriately, they were headed toward the town of Hard Times, Louisiana, to make a crossing well below Vicksburg so that they could then approach the fortified port from the south and east. Grant used Flag Officer David Porter and his small fleet of river-gunboats and transports to get his men across to the Mississippi side of the river. Under intense Confederate fire, Porter had to pass Vicksburg twice,

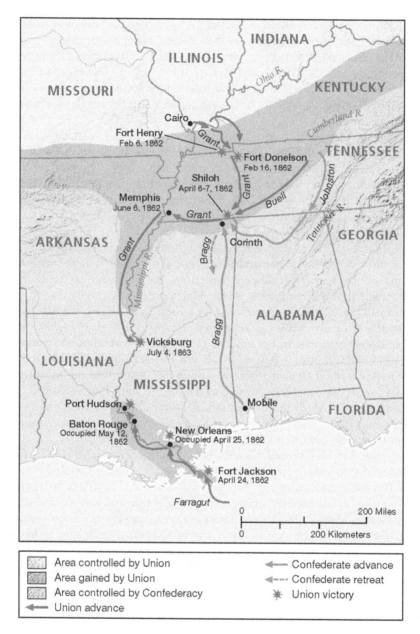

Figure 8.3 Major Battles in the West.

once going upriver from New Orleans and again going downriver to link with Grant at Hard Times.

Grant then moved on the state capital at Jackson rather than striking directly at Vicksburg against the Confederate commander there, Lieutenant General John C. Pemberton. Grant sent the corps of Major Generals William Tecumseh Sherman and James B. McPherson on to Jackson, which they took on May 14. Sherman's corps held Jackson to prevent Joseph Johnston from relieving Vicksburg from the east. McPherson and Major General John McClernand's army turned back toward Vicksburg, where Pemberton was moving to block Grant's advance. After engagements at Champion Hill and Black River Ridge, Pemberton withdrew into his defenses around Vicksburg.

Grant tried a direct assault on Vicksburg from the east on May 18, and again on May 22, but then wisely decided to besiege the city. Grant's force slowly dug its way toward the Confederate works, while Pemberton's troops and the remaining civilians began to run out of food. By July 1, after six weeks of siege, the Confederates were in dire straits. Pemberton surrendered to Grant, who took control of Vicksburg on July 4, the day after the great battle at Gettysburg ended.

The Union now controlled the Mississippi River and had repulsed Lee's invasion of Maryland and Pennsylvania. The Confederates lost a significant army at Vicksburg—it was a loss they could ill afford. Later that summer, the Army of the Cumberland under Union General William Rosecrans advanced toward Chattanooga, where Lieutenant General Braxton Bragg abandoned the town without a fight on September 9. With reinforcements from Longstreet, Bragg regrouped and tried to retake Chattanooga. On September 18, Rosecrans and Bragg clashed along Chickamauga Creek just south of Chattanooga. For two days, the armies battered each other until a gap opened in the Union lines. Exploiting the opening, the Confederates would have defeated Rosecrans in detail were it not for the gallant efforts of Major General George H. Thomas, who fought a rear-guard action that protected the remaining Union forces as they withdrew to Chattanooga. The Battle of Chickamauga resulted in more than 16,000 Union casualties and at least 18,000 Confederate dead, wounded, and missing.

Bragg positioned his victorious Confederates on a line running from Lookout Mountain to Missionary Ridge, hoping that Rosecrans would withdraw entirely from Chattanooga. Meanwhile, Lincoln placed Grant in command of the new Division of the Cumberland. Grant immediately relieved Rosecrans, replacing him with Thomas, and went to Chattanooga to take personal control of the situation. As Grant arrived, Longstreet left with his two divisions to attack Knoxville. Beginning November 23, Grant attacked Bragg on Lookout Mountain and Missionary Ridge. On November 25, a charge led by Major General Philip

H. Sheridan broke the Confederate line to force Bragg to withdraw from the field to retreat into Georgia.

The Naval War

The U.S. Navy grew to record levels during the Civil War and played an essential role in blockading Southern ports and conducting river operations in conjunction with Union armies. The fledgling Confederate Navy had little success in the war. Always undermanned and with few ships, Confederate naval policy relied upon commerce raiding and blockade running.

Lincoln's Secretary of the Navy Gideon Wells rapidly built up Union naval capacities with Congress's record appropriations. With only 42 ships operating in 1860, by 1864 the Navy had more than 650 vessels, including more than 70 ironclads. Wells included numerous steam-powered ships in his building program. The Confederate Navy, on the other hand, never matched its Northern counterpart, forcing the South to pursue primarily *guerre de course*.

As the U.S. Navy attempted to make the announced blockade of the Confederacy real, the Confederacy turned to commerce raiders and blockade-runners as a means to keep supplies coming in by sea. At ports like Wilmington, Mobile, and Charleston, the South hoped to maintain a lifeline to Europe. At first, Southern blockade-runners were effective, using fast ships that could easily outrun the Union blockade squadrons. By 1864, however, the blockade had a more significant effect, severely distressing the Southern economy and war production capacity.

With so many Union naval vessels on blockade duty, fewer were available to protect Northern merchant ships on the high seas. The Confederate raider *Alabama* had great success, capturing more than 60 merchant ships before being sunk in 1864 by USS *Kearsarge* off Cherbourg in the English Channel. The commerce raider *Shenandoah* focused its efforts on the lucrative Yankee whaling fleet and was never captured. While Confederate commerce raiding had little negative effect upon Northern trade, the fear of raiders increased insurance rates to record high levels.

In addition to blockade duties and river operations such as that at Fort Donelson and Vicksburg, the U.S. Navy played a significant role in securing Confederate ports for Union use. The Navy either captured or helped capture every major Southern port except for Galveston, which remained under Confederate control until the war's end. Union naval officers such as Rear Admiral Samuel F. DuPont and Captain David Porter (given the honorary rank of Commodore) helped establish the United States Navy's reputation as a versatile and effective fighting force.

The most famous Civil War naval engagement took place on March 9, 1862, as the ironclad gunboats USS *Monitor* and the Confederate *Virginia* battled off Hampton Roads, Virginia. The *Virginia* had been rebuilt from the hull of the burned-out steamship USS *Merrimack*, while the *Monitor* had been designed and built from the keel up at Long Island. Both were literally iron clad, with the *Virginia* boasting ten guns to the *Monitor's* turreted two. The two odd-looking vessels battered each other for hours. Each vessel's shots simply glanced off the other's armored sheeting, and neither did much harm to the other. The battle between the *Monitor* and the *Virginia* ended in a tactical draw, but the *Virginia* no longer had free rein in the Chesapeake Bay. In May 1862, the *Virginia* was scuttled to prevent its capture when Union forces occupied Norfolk. The *Monitor* also met an inglorious end, foundering while under tow off Cape Hatteras in December of the same year.

Grant Takes Command

As 1864 began, Lincoln believed that victory was in sight. He lacked, however, a commander who he thought could deliver victory. Lincoln had noticed Grant's successes in the West, and in March 1864 gave him command of all Union armies. As General-in-Chief, Grant had two objectives—divide the Confederacy further by driving south and east from Chattanooga, taking Atlanta, which was probably the most important city in the South, and destroy Lee's Army of Northern Virginia. Progress toward winning the war was critical for Lincoln, who faced political criticism of his approach to the war and possible defeat in the 1864 presidential election.

Under Grant's command, the Union delivered war to Southern civilians. Grant ordered Sherman to drive toward Atlanta, the center of Confederate rail transport and industrial hub. With 100,000 troops, Sherman began his march to Atlanta in early May. Joseph Johnston's more than 50,000 Confederates stood between Sherman and the Georgia city. Union and Confederate forces clashed at several places, including New Hope Church and Kennesaw Mountain, with Johnston withdrawing steadily toward Atlanta. Finally, President Jefferson Davis could no longer tolerate Johnston's withdrawal, relieving him in favor of Lieutenant General John Bell Hood of Texas in July. The Battle of Atlanta began July 22, ending only when Hood was forced to abandon the city on September 1.

From Atlanta, Sherman began his 'March to the Sea,' taking Savannah on December 21, destroying in his army's path anything integral to the South's economy and will to fight. Living off the land, Sherman's force foraged with impunity, leaving little food or livestock for the inhabitants. The Confederacy had been split again. Hood's army tried taking Nashville but failed, retreating to the relative safety of Mississippi. From this point forward, Confederate action in the Western Theater was severely limited. Now, Sherman could move northward through the Carolinas and into Virginia, where Grant planned a war-

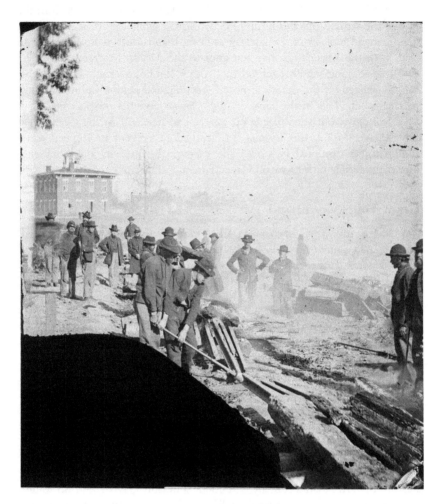

Figure 8.4 Sherman's troops destroy rail tracks in Atlanta, Georgia, November 1864.
Photograph by George N. Bernard.

Source: Library of Congress.

ending campaign to trap Lee between Sherman's army and the Army of the Potomac.

In May 1864, Grant ordered Meade, nominally in command of the Army of the Potomac since Grant traveled with it, to begin the move on Richmond. With 120,000 troops to Lee's 63,000 (probably far fewer, considering desertion and sickness), Meade struck Lee's army in the wilderness. From May 5 through May 7, the two armies battled in the dense growth where they had fought the year before. Casualties were again horrific—17,500 for the Army of the Potomac and 7,500 for the Army of Northern Virginia. Unlike previous Army of the Potomac commanders who either withdrew in defeat or refused to give chase, Grant forced Meade and the Army of the Potomac to press on in what became a relentless, almost year-long pursuit of Lee and his Army of Northern Virginia.

From May 9 through May 19, Grant repeatedly hit Lee at Spotsylvania, where the Army of Northern Virginia had dug in to prevent Grant from directly assaulting Richmond. Wanting to force Lee off the defensive, Grant began maneuvering to the Confederate left toward Richmond on May 20, compelling Lee to counter him at every move. At Cold Harbor on June 3, an impatient Grant tried to punch through Lee's defenses. It was a bloodbath, with several thousand Union troops falling in a matter of minutes. Grant's push on Lee's army had cost him 55,000 casualties in less than a month; Lee had suffered 32,000. By June 18, Grant accepted that he would have to begin a siege to starve Lee's army into submission. Petersburg became the central point of siege operations until the spring of 1865. Under Grant, the Union was bleeding the Confederacy white.

A brief Confederate foray into Maryland that threatened Washington convinced Grant that unity of command was paramount if the Union were to win. Accordingly, he abolished the various departments in the Eastern Theater and created a single command. In February 1865, Davis appointed Lee commander of all Confederate armies, although by that point the Army of Northern Virginia was really the only remaining force of consequence. Meanwhile, Sherman made his way toward Richmond, cutting a path of devastation as he took Columbia, South Carolina, and Wilmington, North Carolina. In March, Grant decided to end the siege and force Lee out of his defenses around Richmond. Capturing Richmond undoubtedly would have been a grand prize, but no matter who controlled the city, the Army of Northern Virginia had to be annihilated on the battlefield to smother all Confederate hope.

Grant began his final assault on Lee's lines on April 2. The Confederates collapsed, forcing President Davis to flee Richmond. Lee abandoned both Petersburg and Richmond and tried to get to Lynchburg's railroad to link with Joseph Johnston's remaining forces. With Lee now in the open, Grant gave chase and by April 6 had enveloped the Army of Northern Virginia near Appomattox Court House. Lee's troops were ragged, exhausted, and hungry, and many were shoeless. The Confederate commander decided that further resistance was futile. Meeting on April 9 at the McLean House, Grant and Lee agreed to terms that were generous toward the Confederates. President Lincoln had planned for a fraternal reunification of North and South, and Grant understood that the terms of surrender were the first steps toward that goal. The men of the Army of Northern Virginia were paroled and allowed to keep their horses.

Johnston surrendered to Sheridan on April 26, and the last Confederate holdouts capitulated by late June.

Preserving the Union and ending slavery had cost the Union more than 350,000 dead, including more than 130,000 killed in battle. More than 280,000 Union troops had been wounded. The Confederacy lost more than 160,000 dead from fighting and disease with at least 250,000 wounded. Because of still-unsophisticated surgery, many of the wounded endured amputations, and because of poor sanitation large numbers of

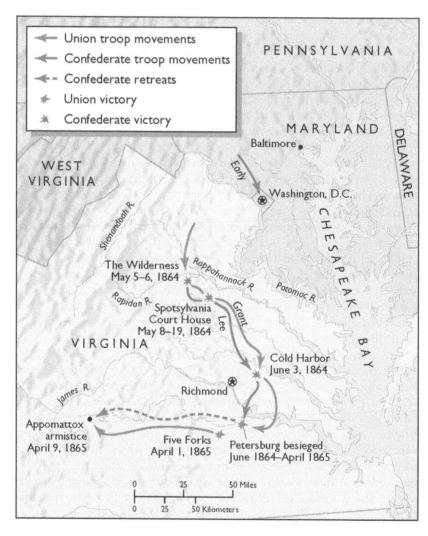

Figure 8.5 The Virginia Theater 1864–1865.

amputees died. As many as 50,000 Confederate and Union prisoners of war died in squalid prison camps, the most infamous of which was at Andersonville, Georgia. Battles of varying size and importance had been fought from as far north as Maine to as far west as New Mexico. The Civil War truly engulfed the American nation.

Reconstruction—A New Job for the Army

Jubilation at the war's end was brief. President Lincoln was assassinated just days after Lee surrendered at Appomattox, plunging the Northern states, at least, into deep mourning. The former Confederate states required military occupation to enforce reconstruction policies. This duty placed the Army in yet another nontraditional role as nation builders.

Typically, demobilization was quick. By 1866, most volunteers had been mustered out, leaving the Army with only 57,000 troops. By 1876, it had an authorized strength of only 27,000. The Navy likewise demobilized, going from more than 700 ships and 60,000 officers and sailors to just 48 ships and 8,000 officers and sailors by the end of the 1870s. With this downsized force, the American military had to patrol the Mexican border, garrison frontier posts, defend the American coast, and carry out Reconstruction duties in the former Confederate states.

Lincoln had wanted a quick restoration, establishing civilian governments in the rebel states as soon as practicable. With Lincoln's assassination, however, the Radical Republicans in Congress dismissed this policy. President Andrew Johnson attempted to put in place an even more lenient policy than what Lincoln had proposed but quickly ran afoul of Congress. Both Lincoln and Johnson believed that reconstruction in the South was a presidential rather than congressional prerogative. The Army, more specifically Grant, disagreed with the leniency of Johnson's proposals and thus courted Congress to make Reconstruction more demanding on the Southern states. Johnson was a weak president, and as such he gave the Radical Republicans in Congress the opportunity to take control of Reconstruction.

Before the war ended, Congress established the Bureau of Refugees, Freedmen, and Abandoned Lands, more commonly known as the Freedmen's Bureau, to handle the vast numbers of newly freed slaves, perhaps as many as four million, who had little to no means of subsistence. The War Department administered the Freedmen's Bureau until its termination in 1871. Under the leadership of General Oliver O. Howard, the Freedmen's Bureau provided food, medical assistance, and, most notably, education for freed slaves across the South. Resistance to the Freedmen's Bureau among many white Southerners grew fierce after the end of the war and contributed to the resurgence of Black Codes and the many Jim Crow laws adopted by several states following Reconstruction.

The Radical Republicans passed several measures to enforce a long process in the former rebel states. The Command of the Army Act of 1867 established a chain of command from the president as commander-in-chief, to the general-in-chief of the Army, and then to field commands. The general-in-chief could be removed only with the approval of the Senate. The Tenure of Office Act, also passed in 1867, declared that the Senate had to approve the removal of cabinet officers. Both of these acts were directed at President Johnson, who wanted to fire several of Lincoln's appointees and take power away from Grant and Secretary of War Edwin M. Stanton. As it was, Grant and Stanton, rather than President Johnson, virtually controlled the Army through Congress. This was an exciting twist in the evolution of civil–military relations in the United States.

The Reconstruction Acts passed by the Radical Republicans created five military districts to govern the now-defunct Confederacy. A major general commanded each district; thus this period of Reconstruction became known as the 'Rule of the Major Generals.' These commanders administered martial law that superseded all civilian law in each of the Southern states. Congress also authorized each of the military governments to register all recently freed male slaves to vote. Acting outside his authority, Grant, as general-in-chief, ordered each of the five major generals to accept orders only from Congress. President Johnson angrily resisted such usurpation of executive power, thus openly ignoring both the Command of the Army Act and the Tenure of Office Act. Johnson's response led to his impeachment in the House of Representatives and a trial in the Senate that ended only one vote short of convicting Johnson. If convicted, Johnson would have been removed from office.

Reconstruction under military rule in the South seemed harsh. Lawlessness and resistance to military rule and the Freedmen's Bureau, in particular, inspired violent reactions from white Southerners. Clandestine terrorist organizations, such as the Ku Klux Klan and the Knights of the White Camellia, terrorized free African Americans as well as the whites who tried to help them, especially those working with the Freedmen's Bureau. With only about 17,000 troops to occupy the South and administer Reconstruction policies, the Army was ill-equipped to carry out these nation-building duties. State militias composed in part of freed slaves were restored across the South as part of Reconstruction to help establish law and order, but because the new militias were tied to the Radical Republicans, many Southerners violently resisted the efforts of state militias to reestablish federal control in the former Confederacy.

Reconstruction ended with a political bargain as a result of the election of 1876. Grant was elected president in 1868, serving two controversial terms that allowed Radical Republicans a free hand in Reconstruction. By 1876, however, both North and South had grown weary of Reconstruction and simply wanted the whole thing to end. In a contested election,

Rutherford B. Hayes, a Civil War veteran, promised to end Reconstruction as soon as he took office. The promise worked, and Congress gave the election to Hayes. In 1877, occupation troops withdrew from the South and were reassigned to other posts, many on the western frontier where conflict with Native American tribes in the region had already begun. Without strong federal authority in the South, old habits returned, as African Americans were subjected to Jim Crow laws and other state policies that made them second-class citizens. Reconstruction had been a failure, and although it was not solely at fault, the Army received a great deal of the public blame.

Women and African Americans

Women played more substantial roles in the Civil War than they had in past American wars, including serving in military hospitals as nurses and organizing clubs and other organizations to provide troops with clothing, fresh food, and books. Some women even passed themselves off as men and served in armies on both sides. Masquerading as men was often easier than students of the twenty-first century might imagine. Many women were accustomed to hard labor and long hours so that enduring a soldier's life was not unusually trying. Evading discovery also proved relatively easy because many of the women were fighting alongside fathers, brothers or husbands who helped shield their identity.

Moreover, there was little expectation that there were women in the ranks. You don't see what you aren't looking for. Women fought in every major battle of the war, fulfilling the same duties and meeting the same expectations as their fellow soldiers. There were at least 250 women who served in the uniformed ranks, with at least six who did so while pregnant. On the occasions they were discovered, their officers opted not to court-martial them, either sending them home or employing them in tasks more in keeping with the nineteenth-century understanding of women's work. Called 'daughters of the regiment,' such women cooked, washed, and mended.

Women were also highly successful as spies. Typically, no one expected women to spy, so again, they did not see what they did not expect. Rightly anticipating that gentlemen would be reluctant to search a woman's clothing, female spies often hid messages among their crinolines or corsets. When discovered, women spies were imprisoned or paroled home. Harriet Tubman, famous for her work with the Underground Railroad leading slaves to freedom, also ran a network of slaves who spied for the Union. The Confederacy's most renowned woman spy was Belle Boyd, who, while working in her father's Virginia hotel, gathered valuable information for Stonewall Jackson.

Far less romantic, but far more critical to individual soldiers, were the thousands of women who served as nurses. More than 20,000 women either volunteered or worked as nurses. Despite their vital tasks, their

Figure 8.6 Dr. Mary Edwards Walker was the first woman awarded the Medal of Honor, for her work as a surgeon during the Civil War.

Source: Library of Congress.

work and the women were often looked down upon, and early in the war most surgeons did not trust that women could emotionally or physically withstand the suffering of wounded soldiers or the endless blood and vomit-filled hours of care the wounded required. Because the Sanitary Commission and Army Medical Department could not meet the demand created on the battlefield, women like Dr. Elizabeth Blackwell and Clara Barton gathered and delivered needed bandages and medicines to Army hospitals. Blackwell also trained nurses for war service and Clara Barton served in Army hospitals. Dr. Mary Edwards Walker served as the only female surgeon, eventually spending months in a Confederate prison on charges of spying for the Union. After her release, she was awarded the Medal of Honor.

Calling out particular women does not detract from all of the women during the Civil War who remained at home. They were the women who helped keep the economy running, retained customs and traditions, knitted and sewed needed clothing for men in uniform, and wrote letters to their soldiers. As the war dragged on, they also endured the privations of wartime economies and became weary with worry about the living and grief over the dead.

The gentlemen's agreement at Appomattox did not end women's association with the military. After the war, Union war widows received a 'widow's pension.' In the South, women petitioned for reimbursement for real property lost during Sherman's March to the Sea. Many Southern women were also daily reminding the Confederacy that it was beaten because of the presence of occupation soldiers. For women in the northern United States and in the southern United States, war and the military rarely left their thoughts as they worked to memorialize the men who had fought and died during the war.

From the beginning of the war, prominent abolitionists urged Lincoln to allow free African Americans to serve in the Union Army and to enlist slaves who had escaped into Union lines (known as contraband) as soldiers. The most Lincoln accepted was the use of contrabands as laborers in the Army. He also allowed the Navy to continue to enlist African American sailors—a practice the Navy had long used because of the shortage of white volunteers for the privations of life on a ship. At sea, African American and white sailors shared quarters and the same mess. Approximately 20 percent of the Union Navy was made up of African American sailors, who shared quarters and the same mess with white shipmates.

Despite the president's prohibition of enlisting African American men in the Army, there were large areas where local Union commanders decided to recruit escaped or abandoned slaves. Notably, in Missouri, Free Soil leaders raised approximately 500 African American soldiers, who were hastily trained before engaging a Confederate force of roughly equal size at Butler, Missouri. When Southern reinforcements arrived the Union soldiers were driven off.

African Americans, both free and slave, were eager to fight with the Union Army but were forbidden to enlist until the Emancipation

Figure 8.7 William Harvey Carney, 54th Massachusetts Infantry, ca. 1864, photograph by John Ritchie.

Source: National Museum of African American History and Culture.

Proclamation. With the proclamation, recruitment of African American soldiers began with energy. Secretary of War Edwin Stanton directed the establishment of a Bureau of Colored Troops to organize enlistment of former slaves under the Army's Adjutant General. Massachusetts raised two African American regiments, the most famous of which is the 54th Massachusetts, commanded by Colonel Robert Gould Shaw, a prominent white abolitionist. The regiment's defining moment was their attack at Fort Wagner. Although the attack failed, with half the regiment including their admired commander falling dead, the fighting there showed that African

American soldiers were good, determined fighters. A memorial to Shaw and the 54th stands on Boston Common, and the movie *Glory* (1989) is a popular telling of the 54th's action at Fort Wagner. Tens of thousands of other African American soldiers fought well and bravely. Twenty-five African American soldiers and sailors were awarded the Medal of Honor, 14 of them for actions at the Battle of Laurel Hill, Virginia, in 1864.

As the Confederacy drained its limited pool of potential soldiers, many Southerners began urging that slaves be manumitted in exchange for service in the Confederate Army. Although the Southern economy depended upon the labor of slaves, some influential Confederates thought that preserving the Confederacy was worth abolishing slavery. Eventually, even Robert E. Lee accepted the idea that any hope of winning rested with the abolition of slavery and enlistment of African American soldiers. Before African Americans were taken into the Confederate Army, however, the Union defeated the Southern forces. There were never African American Confederates.

More than 186,000 African Americans served in the Union Army during the war, plus another 19,000 in the Navy. As many as 40,000 died, including approximately 30,000 from disease, in the conflict that ultimately ended slavery in the United States.

Conclusion

Many historians consider the Civil War the first modern war, foretelling the horrific industrialized conflicts of the late nineteenth and twentieth centuries. The effect of new technology and the harnessing of industrial production in the North certainly support this view. The tactics and strategies, however, harkened backward instead of into the future as both Union and Confederate military and political leaders drew upon the Napoleonic Wars and other conflicts of the early nineteenth century as their guide to conducting operations in the Civil War. The Civil War was a significant turning point in the political and social history of the United States. It was also a turning point in American military history, for mass mobilization, civil–military relations, professionalization, and centralized planning and control all evolved dramatically as a result of this fratricidal war. Perhaps most critical for future warfare, the Civil War formally introduced the United States to the concepts of total war and nation-building; practices that became part of the strategic toolbox of the evolving American way of war.

Further Reading

Blanton, DeAnne, and Lauren M. Cook. *They Fought Like Demons: Women Soldiers in the American Civil War.* Baton Rouge, LA: Louisiana State University Press, 2002.
Dobak, William A. *Freedom by the Sword: The US Colored Troops, 1862–1867.* Alexandria, VA: St. John's Press, 2016.

Fowler, William M. *Under Two Flags: The American Navy in the Civil War.* New York: Norton, 1990.

Giesberg, Judith. *Army at Home: Women and the Civil War on the Northern Homefront.* Chapel Hill, NC: University of North Carolina Press, 2009.

Glatthaar, Joseph. *Forged in Battle: The Civil War Alliance of Black Soldiers and White Officers.* Baton Rouge, LA: Louisiana State University Press, 2000.

Glatthaar, Joseph. *General Lee's Army: From Victory to Collapse.* New York: Free Press, 2009.

Hagerman, Edward. *The American Civil War and the Origins of Modern Warfare.* Bloomington, IN: Indiana University Press, 1988.

Luraghi, Raimondo. *The Southern Navy: The Confederate Navy and the American Civil War.* Annapolis, MD: Naval Institute Press, 1995.

McPherson, James. *Battle Cry of Freedom: The Civil War Era.* New York: Oxford University Press, 1982.

Reardon, Carol. *Pickett's Charge in History and Memory.* Chapel Hill, NC: University of North Carolina Press, 1997.

Reid, Brian Holden. *America's Civil War: The Operational Battlefield, 1861–1863.* Amherst, NY: Prometheus Books, 2008.

Schultz, Jane E. *Women at the Front: Hospital Workers in Civil War America.* Chapel Hill, NC: University of North Carolina Press, 2004.

Sears, Stephen W. *Landscape Turned Red: The Battle of Antietam.* Boston, MA: Houghton Mifflin, 1993.

Sears, Stephen W. *Gettysburg.* Boston, MA: Houghton Mifflin, 2003.

Stoker, Donald. *The Grand Design: Strategy and the U.S. Civil War.* New York: Oxford University Press, 2010.

Trudeau, Noah Andre. *Southern Storm: Sherman's March to the Sea.* New York: Harper Perennial, 2009.

Woodworth, Steven E. *Jefferson Davis and His Generals: The Failure of Confederate Command in the West.* Lawrence, KS: University Press of Kansas, 1990.

Woodworth, Steven E. *The Art of Command in the Civil War.* Lincoln, NE: University of Nebraska Press, 1998.

9   Becoming a Modern Military

Introduction

In 1877, Henry O. Flipper, of Thomasville, Georgia, became the first African American to receive a commission from the U.S. Military Academy at West Point. The Army assigned Flipper to the 10th Cavalry, one of two all-African American but mostly white-officered cavalry regiments—the mounted counterparts to the two all-African American infantry regiments in service since 1869. Flipper joined an Army that was entering one of the most unusual periods in its history. Between the Civil War and the Great War, the Army returned to frontier duties, including long, brutal wars against Native Americans; put down domestic disorders; and fought the Spanish in a brief conflict that exposed serious problems within the Army that limited its ability to conduct operations outside the United States. Despite these challenges, the Army continued to professionalize.

Similarly, the Navy found the post-Civil War years challenging. While struggling to incorporate modern technology into its fleet, Navy intellectuals sought a doctrine to guide planning for the defense of the United States and its newly acquired American possessions overseas. In 1890, Captain Alfred Thayer Mahan provided that guidance when he published *The Influence of Sea Power Upon History*. Mahan's work helped transform naval thought not only in the United States but throughout the Western world and Japan. Congressional support for the Navy further assisted the service's advancement. As a result of the Navy's pivotal role in the Spanish–American War in 1898, Congress supported building a modern battleship fleet rivaling that of the Royal Navy.

Developments during the period between the Civil War and the Great War of 1914–1918 primarily determined the character of the twentieth-century American military. The old and new often clashed in a period during which the military attended to familiar problems while trying to adjust to increased responsibilities, new technologies, and the United States' growing involvement in world affairs.

The Indian Wars

From the end of the Civil War to 1890, the U.S. Army undertook a long, arduous, and harsh war against Indians. After Reconstruction ended in 1877, Congress reduced the authorized strength of the Army from more than 57,000 to only 27,000 men. With this small force, the Army was responsible for fortifying not only frontier posts but also coastal fortifications. West of the Mississippi River, wagon trails and new railroad routes were flooded with waves of migrants hoping to farm, mine, or otherwise cash in on the explosion of western development following the Civil War. New settlers increasingly encroached upon land already occupied by Indians.

Native American tribes on the Plains and in other areas resented the intrusion of settlers onto lands the tribes understood as theirs in perpetuity by treaty with the U.S. government. Because of the pressure brought to bear on indigenous peoples by westward migration, tribes faced difficult and calamitous choices. They could either assimilate into white society or resist encroachment upon their lands. Either option held the threat of extinction. While some Indians looked for peaceful ways to deal with the competition for land, others chose to fight. As settlers and Indians clashed, the Army once again found itself in the role of a frontier constabulary tasked with maintaining an uneasy peace. While the frontier Army spent a great deal of time and energy fighting what it deemed hostile indigenous peoples, it also had its hands full protecting peaceful tribes from harassment and encroachment by settlers.

The federal government's attempts to prevent conflict between Native Americans and settlers typically favored the settlers. The Indian Bureau, part of the Department of the Interior, tried to force assimilation of Indian tribes. For example, the bureau encouraged railroads and hunters to destroy the massive buffalo herds that were central to the Plains tribes' economy and then tried to turn the Plains Indians into farmers. Farming was an occupation more compatible with new settlement. Also, the War Department used force to keep indigenous peoples on reservations by policing tribal lands and returning renegade bands to the reservations. Combined with frequent military campaigns against the tribes, these efforts ended Native American resistance by 1890.

Returning to the rudimentary and neglected pre-Civil War frontier post-and-road network, the Army reorganized its administrative structure in the West into two divisions: the Division of the Missouri, and the Division of the Pacific. A separate Department of the Gulf administered military affairs in Texas. Without an extensive rail network like that in the East, logistics and communication rivaled the indigenous population as the Army's principal problem. The extremes in climate from season to season and the rough and varied terrain in the West also made campaigning over great distances extremely difficult.

The Army invested a good portion of its small budget into new posts along major wagon trails and the new railroads, as well as into housing for the military detachments on reservations. Most frontier posts were not the large stockades often seen in Hollywood westerns, but tent encampments with only a few permanent structures. Most frontier posts were occupied for only a few years before the units moved to new posts closer to whichever tribe was most troublesome. With limited manpower and other resources, this was the best the Army could do.

Most officers, such as Lieutenant Colonel George Armstrong Custer, and soldiers who served in the Indian Wars had little frontier experience because they entered the Army during the Civil War. A few, like General George Crook, had pre-Civil War frontier experience. Thus, the frontier force had to alter its understanding of campaigning and combat developed on Civil War battlefields to fit the altogether different conditions of the Indian Wars.

Despite these difficulties, the frontier Army carried out extensive military campaigns against the Comanche, Kiowa, Arapaho, Cheyenne, Apache, and the Sioux tribes, among others. Facing a cunning and resourceful—and often well-armed—indigenous enemy, the Army found that as in the colonial era wars, winter campaigns that destroyed encampments and wiped out Native American supply stores were particularly useful in subduing recalcitrant Indians. The Army also used Native Americans in the fight against Native Americans. Friendly Indians, however, were mainly employed as scouts rather than as fighters. When chasing renegade bands, the Army tried to converge multiple units and maneuver the Indians into a corner to force a decisive action.

Clashes began between white settlers and Native Americans before the Civil War ended. Migrant trails through Wyoming and Montana brought thousands of settlers and gold miners into contact with the Sioux, Cheyenne, and Arapaho tribes. Responding to Indian raids against mining camps and settlers along the Oregon and Bozeman trails, the Army ordered the Powder River campaign in 1865. When the campaign ended in disaster for the Army, the federal government began treaty negotiations at Fort Laramie with the tribes in the Powder River region. Some indigenous leaders agreed to terms, but others refused. Chief Red Cloud, a Sioux, was notable among those who rebuffed government terms.

While at Fort Laramie, the Native American representatives learned that the Army was sending an infantry column under Colonel Henry B. Carrington to establish forts along the Bozeman Trail. Angry, Red Cloud and his followers left Fort Laramie in 1866 without signing a treaty with the U.S. government. Red Cloud's band retaliated against government actions by harassing the outposts that Carrington established, particularly Fort Phil Kearny.

In December 1866, one of Red Cloud's most talented warriors, Crazy Horse, led a band of Sioux in attacking a small wood-gathering party outside the fort in the hope of drawing a large column of troopers into an ambush. Eighty men under Captain William J. Fetterman were organized to relieve the beleaguered soldiers. Just a few miles outside—and out of sight—of the post, the Indians fell upon Fetterman and his men, completely wiping them out. Acting as decoys, warriors led by Crazy Horse lured Fetterman and his men into a trap. Fetterman ordered his column to give chase as the decoys disappeared behind a ridge. As the troopers crested the ridge, they encountered hundreds of Indian warriors. The battle was over in a matter of minutes.

The Fetterman Massacre gave the Army an excuse to launch a punitive campaign against the Sioux and their Cheyenne allies, but as it developed, only minor engagements took place. Without the manpower or the political will to mount an effective offensive campaign against the Sioux and Cheyenne in Montana, the United States chose to abandon Fort Kearny and the other outposts in 1868.

Meanwhile, in the Southern Plains, commander of the Division of the Missouri Lieutenant General William Tecumseh Sherman complained that he would need an army of more than 100,000 to satisfy the demands for protection of every settlement, ranch, and farm along thousands of miles of frontier and desolate trails. Instead, he had to thinly spread his force in small units across a vast territory. Comanches, Kiowa, Cheyenne, and Arapaho raided settlements, ranches, and farms, and ambushed travelers along the trails. Mindful of white encroachment on their treaty lands and the memory of such tragedies as the Sand Creek Massacre in 1864, these bands had little interest in living on reservations.

Major General Philip H. Sheridan, one of Sherman's subordinates, ordered a bold campaign of three converging columns to attack Indian winter camps in the Red River region near the Texas Panhandle. On November 19, 1868, one of these three columns, the 7th Cavalry under the command of George Armstrong Custer, surprised Chief Black Kettle's Cheyenne encampment on the Washita River. Custer himself was surprised, however, when he discovered that several bands of Cheyenne, Kiowa, Comanche, and other tribes also had winter camps along the river. During a hard day's fighting, Custer burned the village, slaughtered hundreds of Indian ponies, and killed Black Kettle and his wife. The 7th Cavalry then withdrew under cover of darkness. Sheridan's campaign began a six-year-long struggle to bring the Plains tribes under control.

Although living on reservations in Indian Territory, the Kiowas, for example, raided into northern Texas in 1871. By 1874, with Sherman now General of the Army and Sheridan in command of the Division of the Missouri, a fully-fledged war broke out between the Army and the loosely organized Comanche, Kiowa, Arapaho, and Cheyenne tribes along the Red River. In the ensuing Red River War, Sheridan again ordered a multicolumn attack on the Indians' winter campgrounds along the Red River. Under the command of Colonel Nelson A. Miles, five columns converged on the area, trapping the remaining Indians in Palo Duro Canyon. As a result, the Army forced the Indians back to their reservations.

In the Northwest, the Army fought Indians across a wide range of territory, from Utah to Idaho, in Oregon, and as far south as California. The Modoc War of 1872–1873 began when the Modocs left their reservation in Oregon to return to their homeland near the Lost River in California. Four significant battles involving hundreds of troops and Modocs gave neither side a definite advantage. Peace negotiations also were fruitless until the federal government's primary negotiators, General Edward Canby and Reverend Eleazer Thomas, were murdered while meeting with Modoc leaders. Fearing extreme reprisals, the Modocs gave up the fight and returned to the reservation. Four Modoc leaders were tried and executed for the murders.

In the Southwest, the Army faced what may have been its most challenging enemy in the most expansive and difficult of theaters. Across Arizona, New Mexico, western Texas, and even into Mexican territory, the Army spent more than 20 years trying to bring the fierce Apache under government control. Cochise, chief of the Chiricahua Apache, kept General Crook and the Army occupied in Arizona; but through relentless campaigning, using mule pack trains instead of wagons, establishing the equivalent of modern small rapid reaction forces, and making administrative improvements on reservation lands, Crook brought relative peace to Arizona by the time he was reassigned in 1875.

Crook's departure, however, ended the uneasy peace. Corruption among the agents representing the Bureau of Indian Affairs was prevalent; Indian agents in Arizona took advantage of Crook's absence to line their pockets by selling the region's best land and prime beef to speculators, leaving the worst of both for the Indians. The convoluted authority made the situation worse. By leaving administrative jurisdiction with the Bureau of Indian Affairs in the Department of the Interior, and law enforcement authority with the War Department, the federal government had created a dual power over Indian affairs that simply did not work.

By the early 1880s, the Apaches began leaving the reservations in Arizona. The War Department sent Crook to repair the damage done by corrupt administrators and return the renegade bands that had fled the reservations. Crook worked long and hard on both assignments until the Apache leader Geronimo was the only holdout. Crook tracked Geronimo and his band into the Sierra Madre Mountains of northern Mexico and arranged their surrender, but the federal government reneged on the terms, leaving Crook embarrassed and appearing as untrustworthy to the remaining Apache holdouts. In protest, Crook asked to be relieved.

Nelson Miles replaced Crook and vowed to capture Geronimo, sending a small force under Captain Henry W. Lawton after the Apache leader. Throughout the summer of 1886, Lawton's force chased the Apache band deep into Mexico, traveling more than 2,000 miles. Lawton lost more

Figure 9.1 Conflicts in the West.

than two-thirds of his command to desertion or being unfit for duty because of sickness and exhaustion. The chase also took its toll on Geronimo's band, and in August he stopped running. Agreeing to terms that included his incarceration in federal prison at Fort Pickens in Florida, Geronimo formally surrendered to General Miles in a ceremony complete with a regimental band. Geronimo rode in President Theodore Roosevelt's 1905 inaugural parade, and in 1909, at the age of 80, he died at Fort Sill, Oklahoma.

By far the most well-known of the Indian Wars was the great Sioux War of 1876. The conflict began with disputes over the Northern Pacific Railroad's right of way through Sioux lands in 1873 and the discovery of gold by Custer's expedition into the sacred Black Hills in 1874. Despite the Army's best effort, it could not prevent prospectors from pouring into the Black Hills region. Encroachment by new settlers once again made previous treaties meaningless and attempts to negotiate a new settlement with the Sioux failed. Following the example of the Sioux leader Sitting

Bull, the Sioux and Cheyenne left their reservations. The federal government issued an ultimatum demanding that they return by January 1, 1876. It is doubtful that many of the bands ever heard of the warning because they were in winter encampments scattered across Dakota Territory, Wyoming, and Montana. In any event, few returned to the reservation.

General Sheridan ordered three columns—one under Brigadier General Alfred Terry from Fort Lincoln in Dakota Territory, one from Fort Ellis in Montana under the command of Colonel John Gibbon, and the last from Fort Fetterman in Wyoming under General Crook—to converge on the largest concentration of Sioux and Cheyenne in the Powder River area. Crook's force of 1,000 men and 300 Indian scouts clashed with 1,500 Sioux and Cheyenne warriors at the Battle of Rosebud Creek in June 1876. After an intense, six-hour-long engagement, Crook finally ordered a retreat to a supply base.

Unaware of Crook's retreat, Terry and Gibbon met at the confluence of the Yellowstone and Powder Rivers. Scouts found evidence that pointed to a large Indian encampment somewhere along what the Indians called the Greasy Grass and what the Army referred to as the Little Bighorn River. Aboard the steamer *Far West* on the Powder River, Terry, Gibbon, and other officers, including Custer, planned to find and attack the encampment. Terry and Gibbon were supposed to march up the Yellowstone and Little Bighorn to prevent the Indians from escaping to the north. Custer and the 7th Cavalry would approach from the south to complete a pincer-like movement to trap the Sioux and Cheyenne. The column that made contact first was to engage and drive the Indians into the other column.

At least 7,000 Sioux and Cheyenne, probably nearer 12,000 and including at least 3,000 warriors, were camped on the banks of the Little Bighorn. On June 15, 1876, Custer's 7th Cavalry located what it assumed was an isolated, small village of Sioux. Custer did not realize, nor did he bother to ascertain, that this was the first camp of a longer string of camps along the river. Believing that he had the advantage of surprise and fearing that if his force was discovered the Sioux would break into numerous small parties and flee, Custer decided to press the attack.

Custer ordered Captain Frederick W. Benteen and three companies to scout a few miles to the west of the 7th Cavalry's main column. A couple of hours later, Custer ordered Major Marcus A. Reno and three more companies to cross the Little Bighorn and charge the south end of the village. Custer then moved five companies along a ridge, where they took cover in several ravines and gullies that formed folds in the landscape. Perhaps hoping to flank the Indians while they were tied down defending against Reno's attack at the bottom end of the village, Custer rushed to get into an attacking position before he was discovered by Sioux and Cheyenne scouts. Custer sent messengers back to Benteen directing him to bring up the pack train.

Custer had divided his already outnumbered force of about 600 troopers. He did not know the terrain, nor, apparently, did he realize the size of the village along the river below him; he had apparently either ignored intelligence or simply failed to gather this vital information. It proved his undoing. Reno's force ran directly into a large band of warriors who attacked with skill and overwhelming force. Reno's detachment had no choice but to halt its charge, dig in, and fight for survival. Reno conducted at least three fighting retreats, losing half his men. Seeing

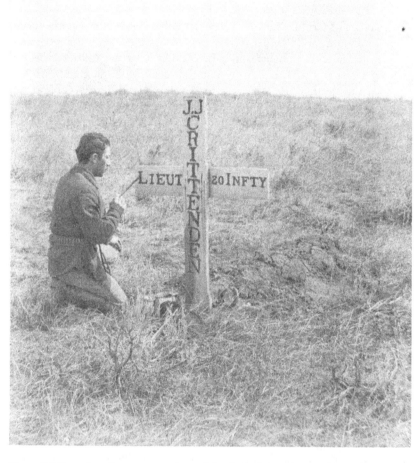

Figure 9.2 Lettering the grave marker of Lt. J. J. Crittenden at the Little Bighorn battlefield. Photograph by Stanley J. Morrow, ca. 1879.

Source: Library of Congress.

Reno's force engaged, Custer, still four miles away, began to advance, but not before being spotted by the Indians below. From the South, Chief Gall led a large force of warriors toward Custer's command, while Crazy Horse bore down on Custer from the north. Outnumbered by at least 20 to one, and outgunned, Custer and his 230 troopers perished in less than an hour.

When Reno and Benteen finally reunited, they heard the gunfire from over the ridge, but knowing neither their own position nor exactly where Custer was, they decided to remain where they were and hold out. Throughout the remainder of June 25, and well into June 26, the remaining 350 or so men of the 7th Cavalry fought for their lives. Finally, on June 27, Sitting Bull ordered the village to move south as scouts warned that Terry's and Gibbon's columns were advancing from the north. Custer's men, strewn about his own naked but otherwise unmolested body, were found mutilated. The Battle of the Little Bighorn was an unqualified disaster for the Army and its campaign to bring the Indians of the Northern Plains under control. Custer's death shocked the nation—he was a well-known and popular figure. In the end, Crazy Horse and Sitting Bull and their Sioux and Cheyenne warriors outmaneuvered and outfought Custer and his 7th Cavalry troopers. It is a great irony that as the nation celebrated its centennial of independence with expositions highlighting the industrial progress and modern advancements of the still-young United States, the nation's military forces suffered such a tremendous defeat at the hands of people whom many at the time considered savages.

Custer's defeat was also a disaster for Native Americans because it spurred the federal government into stronger action. The War Department sent more than 2,500 men into the Powder River area to chase down the Little Bighorn Indians. By 1877, a lack of provisions began to tell on the Sioux and Cheyenne. Desperate, Sitting Bull escaped with his band of Sioux into Canada. Spotted Tail and other leaders gained power over the war factions and sued for peace. Crazy Horse brought his band into the Red Cloud Agency and was later arrested by Crook, who feared that the great leader would foment a rebellion at the agency. In September 1877, Crazy Horse died in a fight between some Indians and their cavalry guards. By 1879, after several more skirmishes and intense negotiations, the Sioux and Cheyenne surrendered. Sitting Bull finally returned to the United States in July 1881.

The Nez Perce War of 1877 was one of the more remarkable of the Indian Wars. Evicted from the Wallowa Valley in Oregon, their homeland, guaranteed by treaty since the early 1800s, the Nez Perce resisted the federal government's order that they move to a reservation in Idaho. Under Chief Joseph, the Nez Perce led the Army on a winding chase of more than 1,700 miles. In major engagements at places such as White Bird Canyon and Bear Paw Mountain, and in fights across recently established Yellowstone National Park (where Army units, stationed to administer the nation's first national park, gave chase), both sides suffered significant casualties.

Living off the land, the Nez Perce maintained the initiative throughout the campaign; for its part, the Army had to rely on long, exposed logistical lines across incredibly challenging terrain. Technology, however, turned the tide toward the Army. Gatling guns and artillery finally overcame the Nez Perce. Unrelentingly pursued by the Army, the Nez Perce had difficulty gathering food. Low on provisions, with many of the band's women and children sick, Chief Joseph finally surrendered. After a battle at Bear Paw Mountain, just 40 miles from the Canadian border and refuge with Sitting Bull, Joseph agreed to terms. In the end, Chief Joseph vowed to 'fight no more, forever.'

The final tragedy of the Indian Wars grew out of the Ghost Dance movement in 1890. Believing that returning to traditional ways would bring back the buffalo and their old life, a Sioux shaman named Wovoka began the Ghost Dance movement on Sioux reservations. At the Pine Ridge Reservation in particular, the Ghost Dance took a fanatical turn, as its adherents preached the total destruction of the white man. Even Sitting Bull became enthralled with the Ghost Dance and was arrested at the Standing Ridge Reservation. Negotiations broke down between the Army and Sioux leaders Short Bill and Kicking Bear. During the arrest of Sitting Bull, carefully conducted by reservation police, things went horribly wrong and Sitting Bull died at the hands of a fellow Indian.

The final act of the Ghost Dance occurred along Wounded Knee Creek in December 1890. Nelson Miles misunderstood Chief Big Foot's decision to come into the reservation to persuade the Ghost Dancers to put an end to what he considered useless mysticism. Miles thought that Big Foot was planning to join forces with the Ghost Dance leaders and start a widespread rebellion. More than 500 troops, mostly from the 7th Cavalry, found Big Foot and his band of 300 encamped at Wounded Knee Creek. Colonel James W. Forsyth had orders to disarm the Indians and transport them to a safe area on the reservation. Forsyth surrounded the camp, trained four Hotchkiss guns on the camp, and ordered his men to move in and disarm the Indians. As the soldiers searched for and collected weapons, some Indians began performing the Ghost Dance and taunted the soldiers. One warrior boldly held his Winchester rifle above his head and challenged the soldiers to take it from him. When they did, a shot rang out. The heavily armed soldiers and lightly armed Indians opened fire on each other. The Hotchkiss guns opened up on women and children fleeing the melee in the camp. In less than an hour, Big Foot and 150 other men, women, and children lay dead. More than 50 troops had been killed or wounded, many by friendly fire. At least another 150 Indians died of exposure after escaping the camp.

The massacre at Wounded Knee, along with similar massacres at Sand Creek, Bear River, and other sites, has come to epitomize the Indian

Figure 9.3 Burial of the dead after the massacre of Wounded Knee, 1890. Photo
published by Northwestern Photo Company, Chadron, Nebraska.

Source: Library of Congress Prints and Photographs Division.

Wars. The Army and the Indians had been placed in a no-win situation by unfortunate timing and circumstances. For the Indians, the choice was to accept assimilation on reservations or to fight for their independence. Neither option offered hope for a happy outcome. A poorly coordinated and often conflicting policy of pacification and military action placed the Army in an unpopular situation. For many soldiers and officers, forcing a people to give up their indigenous ways and live on squalid reservations held no honor, nor did fighting an enemy who most of the time was outgunned and outmanned. Despite the well over 1,000 engagements during the Indian Wars, frontier duty was boring and tedious in the extreme, leading to poor morale, glacial promotion rates, and high turn-over among the thousands of immigrants, former slaves, and other men of lower socioeconomic status who served in the Army during the latter half of the nineteenth century.

Black Soldiers in the West

After the Civil War, the U.S. Army retained African Americans in the ranks, in segregated units commanded by whites, and assigned almost entirely to the undesirable and dangerous locations in the Southwest. The 9th and 10th Cavalry fought the Cheyenne and Apache in Texas and New Mexico. Native Americans gave the cavalry troopers the name Buffalo Soldiers out of respect for their fighting abilities, and loyalty to their duty. The several African American infantry units were also commanded by white officers and assigned to the most arduous tasks. Even when African American units were assigned to stations so that they could rest and retrain they found themselves at isolated posts, such as Fort Riley, Kansas. 'Scientific' bias argued that African Americans could survive only in the hot, humid climate of the South and Southwest. Nearer the end of the nineteenth century, however, African American units were sent to the Dakota Territory and Alaska, where they continued to serve with distinction. One of the most well-known Buffalo Soldiers is Cathy Williams, who enlisted under the name of William Cathay after the Civil War. She served honorably for several years before letting her sex be discovered. After that, she continued to work for the Army in more traditional roles.

During their service on the frontier, at least 17 African American soldiers were awarded Medals of Honor for action on the battlefield; later, two African American infantrymen were awarded for their bravery while defending a payroll shipment from outlaws. A monument to the Buffalo Soldiers' service stands at Fort Leavenworth, Kansas.

Between 1870 and 1880, 25 African Americans received appointments to West Point, but only three graduated. African American cadets endured social harassment and sometimes brutal physical attacks. Johnson Whitaker Chestnut suffered a brutal beating and was then court-martialed for staging his own assault. Although the conviction was overturned, Chestnut was ultimately dismissed from the Academy because of poor grades. His direct descendants served as U.S. Army officers during the two world wars.

Henry O. Flipper, the first African American to graduate from West Point (1879), was later court-martialed because of charges relating to irregularities with commissary monies he oversaw. Although dismissed from service he built a successful career as an engineer. In 1887, John H. Alexander graduated from the Academy, served for several years with the 9th Cavalry, and was then assigned to teach military science at an all-black college in Ohio. Charles Young graduated two years after Alexander and followed a similar career path. Almost 50 years passed before another African American graduated from West Point.

The National Guard

Labor unrest during the late nineteenth century aided the development of the modern National Guard. With industrialization underway in the northeastern United States and cities bulging with foreign immigrants and rural newcomers, labor disputes and other domestic disturbances often erupted in violence. Factory owners usually turned to private

Figure 9.4 Henry O. Flipper, the first African American graduate of West Point.
Source: National Archives and Records Administration.

security forces, such as that provided by the Pinkerton Agency, to maintain order in and near their factories during strikes. Occasionally, violence from labor strikes became widespread. In such cases, local and state authorities relied first on local police and then on state National Guard units to restore order. After the Civil War, the National Guard Movement gained rapid popularity among Civil War veterans who had served in units raised by the states. In continuation of the militia tradition, National Guard units remained state-run organizations. The National Guard Association, founded in 1879, lobbied Congress for federal funding to support state Guard units. By 1892, every state had a National Guard in place, and several had established naval equivalents. The National Guard promoted itself as an at-the-ready militia that could respond to domestic crises that the regular Army could not because of constitutional and congressional restraints. By the end of the nineteenth century, the aggregate manpower of National Guard units across the United States surpassed the total enlistment for the regular Army.

Both the National Guard and the Army were called upon to restore order because of strike-related violence. The national railroad strike in 1877 forced President Rutherford B. Hayes to use soldiers and marines to protect private property and to run rail lines that were shut down because employees had walked out. In 1894, President Grover Cleveland used troops commanded by Indian fighter Nelson Miles to restore order in Chicago during the violent Pullman Strike. Cleveland resorted to using regular Army soldiers because Illinois Governor John Peter Altgeld refused to call out Illinois National Guard units because he thought that a military presence would inflame the situation.

Frequently, issues of state versus federal authority led several of the more industrialized states to rely on their own Guard units rather than the regular Army to restore law and order during labor unrest. National Guard units mobilized to deal with more than 300 separate incidents from 1877 through the early 1900s. Putting down labor unrest was unpopular duty with both regulars and guardsmen. Most significantly, however, using the Guard in this manner had the unintended consequence of establishing the National Guard as part of the national defense apparatus. This development forced the War Department to rethink national mobilization plans as well as reconsider training for this new iteration of citizen–soldier.

In 1903, Congress passed the Militia Act, officially establishing a National Guard system under the War Department, complete with guidelines for mobilization and training per standards set by the War Department. With federal funding, the Militia Act created a National Guard of Organized Militia and a Reserve Militia. National Guard units trained at least twice a month and participated in maneuvers with regular Army units. Regular Army officers served periodically with Guard units. Shortcomings in Guard service on the Mexican border and less-than-efficient Guard mobilization in 1917 prompted Congress to continue reform measures. By the 1920s, the War Department had both the National Guard and the newly formed Reserves under more centralized control and authority, which helped address traditional problems between the regular Army establishment and the 'militia.'

Renewed Push Toward Professionalism

With industrialization in the United States and Western Europe, the advent of new weapons technology, and lessons learned from the Civil War, the American military engaged in another push toward professionalization similar to what it had experienced in the decades following the War of 1812. Progressives in both the Army and Navy struggled to bring their respective services up to date with modern military technology and military thought.

Studying military developments in England and Germany, Army Progressives argued that in the modern industrialized world, relying on a skeletal standing army filled out by militia would no longer suffice to defend American security and national interests. Moreover, they contended, the inefficiency caused by the traditional rivalry between staff and line officers had to be fixed with a staff system based on the German model, which promoted officers by merit rather than by seniority. For the Army, such reform was indeed radical.

In 1903, the Army adopted a general staff model that promoted better cooperation between the various bureaus and field commands. Secretary of War Elihu Root, serving under President Theodore Roosevelt, strongly supported such reforms in the interest of professionalization and national security. Also, the Dodge Commission's (named for its chairman, Major General Grenville M. Dodge) criticism of the Army's organization and command structure during the Spanish–American War made reform seem imperative. Under Root's tenure as Secretary of War, Congress passed the General Staff Act of 1903, which replaced the General of the Army position with a chief of staff to oversee war planning and the conduct of combat operations.

To have such a staff system led by professional officers, the Army had to invest in professional military education, a concept that it had haltingly accepted over the nineteenth century. General of the Army William T. Sherman, one of the original Army Progressives, kick-started the movement. He established engineering and artillery schools, as well as schools for the Signal Corps and the Medical Corps. In 1881, he established the School of Application for Infantry and Cavalry, the forerunner of the Command and General Staff College at Fort Leavenworth, as the senior service school for the Army until the creation of the Army War College in 1903. Sherman intended that the Army War College would educate senior officers on the new staff structure and reduce the influence of the traditionally entrenched bureaus.

Emory Upton provided the energy behind much of the Army reform movement. An 1856 graduate of West Point, Upton served as an officer in the Union Army during the Civil War, seeing action at Antietam, Gettysburg, and Cold Harbor, among other significant battles. By the end of the war, he had risen to the rank of brevet major general. After the war, Upton served as commandant at West Point and at the Presidio in California and instructed at the Army Artillery School. Perhaps his most significant scholarly experience was a two-year-long trip across Europe and Asia to study military organization.

Upton had an immediate and direct effect upon the reform debate even after his death in 1881. He wrote a controversial and extensive study of American military policy after his trip abroad that offered for the first time a strong and well-supported argument against the American militia tradition. The militia was political, poorly led, and poorly trained, all of which contributed to an overall poor combat record. In the modern, industrialized world of the post-Civil War era, reliance upon such a force was foolhardy. Upton instead supported an expansible army concept similar to that promoted by John Calhoun after the War of 1812. Upton envisioned a professional, highly trained and educated army, with a general staff that could mobilize and train a ready reserve of militia under federal rather than state control. Most controversially, Upton called for the complete independence of the Army from meddlesome political control.

As much sense as most of Upton's plan made, and as popular as his ideas were among Progressive reformers in the Army, Congress remained tied to the pro-militia fear of a standing army and anti-professional officer corps traditions that had characterized American military policy since the colonial era. Moreover, Congress had no intention of interfering with civilian control of the Army established in the Constitution. While 'Uptonians' may have been vindicated in the General Service Act of 1903, the Militia Act of 1903 did not fulfill Upton's original vision of the organization and role of a national guard. Military policy in America had always been, and remains, highly politicized. Arguments supporting direct commissioning of officers, for example, even went so far as to recommend closing the academies at West Point and Annapolis to prevent the creation of an elite officer corps.

Technology and tactics also received some overdue attention in the Army; nonetheless, the Army remained technologically backward compared to its European counterparts. Only in 1892 did the Army begin replacing the old black-powder, breech-loading 1872 and 1873 Model Springfields with the more modern .30 caliber, smokeless-cartridge-firing Krag-Jørgensen rifle. In 1903, the Army began replacing the Krag-Jørgensen with the new clip-loading, high-velocity Springfield. Machine guns designed by Hiram Maxim, Isaac Lewis, and John Browning were adopted by armies in Europe, but the U.S. Army did not procure a modern machine gun until 1917. The Colt .45 caliber pistol replaced the weak .38 caliber revolvers as the Army's sidearm of choice in 1911. The Army continued to lag behind European armies in artillery and in using smokeless powder. Likewise, the Army was slow to invest in motorized vehicles and airplanes, despite purchasing a few 1909 Wright Flyers, before entering the Great War in 1917.

Building a Modern Navy

Naval modernization also occurred in fits and starts. The significant advances in maritime technology so eagerly adopted by the U.S. Navy during the Civil War were unceremoniously pushed aside after the conflict. The 'old salts' and 'mossbacks' of the Navy, its sail-loving admirals, looked upon steam-powered ships with suspicion. They argued that these modern vessels wasted valuable space for fuel that sailing ships more efficiently used for guns, crew, and storage. Steam engines could break down, but a sail could easily be replaced. With so little enthusiasm for modern naval ships at the top of the Navy, it is little wonder that the Navy nearly foundered on its sail-based fleet in the 1870s.

Industrial growth and its corresponding increase in American trade abroad, however, demanded a more substantial, modern fleet of naval vessels to protect American shipping and trade interests beyond the waters of the United States. Moreover, as European navies, particularly the Royal Navy, eagerly adopted coal-fueled, steam-powered vessels complete with steel hulls and massive guns, the coast of the United States seemed at higher risk of foreign attack than ever before. To address these genuine security concerns, the Navy had to modernize.

In 1882, a naval board recommended a bold program of modern shipbuilding. Unwilling to make such a substantial investment in expensive ships, Congress would authorize only the ABCD steel-hulled, steam-powered ships—the *Atlanta*, *Boston*, *Chicago*, and *Dolphin*—in 1883. Without a strong ethic of professionalism and little in the way of a reform movement, the Navy could not make much progress against such a robust budgetary headwind and traditionalist tide.

When Secretary of the Navy William E. Chandler established the Naval War College in 1885, the Navy began to reform more steadily. Two notable proponents of modern American naval thought, Rear Admiral Stephen B. Luce and Captain Alfred Thayer Mahan, found that the War College was the perfect environment to promote their bold views on naval reform.

Luce was instrumental in establishing the Naval War College. Inspired by what Sherman and Upton were doing in the Army reform movement, Luce had earlier helped establish the U.S. Naval Institute in 1873 as the center for professional naval education. Professionalism reigned at the Naval Institute, as officers studied naval strategy and tactics and published articles in the Institute's *Proceedings*, which remains one of the leading naval journals in the world. When the Naval War College opened in 1885, Luce was named its first president. For Luce, the principal and direct objective of the Naval War College was to create a doctrine for steam-powered naval warfare.

Luce found his greatest disciple in a naval officer who abhorred sea duty—Captain Alfred Thayer Mahan. Mahan was the son of Dennis Hart Mahan, and the namesake of Sylvanus Thayer, both of whom were influential military thinkers at West Point before the Civil War. When Luce asked Mahan to lecture at the Naval War College, it was an offer the intellectual Mahan could not refuse.

Mahan's lectures were collectively published in *The Influence of Sea Power upon History, 1660–1782* in 1890, and ultimately translated into several languages, including German and Japanese. Mahan suggested that the genuinely great maritime empires of the world achieved such status through supreme naval power. For the United States to break out of its continental shell and become a legitimate world power, it had to marry trade and naval superiority. In other words, the United States had to invest in a modern battleship fleet and naval bases to support the new fleet in strategic locations around the globe.

To accomplish this, Mahan concluded, the United States had to enter the imperialist race—a competition that had been going full bore among European powers for much of the nineteenth century. Accordingly, he recommended annexing Hawaii, and building and controlling a Central American canal. Most importantly, however, he urged the creation of a battleship fleet. Disavowing commerce raiding, Mahan suggested that only a fleet of battleships, acting in concert in a decisive naval battle against a rival's fleet, could guarantee American superiority on the high seas.

Little of what Mahan said was original. Several American naval officers and other naval thinkers had expressed similar opinions since the Civil War. To draw naval lessons from the British experience of the seventeenth and eighteenth centuries and apply them to the American situation in the late nineteenth century was a stretch, at best. Mahan was trying to apply Napoleonic warfare concepts for land war to war at sea.

Still, Mahan helped give big-navy thinking a popular voice. A young New Yorker named Theodore Roosevelt, who had given a guest lecture for Mahan based on his recent history of naval action in the War of 1812, was greatly influenced by Mahan's work. Under the guidance of Mahanian Secretaries of the Navy, such as William C. Whitney and Benjamin F. Tracy, Congress cautiously authorized a handful of modern ships. By the early 1900s, the U.S. Navy boasted a modern fleet that included the 6,000-ton cruiser *Maine*; the battleships *Texas, Oregon, Indiana*, and *Massachusetts*; and the still larger *Kentucky, Illinois, Alabama*, and *Wisconsin*, each with modern guns and substantial armament. It is important to remember, however, that American naval building barely kept pace with that of Great Britain, Germany, and Japan throughout the late 1890s through the 1920s.

Battleships, however, were not the only naval advancement. Navy recruiting began targeting young men from the interior of the nation, giving the Navy a more national flavor. With the Naval Personnel Act of 1899, the old seniority promotion system gave way to a merit-based system. The Navy invested personnel and funds into new cutting-edge fields, such as scientific management and hydro-electronics. One of the first agencies of its kind, the Office of Naval Intelligence was created in 1882.

By 1898, the U.S. Navy was on the verge of becoming a world-class sea power. Progressive officers who strongly supported and carried out naval reform had a revolutionary impact. When war broke out with Spain, the Navy was much better prepared and equipped for war than was the Army.

War with Spain

The Spanish–American War of 1898 is considered a significant turning point in American military and diplomatic history. In this brief but pivotal conflict, the United States enforced the old Monroe Doctrine, became the unquestioned master of the Western Hemisphere, exhibited its new naval strength, exposed weaknesses in mobilization and preparedness in the Army, gained possessions in the Caribbean and the western Pacific, and solidified its role as a significant player in the Far East. With victory in the Spanish–American War, the United States began its steady rise to world power status and took a bold step onto the world stage. The swiftness and suddenness of success led many in the United States to become over-confident of American military prowess. In the Philippines, this led to one of the more regrettable military experiences in American history.

President William McKinley asked Congress for a declaration of war against Spain in April 1898, which Congress readily granted. The war began over Cuba, a poverty-stricken remnant of the once-great Spanish empire in the Western Hemisphere. Americans had long coveted the island just off the southern Florida coast. Southern filibusters had tried to take it before the Civil War. As president, Ulysses S. Grant attempted unsuccessfully to buy it from Spain. President Grover Cleveland had offered mediation to end the widespread rebellion that had enveloped the island since 1895.

During President McKinley's first two years in office, Spanish policy to end the rebellion in Cuba took a brutal turn. The public outcry to end the suffering of the Cuban people, promoted by 'yellow journalism' and a vociferous Cuban community in the United States, came to a head in 1898. McKinley seemed reluctant to go to war over Cuba; he gave diplomacy every chance to avoid a conflict with Spain. Hoping to find a solution that would grant Cuba at least nominal independence from Spain, McKinley worked untiringly to bring an end to Cuba's troubles. Such a settlement, however, became increasingly unlikely, as the American public grew more outraged at each Spanish atrocity, whether alleged or genuine. Captain-

General of Cuba Valeriano Weyler committed an act that particularly aroused American sympathies. To finally destroy the Cuban rebels, Weyler rounded up Cubans from the countryside and resettled them in concentration camps, where tens of thousands perished from disease, starvation, and exposure. Declaring people who remained outside the camps as rebels, Weyler initiated what was mainly a 'search and destroy' campaign against rebel bands.

In a show of 'gunboat diplomacy,' McKinley ordered the cruiser *Maine* to Havana in February 1898. Ostensibly there to evacuate American citizens if the need arose, the presence of the great American naval vessel increased the tension substantially. On February 15, the *Maine* exploded, sinking to the bottom of Havana harbor in a matter of minutes, taking 250 American sailors and marines with it. American newspapers quickly claimed that Spanish agents had planted a mine or a torpedo to destroy the ship. Investigations by the Navy and the Spanish government followed; both failed to find the cause of the explosion, but the Navy concluded that the blast had been external. That conclusion came too late, as the press quickly convinced the American public that Spain was to blame. Later investigations confirmed that an internal explosion, probably caused by spontaneous combustion in the coal room, sank the *Maine*.

When Spain failed to respond satisfactorily to his peace offers, McKinley reluctantly asked for a declaration of war. Congress passed the declaration but added the Teller Amendment stipulating that the United States would not annex Cuba. McKinley immediately ordered the Navy to blockade Cuba and signed into law a mobilization act to get the Army ready for action. Initially, the Army wanted only 100,000 men to occupy Cuba after the Navy's Atlantic Squadron destroyed Spanish naval reinforcements in a Mahan-style decisive sea battle.

Congress, however, dashed the Army's hopes for speedy mobilization by allotting volunteer slots to National Guard units from the states. States protested that their Guard units could not, by law, serve overseas, so the federal government allowed guardsmen to volunteer to form new units within the regular Army. The Army itself expanded from a scattered 27,000 troops to 59,000 men plus more than 200,000 volunteers (whom the Army had not requested in the first place). Politics played a hand in the mobilization, catching the Army utterly unprepared for a force of that size. With inadequate equipment and supplies even for training that number of men, and with insufficient rail stock for transporting them to Tampa, Florida, for embarkation to Cuba, the Army experienced a logistical nightmare during the brief four-month war.

Americans reasonably assumed that Cuba would be the primary theater of operations. Few anticipated that the Pacific, notably the Philippine Islands, would also become a major theater. Speculating that war with Spain was imminent, Assistant Secretary of the Navy Theodore Roosevelt, heavily influenced by Mahan's writings, had earlier ordered the commander of the American Asiatic Squadron, Commodore George Dewey, to

Figure 9.5 The USS *Olympia*, Dewey's flagship at the Battle of Manila Bay, photograph
taken in 1902.

Source: U.S. Navy.

refuel his fleet in Hong Kong for possible action in the Philippines. When
Congress declared war, the Navy Department ordered Dewey to steam to
Manila and destroy the Spanish fleet there. On May 1, Dewey struck the
still-anchored Spanish fleet, literally destroying it in a matter of hours.
Dewey lost only one man, to heat exhaustion, while the Spanish lost
seven ships and 350 killed. Although the Spanish fleet was dilapidated,
Dewey's victory in the Battle of Manila Bay was nonetheless a triumph of
the new modern Navy.

Dewey controlled Manila Bay and occupied the Cavite Navy Yard,
across the bay from Manila. Manila, however, remained in Spanish hands,
forcing Dewey to wait until Army reinforcements arrived to take the
Spanish-controlled city. Dewey became an overnight sensation in the
United States—perhaps more popular than any other military officer in
American history to that point. He was even lauded as a possible candidate
for the 1900 presidential election.

Meanwhile, on the Cuban front, action progressed more slowly. The
Spanish Atlantic fleet had left the Cape Verde Islands for the Caribbean at
the end of April. Not knowing the fleet's location or ultimate destination,
Rear Admiral William Sampson guessed that Spanish Admiral Pascual

Cevera would take his fleet to San Juan, Puerto Rico. Learning that Sampson was waiting for him off Puerto Rico, Cevera instead went to Santiago Bay on the southeastern coast of Cuba. Santiago Bay was heavily fortified with shore batteries, thus giving the Spanish fleet protection. This protection, however, came at the cost of freedom of movement. Once Sampson found Cevera, he bottled up the Spanish fleet in Santiago Bay while staying out of range of Santiago's shore batteries.

Sampson understood that he could not destroy Cevera's fleet unless the shore batteries were knocked out, a task that required the Army's help. Commanding General of the Army Nelson Miles originally wanted to assault Havana with a 70,000-man force in October, after the rainy season, when the roads would be dry and tropical fevers less virulent. Spanish men under arms on the island numbered more than 200,000, although many were Cuban conscripts. The American public and Secretary of War Russell M. Alger, along with Admiral Sampson, prodded Miles for more immediate action. Mobilizing such a sizable force in June, however, was impossible. Under such pressure, Miles canceled his Havana plan and instead agreed to cooperate with Sampson to assault Santiago.

Departing from Tampa, where the logistical problems reached unprecedented levels of confusion and incompetence, the 17,000 troops of the Army's V Corps under the command of Major General William R. Shafter arrived east of Santiago during the second week of June. After a harrowing two-day disembarkation at Siboney and Daiquirí, eased only by the absence of Spanish resistance, Shafter began the march to Santiago. Although the Army undertook this operation to help the Navy defeat the Spanish fleet at Santiago, cooperation between the two services ended as soon as the Army was ashore.

While Sampson wanted V Corps to use the coastal road to approach the shore fortifications around Santiago Bay, Shafter instead insisted upon an inland approach from the northeast of Santiago. From Siboney and Daiquirí, Shafter's force, comprising mostly regulars and the Rough Riders (Theodore Roosevelt's volunteer cavalry), made their way on foot over unfamiliar roads through rocky terrain and dense undergrowth. At Las Guásimas, Major General Joseph Wheeler—a Confederate veteran of the Civil War brought out of retirement in a show of regional solidarity—and his advance force of 1,000 made the first contact with the Spanish. After a brief fight, the 1,500 Spanish evacuated the small town. On July 1, as the Americans approached the San Juan Heights around Santiago, Shafter divided his force, sending Brigadier General Henry Lawton and more than 6,000 troops to prevent the Spanish garrison at nearby El Caney from harassing the American rear. The remainder of the American force advanced on Spanish positions on the Heights. The intent was to coordinate the attacks, with Lawton's attack on El Caney to take only two hours so that he could then support the assault on the Heights. Instead, the Battle of El Caney lasted nearly 12 hours.

Figure 9.6 The Spanish–American War.

Despite the absence of Lawton's 6,000 men, Shafter proceeded with his plan. With more than 8,000 men, including the all-African American 9th and 10th Cavalry (the Buffalo Soldiers) and Roosevelt's Rough Riders, Brigadier General Jacob F. Kent's division attacked on the left of the Heights while Wheeler's dismounted cavalry assaulted the right. The attack began at dawn on July 1, going badly from the start. A Signal Corps balloon tethered among advance units alerted the 500 Spanish on the Heights to the American position, while the black powder from their old Springfields provided clear targets for Spanish riflemen. After a morning's fighting marked by heat and dwindling water supplies, Wheeler's force made it to the top of Kettle Hill, forcing the Spanish defenders to retreat. Seeing Kent's assault on San Juan Hill foundering, Roosevelt and the Rough Riders charged, on foot, up San Juan Hill alongside the Buffalo Soldiers. The Spanish retreated to Santiago, but not without exacting a heavy toll—205 Americans killed and 1,180 wounded. Spanish casualties were 215 dead and 376 wounded.

With Santiago now vulnerable from the northeast, the Spanish began to run out of options. Not knowing that the American force was decimated by disease, exhaustion, and limited supplies, the Spanish withdrew to a formidable defensive line around Santiago. Conditions in Santiago deteriorated as well, as food and ammunition both ran dangerously low. Cevera was ordered to take the fleet out of the bay and make a run for safety, but the U.S. fleet picked off the Spanish ships as they attempted to escape. In less than two hours, the American fleet of six ships ran two Spanish ships aground, sank two, and severely damaged three more, all at the cost of—like Dewey's victory—one sailor to the loss of 300 Spanish killed. Despite the destruction of the Spanish fleet at the Battle of Santiago Bay, Shafter could not advance against the strong defenses surrounding the city. General Miles arrived with reinforcements, however, which convinced the Spanish to surrender on July 16 on the condition that they return to Spain.

On July 21, Miles sailed with a force from Guantánamo to Ponce, Puerto Rico, planning to capture the island. Disease had so weakened V Corps that Miles could take only 3,000 troops, hardly an adequate force with which to challenge the 8,000 Spanish troops garrisoned at San Juan. When 10,000 reinforcements arrived in early August, Miles divided his army into four columns and advanced toward San Juan. Meeting little resistance, Miles reached San Juan just as word came that an armistice had been agreed to on August 12.

In the Philippines, American forces faced a complicated political situation. By July, 15,000 men under Major General Wesley Merritt arrived near Manila, convincing the Spanish commander there that resistance was futile. Filipino rebel leader Emilio Aguinaldo had positioned his 10,000 insurgents around Manila, keeping the Spanish bottled up in the city by land, while Dewey's fleet prevented escape by sea. Their actions were inspired in part by a vague promise from Dewey of Filipino independence after the Spanish were defeated.

Despite Aguinaldo's cooperation with Dewey, the McKinley administration decided against giving the Filipinos their independence and instead chose to keep the islands. Strategically, the United States had little choice if it wanted influence in Asia and the western Pacific. After Aguinaldo learned there would be no independence, he took the initiative. In August, he established a revolutionary government, with him as president. Relations between Aguinaldo and the American military command began to break down, leaving doubt about how the Filipino insurgents would react when the Army commenced its attack on Manila.

As Merritt positioned his forces around Manila and talks began with Aguinaldo to convince him to keep his troops out of the ensuing fight, the Spanish wanted to surrender but were under strict orders from Madrid to at least make a show of resistance before capitulating. To preserve some modicum of Spanish honor, Merritt agreed to what amounted to a brief staged battle, after which the Spanish would lay down their arms and surrender Manila. Aguinaldo reluctantly decided to remain on the sidelines during what was mainly a demonstration. On August 13, the day after the armistice, Merritt began the land Battle of Manila. For a short time, it seemed that the confrontation might become a real battle because some of Aguinaldo's men joined in what they thought was an actual fight. Order was gradually restored, and after a few hours of fighting, during which several American soldiers were killed because of the confusion caused by the Filipinos, the Spanish surrendered.

The Treaty of Paris in December 1898 formally ended the war between Spain and the United States. Cuba gained its independence, while Spain handed over Puerto Rico and Guam to the United States. As for the Philippines, the United States paid $20 million to Spain for the islands. In just the span of a few weeks, the United States had acquired an empire.

War with Spain cost 400 American combat deaths and more than 2,000 dead from disease. In Cuba, typhoid, yellow fever, and malaria so decimated American troops in Santiago that officers sent a joint letter to Shafter recommending that the Army be withdrawn from Cuba immediately. Unfortunately, the press published the letter before Shafter saw it, creating an embarrassment for the Army and widespread outrage. The evacuation of American forces began sooner than initially planned. A sick camp established at Montauk Point on Long Island held the troops from Cuba under quarantine but under appalling conditions. For the Army Medical Corps, tropical disease became a topic of study that ultimately resulted in effective preventive measures for yellow fever and malaria.

Insurrections and Rebellions

After the Spanish–American War, the United States was placed on the world stage, a role that obligated the military to undertake more duties outside the territorial United States. Imperialism increased the need to protect American citizens and property abroad, more significant roles in maintaining order and promoting nation-building in the new American possessions, and rare situations where it was necessary to cooperate at unprecedented levels with other foreign powers in times of crisis.

Following the end of the war with Spain, the Philippine Insurrection placed the U.S. Army in an extremely delicate situation. Aguinaldo's rebel forces remained intact and vowed to resist American occupation. To maintain order, the Army had to either negotiate a settlement with Aguinaldo or force an end to rebel resistance. Remote islands peopled by other groups who did not see eye to eye with Aguinaldo further complicated the political and military situation in the Philippines. During the two years of open insurrection, the Army had to maintain in the Philippines a force that was many times the size of the one that had defeated the Spanish at Manila. Maintaining a logistical line not only from the United States to the Pacific but also among the major islands in the Philippines taxed American resourcefulness. Moreover, the brutal nature of the insurrection, combined with multiple atrocities committed by both sides, further complicated the challenge.

Fighting began after Aguinaldo established the new Republic of the Philippines. In February 1899, insurgent and American patrols clashed;

then, violence broke out in Manila. Major General Elwell S. Otis, Merritt's replacement, had only 12,000 troops to defend Manila against 40,000 rebel insurgents under Aguinaldo. As Aguinaldo's forces withdrew from around Manila, the conflict quickly deteriorated into a guerrilla war fought in the thick jungles of Luzon and surrounding islands where the insurgents had a clear advantage. To make matters worse for the Americans, the Moro peoples of the southern Philippines also violently resisted American rule. The Army was ill-prepared and ill-suited for countering such an insurgency.

New American regular and volunteer regiments arrived as old ones were sent back to the United States for postwar demobilization. Within a short time, Otis had an entirely new and mostly inexperienced army under his command. Otis focused on gaining control over major population centers and logistical routes and then establishing stable government in those areas. The Army built schools, hospitals, and other public works projects. The Army was fighting and nation-building at the same time. During 1899, Otis made significant progress against Aguinaldo, using columns under General Lawton to control the Santa Cruz region and under Major General Arthur MacArthur (Douglas MacArthur's father) to suppress insurgent activity in the San Fernando region.

After these areas were secure, Otis went after Aguinaldo, who had holed up in the northern mountains of Luzon. A three-column approach ultimately defeated the bulk of the rebel forces, but Aguinaldo escaped. Boldly posing as a captured American soldier, Brigadier General Frederick Funston finally captured Aguinaldo in March 1901. With the rebel leader's capture, organized resistance in Luzon mostly ended. Nonetheless, MacArthur, who replaced Otis in 1900, had to continue operations to put down isolated pockets of insurgency. In these small, hard-fought engagements, the Army incurred more casualties than it had during the open insurrection.

In Samar, the Moro peoples continued their resistance. If the war in Luzon had been bitterly fought, the war against the Moro was even more so. Employing tactics reminiscent of the colonial wars, including the destruction of entire villages and ambushes, the United States finally brought Moro insurgency to an end. It was in this campaign that Captain John J. 'Black Jack' Pershing, who as a white officer fought alongside the all-African American 10th Cavalry at San Juan Hill, gained a reputation not only for his fighting skill but his ideas on pacification. Even the Army grew uncertain about the morality of its campaign in Samar, court-martialing Brigadier General Jacob Smith for the excessively brutal tactics used to overcome the Moro.

More than 125,000 American troops were involved in the Philippine Insurrection, and 4,500 of them died. Estimates for Filipino losses from combat, starvation, and disease range from 200,000 to as high as 600,000.

The war became increasingly unpopular in the United States, creating an ardent and persuasive antiwar and anti-imperialist movement. Few anticipated the intensity and cost that keeping the Philippines would entail.

Meanwhile, the Boxer Rebellion erupted in China in 1900, threatening the lives and property of foreigners across China and in particular, the capital city of Peking. The 'Boxers,' as they were called by Westerners, resented foreign influence in China, especially that of Christian missionaries. With the indirect approval of China's Dowager Empress, the Boxers

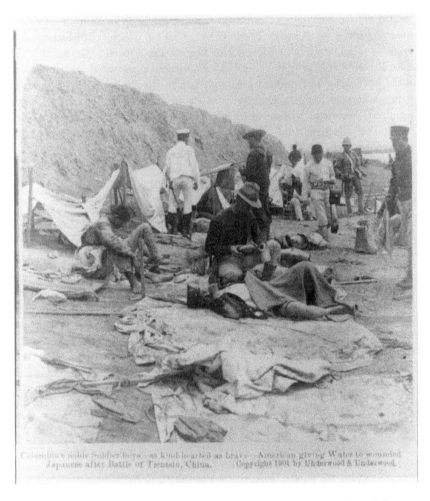

Figure 9.7 An American soldier gives water to a wounded Japanese soldier following a battle in the Boxer Rebellion. Photograph by James Ricalton, for Underwood and Underwood, New York.

Source: Library of Congress.

attacked mission outposts in the countryside, killing missionaries and several of the Chinese converts. They then besieged the Diplomatic Quarter of the Imperial City, forcing the legation staffs and their military guards to band together to defend themselves from absolute slaughter if the Boxers broke through their defenses. Small units of American, British, and Japanese troops tried to reach the city, but all failed.

As the besieged legations held on, an international expedition was formed comprising 19,000 British, French, Japanese, Russian, German, Austrian, Italian, and American troops—including the 9th Infantry, 14th Infantry, and 6th Cavalry from the Philippines—to relieve the legations in Peking. Disembarking at Tientsin in August, the relief force fought its way over 70 miles to Peking. There, in a series of poorly coordinated and costly attacks, it finally reached the Diplomatic Quarter on August 15. The Boxer Rebellion broke apart into scattered pockets of resistance that were eventually put down by foreign troops. Lacking a security contingent, American forces withdrew from Peking as quickly as possible. Two hundred American troops were killed or wounded in the operation in which, for the first time since the American War for Independence, the United States had militarily allied with foreign forces.

Conclusion

In 1907, a modern American battleship fleet left for a world tour. Passing in review off Long Island before a very proud President Theodore Roosevelt, the fleet, painted a brilliant white with pennants fluttering in the breeze, must have been a spectacular sight. The Great White Fleet, as it was called, was a symbol of American power in the modern industrialized world and a clear warning that the United States was going to be a significant player in world affairs. The U.S. Army and Navy had struggled through a tumultuous transformation since the Civil War. Both had adopted new technology and new ideas, both had survived serious tests of their abilities, and both emerged modernized. Moreover, a new spirit of professionalism now pervaded both services. The foundation for American military power in the twentieth century was firmly laid.

Further Reading

Cooper, Jerry M. *The Rise of the National Guard: The Evolution of the American Militia, 1865–1920*. Lincoln, NE: Bison Books, 2002.

Cozzens, Peter. *The Earth is Weeping: The Epic Story of the Indian Wars for the American West*. New York: Vintage Books, 2017.

Dobak, William, and Thomas D. Phillips. *The Black Regular, 1866–1898*. Norman, OK: University of Oklahoma Press, 2001.

Greene, Jerome A. *American Carnage: Wounded Knee, 1890*. Norman, OK: University of Oklahoma Press, 2014.

Hoganson, Kristin L. *Fighting for American Manhood: How Gender Politics Provoked the Spanish-American and Philippine-American Wars.* New Haven, CT: Yale University Press, 1998.

Leeke, Jim. *Manila and Santiago: The New Steel Navy in the Spanish-American War.* Annapolis, MD: Naval Institute Press, 2009.

Linn, Brian. *The Philippine War, 1899–1902.* Lawrence, KS: University of Kansas Press, 2000.

Reardon, Carol. *Soldiers and Scholars: The U.S. Army and the Uses of Military History.* Lawrence, KS: University Press of Kansas, 1990.

Reckner, James R. *Teddy Roosevelt's Great White Fleet.* Annapolis, MD: Bluejacket Books, 1988.

Shellum, Brian G. *Black Officer in a Buffalo Soldier Regiment: The Military Career of Charles Young.* Lincoln, NE: University of Nebraska Press, 2010.

Silbey, David J. *War of Frontier and Empire: The Philippine-American War, 1989–1902.* New York: Hill and Wang, 2007.

Silbey, David J. *The Boxer Rebellion and the Great Game in China: A History.* New York: Hill and Wang, 2012.

10 'Over There'

Introduction

The Great War posed enormous challenges for all the armies that fought in it, and for the governments and societies that raised and fielded them. American involvement in the war, while belated, brought the United States firmly into the affairs of Europe—a process that is ongoing a century later. The American military, and notably the U.S. Army, was afforded a brutal introduction to the realities of modern industrial warfare while the administration of President Woodrow Wilson assumed a leading role in the attempt to forge a postwar settlement, although the opportunity was unfortunately squandered.

The Punitive Expedition

In 1914, Americans were concerned as much with the state of relations with Mexico as with those between the great European powers, and war with the former seemed more likely. The Mexican revolution of 1911 degenerated first into reaction and then into civil war; the Wilson administration sought to influence the course and nature of events in Mexico, not least because it feared intervention by other powers— Germany or even Japan—taking advantage of Mexico's troubles. The earlier, relatively small-scale mobilization of forces in 1911 and 1913 had resulted in generally fruitless attempts to confine the conflict to the Mexican side of the border. In April 1914 Wilson intervened more directly, sending a force of Marines to the coastal city of Veracruz, which was bombarded and occupied till the end of the year. Mexican civilian casualties were extensive, while U.S. forces lost 19 killed and 47 wounded. The death toll in the city served merely to inflame anti-American feelings in the country, although the American presence enabled the Wilson administration to arm and equip the constitutionalist faction within the country that then went on to defeat a number of its rivals.

The 1916 Punitive Expedition was prompted by an incursion into New Mexico by the forces of Francisco 'Pancho' Villa that included a raid on the town of Columbus in March, resulting in 15 deaths among its citizenry and local soldiers. Villa was a frustrated presidential rival, and his force numbered little more than 500. The response was disproportionate: a 'punitive' expeditionary force of some 12,000 troops, equipped with reconnaissance aircraft and motorized transport, commanded by Brigadier General John J. Pershing, that penetrated over 400 miles into Mexico. Mexican nationalism was galvanized by the American intervention, and although there were few real engagements (the most notable being at El Carrizal, which was a technical victory for the Mexicans), the expedition found itself fighting both Villa's troops, which multiplied in number, and units of the Mexican federal army dispatched by the interim president, Venustiano Carranza. The American incursion, and the local response to it, also generated a flow of refugees—Americans resident in Mexico—back across the border into the southern United States.

To enable the use of regular units and maintain border protection against bandits and armed bands, the government called up and federalized the National Guard in Texas, Arizona, and New Mexico in May and, when this proved inadequate to the task, called up guardsmen nationally in

Figure 10.1 In March 1916, the 1st Aero Squadron was deployed to Mexico for aerial observation with eight Curtiss JN-3s, or 'Jennies,' during the Punitive Expedition of 1916–1917.

Source: Library of Congress Prints and Photographs Division.

mid-June. The mechanism used to accomplish this, the newly legislated National Defense Act of 1916, had significantly increased federal powers over the National Guard but had done little to improve its efficiency or effectiveness. Many National Guard soldiers declined call-up because they were either unwilling to accept duty under federal control in circumstances short of war or disliked the tedious and unromantic tasks they were allocated on the American side of the border. Of around 95,000 men on the National Guard's muster rolls, half failed to report, and another 24,000 failed the medical exam.

Recruiting to make good the shortfall was disappointing, a reflection, in part, of disenchantment with the tasks allocated to the men. The shortcomings in the mobilization of the National Guard, which to some extent reflected the old culture of the National Guard that had been exposed during the mobilization for the Spanish–American War in 1898, confirmed for many regular officers that the National Guard was ill-suited to the role of a reserve able to be utilized effectively in a national emergency.

In January 1917, Washington ordered the withdrawal of Pershing's force. Following the promulgation of a new constitution and the election of Carranza as president in March, the U.S. government extended official recognition to Mexico; the tensions that had characterized American–Mexican relations began to recede. Increasingly strained relations with Germany had by now taken their place.

'Over There'

Although the Punitive Expedition had made early use of emergent military technologies such as aircraft and had demonstrated some benefits of the introduction of motorization, the U.S. Army in 1917 was not a modern army. The benefits of recent field service in Mexico were undoubted but should not be overstated. Pershing confirmed the high estimation in which he was held through the skillful discharge of a difficult command hedged by complex political influences and pressures, but these were a mild foretaste of the situations he would encounter in Europe.

Isolationist sentiment and a sense that the squabbles of the Old World had nothing to do with the New World were quickly replaced in significant quarters by a belief in the desirability of an Allied victory. Economic issues were paramount: Supplying the industrial war needs of the Allies was enormously profitable for the United States, and the transfer of capital and assets that took place as a result marked the beginning of Western Europe's financial net indebtedness to the United States that was to accelerate even more markedly in the next world war. The effect of German submarine warfare in the Atlantic on American opinion is well known—especially the furor over the sinking of the passenger liner *Lusitania* in May 1915—but the successful and shrewd British-organized propaganda that depicted German atrocities during the advance into Belgium in the war's opening weeks also turned public opinion in many quarters against Germany.

German naval activity and the threat it posed to freedom of navigation on the high seas persuaded the Wilson administration to scrap existing plans for modernizing, but not enlarging, the U.S. Navy in favor of a new fleet expansion program that would see the creation of a navy to rival the Royal Navy—a navy 'second to none,' in the slogan of the day. Enabled by the Naval Act of 1916, the program emphasized capital ships and surface warfare fashioned to meet a Japanese threat in the Pacific and to defend the waters of the Western Hemisphere; the war at sea that was actually being fought as part of the war in Europe hinted at the decline of the battleship and the need to counter the threat posed by the submarine.

Germany's renewal of unrestricted submarine warfare led directly to American entry into the war in April 1917, and it was a threat with which the Navy initially was ill-equipped to deal. Naval technologies had also undergone a revolution. Oil replaced coal, naval gunnery had built on prewar advances, and there were further developments in areas such as communications at sea, most of which were only partly absorbed or poorly understood by the Navy in April 1917.

The U.S. Army in 1914 was tiny in comparison to its European counterparts. Like the British, but unlike the major European powers, a general staff model was a recent phenomenon—created in the Root Reforms of 1903 in response to shortcomings revealed in the Spanish–American War. Ranking 17th in the world and with a strength of 135,000, the U.S. Army lacked modern weaponry—tanks, aircraft, chemical weapons, heavy artillery—and modern warfighting experience, the Punitive Expedition notwithstanding. The armies of Europe did not rate it highly, if at all.

By the time the United States entered the war, the strategic direction of the Allied war effort had been decided, and the United States exercised little influence over it (a fact that applied equally to the smaller belligerent powers). The decisive theater for the western Allies (Britain and France, since the Russians were in the process of withdrawing from the war by the middle months of 1917) was the Western Front in France and Belgium, and it was there that the main effort against the main enemy army would continue to be made. Heavily reliant upon the Allies for military equipment, the American Expeditionary Force had little choice about conforming to the broad thrust of Allied strategy.

The Joint Army-Navy Board that had emerged from the 1903 reforms had given the United States the beginnings of national security policy machinery charged with planning for the defense of the United States and the Western Hemisphere, but this had little to do with the conduct of the war in Europe. Herein also lay the early development of the so-called Color plans—contingency planning for war with Germany, with Japan, and even with Britain. Plan Orange, for the conduct of war with Japan in the Pacific, laid the basis for the U.S. Navy's operations in the Pacific War in the *next* generation but had little impact on the conduct of the war about to be fought.

The fighting in 1916 had been enormously costly for the British and French, and the campaigns of 1917 were as bad, if not worse. From the perspective of the Western Allies, the need was for immediate reinforcement of their own, sorely debilitated ranks; London and Paris expressed a preference for American units that could be incorporated and subsumed into their own armies as quickly as possible. This was generally unacceptable to American opinion and policymakers, for several reasons. Having steered a political course that sought to avoid commitment to the war, President Wilson now needed to galvanize American opinion in support of involvement, and this was much easier to do if the American military effort was clearly identifiable. Irish-American opinion was a factor, given the suppression of the 'Easter Rising' in Dublin in 1916 and the ensuing Anglo-Irish War between British forces and the armed wing of Irish Nationalism. Professional military opinion within the United States equally would not accept the implicit slur on its capabilities and standing implied by subordination to the militaries of other nations, especially ones whose achievements to date left room for doubt. As Commander-in-Chief of the American Expeditionary Force, Pershing determined that American arms should play a decisive part in securing the defeat of Germany. Wilson's enunciation of the Fourteen Points as the basis of American war aims likewise implied minimal alignment with the war aims of the Allies, also reflected in the fact that the United States entered the war not as an ally but rather as an associated power.

The recruitment, deployment, and maintenance of the American Expeditionary Force represented the most enormous military challenge in American history to that time and the most complex since the Civil War. Pershing arrived in France with a small staff in late May 1917 and concluded that an American army of at least one million men should be in the field within 12 months, with the ultimate goal of deploying a force of up to three million men in Europe. Three key issues confronted the Army and government in achieving these aims: manpower, force structure, and training, to which could be added equipment, inter-Allied relations, and the selection of an appropriate area of operations. All proved taxing.

European military systems were based on a conscript system, with annual intakes serving lengthy periods of reserve obligation after their conscript service ended. It was this system that had enabled the French, Germans, Russians, and Austro-Hungarians to field such large armies so quickly in the war's opening months. Britain had long relied on an army based on long-service regular enlistments, while the constituent parts of the Empire had no standing forces worth speaking of before the war's outbreak. Such systems, and the rejection of conscription as 'un-British,' could not be sustained in the face of the demands of modern industrial warfare waged by mass armies and replete with mass casualties. By 1916, Britain and the Dominions were forced to embrace conscription, however reluctantly, with all its attendant changes and implications.

In the United States, talk of conscription brought memories of the anti-draft riots during the Civil War. Secretary of War Newton D. Baker implemented a selective service scheme as the basis for American man-power policy, reflected in the Selective Service Act of May 1917. With the decision to conscript in this manner, the Army became a truly national army for the first time, with over 70 percent of its troops drafted, a fact that in turn altered the nature of the Army as an institution. Reflecting the political difficulties that accompanied the decision for war, the Wilson administration placed much of the responsibility for overseeing the draft in civilian rather than military hands and granted generous exemptions.

Personnel demands drive force structure, and initially Army authorities did not envisage raising the mass army that would ultimately take the field by late 1918. Tasked with estimating the resources needed to ship 500,000 troops across the Atlantic, the War College Division of the General Staff concluded in March 1917 that the war would need to continue into 1919 to move beyond naval and economic participation and bring to bear an organized and trained ground force in Europe. The logistical and organi-zational problems of building such an army would be overcome later rather than sooner, so the thinking went. Pershing's headquarters moved to France in June 1917, and from there he planned for an American Expeditionary Force of 30 divisions, numbering around 1.1 million men, for use in a substantial offensive early in 1919 aimed at breaking German resistance and ending the war on Allied terms.

The economic mobilization of the United States in support of such an ambitious and complex undertaking involved creating a partnership between government and business during a period when Progressive-Era government regulation of business was just beginning to take hold. During the war, American industry mainly regulated itself within parameters set by the administration and by Congress, the whole being driven by the enormous and growing demand for materiel emanating from federal government agencies. All of this was overseen by the War Industries Board, itself answerable to Wilson, and various other, mostly competing, agencies. The war provided business and industry with numerous oppor-tunities, both for profit and the enhancement of political and adminis-trative muscle within the private sector. Big business probably economically benefited from the war more than any other segment of American society.

These benefits flowed not only from supplying and underwriting American mobilization but also through the growing economic support of an increasingly financially embattled alliance, principally Britain and France. To take but one example, the war made J. P. Morgan and

Company the world's biggest buyer of goods, one whose purchases for the Allied powers between January 1915 and April 1917 were valued at $3.16 billion in a series of transactions that further involved almost 20,000 other firms in subcontracting roles. Such strong growth *before* the entry of the United States into the war, however, meant that in critical areas of the economy there was little room for fast growth after April 1917; this, in turn, produced distortions in the American economy, at least while the war lasted.

In strategic terms, 1917 was another desperate year for the Allies, with little sign by year's end that the United States was in much of a position to make a difference—the American Expeditionary Force still numbered fewer than 200,000 men in December 1917. The great German offensive of March–April 1918, part of Germany's last strategic gamble to win the war before the American Expeditionary Force could get fully mobilized, was defeated by the weary French and British Empire armies, as well as through strategic miscalculation and overreach on the part of the German High Command.

The relative failure of American mobilization in 1917 prompted changes to both economic and industrial regulation and the capacity of the War Department to deal coherently with business, as well as to the organization of the Army and the system of draft registration and induction. Many of these problems mirrored those in Britain and elsewhere earlier in the war, while the creation of a mass army from scratch in a short space of time taxed every combatant nation that attempted it.

The Allied manpower situation had been difficult at the end of 1917, and following the defeat of the German offensives it was dire. The U.S. Army had generated large numbers of men in uniform but still exercised little real combat power or offensive capability. Its units and formations were much larger than those of their Allied counterparts because of the organizational assumptions under which the Americans operated—battalions included 1,000 men, and divisions numbered over 26,000. The British could transport U.S. soldiers across the Atlantic while the French could equip them; and under extreme military, political, and social pressures after nearly four years of war, they proposed incorporating American units into British and French divisions, in the interests of economy, efficiency, and suspicion of American capabilities. An independent U.S. Army, however, was central to Wilson's desire to dictate the ensuing peace in terms of the Fourteen Points and to remake the old-world order.

The real architect of the independent American military force and the dogged defender of American military reputation was the Commander-in-Chief of the American Expeditionary Force, Pershing. Field Marshal Sir Douglas Haig, commanding the British armies in France, noted Pershing's obstinacy on this point in May 1918, further observing that Pershing wanted an independent command though he had no army, nor even a corps, at the time to command. Still, Pershing could play the role of courtier with Allied commanders and politicians while commanding an army at the same time. Arguably, Pershing was the only American general officer who could command the American Expeditionary Force. Although he did not fully appreciate the tactical situation on the Western Front, few officers in any of the fighting armies did. He had a strong personality, perhaps strengthened by the death of his family in a fire in their home at the Presidio in 1915, and he could be inflexible, impatient, and even ruthless toward his subordinate officers and staff.

Pershing's contemporaries in the Allied high command criticized him because to them he seemed single-minded in his pursuit of American goals at the expense of Allied objectives. Pershing, in some ways, was a flawed commander. His stubborn self-righteousness, his unwillingness to correct initial misconceptions such as those that marred the doctrine and training of the American Expeditionary Force, and his stormy relationship with Allied military and civilian leaders hurt the military and political effectiveness of his army.

The American commitment to an independent American army in France often meant relearning the lessons already paid for in Allied blood. Pershing argued that the American Expeditionary Force should occupy a section of the front to the south of the French, positioned between the Argonne Forest and the Vosges Mountains. The AEF's objective, as he saw it, was to dislodge the Germans around Metz and threaten industrial centers in the Saar valley, without which Germany could not continue the war. This was indeed the eventual area of operations for the American Expeditionary Force, but with it came an implicit assumption (in Pershing's case, explicitly expressed) that operations in this sector would involve 'open warfare' rather than the relentless attritional grind of the trenches associated with the warfare of previous years.

Pershing held the Allied armies in low regard, believing that the American Expeditionary Force had little of value to learn from them; he was altogether wrong. He insisted on high standards of drill, discipline, and marksmanship among American units, which was fine as far as it went, but he missed the point about the value of massed and coordinated fire against area targets rather than the traditional aimed fire against point targets emphasized in American training doctrine. His invocation of the importance of skill with the bayonet was irrelevant and straight out of 1914. Nor did senior American officers always appreciate or understand the need for careful preparation and the evolution of battle techniques within the British and French armies. Pershing dismissed the cautious approach to 'bite and hold' limited-objective offensives that had evolved from bitter experience in the British sector, and he advocated a return to the concept of unlimited assaults—an approach that had died in the other armies, along with many of its proponents, in the war's early years.

As part of the argument within the Allied high command over the utilization of American troops in combat, and their preparation for it, Pershing agreed in early 1918 that six American divisions would be brought to France on British shipping to train with the British and French armies while their equipment caught up with them, after which they would return to the American Expeditionary Force in the summer. Pershing was thus able to concentrate more significant numbers of American soldiers in France more quickly than the American shipping schedules would allow, while the divisions grouped under the American II Corps headquarters were exposed to tactical methods and thinking in advance of anything then being taught in the American Expeditionary Force's schools of instruction.

Still, Pershing remained highly suspicious of Allied intentions toward American units under their temporary command. He refused permission, for example, for the participation of several infantry companies in an attack at Hamel by the Australians, with whom they had been training, on July 4, 1918 (some of the Americans went in anyway). His refusal undoubtedly reflected the renewed pressure for incorporation of American troops into Allied formations during May and June, and also reflected both British and French desperation over manpower and the general state of inter-allied relations at the most senior levels of the Allied high command. Pershing engaged in a great deal of 'horse-trading' with the French, offering short-term reinforcement in exchange for their support in forcing changes to British shipping schedules; doing so enabled him to concentrate more units and formations in France, where he might finally begin to form an American field army more quickly.

This rapid expansion brought additional problems, ones that the British armies, again, had faced in the first half of the war. As Haig had pointed out, large armies consume skilled manpower at an exponential rate, one that the tiny prewar American military was entirely ill-equipped to meet. The obvious solution to this was training. The American Expeditionary Force, like its Allied counterparts, created an elaborate system of schools and courses to train officers, in particular, for both tactical command and higher staff functions. The existing core of prewar regular officers proved to be invaluable, especially those who had received higher-level schooling at the Command and General Staff College and the Army War College; but as the British had also found, there were never enough of these educated officers to go around, and they were generally overrepresented at the senior levels of the American Expeditionary Force. By the end of the war, over 80 percent of chiefs of staff at the army, corps, and division levels were Staff College graduates. Attendance at courses of instruction in France took officers away from their units and formations while they trained, however, and the standard remained uneven in any case. As late as August 1918, senior American staff officers, after reviewing divisions at the front, noted the absence of uniform organization and function among division staffs.

Three elements of the American Expeditionary Force posed additional problems for the high command: the National Guard, the U.S. Marines, and African American soldiers. Regular–militia relations presented all the old difficulties anew, ones to which Pershing was keenly attuned. Some regular Army officers hoped that the war would result in termination of the militia movement once and for all. Neither the Guard nor the War Department was prepared for the remobilization of state forces so soon after the Punitive Expedition. The necessary reorganization of Guard units and formations to conform to that being applied in the American Expeditionary Force led to the merger, disbandment, or conversion of units, with concomitant reduction of responsibilities or loss of command among many citizen officers, all without much regard by regular Army officers toward their Guard brethren.

Unhappiness at their changed circumstances was understandable but also reflected the age-old problem of the provincial nature of the National Guard. Some 12 percent of the wartime army had enlisted as guardsmen, and they made up nearly a fifth of the American Expeditionary Force, but their distinctive identities were erased by and through wartime service, and they never again dominated the army structure. But the National Guard, or at least its political backers, did not go quietly; to rebut criticism of the firing of senior Guard officers from commands in France, Pershing had dossiers compiled to show that relief from command was invariably for cause, and favored neither Guard nor regular officers over the other.

The Marines, as usual, provided magnificent combat soldiers, perhaps at times given to excesses of martial ardor such as at the Battle of Belleau Wood. Two Marine regiments formed a brigade of the 2nd Infantry Division, but the Marine Corps' desire to create a separate Marine division was frustrated by Pershing for institutional and political reasons. It may have been some comfort to the Marines to know that the 4th Brigade represented the single most substantial accrual of combat power in the history of the Corps to that point. The overall strength of the Corps grew from around 10,000 to more than 75,000 during the war.

The experiences of African American soldiers in a persistently 'Jim Crow' military were of a different order entirely. Extreme incidents, such as that of the 1917 race riot in Houston, Texas, involving several African American soldiers, served only to heighten distrust African Americans and whites. In that particular case, a riot began when several African American soldiers tried to assist civilians being mistreated by white police officers. When the violence ended several people had died or been severely injured. Many of the African American soldiers involved were court-martialed for mutiny. Nineteen soldiers were executed, and 41 served prison terms.

Racial prejudice in the American military reflected much peacetime and civilian practice in the United States, although it puzzled many European observers. Both the French and British armies made widespread use of non-white colonial soldiers in combat formations. While racism was institutionalized in both of those armies and the broader societies they represented, British attitudes toward Indian soldiers, for example, conveyed a healthy level of respect and were seldom characterized by the viciousness apparent in race relations within the United States. Indeed, African American soldiers were not the only ones who discovered that there was a much less vicious racial environment in Europe than in the United States: many American jazz musicians, who pursued highly successful careers in Europe from the 1920s to the 1960s, encountered similar experiences.

The Army made a conscious decision to utilize the majority of African American soldiers in noncombatant supporting roles, often as little more than laborers. Attempts at more-or-less complete segregation failed, since African

Figure 10.2 Officers of the 366th Infantry. From left to right: Lieutenant C. L. Abbot, South Dakota; Captain Joseph L. Lowe, Pacific Grove, California; Lieutenant A. R. Fisher, Lyles, Indiana (awarded the Distinguished Service Cross); Captain E. White, Pine Bluff, Arkansas.

Source: National Archives and Records Administration.

American as well as white soldiers found themselves in proximity to each other on troopships, in training camps, and in French urban centers when on leave. Many white soldiers resented this, while many African American soldiers objected to the demeaning status often accorded them. They also objected strenuously, if ineffectively, to how the disciplinary system protected white soldiers who attacked and abused them. The relative social freedom that African American soldiers enjoyed while on leave in France infuriated many Southern whites, as did their open interaction with French women.

More than 200,000 African American soldiers served in Europe as part of the American Expeditionary Force. Only two groups, in the main, had the opportunity to see combat. In a rehearsal of similar problems and outcomes in the Mediterranean theater in the next world war, the Army formed the 92nd Division for active duty, but its men were poorly trained, its officers were divided along racial lines, and its performance at the front was poor. Four regiments formed from existing National Guard divisions—the 369th, 370th, 371st, and 372nd—fought with French formations, including a Moroccan division. Officered mainly by African Americans, these units distinguished themselves repeatedly, with many members receiving French gallantry decorations. The contrast provided by the 92nd Division once again demonstrated that indifferent leadership and inadequate training produces undermotivated and ill-prepared soldiers; it was the 92nd Division that the interwar army remembered, not the regiments in French service. The 92nd Division was raised through a racist process, and its performance reflected the racist context in which it operated.

Women served the American armed forces in unprecedented numbers, mostly as nurses. When the Great War began, the U.S. Army and U.S. Navy already had nurse corps, although the nurses were not allowed full military status until World War II. During World War I, both nurse corps expanded substantially—the Army nurse corps grew from a few hundred to 20,000, while the Navy nurse corps expanded from less than 500 nurses to 1,400 women. Nurses served across the globe, especially Army nurses, in field hospitals, mobile hospital units, and convalescent hospitals. Although noncombatants, they experienced all the horrors of the first truly industrial war. Nurses, just as soldiers, carried the experience through the rest of their lives. A substantial number of nurses were highly decorated, being awarded American and foreign medals. The Army awarded three nurses the Distinguished Service Cross, a combat medal second only to the Medal of Honor.

With the high demand for fighting men, a shortage of administrative personnel posed a challenge. In response, the Secretary of the Navy Josephus Daniels decided to enlist women to fill the gap. In March 1917, the Navy officially began recruiting women as yeomen (unofficially called 'yeomenettes'), and other non-combat, but essential ratings. A year later, the Marine Corps also began enlisting women into similar positions. The

Coast Guard also enlisted women. The War Department refused, however, to accept women into Army ranks except for nurses.

As women showed their mettle, their duties expanded to include work
as translators, recruiters, and in intelligence, with many serving overseas.
Pershing's need for clerical and administrative staff was ultimately filled by
personnel from the United Kingdom's Women's Auxiliary Army Corps as
well as over 5,000 volunteers recruited from American welfare organizations. The latter proved a blessing and a hindrance because the Army had
no authority over these volunteers. While the women contractors and
volunteers were rightly proud of their activities, they were not eligible for
the care or pensions available to uniformed women after the war. Legislation pushed through during World War II eliminated what many considered an injustice by allowing women to enlist in all of the services, thus
allowing them the benefits afforded to all uniformed personnel.

The Fight in 1918

Although the March 1918 offensive is the best known, the Germans
mounted a succession of increasingly weak and unsuccessful assaults
between March and July. These were defeated by the combined efforts
of the British and French armies with minimal assistance from the American Expeditionary Force, although in May the American 1st Division
captured positions around Cantigny while fighting in the French sector of
the front, at the cost of 1,067 casualties. Although ultimately failures,
several of the German post-March offensives placed the Allied armies
under severe pressure. For a week in May–June, the German assault
pushed the outnumbered French and British divisions back across the
Marne to again threaten Paris. The American 2nd Division, which
included the Marine regiments, and the 3rd Division were temporarily
placed under French command to defend the crossings at Château-
Thierry.

The advent of the oversized American division made a considerable
difference to a faltering and demoralized French defense. It was during this
consolidation of the defensive positions that a Marine famously responded
to a French order to withdraw with 'Retreat, hell. We just got here.'
Going over to the attack, the Marine brigade assaulted and took Belleau
Wood at the cost of 1,087 casualties and then beat back German counter-
attacks for a further 20 days through most of June, while suffering a total
of 5,200 casualties, including 750 killed. These casualties amounted to
more than half the brigade's strength.

The Marines received the bulk of the publicity because of an American
Expeditionary Force policy that prohibited press mention of specific units
or branches of the Army, even though the other brigade in the 2nd
Division, the Army's 3rd Brigade, suffered 3,200 casualties of its own in
the fighting in this sector. Heavy losses in such grueling fights for

otherwise unimportant positions were inevitable (and incurred by all combatant armies), but it is equally clear that senior officers in the 2nd Division paid less attention to careful artillery preparation than their experience on the Western Front warranted and perhaps placed too high a reliance on 'vigor' and a willingness to keep going forward when heavy and sustained casualties suggested otherwise.

The period from late July 1918 to the end of the war in November is called the Hundred Days Offensive, during which the Allied armies mounted a series of offensives that broke through successive German defensive lines, pushed German formations back into a rolling series of retreats, and culminated in the defeat of the German Army in the field to the extent that Germany agreed to an armistice in November. It was during this final phase of the war that the American Expeditionary Force began to come into its own, certainly as an independent and increasingly powerful military presence on the front lines. American divisions took a leading part in the French offensive along the Aisne and Marne rivers in late July, negating earlier German advances. French tanks in significant numbers assisted the American assaults toward Soissons, which were otherwise characterized by lack of artillery preparation, breakdowns in communications, and tactical ineptness. The French, however, took notice of their American brothers in arms, noting that their courage often bordered on recklessness. This remained a valid criticism to the war's end.

Figure 10.3 The Western Front 1918.

The American 1st Army, comprising five French and 15 American divisions, was activated on August 10, in an unambiguous communication of Pershing's long-held resolve to maintain American independence in the field. He was less successful, however, in persuading the British and French to accept his strategic conception for its use. The St. Mihiel Offensive was intended originally to reduce the salient in that area and drive toward German positions around Metz; these objectives were reduced when the Supreme Commander, Marshal Ferdinand Foch, accepted Haig's plan for an envelopment of the German Army that required U.S. forces to drive north through the Meuse-Argonne region and cut German communications around Sedan. The resulting offensive eliminated the salient. This success, however, came at the loss of 7,000 U.S. casualties while inflicting some 17,000 on the Germans (most of them prisoners). The campaign further exposed shortcomings in command, staff work, and appreciation of what was actually possible in an offensive, even in the latter days of the war.

Over a million American troops, most of whom lacked combat experience, fought in the Meuse-Argonne Offensive. This inexperience combined with a stubborn German defense to cause severe casualties. The offensive demonstrated both the strengths and weaknesses of the American Expeditionary Force. Few of the divisions that took part in the initial assaults were combat-experienced; in at least one division—the 79th—half the enlisted men had been in uniform for less than six months. Senior commanders and staffs were generally good, but there remained weaknesses in command and administration at lower levels, compounded by disparities in training.

By mid-October, the defensive lines of the *Kriemhilde Stellung* had been taken, and with the activation of the U.S. 2nd Army, Pershing relinquished the cumbersome 'dual hatting' system that had seen him commanding both the American Expeditionary Force and the field army rather than fulfilling his duties as head of a national expeditionary army. The commanders of the two field armies, Generals Hunter Liggett and Robert L. Bullard, were able and experienced officers of considerable attainment.

The hard slogging and heavy casualties in the first phase of the offensive earned criticism and snide remarks from some of the Allied high command, but the genuine difficulties experienced by American formations reflected both weaknesses specific to the American Expeditionary Force and the challenges of coming to terms with the tactical and operational challenges of the Western Front. In the war's last days, the 1st Army reached positions around Sedan while the 2nd Army launched assaults toward Metz, as Pershing had initially intended. Hammered from three directions by Allied armies, and with manpower losses long past the critical point, the German government sued for an armistice, which came into effect on November 11. This final phase of the war cost the American Expeditionary Force more than 26,000 dead and close to 100,000 wounded.

Figure 10.4 Gun crew from 23rd Infantry, firing a 37mm gun during an advance against German positions, 1918.

Source: National Archives and Records Administration.

The Navy in the Great War

The war at sea tends not to receive the attention often lavished on the Western Front, but the control of sea lines of communications and the neutralizing of the German fleet by the Royal Navy were critical to the Allies' capacity to fight and win the war. The ability of the American Expeditionary Force to take the field at all was dependent on sea transportation, and the greatest threat to this was posed by the successive German submarine offensives blockading Britain and attempting to cut the sea links across the Atlantic. Although the threat posed by the submarine, both potential and actual, should have been clear following German successes in 1915, the 'battleship mentality' was still predominant within the senior ranks of the U.S. Navy when the nation went to war in 1917.

Senior American naval opinion was by no means entirely backward-looking. In particular, while on a special mission to the Admiralty in London in March 1917, Admiral William S. Sims, serving as president of the Naval War College at the time, argued forcefully in support of those

British naval officers who advocated a convoy system as the key to defeating the submarine menace. Experimental convoying in May 1917 proved the point, and after that, the U.S. Navy and merchant fleet contributions to the convoy system and the anti-submarine campaign were fundamental to Allied success in this dimension of the war. The American industrial effort provided dramatically more numbers of merchant vessels and escort ships, and American ships played an important part in laying the mine barrage in the North Sea between Scotland and Norway to restrict German submarines' freedom of movement. The U.S. Navy increased to an unprecedented size of almost half a million men and over 2,000 ships, ranging from simple transports to battleships.

As Commander of U.S. Naval Forces Operating in European Waters, Sims had his headquarters in London, with a large staff and constant interaction with his British counterparts. This was not how the U.S. Navy had initially conceived of its role in the war, planning instead to safeguard the coastal waters of the Western Hemisphere, but it reflected the reality of the naval war in the latter years of the conflict and the pressing needs of the Allied war effort. Aircraft were also pressed into embryonic service in the anti-submarine campaign. The U.S. Navy's principal role—safeguarding convoys—was not the glamorous 'big ship' mission envisaged by many before the war, but it was a vital contribution to winning the war at sea.

The American Air War

If the war at sea failed in large part to realize the aspirations of that generation of naval officers, the same could not be said of the war in the air. In common with other Western militaries, American forces had begun to develop military aviation capabilities before 1914, but these were still nascent when the United States entered the war three years later. Young Americans keen to fly impatiently volunteered for service with the Royal Flying Corps and the French aerial service (in the latter case forming the Lafayette Escadrille) before the United States entered the war, and subsequently provided a small core of combat-experienced aircrew to the American Expeditionary Force's Air Service. Like its British counterpart, this service quickly became the plaything of ambitious and influential personalities, including Colonel Billy Mitchell, relatively young and junior in rank due to the lack of a prewar senior officer corps interested in what many before the war derided as a 'pastime' with little military application.

Like much of the rest of the American Expeditionary Force, the Air Service only really made an impression at the front from the middle of 1918, and while its wartime expansion was both rapid and exponential, its roles and missions emphasized reconnaissance and countering the threat posed by German fighters rather than offensive action through aerial bombardment. In this, the visionaries in its ranks shared many of the frustrations of their wartime comrades in the British Royal Air Force, which, thanks to the efforts of General Hugh Trenchard, had become an independent service in the British military. Still, the American flyers provided good propaganda for the folks at home. Aces—like race-car driver Eddie Rickenbacker, who shot down 26 German planes—became celebrities.

Impact of the AEF in the Great War

In intervening in the First World War, the United States had mounted a massive effort in its own terms, but one that impressed its war-weary and sorely damaged allies much less than it did many Americans. From their perspective, the Americans entered late and did relatively little, which was both fair and wrong in roughly equal measures. The 60,000 combat deaths suffered by American forces paled beside those incurred by the French, Russians, or British; and the United States had known neither enemy occupation nor the devastation of countryside and infrastructure fought over repeatedly; neither aerial bombardment nor the bitter aftermath of defeat, collapse, and revolution. American intervention in the affairs of the 'Old World' in 1917–1919, and the beginnings of the shift in economic, military, and diplomatic power that this presaged, did not necessarily impress the other victorious powers who met at Versailles in 1919 to divide the spoils.

U.S. forces took part in the occupation of the Rhineland in western Germany alongside the French and British, reaching a high of 262,000 troops in February 1919. When it became clear that there would be no civil disturbances in the occupied areas and that the German government would, however reluctantly, sign the Treaty of Versailles, the demobilization of the American Expeditionary Force (AEF) in Germany began in earnest; by November 1919, there were only 15,000 American soldiers left in Germany, and all remaining U.S. troops had departed the occupied zone by January 1923, their responsibilities assumed by the French. Those not tasked with occupation duties looked forward to speedy repatriation and demobilization in the United States, and like the soldiers of every army that had traveled from outside Europe, were frustrated by the shortage of shipping and conflicting priorities for its use.

Pershing initially insisted on maintaining wartime standards and requirements and the substitution of drill for purposeful military activity; this not only made him profoundly unpopular but severely affected morale in a climate where soldiers in some armies were staging protests and even mutinies in response to the apparent dilatoriness and lack of concern for their welfare exhibited by the high command. Pershing soon relented and introduced sports and educational programs, in line with the British and Empire armies also waiting homeward shipment. The majority of American soldiers did not leave

Europe until the spring of 1919. Once the repatriation process got underway, however, the shipment of troops accelerated rapidly; the last combat division sailed from France for the United States in August of that year, although the last Americans did not depart until the beginning of 1920.

The 'war to end all wars' was, of course, nothing of the sort. Wars never end tidily. Even before the armistice, the Allies—the United States included—found themselves being dragged into Russian affairs following the October revolution that brought the Bolsheviks to power, initially at least in the major urban centers. Opposition to Communist rule by a loose and often conflicting coalition of non-Communist, nationalist, and monarchist elements grouped under the label of 'White Russians' dragged the country into a horrendous civil war that lasted until the early 1920s.

American forces were committed in two distinct theaters and for two different reasons. The 339th Infantry regiment and supporting units, about 5,000 men in total, were deployed to North Russia as part of an allied expeditionary force initially designed to prevent the vast stockpiles of military supplies stored there to support the old tsarist army from falling into German hands. Inevitably, the American contingent, under British command, became drawn into the murky processes of the civil war in

Figure 10.5 American soldiers in front of a blockhouse, near Archangel, North Russia, 1919.

Source: Library of Congress.

support of the Whites; the American units saw considerable, if sporadic, action against Soviet forces in the area, as their casualties of 139 killed and 266 wounded attested. They also suffered from poor morale and discipline problems after the armistice came into effect because they were not withdrawn from Russia until the summer of 1919 and had to endure the harsh Russian winter while waiting to be relieved.

Another 9,000 men of the 27th and 31st Infantry Regiments and supporting units were committed to Siberia at the same time, initially in what could be described as the first occasion on which the United States used military force in support of purely diplomatic ends. In addition to assisting the Czech Legion, whose efforts to get eastward to a warm-water port and take ships to Europe to fight the Germans and Austro-Hungarians had captured the popular imagination in the United States, the American role in the intervention in Siberia also was intended to deter Japanese expansionist tendencies in the region. Inevitably, again, the intervention force became involved in the civil war in aid of the White armies, although it saw much less combat than did outside forces elsewhere in Russian territory. The Americans there suffered 35 killed and 52 wounded. They were withdrawn in early 1920 after the Whites in the area collapsed, leaving the Japanese to meddle in Russian affairs for several more years until they, too, withdrew following the Red victory in the Russian civil war.

Conclusion

American involvement in the Great War was far more important to and for Americans than for anyone else, but this is true mainly because the war ended when it did in November 1918. Had the war gone on into 1919, as some senior Allied figures at the time certainly believed likely, then the weight of American numbers and the sharp increase in American combat capability that was the inevitable fruit of broader experience would have proven irresistible, coupled of course with the rapid decline in German manpower stocks and military effectiveness that would have benefited Allied arms generally. Pershing, in fact, lamented that the war ended in 1918 because, in his estimation, the American Expeditionary Force was just approaching maturity as a capable fighting force when the armistice suddenly ended the fighting.

Pershing was unmistakably the creator of the American Expeditionary Force, and it bore his stamp, for both good and ill. The experience of the American Expeditionary Force, and the disastrous military and exceedingly slow industrial mobilization, greatly affected American military and mobilization plans in World War II. The Great War experience of the Army and the Navy would have implications for the peacetime development of American arms in the war's aftermath and through the long, and sometimes bitter, years of peace. Their fullest fruit, as in other armies, would not be harvested until the next world war.

Further Reading

Axelrod, Alan. *Miracle at Belleau Wood: The Birth of the Modern U.S. Marine Corps.* Guilford, CT: Lyons Press, 2018.

Dumenil, Lynn. *The Second Line of Defense: American Women and World War I.* Chapel Hill, NC: University of North Carolina Press, 2019.

Faulkner, Richard S. *The School of Hard Knocks: Combat Leadership in the American Expeditionary Forces.* College Station, TX: Texas A & M University Press, 2012.

Grotelueschen, Mark E. *The AEF Way of War: The American Army and Combat in World War I.* New York: Cambridge University Press, 2007.

Halpern, Paul G. *A Naval History of World War I.* Annapolis, MD: Naval Institute Press, 1994.

Harris, Stephen L., and Rod Paschall. *Harlem's Hell Fighters: The African-American 369th Infantry in World War I.* Lincoln, NE: University of Nebraska Press, 2005.

Keene, Jennifer. *Doughboys, the Great War, and the Remaking of America.* Baltimore, MD: Johns Hopkins University Press, 2001.

Sarnecky, Mary T. *A History of the US Army Nurse Corps.* Philadelphia, PA: University of Pennsylvania Press, 1999.

Williams, Chad L. *Torchbearers of Democracy: African American Soldiers in the World War I Era.* Chapel Hill, NC: University of North Carolina Press, 2013.

Yockelson, Mitchell A. *Borrowed Soldiers: Americans under British Command, 1918.* Norman, OK: University Press of Oklahoma, 2008.

11 Learning and Preparing
The 1920s and 1930s

Introduction

The Great War of 1914–1918 forced several nations to reconsider their diplomatic and military traditions. Disgusted and ashamed of the death and destruction of four years of total industrialized warfare, the great powers sought ways to prevent such a war from happening again. The world had changed for the European powers, for Japan, and perhaps most dramatically for the United States. Even though the United States Senate had rejected the Treaty of Versailles and President Woodrow Wilson's League of Nations, the United States was far from isolationist following the war. Instead of being bound by treaty to a collective security arrangement that might not be in its best interests, the United States pursued diplomatic and military policies that allowed for unilateral action while using multilateral approaches when necessary. Following this trend, the United States would be a leader in the disarmament movement of the 1920s but would also slowly increase its own military capabilities to unprecedented levels.

The war in Europe stretched American military and industrial mobilization to its organizational limits, with less-than-spectacular results. During the 1920s and 1930s, the United States would develop new strategies to improve both systems in case of another conflict. Despite having fought a war for the first time on European soil, the United States continued to see the Atlantic and Pacific Oceans as its vast security moat and continued to invest heavily in capital ships. The advent of airplane technology, however, forced the United States to incorporate this power of seemingly unlimited potential into its arsenal and develop doctrine regarding its use in war.

Postwar Duties

The sudden end to the war in November 1918 sped up plans for demobilizing the massive force that the United States had built mostly from scratch in 1917. The problem with disbanding such a large army was finding a rate of discharging servicemen that brought the boys home as soon as practicable but did not do undue harm to the American economy or endanger postwar occupation responsibilities. War industries also demobilized and returned to peacetime production. Because industrial mobilization had been so slow and somewhat disorganized, war industries had just approached peak production levels when the war abruptly ended. Thus, vast surpluses of equipment, weapons, ammunition, and other war materiel packed bulging warehouses at the end of the war. The War Department decided to maintain a large amount of this equipment for future use, especially for outfitting the Guard and Reserve. An unintended consequence of maintaining this circa-1918 equipment, however, was that throughout the 1920s and 1930s the military was slow to procure new, more modern weapons and other equipment.

With its demobilized force, the Army still had duties to perform. It continued to patrol the Mexican border and help quell domestic disturbances. In addition to assisting local law enforcement in restoring order in some of the violent race riots, the Army dispersed the controversial Bonus Army in Washington in the summer of 1932. Overriding President Calvin Coolidge's earlier veto, in May 1924 Congress had passed the World War Adjusted Compensation Act to give veterans of the Great War a one-time bonus payment of up to $500 for domestic service and a maximum of $625 for serving overseas. Each qualified veteran was issued a bonus certificate that could be redeemed upon maturation in 20 years. With over 3.6 million veterans eligible to receive payments, the government had to build a trust fund of over $3.64 billion, over $53 billion in today's dollars, to cover the disbursement. By 1931, a veteran could borrow against half of the certificate's value, but with the Great Depression deepening each passing month, more veterans began calling for Congress to authorize early redemption of the full amount of the certificates.

The American Legion, Veterans of Foreign Wars, and other veterans' groups added their weight to the call for early payment. By June 1932, over 17,000 veterans, their families, and other protesters had descended upon Washington, D.C., making camp in a well-organized 'Hooverville' on Anacostia Flats. While the House of Representatives passed a bill authorizing early payment, the Senate on June 17 defeated a similar measure. While the Bonus Army marchers had been mostly peaceful, the atmosphere grew tense. On June 28, Washington, D.C., police attempted to disperse the marchers, who resisted. Police shot several protesters, two of whom, both veterans, later died from their wounds. Based upon FBI Director J. Edgar Hoover's fear of anarchists believed to have infiltrated the Bonus Army camp, President Herbert Hoover ordered Army Chief of Staff General Douglas MacArthur to break up the Bonus Army's camp. MacArthur himself commanded the force of 600 troops, including a cavalry regiment commanded by Major George Patton, as it moved in on the camp with tear gas and fixed bayonets. Much of the shantytown burned to the ground, and several shoving matches between the regulars and the veterans broke out. One of MacArthur's aides, Major Dwight Eisenhower, objected to MacArthur participating in breaking up the camp but to no avail. It was a controversial event from which the Army, and MacArthur in particular, took some time to recover. In 1936,

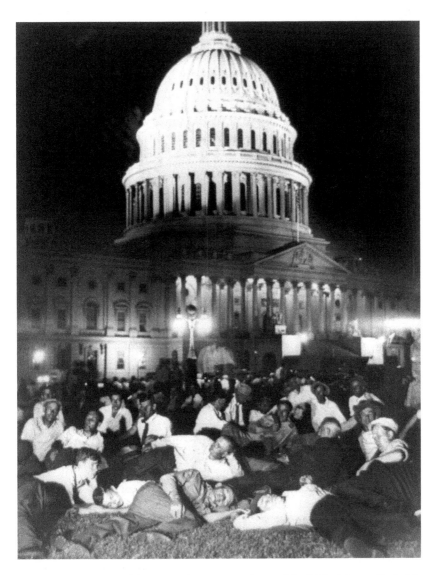

Figure 11.1 Members of the Bonus Army on the lawn of the United States Capitol in Washington, D.C., 1932.

Source: Library of Congress.

Congress passed the Adjusted Compensation Payment Act, which authorized payment of the bonus certificates.

In a more positive development, the Army coordinated the Civilian Conservation Corps (CCC), one of President Franklin Roosevelt's New Deal work programs to ease the effects of the Great Depression. In 1933, the Army helped run more than 1,000 camps across the United States for over 250,000 young men participating in the CCC. While the Army was lukewarm to performing this duty, thousands of officers gained invaluable organizational and managerial experience in running the camps. Although the CCC did not significantly affect the economic crisis, it did pay thousands of unemployed young men a subsistence wage, complete beneficial public works projects, and give the American people a sense that the federal government was at least trying to alleviate the effects of the Great Depression. Perhaps most significantly, during World War II, men who worked for the CCC were fast-tracked to the rank of corporal and sergeant due to their experience in working with regular and reserve officers in the CCC.

The Army of the United States

The American experience in the Great War convinced many in military and political circles that the military establishment needed a significant overhaul. The expansible army concept, dating back to the early nineteenth century, had not worked well in the massive mobilization effort required in 1917. Industrialized warfare required new and improved military organization. In 1920, Congress passed a new National Defense Act that radically altered the organizational structure of the Army and provided for a better-trained and better-prepared military force should war again threaten the United States.

The National Defense Act of 1920 created what it called the Army of the United States, which included a Regular Army of professionals, a civilian-based National Guard, and an Organized Reserve of both officers and enlisted personnel. The new Regular Army had an authorized strength of over 17,000 officers and 280,000 enlisted personnel—although throughout the 1920s and into the early 1930s, lack of a real security threat and then the Great Depression kept the Army at well below its authorized strength. Included in the Army were new air, chemical warfare, and finance branches.

The Army would be administered through a general staff system, much like the one that Pershing had used in commanding the American Expeditionary Force in France. The War Department would be responsible for mobilization and war planning, dividing the responsibilities between the Chief of Staff and the Secretary of War's office. In 1921, Pershing became Chief of Staff and reorganized the General Staff into specific divisions: G-1 was for personnel; G-2 handled intelligence; G-3 trained troops and conducted operations; and G-4 organized logistics and supply. Pershing also added a War Plans Division to carry out planning functions mandated by the National Defense Act.

The new Army would be spread across nine commands, or corps, each with one regular, two National Guard, and three Reserve divisions. Also, the Army established military departments in Panama, Hawaii, and the Philippines. Because the Army was under strength, many tactical units remained skeletal, while some only existed on paper. With new mobilization plans, however, National Guard and Reserve units could quickly fill out the Army to more than two million men in a matter of just a few months. Thus, while the expansible army concept remained, it was much better organized, trained, and outfitted than it had been in the nineteenth century.

The new National Guard became a vital component of the Army of the United States, one that both addressed defense needs and reassured states that their right to maintain a militia had not been eroded by the 1917 mobilization of state guard units. The National Defense Act authorized a National Guard of over 400,000 troops, but throughout the 1920s the National Guard typically maintained only about 180,000. The massive surplus of materiel after the war made equipping Guard units quite easy. Regular Army officers trained Guard units, including 48 times a year at their respective armories and for two weeks each year in the field. Importantly, the National Defense Act required the Army staff to include Guard and Reserve officers, providing invaluable training and experience as well as input into planning and policies affecting the Guard and Organized Reserve.

The National Guard and regular Army were augmented by the Reserves, also established by the National Defense Act. The Organized Reserve did not experience the postwar prestige that came with Guard service but nonetheless provided continued training and readiness for thousands of men, mostly veterans of the Great War, who already had military training and experience. More successful was the Officers' Reserve Corps, made up of veteran officers as well as a steady stream of newly commissioned officers. Later, in 1940 and 1941, such a large pool of trained soldiers made mobilization for World War II much more effective and efficient.

While the Military Academy at West Point remained the more elite and prestigious officer commissioning institution for the Army, the Reserve Officer Training Corps (ROTC) and the Citizens' Military Training Camp program (CMTC) became the primary training ground for commissioning new officers. The National Defense Act increased the number of ROTC programs at colleges and universities across the United States. Over 325 schools had ROTC programs by 1928, commissioning over 6,000 new second lieutenants annually. The CMTC worked through summer training camps rather than colleges and universities. Completing a four-week summer training camp each year for four years qualified one for commissioning in the Reserves. Over 30,000 participated in this alternative commissioning program. Both the ROTC and CMTC greatly helped the Army maintain its officer needs for the Reserves and the National Guard, as well as for the regular Army.

Professional military education in the Army was reinvigorated to levels not seen since the 1880s. In addition to officer training programs at West Point and in ROTC programs across the United States, over 30 Army schools provided specialized training for most branches of the Army. Primarily directed toward officers, these schools educated not only regular officers but officers from the Reserves and Guard components as well. Like the professional military education schools in Great Britain and Germany, the U.S. Army Command and General Staff College, the Army War College, and the Army Industrial College provided advanced education and training to more senior officers. The purpose of these schools was to produce competent officers who could command at various levels during war rather than to allow for in-depth study of war theory. Career officers in the Army, Guard, and Reserves were among the best-educated and trained in the world.

Perhaps the greatest weakness of the Army of the United States was its lack of interest in armor during the 1920s. Infantry, with its rifles and bayonets, remained the 'Queen of Battle,' as it had under Pershing's command in France during the Great War. Despite the impact of new tank technology, Army strategists saw little use for the vehicles beyond infantry support. As a consequence, the infantry absorbed the Tank Corps after the war. Little valuable research and development funds went toward tank warfare. Only one experimental tank brigade existed during the 1930s, and as World War II approached, the Army had only four mechanized units.

Great Britain and Germany, on the other hand, recognized the tank's strategic and tactical potential in combat operations. Convinced that armor could operate as mechanized units on a battlefield and break through enemy lines, British military leaders gave armor a role independent of infantry support. Germany pioneered tank tactics by concentrating large but fast armor units to achieve a sort of 'shock and awe' impact on the enemy. Ideas and techniques developed in concert with the Soviet Red Army in the 1920s during the so-called 'Black Reichswehr' period gave both the Germans and Soviets a distinct edge in armor doctrine and practice. While the British, Germans, and Soviets developed new, faster, and more lethal tanks and other armored vehicles during the 1920s and 1930s, the United States did comparatively little. Equally, the financial strictures of the 1930s imposed severe interruptions for developments in all Western armies, while political interference in the Soviet Union mostly killed innovation there in the same period.

Doctrine for Airpower

The rapid advancement of aviation technology during and after the Great War challenged airpower advocates and detractors alike. The Army's traditional role as land force and the Navy's time-honored function as ocean fleet did not allow for the smooth integration of aircraft into their strategic or operational thinking. Airpower enthusiasts went so far as to suggest that armies would be obsolete, as aircraft alone could bring an industrialized nation-state to its knees through strategic bombing. The main disagreements centered on how airpower should be used.

Among these enthusiasts were British General Sir Hugh Trenchard, Italian Air Chief Guilio Douhet, and American Brigadier General Billy Mitchell. Trenchard had been instrumental in establishing the Royal Air Force as an independent service and served as the first Chief of the Air Staff in 1917. Douhet wrote extensively on the use of airpower and theorized that bombers targeting civilian populations, in addition to industrial targets, could force such political chaos in a country to make its government come to terms. Wars would be shorter and ultimately less destructive, which was precisely the remedy that war-weary people sought after the seemingly endless slaughter of the Great War. Critics, however, rightly questioned the ethics of bombing civilians.

General Mitchell enthusiastically shared these ideas. Typical of bureaucratic organizations the Army and Navy resisted radical change and instead promoted a more conservative doctrine that aircraft could be useful in supporting air and naval operations through missions involving the pursuit of enemy aircraft, bombardment of enemy positions, attack on enemy forces in battle, observation of enemy troop movements, and artillery support. There was no concept of joint Army and Navy air operations and only minimal thought given to how airpower could be used to repel a seaborne invasion of the United States. Mitchell, on the other hand, radically suggested that airpower alone could not only defend the United States but win future wars in which land and sea forces would be obsolete.

Like Trenchard, Mitchell wanted an independent air force that would train, maintain, and operate all American military air assets, and more controversially overtake the Navy's fleet as America's first line of defense. To Mitchell, spending more money building battleships took funding away from building his independent air force. To gain support for his radical ideas, Mitchell boldly dared the Navy to allow Army aircraft to attack a battleship. Mitchell hoped to prove once and for all that battleships were devastatingly vulnerable in the new age of air. The Navy had already conducted staged-air attacks against mothballed vessels in 1920 and 1921, but eagerly accepted Mitchell's challenge. Off the Virginia Capes in 1921, Mitchell got his chance as the Army and Navy agreed to a demonstration as part of a more substantial joint exercise. Using a stationary, unmanned German battleship, the *Ostfriesland*, as his target, Mitchell organized a squadron of Army bombers from Langley Field to 'attack' the battleship. The Navy had set strict rules to guide the experiment. Only one bomb could be dropped at a time. After each bomb drop, investigators would board the ship to examine the damage, if any. Mitchell probably never had any intention of following these rules. Dropping over sixty 2,000-pound bombs at the anchored vessel, the Army bombers scored 16 direct hits, none of which were strictly observed by the Navy board of investigators according to the predetermined rules. Mitchell sank the battleship, but he and the Navy disagreed on the meaning of the result. Mitchell claimed his point proven—battleships were vulnerable to air attack. The Navy rightly claimed that Mitchell's test had been in a controlled environment. The weather was perfect, the ship at anchor, and no anti-aircraft fire dissuaded the attacking bombers. For the Navy, Mitchell had just proven how difficult it would be for aircraft to successfully attack a battleship, much less a fleet of warships.

Mitchell was a maverick who enjoyed talking to the press. When the War Department and Navy Department would not yield to what seemed to him overwhelming evidence of air superiority, he went to the public to plead his case. In an attempt to at least quiet the outspoken aviator, the War Department transferred Mitchell to San Antonio, Texas, in 1925, demoting him from his wartime rank of brigadier general to colonel, an act many considered a punishment for Mitchell's increasingly outspoken support of airpower. He had already flirted with insubordination against his superiors, but in September 1925, he crossed it for good. On the morning of September 3, the Navy airship *Shenandoah* crashed during a storm in Ohio, adding to a string of recent air accidents. Fourteen crewmen were killed. Outraged at what he considered needless loss of life, Mitchell spoke to the press, going so far as to claim the Army and Navy were incompetent, even criminally negligent. The Army charged Mitchell with insubordination. His court-martial was a public sensation. Convicted, Mitchell resigned his commission in the hope of being able to promote airpower unhindered by a military chain of command.

Mitchell's was not a voice in the wilderness, just too radical a one. Many in the Army and Navy, as well as in Congress, recognized the importance of airpower to future conflict. Still, Congress and a special investigating board appointed by President Calvin Coolidge rejected the idea of an independent air force. Whatever air development would come would be done under the current military structure.

Unconnected to Mitchell's pleas for an independent air arm, Congress did create the Army Air Corps in 1926, with an authorized strength of over 17,000 officers and men and 1,800 aircraft. Congress also instituted a five-year expansion and modernization program for the Air Corps. This program paid reliable dividends, for, throughout the 1930s, Army aircraft improved in both type and efficiency; and by the beginning of World War II, the United States indeed had one of the best air forces in the world. Moreover, by creating an Army Air Corps, Congress had removed the stigma of air service in the Army and helped establish a culture open to sound strategic and tactical ideas. By the late 1930s, the Army Air Corps Tactical School thrived at Maxwell Field in Alabama, training a generation of tactical and strategic air thinkers that would have much success in

Figure 11.2 General Billy Mitchell at his court-martial, 1925.
Source: United States Air Force.

World War II and beyond. It is intriguing that the Army ultimately advocated airpower but did not exercise similar enthusiasm for armor.

Naval aviation did not experience the Army's internal and public travails in seeking a mission for airpower. The Naval Air Service had been created in 1917 and understandably blossomed during the war to over 50,000 officers and men with over 2,000 land- and sea-based aircraft. After the war, the Navy issued a doctrinal statement that called for a Naval Air Service capable of accompanying and protecting the fleet wherever it might be in the world.

Mitchell's highly publicized sinking of the *Ostfriesland* inspired and even converted some senior naval officers, such as Admirals William Fullam and William S. Sims, to the notion that maritime airpower had a role in fleet operations. Sims had already studied what might happen if two fleets of equal strength in capital ships faced each other, with one side having more aircraft carriers than the other. He concluded that the superiority lay with the fleet that had more aircraft carriers. Air superiority at sea would expose the enemy's fleet to massive air assault and battleship bombardment, the combination of which would be decisive. At a public demonstration of military aircraft in San Diego, Fullam noted how easily ships in San Diego Bay could have been destroyed. With the strong support of the Navy's Chief of Aeronautics, Rear Admiral William A. Moffett, the Navy built its first carrier, the *Langley*, from a converted collier. The carriers *Lexington* and *Saratoga* were both converted heavy cruisers.

The Navy wholeheartedly embraced airpower as a complement to fleet operations. Congress increased budgets for naval aviation, adding more planes to the fleet. New carriers were built. At the Naval Academy at Annapolis, students received aeronautical instruction, including flight and navigation training, and air service billets grew to equal the importance of sea duty. Naval aviators even became celebrities. It had been a Navy pilot—Lieutenant Commander A. C. Read, flying a Curtis airplane—who made the first transatlantic flight (Newfoundland to the Azores to Portugal) in 1919. The polar explorer Commander Richard E. Byrd flew over the North Pole in 1926 and over the South Pole in 1928. Navy flyers routinely won the air races and competitions that were so popular across the United States in the 1920s.

First Line of Defense: the Fleet

The Navy remained the first line of defense for the continental United States. The notion of a navy second to none, heralded by the Navy Act of 1916, remained in place after the war. The Naval Act of 1919 was intended to continue the building program of the prewar 1916 act. But in the postwar disarmament environment, both the United States and Great Britain, the world's leading naval power, considered the financial cost of expanding their navies and agreed in principle to some sort of naval limitation to avoid setting off another arms race.

Moreover, some naval strategists began to question the Mahanian focus on the battleship fleet as the primary means of naval maneuver. The devastating use of submarines by Germany and the advent of military aviation during the war could indeed ultimately make battleships obsolete, as Mitchell believed he had demonstrated. As had been the case in the past, however, overcoming traditional doctrine with new technology proved extremely difficult.

With the American and British fleets still building new ships, and Japan solidifying its position as a naval power in the western Pacific, representatives from the United States, Great Britain, Japan, France, Italy, China, Belgium, the Netherlands, and Portugal met in Washington in late 1921 to discuss the concept of limiting naval arms and maintaining the balance of power in Asia and the Pacific. It is worth noting that the idea of scrapping American battleships already under construction and limiting future building came from the State Department, not the Navy Department. Nonetheless, the idea of arms reduction struck a popular chord in the postwar world.

Three agreements came from the Washington Naval Conference of 1921–1922. First, Great Britain, the United States, Japan, France, and Italy agreed to a naval limitation treaty based upon a tonnage ratio of

5:5:3:1.7:1.7, respectively, for battleships and, interestingly, aircraft carriers. The so-called Five-Power Treaty also called for a ten-year moratorium on building battleships and cruisers. The agreement recognized that Great Britain and the United States had more extensive geographic and economic security interests and that Japan had significant regional security interests, though Japan protested its relegation as a second-rate power in the agreement. Great Britain, the United States, France, and Japan also signed the Four-Power Treaty that called for a conference of the signatories to settle any disputes over possessions in the Far East. Finally, the Nine-Power Treaty obligated each signatory to respect the Open Door policy in China, in what turned out to be a vain attempt to recognize the territorial integrity and sovereignty of China.

The United States Navy came out of the Washington Naval Conference in comparative shipshape, considering the age of the British fleet and the relatively small size of the Japanese Imperial Navy. To meet the stipulations of the treaty, the Navy had to scrap 15 old battleships, most of which would have been decommissioned regardless of the agreement. Additionally, two new ships and several in various stages of construction had to be dismantled, many of which might not have otherwise seen the sea because of congressional budget cuts. The primary purpose of the accord was to prevent the United States, Great Britain, and Japan from having the overall naval strength to conduct offensive operations in the Pacific. The treaties served an entirely preventive purpose. The Washington Naval Conference had a Wilsonian aspect, as the United States used a multilateral agreement to collectively prevent another world war—or at least a fight in the Pacific, a prospect that many post-Great War strategists feared.

The U.S. Navy in the 1920s, then, was built around the Five-Power Treaty and, in fact, was under the strength allowed in the agreement by as much as 35 percent. The money saved from the treaty limitations, however, allowed the Navy to significantly improve the quality of its fleet at the expense of quantity. In 1933, the Navy boasted only 100 ships and submarines, crewed by 90,000 officers and men.

A 1927 conference at Geneva to further limit cruisers and place limitations on destroyers and submarines came and went without an agreement. In 1930, however, such restrictions were agreed upon at the London Naval Conference. In addition to placing new limitations on cruisers, destroyers, and submarines, the London agreement extended the ten-year capital shipbuilding moratorium to 1936. If any of the signatories believed its security under threat from another nation, however, it could suspend its part of the agreement and add more ships. But if one of the signatories pulled out or broke the deal and built more ships or increased tonnage, the rest of the signatories could do likewise. If one country suspended or broke the agreement, then the whole thing was off.

All of the signatories assuredly violated the spirit of the naval accords, but Japan openly broke the treaties in the early 1930s when it began expanding its sphere of influence in Asia and the Pacific. After 1933, the Washington and London agreements were indeed finished. President Franklin Roosevelt, who had served as Assistant Secretary of the Navy during the Great War, began building a stronger navy as soon as he took office in 1933. As part of the National Industrial Recovery Act of 1933, Roosevelt ordered over $200 million spent on building 32 ships through 1936. In 1934, Congress passed the Vinson-Trammell Act, which authorized the replacement of older vessels, including one carrier, two cruisers, 14 destroyers, and six submarines in 1935 alone, followed by similar replacements through 1942. It is essential to understand, however, that these increases in naval shipbuilding would only bring the U.S. Navy up to its treaty limits, even though the treaties had largely ceased to exist. And with the lead time required to build a capital ship, few of these vessels would actually join the fleet before the early 1940s.

The Marine Corps and the Development of Amphibious Warfare

Despite its expansive role in France as part of the American Expeditionary Force during the Great War, the Marine Corps radically demobilized after the conflict and continued to fine-tune its mission. Intervention operations and occupation duties in Nicaragua, Hispaniola, and China and developing an amphibious warfare doctrine kept the active but still small Marine Corps quite busy during the 1920s and 1930s.

In 1926, the Marines landed in Nicaragua to end political chaos there and did not withdraw until 1933. Disputes between the Nicaraguan Liberal and Conservative politicos over election results in 1924 and 1925 erupted in violence that approached civil war. Throughout 1926, the American legation in Nicaragua used Marine shore parties to protect American lives and property. By late 1926, however, Liberal forces had killed an American citizen and sacked some American-owned warehouses. The Coolidge administration supported the Conservative government that had been elected previously, and in early 1927 the president decided to intervene in Nicaragua. By February, the 5th Marine Regiment was onshore, supported by a six-plane observation squadron. With one battalion defending Managua against Liberal forces, smaller units occupied strategic towns along the railroad from Managua to the coast.

Coolidge sent former Secretary of War Henry Stimson to work out an agreement between the Conservatives and Liberals. With Marine units strategically placed to prevent the two armies from taking advantage of the temporary ceasefire, Stimson brought the two parties together in the so-called Peace of Tipitapa. New elections would be held in 1928, and both armies would disband and be replaced by a new national Nicaraguan army. The 11th Marine Regiment arrived to help implement the peace accord.

Figure 11.3 United States Marines with the captured flag of Augusto César Sandino, 1932.
Source: United States Department of Defense.

Some Liberal bands held out, including one led by Augusto César Sandino, who had refused to sign the Peace of Tipitapa. The Marines were caught in an impossible situation. They had to simultaneously disarm rebel bands, build a new Nicaraguan army, and pacify large regions of the countryside. Sandino presented the most troubling problem. Marine Brigadier General Logan Feland sent a force of over 200 Marines deep into territory controlled by Sandino to bring him in, by force if necessary. Sandino, however, hit first in an attempt to surprise the Marines and their Nicaraguan *Guardia* allies. Fighting in the predawn darkness, the Marines recovered quickly and repulsed several assaults by Sandino's force of over 600 men. With daylight came help from above, as the Marine observation planes strafed and even dive-bombed Sandino's positions. This may have been the first use of dive-bombing techniques in military aviation history. Sandino suffered heavy losses, with perhaps as many as 100 killed to one Marine killed. This incident led to almost five years of war with the so-called *Sandinistas*; it ended finally with the establishment of the Somoza dictatorship in 1933, which remained in power until the late 1970s.

Meanwhile, in China, Marines in 1927 garrisoned Shanghai and Tientsin to protect American lives and property amidst the Chinese civil war and the threat of foreign intervention from Great Britain and Japan. Marine units found themselves caught in a complicated situation between rival warlords and Chinese nationalist forces, not to mention foreign maneuverings, in China. General Smedley Butler returned from a turbulent two-year leave, serving as director of public safety for the city of Philadelphia, to command the 4th Marine Regiment in China. The so-called 'China Marines' stayed on station in China under these conditions until they were withdrawn in November 1941.

Occupation duty for the Marines also included extended stints on Hispaniola in the Caribbean. All told, the Marines lost fewer than 100 officers and men from combat action while fulfilling these often thankless duties as the State Department's 'police force' in the Caribbean, Latin America, and China. Trying to make the most of this challenging duty, the Marines gained valuable experience that would serve them well in the Pacific during World War II. Many Marine officers, such as Captain Lewis ('Chesty') Puller, learned a great deal about small-unit action, guerrilla warfare, and pacification. In 1925 the Marine Corps even published a pacification guide, the *Small Wars Manual*, based mostly upon the writings of Majors Samuel M. Harrington and Harold H. Utley. Occupation and intervention duty, however, convinced many in the State Department and Congress that these duties were the Marine Corps' principal function. As unpopular as pacification became by the 1930s, the Marine Corps needed to distance itself from these missions and refocus on creating a sufficient advance base force for the Navy.

Wanting to narrowly define its unique mission beyond being an imperial constabulary, the Marine Corps boldly took the position that assault from the sea against fortified positions was possible, if not necessary, especially in a war in the Pacific. Holding and maintaining advance bases for the Navy would be paramount, and only the Marines could do it. Under the direction of Commandant John A. Lejune, the Marines studied amphibious assault, learning from experience and the disastrous British campaign against the Turks at Gallipoli during the Great War. Important doctrinal concepts were worked through by Major Earl H. Ellis, especially in his 1921 paper 'Advanced Base Operations in Micronesia,' which was to prove prophetic of the course of operations in the Pacific in 1943–1944.

This study assumed that with the support of naval gunfire and airstrikes against enemy positions, waves of Marines with heavy equipment, such as tanks and artillery, could sweep ashore from landing craft. Landing exercises in the mid-1920s proved problematic since neither the Marines nor the Navy had landing craft or transport to carry the tanks, artillery, and other necessary equipment to successfully assault a beach from the sea. With little funding to put into research and development of landing craft, yet tasked with developing the tactical means to carry out amphibious assaults, the Marines instead spent much of the pre-World War II years developing the theoretical concepts of amphibious assault.

This effort paid off in the early 1930s with the publication of *Tentative Manual for Landing Operations* and the establishment of a Fleet Marine Force within the Pacific Fleet. The *Manual* outlined a doctrine for amphibious assault, including pre-landing bombardment, air support, ship-to-shore communications, and the continual flow of supplies and reinforcements during the landing. By creating a Fleet Marine Force, the Navy and Marines committed themselves to develop landing craft and other support equipment for amphibious operations. It was through this effort that the landing craft familiar in World War II were first developed. The Fleet Marine Force would require a minimum of 25,000 Marines in wartime. In the mid-1930s, the entire Marine Corps numbered just over 16,000 officers and men, making landing exercises recreating wartime conditions all but impossible. Still, when World War II began, the Marine Corps had in place a doctrine to guide island assaults in the Pacific. Amphibious assault had been the butt of many a joke about the Marines among the Army, which ironically found itself indebted to the Marine Corps as it conducted significant amphibious operations in both the European and Pacific theaters during World War II.

War Planning

During the interwar years, perhaps the most critical function undertaken by the American military was updating plans for mobilization and military operations. The military and industrial mobilization for both the War with Spain and the Great War had been nothing short of shameful. The color-coded war plans that had been around since the early 1900s also needed updating. The rise of ideological militarism in Nazi Germany and Imperial Japan in the 1930s created even more incentive for improving mobilization and war plans.

Creating a mobilization plan that coordinates industrial capacity and manpower needs with security requirements is extremely difficult, particularly when war might suddenly befall a nation rather than allow for a gradual buildup. To overcome this difficulty, the Army-Navy Munitions Board sought to coordinate procurement and supply between the two services. The National Defense Act of 1920 made the War Department responsible for mobilization and created a special assistant secretary position in the War Department to carry out this function. Industry representatives and even Bernard Baruch, who had chaired the War Industries Board during the last year of the Great War, assisted the War Department by providing data, ideas on how to transform peacetime production to wartime production, and information on manpower needs that the War Department would have to balance against military manpower needs.

Also, the Army Industrial College, established in 1924, studied logistics and industrial mobilization.

In 1930, the War Department created an Industrial Mobilization Plan to put the nation's industrial might on a wartime footing while the military first ensured the security of the United States and then conducted offensive campaigns to defeat the enemy. The first plan found few supporters in Congress, which thought the plan too decentralized and too advantageous to industry considering the economic crisis devastating the country at the time. A subsequent revision increased centralized planning and gave the War Department apparent authority to put in place price and wage controls, which gave the military near-complete control over the American economy during a war. Although the Industrial Mobilization Plan was much needed, its timing could not have been worse. Aside from the Great Depression, the Senate investigation of profiteering by munitions manufacturers during the Great War made suspect any union between the War Department and American industry, war or no war.

Bringing together American industrial potential with its military might in a cohesive plan continued to elude planners. The 1937 Protective Mobilization Plan, the brainchild of Secretary of War Harry Woodring and Army Chief of Staff Malin Craig, made the most progress toward this end. In addition to organizing American industry for war production, the plan realized the interdependence of the military and the American economy during wartime. Militarily, it used the National Guard and the Navy to provide the first line of defense while the Army mobilized to meet wartime needs. This plan included specific details on training camps for individuals and units to avoid repeating the severe shortcomings of the 1917 mobilization. The plan assumed a mobilization similar in size to that of 1917; in fact, the mobilization that began in 1939 was ultimately over twice that size. The plan also assumed that the United States would be at war almost overnight, rather than envisioning the gradual, escalating crisis the United States faced from 1939 to the Japanese attack on Pearl Harbor on December 7, 1941.

The military needed new equipment. The stockpiles left over from the Great War had long been exhausted and worn out. The economic crisis did not help matters, as the federal government had a difficult time finding the money to update weapons, equipment, and facilities. The Army needed modern artillery, mechanized vehicles, anti-aircraft weapons, and updated infantry arms. The other problem the Army faced was that it could not predict to Congress what type of future war the United States might face. Another war in Europe would require different force structure and equipment than would a war in the Western Hemisphere—say, against Mexico, or an attack on the Panama Canal. Thus, the Army's safest, though not most complete, policy became to spread funding thinly across several types of units and to opt for increased and better-trained manpower over modernization.

A few bright spots surfaced, however, including replacing the 1903 Springfield rifle with the M-1 Garand semi-automatic rifle and adopting modern mortars and howitzers for infantry and artillery use. The horse was finally phased out as a means of transportation, being wholly replaced by motorized transport. Smaller, more mobile divisions took the place of the large, cumbersome division model established in 1917. By the mid-1930s, manpower needs were also at least partially addressed, as the Army increased in size to 165,000 enlisted personnel.

The Air Corps found growth during the mid-1930s as well. In 1931, both the Army and Navy concurred that the Air Corps should be the lead in repelling a seaborne invasion of the American coast. Long-range patrolling from Hawaii and the Philippines, as well as the Panama Canal Zone, was added to the growing list of Air Corps responsibilities. Mitchell's disciples tactfully argued for an expanded bombing mission for the Air Corps. By 1934, the Air Corps boasted 11 attack squadrons, 20 observation squadrons, 17 pursuit squadrons, and 27 bomber squadrons. The new emphasis on pursuit and bombing gave rise to new strategic and tactical doctrine, including daylight precision bombing of industrial targets and formation flying of bombers for self-defense against enemy intercep-tors, which arguably would allow bombers to penetrate deep into enemy territory. New aircraft that utilized mono-wing, closed-canopy designs with more powerful engines made these missions possible. By the eve of World War II, tactical air support for ground operations and strategic bombing, à la Mitchell, had become firmly entrenched in Air Corps doctrine.

The Navy enjoyed some expansion after the collapse of the limitation agreements and increased Japanese naval building. The Naval Act of 1938 authorized a $1.1 billion ten-year building program that would place the Navy at 20 percent over the old tonnage limits and double the size of naval aviation to over 3,000 aircraft. By comparison, in 1939, the Navy had 15 battleships to Japan's ten, five carriers to Japan's six, 36 cruisers to Japan's 37, 104 destroyers to Japan's 122, and 56 submarines to Japan's 62. Japan had 500 carrier-borne aircraft, while the United States maintained over 800. Still, the Navy, especially in the Pacific, was woefully short on adequate forward bases, a problem that was not addressed until war broke out in the Pacific in 1941. Beyond the Western Hemisphere, the fleet would be hamstrung by a tenuous logistical line back to the United States. Manpower also lagged, as the Navy was at only 80 percent strength in 1939 with 125,000 officers and seamen. While strides had been made to improve naval readiness, the Navy, along with the Marines, remained underprepared for major conflict.

War planning during the 1920s and 1930s focused on hypothetical conflict with Great Britain, which was unlikely, and with the Empire of Japan, which was more likely. War Plan Orange supposed a Pacific war against Japan. First proposed in 1903, the joint Army–Navy plan assumed that the conflict would be a naval war in which Japan would quickly overrun American possessions in the Pacific, including Guam and the Philippines. Once fully mobilized, American naval forces and airpower would then retake these possessions and others necessary for basing to finally blockade the Japanese home islands. Exhibiting the influence of Mahan, the plan called for a climactic, decisive fleet action to decide who ruled the waves in the Pacific.

War Plan Orange had many defects, but chief among them was advance basing. Securing advance bases in forward areas was a problem because until the 1930s the Navy and the Marine Corps had little means of doing so. The handful of American possessions in the western Pacific offered basing alternatives, but the Army and Navy could not decide where to establish their primary base. Manila and Guam were the principal candidates. Because the Army and Navy were unable to make a choice before 1922, the Five-Power Treaty made the decision for them, as the agreement included a provision prohibiting the construction of new bases. Pearl Harbor in Hawaii already existed, and though not yet developed enough to base the Pacific Fleet, it was as far west as the United States could get under the agreements. The Navy argued that it could maintain a supply line from Pearl Harbor to keep the hungry Pacific Fleet operating. Disagreement arose regarding whether to defend Manila. The Army, quite naturally, wanted to hold it until reinforced. The Navy debated whether reinforcements could even get to the Philippines in time to save the Army garrison.

Even Pearl Harbor was not invulnerable to attack. As early as 1919, Admiral William B. Fletcher warned that aircraft from a carrier fleet could easily surprise military bases in Hawaii and probably destroy them before any effective defense could be mounted. In 1921, Major General Charles T. Menoher authored a report claiming that Pearl Harbor and other military installations on the island of Oahu were defenseless unless the United States had air superiority, which in 1921 it did not. During the 1930s, per War Plan Orange revisions and in response to Japanese aggression in China, the Navy deployed the bulk of its fleet to the Pacific, including the new carriers *Lexington* and *Saratoga*.

By 1938, it was apparent that the United States might face a simultaneous two-ocean war. The color-coded war plans designed to fight a single enemy would not suffice if the United States had to fight Germany and Japan at the same time. To plan for this worst-case scenario, the War Department ordered a review of all war plans. The recommendations became known as the Rainbow war plans. Five scenarios were studied. Rainbow One called for the defense of the entire Western Hemisphere, not just the United States and its own possessions, as had been the policy in the past. Rainbow Two and Rainbow Three supposed that the United States would fight in the Pacific against Japan, basically following War Plan Orange while its allies, France and Great Britain, fought Germany in Europe. Rainbow Four envisioned an Atlantic war fought by the United States without allies. Rainbow Five assumed an alliance with France and Great Britain and recommended giving primacy to the Atlantic theater while holding in the Pacific. Assuming the loss of Guam and the Philippines, Rainbow Five proposed to defend the Panama Canal Zone, the Atlantic coast, and shipping lanes across the Atlantic as well as conducting land operations in Europe, perhaps even Africa, all while fighting a defensive war in the Pacific. In essence, Rainbow Five was a defeat-Germany-first strategy, and it was this plan that ultimately provided the basis for war planning at the outset of World War II.

Conclusion

In August 1928, Secretary of State Frank Kellogg and French Premier Aristide Briand signed a remarkable agreement called the International Treaty for the Renunciation of War. More commonly known as the Kellogg–Briand Pact, the agreement stated that signatories to the treaty would renounce war as a means of achieving national policy objectives. In all, more than 60 countries signed the pact, including Germany, Japan, and Italy. The only exception for war was self-defense, which was vaguely defined in the treaty. Such a concept, to outlaw war, was certainly understandable following the trauma of 1914–1918. It was, however, naïve and idealistic in the worst of Wilsonian traditions.

In the 1930s, the world again seemed to irrationally tumble toward conflict. Germany rejected the Treaty of Versailles, rearmed, and then undertook an escalating policy of aggression in Europe. Japan disavowed the League of Nations and initiated an overtly aggressive policy of expansion in Asia. Even Italy, a weak and ill-governed state, became enamored with the expansionist urge in its conquest of Ethiopia. Even more troubling was that these states denounced liberal democracy and capitalism for political theories that espoused national socialism and militaristic nationalism. These nations chose their paths for numerous reasons, including the Treaty of Versailles, the Great Depression, and what they perceived as real threats to their national interests and security. The United States responded with a series of neutrality acts passed by Congress that were designed to prevent the nation from being unwillingly pulled into war, as it had been in 1917.

The United States also responded with better military preparedness than it had during the Great War. As the prospect of war loomed ever higher in the late 1930s, the American military was better prepared for conflict than ever before. Although not perfect by any means, the Army and Navy, as well as American political leaders, had learned valuable lessons from mistakes in the Great War. These mistakes would at the very least be minimized as the United States prepared to enter the greatest, costliest, and perhaps most tragic conflict in human history. Still, as the United

States entered World War II, it did so with a military culture built around loyalty and toeing the party line. During the interwar period, the American military had not tolerated mavericks or independent thinkers very well. This rigid attitude toward new and different ideas would have to become more flexible and accommodating for the United States to successfully fight the next world war.

Further Reading

Biddle, Tami Davis. *Rhetoric and Reality in Air Warfare: The Evolution of British and American Ideas about Strategic Bombing, 1914–1945*. Princeton, NJ: Princeton University Press, 2004.

Jordan, John. *Warships After Washington: The Development of the Five Major Fleets, 1922–1930*. Annapolis, MD: Naval Institute Press, 2015.

Koistinen, Paul A. C. *Planning War, Pursuing Peace: The Political Economy of American Warfare, 1920–1939*. Lawrence, MD: University Press of Kansas, 1998.

McPherson, Alan. *The Invaded: How Latin Americans and Their Allies Fought and Ended U.S. Occupations*. Oxford: Oxford University Press, 2014.

Miller, Edward S. *War Plan Orange: The U.S. Strategy to Defeat Japan, 1897–1945*. Annapolis, MD: Naval Institute Press, 2007.

Murray, Williamson, and Allan R. Millett. *Military Innovation in the Inter-War Period*. Cambridge: Cambridge University Press, 1996.

Nasca, David. *The Emergence of American Amphibious Warfare, 1898–1945*. Annapolis, MD: Naval Institute Press, 2020.

Schmidt, Hans. *Maverick Marine: General Smedley D. Butler and the Contradictions of American Military History*. Lexington, KY: University of Kentucky Press, 1998.

Simon, John Arthur. *The Greatest of All Leathernecks: John Archer Lejeune and the Making of the Modern Marine Corps*. Baton Rouge, LA: Louisiana State University Press, 2019.

Tuccille, Jerome. *The War Against the Vets: The World War I Bonus Army during the Great Depression*. Lincoln, NE: Potomac Books, 2018.

Wildenberg, Thomas. *Billy Mitchell's War with the Navy: The Interwar Rivalry Over Air Power*. Annapolis, MD: Naval Institute Press, 2014.

12 World War II

Introduction

If the Spanish–American War brought the United States to the world stage, the Great War gave the United States a leading role in the world. Yet, despite this rather rapid ascendancy, American military power remained potential rather than realized through the 1920s. By 1945, however, the United States had emerged as the leader of the non-communist world and faced only one rival, the Soviet Union, in the competition for world dominance. The trajectory of American power in 50 years was nothing short of remarkable, but this embrace of global involvement brought new challenges and unforeseen costs.

World War II was the greatest war in human history. Fought on a truly global scale, it involved the creation of a grand coalition to defeat and destroy powerful opponents, some of whom personified evil in its purest form. The physical destruction was exceeded only by the human toll. Unlike the Great War of 1914–1918, in which most casualties were sustained by the armed forces of the various combatant nations, in World War II civilian deaths eclipsed military ones, with millions of civilians killed due to purposeful attempts to wipe out whole races or classes of people. Nonetheless, World War II is ironically remembered in the American nationalistic narrative as the 'Good War.'

The Great War had not resolved the 'German problem' in central Europe but had merely checked German power while creating the basis for powerful new grievances among the German people. The Russian revolution and the triumph of Bolshevism, the growth and success of Italian Fascism in the 1920s, and the aggressive expansionist policies pursued by the Japanese from 1931, initially against China, were all legacies of the Great War. All of these contributed to the outbreak of a new world war in 1939 and helped to determine the course and, to some extent, the outcome of that war.

Preparing for War

To a degree, the United States contributed to the deteriorating international situation that developed during the interwar period. Congressional rejection of the League of Nations and a strong resurgence of the isolationist strand in

American popular attitudes made it difficult for the Roosevelt administration to support Great Britain and the first anti-Axis coalition between 1939–1941. Moreover, the likely German dominance of the European continent further increased American reluctance to get involved in events there. Passage of the Neutrality Acts in the late 1930s severely restricted American support to all the belligerents, regardless of whether they were democracies or dictatorships. The United States seemed committed to preventing the mistakes that led it into World War I.

After the German invasion of Poland in September 1939, American policy continued to focus on the defense of the Western Hemisphere— essentially the continental United States and the seaward approaches from the Pacific and Atlantic oceans and the Caribbean. Not until the middle of 1940—with the French surrender, Germany triumphant, the Soviet Union neutralized through a nonaggression pact signed with Germany, and Britain and its empire left alone to face the Axis—was there significant change in American policy. Even then, isolationist sentiment among the public and in Congress constrained the Roosevelt administration; in the second half of that year, however, its policy began to tip decisively toward aiding Britain in its struggle for national survival. Assistance arrived via a 'bases for destroyers' agreement through which the United States transferred 50 mothballed destroyers to the British in exchange for basing rights in British territory in the Western Hemisphere.

Roosevelt also moved to improve military preparedness. The fleet doubled in size, including authorization for 11 additional aircraft carriers, and the Army Air Corps began a major expansion to nearly 8,000 combat aircraft of all types. Neither of these developments made an immediate impact, and most of the new warships only came online in 1943, but these moves laid the foundation of a readiness program that stood the armed forces well once the United States formally entered the war.

The Army underwent the most significant changes. In June 1940, the National Guard was federalized, while the passage of the Selective Service and Training Act in September brought more than half a million draftees into the ranks. In the short term, rapid expansion reduced the Army's capabilities because large numbers of soldiers and officers were diverted to training and administrative duties. Despite the growing pains, by mid-1941 the Army could field 1.2 million men. In September, the Army put the finishing touches to its Victory Program plan for the expansion and organization of the ground forces: a ground army of 213 divisions and an air corps (soon to be re-designated the United States Army Air Forces) of 195 air groups. Almost half the Army was tested in a major exercise in Louisiana in the same month, with rising officers such as George Patton, Dwight Eisenhower, Walter Krueger, and Mark Clark playing key roles in planning and executing the exercises.

Lend-Lease was the final major development in American policy before the United States formally entered the war. Announced in March 1941, the program supported the British war effort by giving London wide-ranging access to American war industry without requiring Great Britain to pay from its rapidly diminishing stock of dollars. Although there were repayment provisions in the legislation, and while Lend-Lease was absolutely vital to Great Britain's war effort, the program ultimately beggared the British economy. In May, its provisions were extended to the Nationalist Chinese and subsequently to the Soviets, the Free French, as well as to other Allied belligerents.

By late 1941, the United States had made considerable advances in preparing for war; even so, it was not at all clear on what basis the Americans would enter the conflict. Roosevelt faced complex strategic choices. There was growing concern about Japanese intentions in the Far East, despite the adoption of a 'Germany First' strategy that assumed a German victory over Britain would pose more significant challenges for the United States than would short-term Japanese gains in the Pacific, as outlined in the Rainbow war plans developed in the 1930s. The surprise Japanese attack on Pearl Harbor on the morning of December 7, 1941, was not the immediate answer to Roosevelt's strategic dilemma; although it pitched the country into the war, it mobilized outraged American opinion against Japan, not Germany. Roosevelt swiftly declared war on Japan on December 8. Within two days, Hitler answered with an act of extraordinary strategic folly, declaring war on the United States in an entirely needless and unprovoked manner that now allowed American resources to be pitched into the conflict alongside the British and Soviets.

The most significant strategic decision concerned the priority that the United States would give to the various combat theaters. American planners recognized that if the Germans defeated Britain, the emerging Allied cause might not prevail; but if Britain could be sustained, they were unlikely to lose, however difficult the fight. British and American planners had worked out the elements of the Germany First strategy in the first months of 1941, while the United States was still out of the war. This approach was further reflected in the final Rainbow war plan. The Washington Conference, which convened shortly after Pearl Harbor in December 1941–January 1942, confirmed these decisions and laid out the essentials of Anglo-American strategy for the rest of the war.

The American war was fought in three main theaters: North Africa and the Mediterranean, the Pacific, and, from June 1944, Northwest Europe. The wars against Germany and Japan were not coordinated efforts in any but the most general sense and competed for priority at different stages of the conflict, especially for essential equipment like airplanes and landing craft.

The War in the Pacific

Relations between the United States and Japan had deteriorated steadily after the mid-1930s, mainly over Japanese actions in China and the retaliatory sanctions imposed by the United States on oil imported into Japan. The Japanese advance into Southeast Asia at the end of 1941 was driven by a need to secure resources, specifically strategic materiels like oil, rubber, and tin to fuel Japanese industry and maintain the armed forces. Dutch and British colonies of the East Indies (now Indonesia) and Malaya (now Malaysia) had the most abundant supply of these resources in the Pacific, and the attacks upon the American Pacific Fleet at Pearl Harbor and American and Filipino forces in the Philippines were intended to preempt American ability to interfere in Japanese ambitions.

Each attack was only partially successful. The Japanese severely damaged the American Pacific Fleet, but the vital aircraft carriers were at sea and untouched, and thus still a serious threat to Japan's plans. Although American and Filipino forces held out on Corregidor for six months—far longer than the Japanese anticipated—the conquest of the rest of Southeast Asia was completed in just three months, well in advance of Japanese timetables. The force deployed by the Japanese was far smaller than those it faced, a testimony to the advantage of surprise, enhanced combat capability derived from the war in China, and the arrogance and over-confidence of the British and Americans.

Figure 12.1 World War II in the Pacific.

The early months of the Pacific War were a disaster for the Allies everywhere. Japan occupied Southeast Asia, overran Burma, threatened the British position in India, appeared to have isolated Australia and Allied positions in the South Pacific, and continued to wage a savage war in China. For the time being, therefore, the Japanese enjoyed the strategic initiative, but their advantages in the longer term were more apparent than real. Japanese industrial capacity could not hope to match that of the United States, and in shipping and aviation alone American building programs dwarfed Japan's, readily replacing the losses sustained in the first months of the war and then overwhelming the Japanese forces with materiel. Throughout the war, Japan maintained significant forces in China, Manchuria and Korea, and the Japanese home islands, and as the American submarine campaign gained in intensity and paralyzed and then gradually destroyed the Japanese merchant marine capability, the forces scattered throughout Asia and the Pacific were increasingly isolated and rendered strategically immobile.

Rivalry within the Japanese high command produced failures of coordination between the army and navy, while Japanese strategy always operated from flawed assumptions and unrealistic expectations. Their advantages were further negated by the American ability to decipher and analyze key communications codes and effectively utilize the resulting intelligence. Some of these factors were evident by mid-1942. The failure to sink the American carriers at Pearl Harbor enabled the United States to stage the dramatic, if strategically irrelevant, air raid on Tokyo by carrier-based B-25 bombers in April (the 'Doolittle raid'), while the involvement of two American carriers in the Battle of the Coral Sea in May prevented Japanese attempts to cut sea lines of communication with Australia. The more decisive Battle of Midway in June, prompted by intelligence intercepts via MAGIC and other naval intelligence cryptanalysis or code-breaking, resulted in substantial losses to the Japanese of planes and aircrew as well as a carrier—losses that they were increasingly unable to replace.

The war in the Pacific overwhelmingly remained an American war, despite the presence and roles of other principal allies such as the British, Chinese, and Australians. The United States enjoyed little real influence with the Chinese despite heavily underwriting aspects of the war effort, and the Chinese military and political levels were corrupt and often incompetent, although there were exceptions. The British dominated Southeast Asia Command and the conduct of the war in Burma as well as the defense of India. Only in the Southwest Pacific, under General Douglas MacArthur, and in the Pacific Ocean area, under Admiral Chester Nimitz, did significant non-American forces from Australia and New Zealand make effective contributions to the struggle against Japan. Even then, the command arrangements remained fundamentally American, and the strategy for the war was determined in Washington and London through the Combined Chiefs of Staff.

MacArthur's theater was dominated by the United States Army and involved a series of advances and amphibious assaults northward through

Figure 12.2 The carrier USS *Lexington* explodes after damage from Japanese air attacks
        during the Battle of the Coral Sea, May 8, 1942.
Source: United States Navy History and Heritage Command.

Papua New Guinea to the Philippines, utilizing American airpower and
American and Australian ground forces. The Pacific theater was dominated by the Navy and the Marines, and in conformity with the prewar
Orange plans for war with Japan, it saw American forces advance westward across the Pacific in a series of surface battles and amphibious
advances dominated by carrier aviation. Both were supported by the
offensive anti-shipping campaign successfully waged by American submarines operating from bases across the Pacific.

The weakness in the Japanese position was demonstrated in the second
half of 1942 and early 1943 in the simultaneous campaigns in the Solomon
Islands and Papua. The terrain in Papua dictated a grim, low-level infantry
war, with the Japanese suffering 90 percent losses by the time the
Australians retook Papua at the beginning of 1943. Although it involved
sustained ground combat as well, the fighting in the Solomons was
dominated by air and naval engagements; and in this area American
forces gradually exerted dominance over the previously unstoppable
Japanese, who suffered heavy losses in aircraft, aircrew, and surface ships.
The critical Japanese weakness, however, was logistical: they were unable

to mount and sustain two campaigns in the South Pacific simultaneously, while the severe losses suffered through defeat in detail in these campaigns further reduced their combat power and effectiveness.

American forces refined and developed their thinking at both the strategic and tactical levels. In the Southwest Pacific area, MacArthur adopted a strategy of selected advances, isolating and bypassing the large Japanese forces based at Rabaul, clearing New Guinea, and forcing the Japanese to choose a new defensive line centered on the Philippines and the Marianas in the central Pacific. The Marines and naval forces under Nimitz gradually mastered the techniques of large-scale amphibious assault, drawing on doctrine fashioned during the interwar period and refining it through trial and error. Casualties in early operations such as Tarawa were heavy, but as new and specialized equipment became available and tactics and techniques were developed to utilize it more effectively, the balance again swung decisively against the Japanese.

MacArthur's objective now became the Philippines, while the Navy focused on seizing the Marianas to establish forward bases from which to mount long-range bombing of the Japanese home islands. This two-pronged approach to the Japanese home islands, combined with actions in the Aleutian Islands, China, and Burma, would force the Japanese to spread their forces even more thinly and give the Allies the opportunity to gradually tighten a noose around Japan.

In contrast with interwar planning and wargaming, the United States thus mounted a dual drive on Japan that culminated in 1944 in a series of stunning advances and crippling defeats for the Japanese. As well as deploying vast air, naval, and ground forces, the United States had created a robust logistics system that enabled it to mount more or less continuous operations, denying the enemy any respite. The Japanese were caught in an increasingly vicious spiral, losing experienced personnel (especially pilots) and equipment that they could not replace and were forced to field inadequately trained and inexperienced troops who then suffered even heavier losses.

During the Battle of the Philippine Sea in June 1944, Nimitz's forces inflicted further devastating losses, affecting Japan's ability to wage aero-naval warfare. In the Great Marianas Turkey Shoot, as it was quickly dubbed, Japanese losses included three aircraft carriers and 480 aircraft, against American losses of just 130 aircraft and only 76 aircrew. The Japanese defensive position was coming unhinged, and the further American victory at the Battle of Leyte Gulf in October, the only battleship-type Mahanian fleet engagement of the Pacific War, ensured the success of MacArthur's landings in the central Philippines. The battle also saw the final destruction of what was left of the Imperial Japanese Navy, ensuring as well that those Japanese ground forces still deployed throughout the Pacific were now effectively isolated from reinforcement and further assistance.

Increasingly desperate, the Japanese introduced tactical changes to counter the overwhelming superiority now enjoyed by American forces. On the ground, defending forces henceforth allowed the Americans to land, then fought them to the death from well-constructed and positioned defenses—bunkers and natural cave systems. The Japanese were all but annihilated in such battles, but American casualties increased sharply as well. First encountered at Peleliu in September 1944, these tactics were to culminate in the costly and horrendous fighting for Iwo Jima (February–March 1945) and Okinawa (April–June 1945) as the Allies drew ever closer to the sacred soil of Japan itself. In the air, and to some extent at sea, the enemy introduced kamikaze units dedicated to inflicting losses through suicide attacks, especially against American ships. Making their first appearance in October 1944, the kamikaze attacks were a further measure of the degradation in the quality of the Japanese military. Pilots now lacked the training and experience to enable them to meet their American counterparts in aerial combat and could inflict losses only through their own intentional deaths.

American advances and capture of territory in the western Pacific provided bases for the Army Air Force to begin the devastation of the Japanese homeland, through both day and night bombing campaigns. The raids on Tokyo in March killed 84,000 people and left large parts of the capital destroyed using incendiary munitions, and by June most of Japan's major urban centers were destroyed; 900,000 civilians were killed, and as much as 80 percent of the infrastructure was wiped out. The Japanese government, however, continued to believe that a defense of the home islands against amphibious assault was both sustainable and capable of bringing victory—or, if not, of ensuring the destruction of Japan and thus avoiding the disgrace of defeat and surrender. American casualties incurred on Okinawa, where roughly 12,000 had been killed and well over 30,000 wounded, together with the knowledge that sizable forces in southern Japan were planning for a determined last stand—with the implications this carried for the civilian population as well—helped persuade President Truman and his advisors to use the atomic bomb as a means of forcing the enemy's surrender. The bombing of Hiroshima on August 6 and Nagasaki on August 9 prompted the Japanese emperor to order the government and armed forces to surrender on August 10.

The Bomb

The decision to end the Pacific War by dropping atomic bombs on the Japanese cities of Hiroshima and Nagasaki remains one of the most controversial episodes of the war. The event had profound implications for the future of warfare and the use of force in the postwar world. Much about the decision and the reasoning behind it is contested. The Manhattan Project, which secretly built the atomic bombs, represented an

Figure 12.3 Standing in the grassy sod bordering row upon row of white crosses in an American cemetery in the Pacific, two Coast Guardsmen pay silent homage to the memory of a fellow Coast Guardsman who lost his life in action in the Ryukyu Islands.

Source: National Archives.

unprecedented level of federal support for scientific research, but this did not overshadow the incredible destructive power of these new weapons.

There were serious concerns at the highest political and military levels about the likely cost of invading the Japanese home islands in late 1945 and early 1946, as the United States planned to do. Large divisions of regular forces heavily defended the southern part of Japan. Moreover, the Japanese government had made extensive preparations, including massed suicide attacks and the utilization of the civilian population, to repulse an Allied invasion. There can be little doubt that a full-scale assault would have been horribly expensive, not merely in American and Allied casualties, but in Japanese ones as well.

Geopolitical considerations also played a part, as Soviet intentions in Manchuria had to be checked. Although the bombs were not dropped simply to send a signal to the Soviets, it is still reasonable to suggest that this was a factor in the decision to utilize these weapons. Nor was the use of the bomb racially motivated, as is sometimes alleged. Many of the scientists who worked on the Manhattan Project were Jewish, and others were refugees from Nazi Germany. Indeed, the bomb was built with its possible use against Germany in mind. The fact is that the successful testing of the device did not occur until July—after Germany's surrender. There were a variety of reasons for using the atomic bomb, and in 1945 scientists and political and military leaders had a less-than-full appreciation of the effects of the weapon, as well as of the moral and other implications of its use.

The Mediterranean Theater and the Rise of American Leadership

The war in the Mediterranean was the most protracted campaign of the war, beginning in 1940 following Italy's declaration of war in June and ending only with the surrender of German and remnant Fascist forces in northern Italy in May 1945. As in the Pacific and Southeast Asia, fighting in the Mediterranean had a colonial warfare dimension, since Italy, Great Britain, and France all held colonies and/or protectorates in North Africa and the Middle East. This complicated matters for American leaders, who did not share the sense of priority accorded the theater by their British ally. Roosevelt and Churchill had agreed to place the untried but highly respected General Dwight Eisenhower in overall command of Allied forces in North Africa. Eisenhower would later be named Supreme Allied Commander of Allied Expeditionary Forces in Europe.

By the time American forces came into action in North Africa in November 1942, the seesaw of advantage in the North African campaign had resolved itself mainly in favor of the Allies, although there was still plenty of hard fighting to be done before North Africa was finally cleared of German and Italian forces. The great virtue of American involvement in this phase was the opportunity it provided to 'blood' units and formations; expose weaknesses in equipment, doctrine, and training; and weed out incompetent combat leaders, especially more senior ones, who were inadequate to the stresses and challenges of modern industrial warfare.

The first taste of the war in Europe for the United States came as part of an Anglo-American invasion of Morocco against the Vichy French, called Operation Torch, which opened a second front to the rear of the retreating Axis forces being driven across North Africa by the British 8th Army, based in Egypt. The political situation in the French colonies was very complex, and the Allies received assistance from supporters of the Free French while nonetheless negotiating an end to the fighting with Vichy authorities. The Germans immediately occupied the southern, Vichy-controlled part of France in response and stalled the American attempt to rapidly move into Tunisia.

The early encounters with the German Wehrmacht—the best-known action being at Kasserine Pass—saw inexperienced and outclassed American units bested and quickly disheartened by better-trained, better-led, and better-equipped German opponents. At this early stage of the American war, the difference between amateurs and deeply seasoned professionals was readily apparent. There were some high-level firings, including the commander of the American II Corps General Lloyd Fredendall, to make room for a new wave of younger, tougher, and better-prepared leaders, including General George S. Patton and his new deputy corps commander, General Omar Bradley.

American dominance of the Anglo-American alliance was less evident at this stage, with the more experienced British winning many of the early arguments on the Combined Chiefs of Staff over strategy and future direction of the Allied war effort. An excellent example of this situation was the continuation and expansion of the war in the Mediterranean, decided at a conference in Casablanca in January 1943. At Casablanca, the Allies approved an invasion of Sicily with the aim of knocking Italy out of the war. This plan, in turn, was later extended to include an invasion of mainland Italy itself. The argument was partly about reasserting British and, to a lesser extent, French supremacy in the Mediterranean and safeguarding strategic routes to India through the Suez Canal. But it also reflected British hesitancy over American advocacy of a cross-channel invasion of France in 1943, which the British judged (probably correctly) to be premature. The surrender of a quarter of a million German and Axis troops in Tunisia in May 1943 meant that resources deployed in North Africa had to be used somewhere, and a further campaign in the Mediterranean seemed the most attractive of the limited options available.

The Sicilian campaign fought in July–August 1943 returned mixed results, as America's early wartime campaigns tended to do. The enormous number of prisoners taken in Tunisia was not replicated in Sicily, with the modest force of German defenders eventually passing quickly across the Straits of Messina to mainland Italy after a vigorous and protracted defense of the island. While Operation Husky also proved to be a useful test for training, equipment, and doctrine, including the use of paratroopers and gliders, the test results were by no means encouraging, and the initial

landings were marked by confusion and needless losses. The least impressive aspect of the campaign, however, was at the highest levels of command and strategic direction. The commanders of the American 7th and
British 8th Armies—Patton and General Bernard Law Montgomery,
respectively—did not care for each other, disagreeing on the best way to
quickly roll up the enemy, and offering little active support to each other.
Their superiors, Eisenhower and General Sir Harold Alexander, allowed
them to get away with it, reflecting the still-nascent nature of inter-Allied
relations at this stage, even at senior levels and between individuals who
got along well personally.

The Sicilian campaign was followed by the invasion of mainland Italy at
Salerno in Operation Avalanche in September 1943, again because the
forces were in place and there was not a convincing alternative. Moreover,
the Allies misread the intensely complicated internal political situation.
Mussolini was removed from power because of the invasion of Sicily, but
this only prompted the Germans to move forces rapidly southward to
counteract or neutralize defeatism in the Italian armed forces and deny the
Allies any easy victories. The Italian surrender in September thus represented no advantage to the Allies while removing several constraints on
the Germans. The Italian terrain proved a gift for the defenders, who
demonstrated all their usual tenacity, defensive, and engineering skill to
vigorously contest every mile of the Allies' northward advance. By the
winter of 1943, the Allied armies were stuck in front of the enemy's
Gustav Line defenses, 100 miles from Rome, and faced strong natural
defenses with which to contend, such as the Rapido River and the heights
of Monte Cassino.

Until its last days, the campaign in Italy offered the Allies a series of
bloody frustrations. The attempted amphibious landing at Anzio in January 1944 nearly proved a disaster. Rather than circumventing the
German defenses and taking the pressure off the Allied advance, the
landing forced the commander of the American 5th Army, General Mark
Clark, to renew the offensive to save the beachhead. Repeated attempts to
take the German defenses at the foot of Monte Cassino prompted the
decision to level the monastery on its heights with heavy bombing. The
Germans at first had respected the monastery's neutrality as a religious
house but then moved into the ruins to create formidable defenses that
had to be captured, laboriously and bloodily, by Allied infantrymen.

Rome finally fell on June 4, 1944, after being declared an open city and
with a calculated political gesture on Clark's part that was designed both to
snub the British and gain publicity in advance of the D-Day landings in
Normandy two days later. Many of the soldiers who fought there believed
that Italy was a forgotten or neglected theater after the main focus
switched to Northwest Europe, and there were indeed grounds for
thinking this. Following the capture of Rome, the Germans reestablished their defenses, formidable as always, along the Gothic Line.

The American high command, increasingly dubious about the worth of the Italian campaign at all, began to shut down its commitment there.

Seeking, at last, to open a second front through an invasion of southern France, Operation Anvil/Dragoon withdrew six American and French divisions from the Italian campaign to be fed into a new advance through the Rhone Valley. There, they were intended to link up with the armies moving eastward across northern France toward Germany. By September, the Gothic Line had been breached in places; but attention had now moved decisively from the Italian theater, rendered now a sideshow, especially from the American point of view. The campaign petered out in the final days of the war and amidst further political complexity, this time represented by surrender negotiations with rogue elements in the German command and uneasy standoffs with Josip Broz Tito's Yugoslavian communist partisans moving into northern Adriatic Italy and bumping against Allied units. The American 5th Army suffered nearly 200,000 casualties during the campaign. Its contribution to final Allied victory against Germany remains controversial.

Northwest Europe (1944–1945)

The American high command had wanted to launch an invasion of Northwest Europe and take the fight to the Nazis in 1942, within months of entering the war. The real war dictated otherwise, a conclusion reinforced by the disastrous British–Canadian amphibious raid at Dieppe, Operation Rutter, that same year. The second-front debate percolated along as part of the Anglo-American strategic dialogue thereafter, with the addition of regular demands from the Soviets to help relieve pressure on the Eastern Front in some of the grimmest periods of the war in the East. The Americans increasingly regarded British enthusiasm for extending the Mediterranean campaign as a means of avoiding the hard fighting that an invasion of France would entail, while the British feared the consequences of an abortive attack on a multidivisional scale before the training, technology, and doctrine were sufficiently developed to deal with the increasingly daunting German defenses in France.

The period in which Operation Overlord developed emphasized the shift in the balance in the Western alliance between the British and the Americans to the latter's advantage. Resources, including divisions and equipment such as landing craft, ships, and aircraft, were earmarked for Normandy at the expense of both the Mediterranean campaign and the Pacific, while after D-Day the American high command strongly argued for the 'second front to the second front' through southern France to assist the main advance and the breakout of Allied forces. The delay in launching the invasion also enabled the Allies to marshal the enormous logistic effort needed to help its success, as well as giving them time to solve the problems presented by so vast an undertaking and to deceive the Germans as to their intentions.

Figure 12.4 World War II in Europe.

The initial landings on June 6 were a success, although for the Americans landing at Omaha Beach a very costly one. After that, things developed less smoothly. The original intention was to take the city of Caen, with its transportation hub, and break out into the open country beyond, but the British moved cautiously and lost the opportunity. Instead of an early campaign of rapid movement, the Normandy fighting quickly degenerated into a brutal contest for small gains in ground through the difficult *bocage* country, small fields lined with thickly wooded hedgerows, that provided ideal defensive terrain for the Germans, who exploited it effortlessly. Within weeks, the Allies had landed more than a million men in northwestern France, and the invasion was an accomplished fact. Nonetheless, it took a further assault, called Operation Cobra, by Bradley's 12th Army Group at the end of July to crack open the weakening German

Figure 12.5 A landing craft disembarks troops of Company E, 16th Infantry, 1st Infantry Division (the Big Red One) wading onto the Fox Green section of Omaha Beach on the morning of June 6, 1944. During the initial landing two-thirds of Company E became casualties.

Source: National Archives.

defenses and begin a rapid and unstoppable advance by Patton's 3rd Army across France toward Paris and beyond. Tactical airpower and heavy 'strategic' bombers, deployed in a tactical role, were central to American success.

Strategic bombing had in fact been the major effort against German-occupied Europe since the beginning of the war. The British had launched bombing raids on targets in Germany and Western Europe because air assault was the only means of attacking the enemy after Germany had conquered Europe, but the early results were limited and expensive in aircraft and aircrew losses. The technology of the time was unable to meet the expectations of airpower's decisive potential as identified by interwar theorists and enthusiasts. These losses dictated one of the fundamental characteristics of the bombing offensive waged by the Royal Air Force's Bomber Command—night bombing of area targets, that is, cities. The losses and damage inflicted on Germany's cities and on German civilians led, in turn, to the development of an increasingly sophisticated air defense system, with advances on one side being matched by technological, tactical, and doctrinal developments on the other.

The Army Air Forces believed in precision daytime bombing on industrial and military targets rather than on civilians in cities. They suffered the same initial loss rates as the Royal Air Force had before it switched to night bombing. In January 1943, Roosevelt, Churchill, and the Combined Chiefs of Staff initiated a Combined Bombing Offensive, designated Operation Pointblank, in which the British would bomb at night and the Americans by day with the idea, among others, that such round-the-clock bombing would place the German air defenses and economy under strain too great to bear.

The Americans also opted to concentrate on the German aircraft industry and the Luftwaffe's airfields to further damage their capacity to counter the bomber streams. This had only limited effect, however, and losses continued to be heavy primarily because the bombers attacking beyond the limits of fighter aircraft range were unescorted for the most dangerous part of the raid and were shot down in considerable numbers as a result. German day and night fighter pilots became increasingly skilled in air defense tasks, and new planes, equipment, and techniques were quickly adopted to maintain the advantage. Life expectancy among Allied bomber crews resembled that of infantry subalterns on the Western Front in 1916–1917.

The critical factor that turned the tide for the Allies was the development and deployment in increasingly large numbers of fighter aircraft with the range necessary to protect the bombers to the target and back again. New types, modifications of existing models, and the addition of external fuel tanks all played a part in this. Another factor was the creation of the 15th Air Force, based in Italy, to complement the 8th Air Force operating from Britain. The Germans now had to deal with two bomber streams and thus divide their defenses. Although in 1944 Germany produced more aircraft than previously because of changes to the organization of labor within aircraft factories, the enemy lacked sufficient numbers of skilled pilots to fly all the planes available while increasing pressure on the air defenses produced an upswing in losses that were now almost impossible to recoup.

In advance of D-Day, Allied bomber forces were assigned numerous targets across France in addition to specific targets just behind the intended invasion area to deceive the Germans and interfere with their ability to move reinforcements easily. These deception raids killed thousands of French civilians, a cost that both Eisenhower and French General Charles de Gaulle both recognized and accepted. The attendant 'transportation plan' was necessary to degrade Germany's ability to successfully counter the Normandy invasion. By early 1945, Allied bomber forces ran out of worthwhile targets to attack.

The rapid advance of the French and American divisions that landed in southern France in August 1944 meant that the Allies quickly formed a continuous front by September, cutting off German forces remaining in southern and western France. Success now hobbled operations, with the logistics system, remarkable though it was, unable to sustain multiple armies advancing on multiple fronts simultaneously. The Germans rationalized their forces and defenses along the Franco-German border region (the so-called Siegfried Line), while the Allies were further diverted by Montgomery's quixotic and unsuccessful Operation Market Garden into Holland to seize crossing points over the Rhine at Arnhem. Faced with manpower difficulties as well as supply problems, Eisenhower gave priority to Montgomery's 21st British Army Group, reinforced it with several American units, and placed operational restrictions on remaining American forces occupied in taking the Siegfried Line to get across the Rhine. The debate at the highest levels over a broad front or narrow front advance was thus resolved in favor of the latter. In doing so, Eisenhower was being a good ally but not necessarily a good strategist.

The fighting in the autumn mud and wet cold was grueling, bitter, and costly as the Germans found new reserves of determination in seeking to deny Allied entry into the Germany. Guilty perhaps of a reasonable belief in inevitable victory, the Allies failed to see the preparations for a major new offensive in the rugged Ardennes against thinly spread American forces. In what is popularly known as the Battle of the Bulge, the revitalized German forces advanced 50 miles in short order, capturing large numbers of prisoners, a group of whom were murdered at Malmedy.

Although initially successful, the Germans could not, in fact, sustain their momentum. When the weather cleared, and Allied tactical airpower could again be deployed against the Germans, the offensive was defeated. American and British armor also played pivotal roles in repulsing the German advance. American losses were heavy, on the order of 100,000 men, while German losses amounted to over 120,000. But the most important consequence was the loss of armor and other heavy equipment that the German war industry could not replace, a weakness that eliminated Germany's ability to mount large-scale, sustained operations against the Allied advance.

As German capacity to resist diminished, Allied offensive capacity increased, with simultaneous offensives launched on both the Eastern and Western Fronts in January 1945. Once the German fronts began to crack, the torrent proved unstoppable; and although resistance continued to the bitter end, the end itself was inevitable. Hitler committed suicide at the end of April, with the Soviets already in the streets of central Berlin and American forces invading Austria and Czechoslovakia. The remaining German authorities surrendered their devastated country on May 7.

Women and Minorities in the War Effort

Great wars often produce short-term social changes with long-term implications. World War II provides an excellent example of this process at work, not just in the United States but among many of the other combatant nations as well. This proved especially true in the case of various minorities in the American population concerning employment, social position, and economic advantage. It also proved true across the population as a whole, of course, with higher wages and increased employment in war industries counteracting the lingering effects of the Depression, but women and minorities also benefited.

Change and opportunity were reflected in two major areas: the civilian economy and the ranks of the armed forces. The expansion in industry and the military quickly soaked up the seven million unemployed, who in turn were joined by millions more outside the formal workforce. The demands for labor provoked internal migration on a large scale, with African American and whites moving from the rural south and other agricultural areas to the hubs of manufacturing industry in the Northeast and Midwest. The industrial workforce grew by ten million workers during the war, while wages increased by 68 percent. The Great Depression of the 1930s essentially vanished. The basis of postwar prosperity was thus laid in wartime prosperity.

The armed forces remained racially segregated throughout the war, but opportunities were still available to women and minorities in a manner and on a scale not previously experienced. Women's auxiliary services had been created during World War I and were reformed in World War II to utilize skilled female personnel and to free men for the fighting forces, from which women remained barred. Women served overseas in significant numbers, and not only in the nursing services: 333,000 women, out of a total of 16 million, served in uniform across the war, and in late 1945 there were still 266,000 in uniform. Women were not included in the draft.

The draft was, however, extended to include African Americans and other racial minorities. Provisions within the Selective Service and Training Act forbade discrimination on racial grounds, but many inside and outside the armed forces resisted attempts to dilute segregation within the military. New African American units were created within the Army and the Army Air Forces, with mainly white officers and African American enlisted men, just as had been the case in the interwar period. Four fighter squadrons and a bomber group were raised and trained separately, at substantial expense, at Tuskegee, Alabama. The fighter squadrons served with great distinction in the Mediterranean theater, but the bomber group never reached operational status.

Three African American Army divisions were also created to absorb the increased number of African American infantry, artillery, and tank units: the 2nd Cavalry and the 92nd and 93rd Infantry. The 92nd eventually saw service in Italy and the 93rd in the Pacific on Bougainville. Some units fought with distinction, others less so—just like the plurality of white units across the army. Soldiers in the combat units were sometimes discriminated against by their own (white) senior command. There was an unofficial policy in the 92nd Division, for example, that no African American soldier was to be awarded the Medal of Honor, even though a number were recommended. Some of these were finally awarded as late as the 1990s. Contemporary racism defined the African American experience in World War II as it had in World War I.

Most African Americans served in quartermaster units within the Services of Supply and in transportation units in Europe and the Pacific. The most famous of these units was the Red Ball Express in Europe, and many of those deployed overseas to Britain or elsewhere in Europe found a refreshing absence of discrimination among the local civilian population, in marked contrast to what they knew back in the United States or within the ranks of the American military.

Two other groups also distinguished themselves in armed service. Navajo soldiers, made famous as the Wind Talkers, were utilized in the Pacific as signalers because their language defied Japanese attempts to interpret it. Japanese Americans, whether Issei or Nissei, fought in Italy where their 442nd Regiment became the most decorated unit in the U.S. Army. Many of these soldiers left families behind in internment camps in the western United States (not including Hawaii) when Japanese Americans were forcibly interned after Pearl Harbor by Roosevelt's Executive Order 9066.

The Homefront

While no large-scale fighting took place on the American mainland, acts of sabotage did occur, notably by teams of German saboteurs landed from U-boats on the Atlantic coast. Few incidents resulted in any significant damage, but the threat was real enough. Americans at home nevertheless felt the effects of war in positive and negative ways.

By early 1942, the United States government began rationing and price control programs to support the war effort but also to control the economy. War often causes high inflation; to combat this, price and wage controls were instituted and proved effective throughout the war. Rationing and recycling probably touched more American lives than any other development on the Homefront. Tires, for example, quickly came under rationing restrictions, as rubber was needed for a whole host of war-related equipment. New tires were not available for purchase during the war, and even used tires became scarce by 1944. In addition to durable goods, such as refrigerators, washing machines, and automobiles, which were not made during the war, day-to-day items like nylon stockings, petroleum-based lipstick, and even shoes were subject to rationing.

Similarly, gasoline was also restricted, requiring a unique lettered sticker on one's automobile to determine how much gas one could purchase, usually three gallons per week. The phrase 'was this trip really necessary' became commonplace, as the government encouraged Americans to cut back on vacation drives and other unnecessary trips. Even auto racing was banned; there was no Indy 500 during the war!

Figure 12.6 A real-life 'Rosie the Riveter' operating a hand drill at the Vultee aircraft factory, in Nashville, Tennessee, working on an A-31 Vengeance dive bomber. Photo by Alfred T. Palmer.

Source: Library of Congress Prints and Photographs Division.

Food rationing was the most intrusive on daily life. Each individual, including children, was issued a ration booklet, obtained from a local rationing board. To prevent hoarding of ration stamps, the coupon booklets had set expiration dates. The food rationing program allotted to each household limited amounts of meat, sugar, flour, butter, milk, coffee, even cheese and jams, per week. Families were encouraged to have 'meatless Tuesdays' to save food for soldiers and sailors serving around the world, and plant 'Victory Gardens' to grow their own vegetables and other foods.

The government also encouraged households to recycle. Cities and towns across the United States held frequent 'junk' drives to collect scrap metals, especially aluminum, copper, brass, and steel. Fenders from derelict cars, worn pots and pans, and empty food cans were saved and collected for reuse in shell casings, aircraft, ships, and military vehicles. Housewives saved fat and grease leftover from cooking bacon, hams, and other meats in cans or glass jars under their kitchen sinks. Each week, Boy Scouts or some other service organization would pass through neighborhoods to collect the congealed fats to be recycled as soap and even explosives, or one could drop off the can or jar at a local butcher's shop for collection. In some ways, recycling in World War II gave birth to the modern recycling movement.

Not surprisingly, a black market developed for all rationed and barred goods. Enterprising individuals and gangs around the country hoarded rationed items to sell on the side at hugely inflated prices. Despite stiff penalties for black marketeering in wartime, the illicit trade of rationed goods flourished, amounting to millions of dollars in goods, especially gasoline, lost each year. This does not include war profiteering, which was also a serious problem during the war. Missouri Senator Harry Truman led the Senate Special Committee to Investigate the National Defense Program, which exposed billions of dollars of wartime corruption. The most famous incident involved exposing shoddy housing for war workers at Winfield Park, New Jersey. Housing for workers at the nearby Kearny Shipyard was found to be barely habitable. Truman's investigators gained a reputation for sniffing out the slightest hint of corruption, so much so that the threat of investigation by the so-called Truman Committee deterred many from engaging in illegal activities. Generally, most Americans obeyed the law; with millions of American in uniform, participating in such activities was risky business.

The rapid and vast expansion of war production across the United States created millions of jobs, so many that with several million young men in uniform opportunities expanded dramatically for women and African Americans, as well as for those not in the workforce, such as teenagers and retired persons. Even young men of draft age were often released or temporarily excused from their military obligation to work in production plants and shipyards, as well as to manage farms and ranches. Unemployment hovered below 1.5 percent by 1943, a far cry from the near 25 percent unemployment rates during the height of the Great Depression just a few years before. Over 6.5 million women entered the workforce, including 2.5 million working in defense plants as 'Rosie the Riveter.' At its height in 1944, more married women worked than single women for the first time in American history.

African Americans, both men and women, also found opportunities in the expanded workplace. Many moved out of the South's agricultural belt to factory jobs in Michigan, Indiana, and Ohio, as well as New York City and California. While racism still pervaded the African American experience during the war (there was a race riot in Detroit in 1943), many did not return to the South, remaining instead in the Midwest and West after the war. The postwar civil rights movement partially originated from the 'Double V' campaign organized by African American leaders during World War II. Showing their patriotism and commitment to democracy through victory over Nazism and Fascism, African Americans hoped to claim victory over racial discrimination at home in the United States as well. This Second Great Migration, as it is known, of over five million

African Americans was one of the more significant movements of people in the United States during the twentieth century. Latinos, especially in Los Angeles, felt the pressure of this migration through increased competition for jobs and housing shortages. Like the race riot in Detroit, the 1943 'Zoot Suit' riots in Los Angeles highlighted the change in labor and migration patterns caused by the war.

Perhaps the more unintended consequence of the expansion of the workforce during the war was savings. More men and women, especially minority men and women, were working and earning a good wage than ever before in American history. With rationing and other purchase restrictions, however, these workers had nothing to buy. This fact, along with the new Federal Deposit Insurance Corporation protecting bank deposits and the very popular purchase of war savings bonds, resulted in individuals and families across the United States having substantial savings at the end of the war. By 1946, once price controls and other restrictions had been lifted, people spent money on new appliances, new cars, new homes, and other items that they had to do without or make do with what they had during the war. This made possible the material consumer culture of the 1950s, including the popularity of the new 'credit' card.

A massive propaganda effort led by the United States government's Office of War Information encouraged all Americans to embrace rationing, buy war bonds, and support the war effort. In addition to exceptionally creative posters and other art produced by government artists, Hollywood did its bit by producing training films for the War Department along with hundreds of feature-length movies dealing with some aspect of the war. Films like *Casablanca* (1942), *Mrs. Miniver* (1942), and *Air Force* (1943) depicted both the evil of the enemy and the heroism of noncombatants and combatants. Movie stars, such as Bette Davis and Ronald Reagan, led bond drives, often appearing in person at movie theaters around the country. Of course, several served, often in combat, including bomber pilot Jimmy Stewart, who was awarded the Distinguished Flying Cross for combat missions over Europe; Clark Gable, who served on a B-17 aircrew; and Henry Fonda, who served in the Navy in the Pacific. Hollywood directors such as John Ford, George Stevens, and perhaps most famously Frank Capra served in the Signal Corps and produced films supporting the war effort. Capra's *Why We Fight* series is still considered a masterpiece of propaganda film-making. Disney and Warner Brothers cartoon studios made animated training films as well as cartoons for public viewing in movie theaters. Donald Duck, Bugs Bunny, and Popeye, and many other animated 'stars,' bewildered both the Nazis and Japanese in racially charged animated features.

The darkest stain on the Homefront experience is the internment of Japanese Americans who lived on the West coast, especially California. Considered a security risk in the aftermath of the Japanese attack on Pearl Harbor, racial prejudice and fear overruled common sense to feed a growing internment movement, especially in California. President

Roosevelt made the controversial decision to move Japanese Americans into internment camps beginning in February 1942. Per Roosevelt's Executive Order 9066, over 100,000 people of Japanese descent, most of whom held American citizenship, were forced to relocate to internment camps organized by the Wartime Relocation Authority working with military authorities on the West coast. Japanese families thus sat out the war in isolated camps in California, Arizona, Utah, Colorado, Wyoming, Idaho, Arkansas, and other locations. While internees were allowed schools, work, and other activities within the camps, internment was nonetheless traumatic and difficult. In 1944, the Supreme Court confirmed the constitutionality of the internment order in *Korematsu v. United States*. Many lost their homes and businesses, and efforts after the war to provide restitution, such as the 1948 American Japanese Claims Act, were inadequate at best. After decades of lobbying and activism, in 1988 Congress passed the Civil Liberties Act, which provided a reparation payment of $20,000 to each surviving internee. Over 81,000 survivors received payment. Today, several of the internment locations are national historic sites managed by the National Park Service.

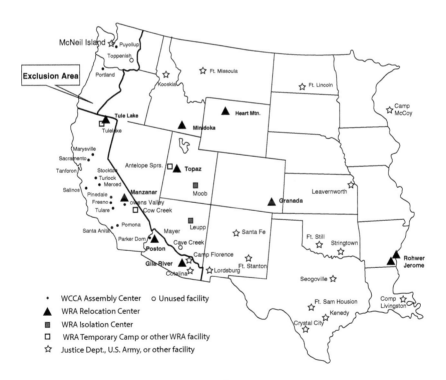

Figure 12.7 Japanese Internment Camps in the American West.

Conclusion

World War II was the greatest and most destructive conflict in history and one that helped to cement the American rise to global dominance. The Allies could not have won the war without the involvement of the United States, and with the United States in the war, they ultimately could not lose it, either. The United States did not win the war alone. Victory in Europe could not have been achieved without the Allies; the Soviets had many more divisions in the field, fought the majority of the German forces deployed on the continent, and tore the heart out of the German war effort in a series of extensive and very costly offensives. Britain provided significant forces but, more importantly, was the primary staging area for the Allied return to Western Europe. The United States was much more the driver of the war against Japan, but even here the Allied efforts by Australia, China, and other Allied nations need to be considered.

By taking a leading part in the occupation of Germany and the overwhelming lead in the occupation of Japan, the United States remade those societies along liberal-democratic and capitalist lines and helped both to create the economic miracles in those countries and to reshape them as participatory democracies and significant allies in the ensuing Cold War with the Soviet Bloc. The seeds of success in the Cold War, ultimately, were sown through the generosity of the Marshall Plan for the reconstruction of defeated enemies and the far-sighted decisions by the Truman administration not to repeat the failures that occurred after 1919 and to remain engaged with the rest of the world.

For the American military, World War II was a triumph of mobilization, procurement, leadership, and combat capability. A staggering 16 million Americans had been equipped, trained, and deployed to fight this war. Over 291,000 of them died in battle, with another 113,000 dead from other causes. Over 670,000 had been wounded. Victory over Germany and Japan, however, did not guarantee lasting peace. A new and different conflict was brewing even as World War II was still being fought.

Further Reading

Atkinson, Rick. *An Army at Dawn: The War in North Africa, 1942–1943*. New York: Henry Holt, 2002.

Atkinson, Rick. *The Day of Battle: The War in Sicily and Italy, 1943–1944*. New York: Henry Holt, 2007.

Atkinson, Rick. *The Guns at Last Light: The War in Western Europe, 1944–1945*. New York: Henry Holt, 2013.

Frank, Richard. *Downfall: The End of the Imperial Japanese Empire*. New York: Random House, 1999.

Hasegawa, Tsuyoshi. *Racing the Enemy: Stalin, Truman, and the Surrender of Japan*. Cambridge, MA: Harvard University Press, 2005.

Herman, Arthur. *Freedom's Forge: How American Business Produced Victory in World War II*. New York: Random House, 2012.

Hornfischer, James. *The Fleet at Flood Tide: America at Total War in the Pacific, 1944–1945*. New York: Bantam, 2016.

Knell, Herman. *To Destroy a City: Strategic Bombing and Its Human Consequences in World War II*. New York: Da Capo Press, 2003.

McManus, John C. *Deadly Sky: The American Combat Airman in World War II*. New York: NAL Caliber, 2000.

Murray, Williamson, and Allan R. Millett, eds. *A War to be Won: Fighting the Second World War*. Cambridge, MA: Harvard University Press, 2001.

Reeves, Richard. *Infamy: The Shocking Story of the Japanese American Internment in World War II*. New York: Henry Holt, 2015.

Rhodes, Richard. *The Making of the Atomic Bomb*. New York: Simon & Schuster, 1988.

Symonds, Craig. *World War II at Sea: A Global History*. New York: Oxford University Press, 2018.

Toll, Ian. *Pacific Crucible: War at Sea in the Pacific, 1941–1942*. New York: W.W. Norton, 2011.

Toll, Ian. *The Conquering Tide: War in the Pacific Islands, 1942–1944*. New York: W. W. Norton, 2015.

Weinberg, Gerhard L. *A World at Arms: A Global History of World War II*. Cambridge: Cambridge University Press, 1994.

Wynn, Neil A. *The African American Experience during World War II*. Lanham, MD: Rowman and Littlefield, 2010.

Yellin, Emily. *Our Mothers' War: American Women at Home and at the Front During World War II*. New York: Free Press, 2005.

13 Postwar Reform and New Challenges

Introduction

World War II had been a stunning success of American combat arms and centralized federally controlled industrial mobilization. In the traditional postwar rush to demobilize, however, the United States faced a new and different enemy: the Soviet Union and its state ideology communism. The total defeat of German fascism and Japanese militarism had not left the world in complete peace. Instead, the United States and its allies in the West, and the Soviet Union, its Eastern Bloc satellite states, and later China entered a new type of conflict that became known as the Cold War. Misunderstandings of the other's security needs, mutual suspicion of the other's political and economic philosophies, and in some ways just old-fashioned realpolitik set the stage for a war that would ultimately be fought regionally, often through proxies, all under the constant threat of nuclear holocaust.

Facing what it considered a threat to American liberty and the free world, the United States had to reorganize its military establishment, create a cohesive grand strategy to fight this war, and convince the American people to finally and fully accept a huge defense organization of unprecedented cost and size. Strategic concepts, such as containment, brought together diplomatic, economic, political, and military strategies to form a multifaceted approach to war different than that of World War II. The Korean War would quickly test this Cold War strategic framework. The United States had permanently broken with its tradition of oceanic security and downsized peacetime forces.

Containment and the Military

World War II ended with a bipolar world system characterized by an ideological contest between the communist Soviet Union and its satellites and the capitalist and democratic United States and its allies. Initially, the atomic bomb made the United States the undisputed global military super-power. With the atomic bomb, the American military could reduce its conventional forces. Thus, American industry quickly reverted to the production of consumer goods, the armed forces rapidly demobilized, and the defense budget shrank. World events, however, forced American foreign policy to become increasingly dependent upon military indemnification.

Allied cohesion, strained during the last months of the war, began to crumble soon after Japan's surrender when the Soviet Union strongly objected to the terms of peace treaties with the former Axis states. On February 22, 1946, an American diplomat to the Soviet Union, George F. Kennan, wrote the Long Telegram. In his top-secret cable, Kennan explained that the deepening American–Soviet estrangement could be traced to the Soviet fear of capitalist encirclement. Stalin zealously believed the two countries could never reach a permanent modus vivendi. Relations worsened over the next several months when the Truman administration refused a reconstruction loan to the Soviet Union because of disagreements about the future of Eastern Europe. Also, in June 1946 the Soviets rejected a proposal for an International Atomic Development Authority, which would have given the United States de facto control over atomic research worldwide. In September, presidential advisor Clark Clifford counseled Truman to prepare for a 'war on all fronts' against Soviet aggression.

Ultimately, the development of America's containment policy made 1947 the pivotal year for postwar American–Soviet relations. Economically devastated, Great Britain announced its withdrawal from commitments in Turkey and Greece despite Western assumptions of Soviet interference in the region. Determined to defend the Free World and fearful that Great Britain's pullout might mean conceding Middle Eastern resources to the Soviets, the president proclaimed what came to be known as the Truman Doctrine. In an address to Congress in March, Truman declared that the United States would 'support free peoples who are resisting attempted subjugation by armed minorities or by outside pressures' and urged Congress to provide millions of dollars in economic and military aid, including military advisors, to preserve Turkish and Greek sovereignty. Indeed, American assistance was mostly military, particularly to Greece.

In July 1947, Kennan anonymously published an article in the journal *Foreign Affairs*. The article, titled 'The Sources of Soviet Conduct,' expanded upon his earlier analysis. Now Kennan urged the United States to develop a coherent foreign policy, centered on using every method short of war to obstruct Soviet expansion. In June, Secretary of State George C. Marshall had introduced the European Recovery Program, known as the Marshall Plan, to jump-start Europe's postwar economic recovery with $16 billion in aid. While the administration genuinely wanted to improve living conditions for people on the devastated continent, it also hoped the program would prevent the spread of communism by establishing strong and stable European economies. As with the

Truman Doctrine, however, Marshall Plan funds mainly went to military aid. In 1951, Congress merged the Plan with the Military Defense Aid Program; a year later, the program became the Mutual Security Administration and continued to provide European nations funding for their armed forces.

Defense Reorganization and a New Air Force

During World War II, bureaucratic tangles, inter-service squabbles, and budget worries prompted then Army of Chief of Staff General George C. Marshall to lay the foundation for postwar defense reorganization. Wartime demands naturally required that serious attention to reform be delayed until the war ended, but after Japan surrendered, the Army and Navy quickly began arguing over the best way to unify command and administration of the defense establishment. In an internal debate that the press dubbed 'The Battle of the Potomac,' the Army supported an independent air force and pressed for the creation of a single cabinet-level office to oversee all three services. In contrast, the Navy opposed both an independent air force and merging the services under a single secretary, preferring a looser arrangement that provided only for coordination of the services. Both services faced budget cuts with a potential third party entering the budgetary fray. The dispute continued until inter-service negotiations and congressional hearings ended in the passage of the National Security Act of 1947.

Enacted in July, the National Security Act reorganized and modernized the national defense establishment, creating the bodies that continue to be responsible for American national security. The most important of these advisory groups would be the National Security Council, comprising, at a minimum, the president and vice president, and the Secretaries of State and Defense. Also, the act created the successor to the World War II Office of Strategic Services, the Central Intelligence Agency, whose director also sat on the National Security Council.

Congress provided for coordination and supervision, rather than unification, of the defense establishment. A new Department of Defense replaced the old War Department, and new Departments of the Army, Navy, and, most controversially, Air Force now existed as part of the Department of Defense. Although the legislation replaced the Secretary of War and the Secretary of the Navy with a single Secretary of Defense, that office was given little power. Given the weak authority of the office and the demands on the military created by the postwar shifts in the balance of power, the first Secretary of Defense James Forrestal (previously Secretary of the Navy) faced an unusually difficult task. Inter-service competition and disagreement reemerged with new vigor as each service scrambled to protect its interests. The National Security Act also provided for a Joint Chiefs of Staff, which included the commanding officers of the Army,

Navy, the new Air Force, and the Marines. The president had the authority to select a chairman of the Joint Chiefs of Staff, who could be from any of the services and whose authority included managing the services and advising the president on military matters.

Because military aviation is inherently expensive, the rivalry between naval aviators and the Air Force was especially malicious, with the Navy contending that the Air Force was maneuvering to eliminate naval air altogether. The Navy also defended its organic air arm with the argument that naval airpower was uniquely suited to its tactical mission to protect the fleet at sea, a defense need that the Air Force ignored with its focus on strategic bombing. Naval aviators were not willing, however, to give up strategic air capabilities. Advocates for the Air Force accused the Navy of using the tactical air argument as a ruse to create a second air force. The Navy was also on the defensive against the Army's claim over control of all ground forces, a move the Navy considered a direct threat to the Marine Corps. Trying for compromise, Forrestal suggested that each service receive an equal portion of the defense budget. Dissatisfied with one-third of a much-reduced defense appropriation, the services took their disputes into the public arena.

Disappointed with Forrestal's inability to resolve the feud, President Truman replaced him with Louis A. Johnson. Truman thought that Johnson's tireless, no-nonsense work ethic and widely recognized talent for administration was what a secretary of defense needed to get the job done. Moreover, Johnson's background as a World War I infantry officer, National Commander of the American Legion, and Assistant Secretary of War under Roosevelt gave him the experience needed to gain the respect of the service chiefs. Indeed, the Army and Air Force were pleased with Johnson's appointment, partly because he was well known for his pro-Air Force opinions. As one might expect, however, the Navy was apprehensive over the new secretary's influence on its future.

Johnson wasted little time. Within two weeks of his appointment, Johnson announced that all public statements by active or retired flag officers had to be approved by the Office of the Secretary of Defense. Naval officers were especially resistant to this requirement because they believed Johnson was purposely preventing them from openly pressing the Navy's case. The secretary further angered the Navy by approving the Air Force's purchase of 36 B-36 bombers in place of fighters and medium-range bombers.

The Revolt of the Admirals

Less than a month after taking office, Johnson sparked the Revolt of the Admirals by canceling construction of the *United States*, the Navy's 1,090-foot-long, 65,000-ton supercarrier, designed to provide naval aviation with a strategic bombing role. Not only would strategic bombing ensure the Navy's relevance, but it also would guarantee that the sea services were given a substantial share of the defense budget. Senior naval officers had pinned the Navy's future on the *United States*; the keel had been laid just days before Johnson stopped the program. Although Johnson discussed the ship's future with the service chiefs and with the chairmen of the House and Senate Armed Services Committees, he did not consult with the service secretaries.

The cancelation order was delivered to Navy Secretary John L. Sullivan and the press at the same time on the morning of April 23, 1949. Sullivan immediately resigned; his letter of resignation lambasted Johnson for not consulting with the Navy on an issue considered vital to its future. Johnson was unruffled, however, because he had taken a big step toward his twin goals of cutting the defense budget and unifying the defense establishment.

Naval officers, especially aviators, were determined to fight for their service's future. An anonymously prepared document (written by Cedrick R. Worth, a special assistant to the Undersecretary of the Navy) made its way to the House Armed Services Committee. The report implicated Johnson and the Secretary of the Air Force in falsifying information on the B-36 program to the benefit of the airplane's manufacturer, Convair. The committee called for an investigation and scheduled hearings for August and October. A long list of witnesses, including Worth, discredited the Navy's charges and reinforced public and congressional support for unification and the Air Force.

Furthermore, amendments to the National Security Act gave the secretary of defense greater authority over the services, easing efforts to enforce economy, especially across-the-board cuts in Navy programs. This new threat prompted the Navy to continue its fight. In early September, Captain John G. Crommelin, a naval aviator serving as a staff officer to the Joint Chiefs, publicly charged that Johnson and the Joint Chiefs of Staff wanted to destroy the Navy. Francis Matthews, the new Secretary of the Navy, rushed to reassure Johnson and the Chief of Naval Operations and convinced Carl Vinson, the Chairman of the Senate Armed Services Committee, to postpone further hearings. However, Admiral Arthur W. Radford intervened to change Vinson's mind.

During the first days of the October hearings, several influential Navy officers—including Admirals Radford, William F. Halsey, Ernest J. King, and Captain Arleigh A. Burke—presented the Navy's case against the Air Force and Secretary Johnson. Secretary Stuart Symington followed to deliver the Air Force's presentation. His evidence was enough to defeat the Navy, but Army General Omar N. Bradley, the recently appointed Chairman of the Joint Chiefs of Staff, gave the Navy a fierce tongue-lashing for its stubborn and shortsighted opposition to unification. Worse, Bradley accused the Navy of rejecting civilian control of the military. The Navy's gamble had failed. Unification proceeded, and the Air Force retained control of the strategic air mission. All the officers involved in the revolt—except for Arleigh Burke, who was promoted to admiral—were punished with reprimands, forced retirements, or resignations. Although inter-service rivalry continued, the Navy's fortunes soon revived as it became clear that sea power remained vital to national defense.

Racial Integration of the Armed Forces

Postwar reform of the military included the integration of African Americans into the armed forces. African Americans had served in every American war but had never been treated as equal to white soldiers. Furthermore, although African Americans wore their uniforms proudly and expected that their efforts would earn social and legal equality for African Americans in the United States, neither their service nor its relationship to the full rights of citizenship was officially recognized. After World War II, African Americans were especially determined that their service and their citizenship be acknowledged, and so they threatened to boycott the armed forces.

This understandable threat held even more prescience following the mob lynching of two African American couples near Moore's Ford Bridge in Walton County, Georgia, on July 25, 1946. One of the men, Roger Malcolm, had been accused of stabbing a white man in nearby Monroe, Georgia. As the couples drove back to their farm after posting bail for Malcolm, they were stopped by a white mob, who bound both couples then shot them over 60 times. As was too often the case, state and federal investigators were unable to charge anyone in relation to the killings, which received national attention. One of the victims, George Dorsey, was a veteran who served in the Pacific. Southern whites did not welcome African Americans who had served in uniform. Such veterans frequently met violence, including death, across the South. African Americans recognized the connection between military service to the country and their struggle for civil rights and equal treatment. If African Americans carried out the service boycott, military recruitment needs would be seriously undercut.

Sympathetic to the need for anti-lynching laws and civil rights legislation, President Truman was equally concerned about military preparedness. Moreover, African Americans traditionally supported the Democratic Party, and Truman did not wish to alienate a key group of voters during the upcoming 1948 presidential campaign. Despite having his anti-lynching bill defeated in the House of Representatives, on July 26, 1948, Truman issued Executive Order 9981 declaring 'that there shall be equality of treatment and opportunity in the armed forces without regard to race, color, religion, or national origin.'

The Navy and Air Force were generally cooperative. During World War II, the Navy had begun integration and proposed to continue that policy. The Air Force had planned to start integrating but recommended using merit to determine which African Americans would serve in white units. Dissatisfied with such a limited approach, Truman made it clear that integration was going to happen and that the services needed to move quickly. By the summer of 1949, the Department of Defense had approved both the Air Force and Navy integration plans, but the Army was dragging its boots. Army officials stubbornly resisted integration and looked for ways to subvert the president's order.

When the order was first announced, Army officers noted that it did not explicitly require integration of the Army. On July 27, Army Chief of Staff Omar Bradley declared that the Army would not integrate until society fully accepted the equality of African Americans, arguing that the Army was not the place to conduct social experiments. Each proposal the Army submitted included provisions for segregated units with ten percent enlistment quotas for African Americans. Finally, in December 1949, the Army agreed to integrate its units but refused to abolish the quotas until February 1950, when Truman consented to let the Army re-establish quotas if too many African Americans enlisted. Clearly, the Army did not intend to fully integrate.

Combat losses in Korea, combined with a breakdown in discipline under fire of the all-African American 24th Infantry Regiment, convinced the Army to assign African American soldiers across the service, thus achieving a de facto integration of the Army. By the end of the Korean War, the Army claimed 95 percent of African American soldiers served in integrated units.

In 1948, Truman also signed the Women's Armed Services Integration Act, which for the first time granted women permanent status in the United States armed forces, though not in combat roles. Although historically women were heavily recruited for wartime service, they had not been allowed to remain in uniform after a war ended. The new law restricted the number of women in the services to no more than two percent of authorized manpower. There were also restrictions on promotions and women could be discharged without cause at any time. Married women and those with children could not serve. While the restrictions eased somewhat over the following decades, real changes did not occur until the Department of Defense adopted the All-Volunteer Force model in 1973.

The Berlin Airlift

While underwriting economic recovery in Europe, the Marshall Plan increased tensions between East and West, particularly on the issue of German reunification. Economic conditions in occupied Germany were so bad that the currency of choice was American cigarettes rather than the hyperinflated Reichsmark. During the summer of 1948, the United States, Great Britain, and France combined their occupation zones to save the German economy; the joined zones quickly became the West German Republic.

Figure 13.1 Secretary of Defense James Forrestal (center) congratulates (left to right) Colonel Geraldine May, Colonel Mary A. Hallaren, Captain Joy Bright Hancock, and Major Julia E. Hamblet, after the passage of the Women's Armed Services Integration Act, the Pentagon, Washington, D.C. Photograph by U.S. Army Signal Corps.

Source: Library of Congress.

With a self-governing West Germany looming, the new Joint Chiefs of Staff pressed Truman to form a Western Europe-based military alliance that could include German troops. The Senate also passed the Vandenberg Resolution, which urged American cooperation with regional collective security agreements, such as the Brussels Treaty, and claimed under Article 51 of the United Nations Charter the right to unilateral or multilateral self-defense. To the Soviet Union, the imminent military alliance between Western Europe and the United States was indeed a security threat.

Increasingly threatened and isolated, the Soviets attempted to divide the Allies by blockading all surface routes into West Berlin. They also disrupted city services by reducing the amount of electricity received by the western part of the city and by freezing West Berliners' accounts in the central bank, which was in the Soviet zone. If the Soviet Union successfully usurped West Berlin, American credibility in Germany, if not the world, would be undermined. Because Soviet forces in Germany outnumbered Allied troops three to one, the confrontation had to be resolved peacefully.

Truman ordered what became known as the Berlin Airlift to supply the beleaguered city and authorized an embargo on vital industrial supplies needed in East Berlin. Between June 1948 and September 1949, American and Allied military planes landed in West Berlin every three minutes, delivering food, medical supplies, and daily necessities. Throughout 15 months, the airlift delivered over 2.3 million tons of supplies on over 275,000 flights into West Berlin. Sixty pilots and aircrew were killed in plane crashes during the operation. The Soviets could do little but watch. Truman gave the impression that the United States was willing to use atomic weapons against the Soviet Union if it interfered with the operation or threatened West Germany.

NATO and NSC 68

Instead of starving West Berlin and forcing the American hand, the Berlin crisis nurtured the alliance between the United States and Western Europe. Despite the traditional American fear of involvement in foreign wars and entangling alliances, on July 21, 1949, the Senate approved American membership in the new North Atlantic Treaty Organization, or NATO. Initially comprising the United States, Great Britain, Canada, France, Italy, Norway, Iceland, Portugal, Belgium, Denmark, Luxembourg, and the Netherlands, NATO was a permanent military alliance that defined 'an armed attack against one or more' of the members as 'an attack against them all.'

The concern voiced by the Senate over membership in NATO was deep-rooted and genuine. Indeed, NATO represented the nation's first formal military alliance with Europe since the American Revolution, as well as its first official peacetime military partnership. Nonetheless, American membership was crucial for NATO's deterrent effect against Soviet aggression in Western Europe because the United States still held a monopoly on atomic weapons.

Still, the real purpose of NATO was to prevent nuclear war. The Mutual Defense Assistance Bill, a $1.5 billion military aid package intended to modernize and enlarge European armed forces, accompanied Senate approval of the NATO alliance. Truman also hoped that NATO would serve as a conduit for the reintegration of the new Federal Republic of Germany (West Germany) into Europe, in part because NATO needed West German manpower, resources, and base sites. Interest in West German membership in NATO increased when the Soviet Union exploded an atomic device in September 1949, thus ending the American atomic monopoly. Creation of the Communist German Democratic Republic of East Germany a month later increased support for West German NATO membership. Unfortunately for the German people, once again Germany was a potential battleground.

Communism also seemed to be making gains in Asia, where the Chinese Communist Party of Mao Tse-tung defeated Chinese Nationalist forces under Chiang Kai-shek in 1949, pushing what remained of the non-Communist army off mainland China onto the island of Taiwan. Considering communist successes, Truman ordered a reassessment of American foreign and defense policy. The National Security Council's Policy Planning Staff prepared National Security Council Study 68, better known as NSC-68, which assumed that the Soviet Union was aggressively expansionist and that its primary target was the United States.

According to NSC-68, conflict was inherent in the ideological disagreement between the Free World and Communism; thus, the United States should adopt a 'bold and massive program' of defense buildup in support of a dynamic global containment policy aimed at defeating the Soviet Union through economic and other means rather than military force. The study also recommended that the United States build more atomic weapons and accelerate the development of the hydrogen bomb. To avert an all-out general war, direct conflict with the Soviet Union was to be avoided, opting instead for contained regional conflict of limited scope and scale, fought preferably by proxy states. Containment thus became an offensive approach rather than a defensive posture. The NSC-68 conclusions provided the foundation for unprecedented peacetime defense expenditures and military buildup and the development of what President Dwight D. Eisenhower would later call the military–industrial complex.

Although American military planning remained focused on a European-based war against the Soviet Red Army, the United States soon found itself fighting in Asia instead. The Korean War ironically served as the immediate justification for implementing the recommendations of NSC-68 and brought to the fore concepts of limited war in a nuclear world.

The Korean War

As Japan collapsed under the horrific weight of the atomic bombs, the Soviet Union declared war against what remained of the Japanese Empire on August 8, 1945. Within two days, Soviet troops had moved into the far northeastern regions of the Korean Peninsula. On August 15, President Truman and Soviet Premier Stalin approved the division of Korea at the 38th parallel, with the Soviet Union to occupy the industrial north and the United States to garrison the agricultural south. The dividing line had been chosen primarily because the Soviet Union agreed not to move south of that demarcation line.

Despite wartime agreements that Korea would be unified as a free and independent state, reunification discussions between the Soviets and Americans quickly broke down. Frustrated at the lack of progress, the United States referred Korean reunification to the United Nations General Assembly, which in turn called for nationwide elections. In the meantime, as was happening in Europe, the occupation governments in both North and South Korea did their best to create political institutions reflecting the ideologies of their occupiers. Although the Soviets refused to hold elections in the North, United Nations elections took place in the South in May 1948.

Syngman Rhee was elected president of the Republic of Korea (South Korea). The elderly Rhee was a staunch nationalist who had been educated in the United States and had lived there for much of his long exile from his home country. Although Rhee's authoritarian character disqualified him as a defender of a free society, the Cold War meant that his reliably anti-communist sentiment outweighed other considerations. Kim Il Sung, backed by the Soviet Union, became prime minister of the Democratic People's Republic of Korea (North Korea) in September.

In December, the United States agreed to continue economic and military aid to South Korea. When World War II ended, the American occupation government in Korea began training a South Korean military. Rhee's clear intent to reunite the peninsula, however, prompted the United States to limit South Korean armaments to light artillery and a few small aircraft, all of which were worn and outdated World War II designs. In contrast, the Soviet Union equipped the North Korean Army with heavy artillery and tanks and had trained North Korean soldiers. However, at the urging of the United Nations, Red Army troops withdrew from North Korea in late 1948, and the United States pulled its occupation forces out of South Korea the following summer. Several hundred Soviet and American military advisors remained to continue training programs.

Although the United States continued to assure South Korea of its support, the Truman administration's actions suggested to the world that South Korea would have to take care of itself. Preoccupied with securing Western Europe against Communist expansion, American policymakers were reluctant to expand commitments in Asia. Military leaders also considered events in Asia secondary to what was happening in Europe. The postwar Army had been reduced to approximately 591,000 men, organized into ten undermanned and poorly equipped divisions. About one-third of the Army was on occupation duty in Germany and Japan, with roughly 108,500 in the Far East.

The United States sent mixed signals to the Soviet Union regarding its policy in Korea. Speaking before the National Press Club in January 1950, Secretary of State Dean Acheson implied that the United States did not consider Korea a vital national security interest. Defining the American defense perimeter in Asia, Acheson included the Aleutian Islands, Japan, the Ryukyu Islands, and the Philippines, but not Taiwan or Korea. He also declared that if nations were attacked, they must rely upon their own resources until the United Nations could assist them. His speech may have been intended as a message to Communist China that the United States wanted to avoid a conflict over Taiwan, but Kim Il Sung also was listening. General Douglas MacArthur, the American military governor of occupied Japan and Commander-in-Chief, Far East Command, also publicly opposed a general Asian war.

For some time, Kim had been pressing Stalin to support the use of force to reunite the peninsula. Acheson's speech appeared to indicate that North Korea could attack the south without fear of American intervention. Finally, after exploding its own atomic weapon and having completed an alliance with Mao's China, the Soviet Union was willing to give Kim the go-ahead. Stalin was not enthusiastic in a reunited Korea; instead, he saw a Korean war as an opportunity to weaken China by forcing it into a fight with the United States. A weakened China would have to take a subservient position to Soviet strategy. Kim also consulted with Mao, but Mao was not kept apprised of North Korean plans. When war came, China was caught by surprise.

Phase I: The United Nations Defensive (June 27–September 15, 1950)

With Stalin's blessing and Soviet military advisors' assistance, North Korea invaded South Korea in the early hours of June 25, 1950. At Truman's request, the United Nations Security Council quickly condemned Kim's action and called for the immediate withdrawal of North Korean forces. Kim refused, and on June 27 the Security Council passed a second resolution asking member states to provide military assistance to South Korea. Seoul, the South Korean capital, fell to North Korean troops the following day.

Despite the American military's lack of readiness, the United States had to act quickly or risk losing credibility with its allies. Ammunition and other equipment were immediately shipped to help shore up South Korean resistance, and on June 26, Truman authorized American air and naval attacks against the invading forces. Two days later, the United States Far East Air Forces (FEAF) began attacking military targets between Seoul and the 38th parallel. The next day, the 3rd Bombardment Group made the first American air raid on North Korea, bombing the airfield at Pyongyang. The FEAF Bomber Command followed this raid with sporadic B-29 missions against North Korean targets through July. Then, in August, B-29s made concerted and continuous attacks on North Korean marshaling yards, railroad bridges, and supply dumps. These raids made it difficult for the enemy to supply, reinforce, and move its front-line troops. On June 30, Truman gave MacArthur the authority to take military action to repel the invasion.

MacArthur was confident that his UN forces would easily turn back the North Korean invasion force. When a task force of 400 infantry, most of whom were untried in combat, failed to block the road to Pusan, American certainty faltered. Task Force Smith—named for its commander, Colonel Charles B. Smith—held as long as it could, but his troops were soon literally running for their lives. MacArthur claimed that Smith had traded space for much-needed time, but in reality, Task Force Smith had been an arrogant tactical disaster that exposed lack of combat readiness among American forces.

On July 7, the United Nations Security Council recommended the formation of a single command over the international forces that would be fighting in Korea. Because the United States would undoubtedly be the dominant member, the Security Council asked for an American commander. MacArthur became Commander-in-Chief, United Nations Command, and the U.S. Eighth Army Commander; Lieutenant General Walton H. Walker, took command of all United Nations ground forces.

Walker's American forces, all under strength and missing entire elements, included the 7th, 24th, and 25th Infantry Divisions, the 1st Cavalry Division, and the 29th Regiment. The unpreparedness of Walker's troops dictated his strategy. Throughout the rest of July and the first few days of August, the Eighth Army fought a defensive war, delaying the North Korean advance as much as possible while waiting for reinforcements. During brutal fighting, the North Koreans steadily drove the Americans and South Koreans southward. Casualties mounted and the numbers of missing multiplied. During the Battle of Taejon, the 24th Infantry Division's commander, General William F. Dean, became separated from his troops and was later taken prisoner by the North Koreans. He remained a prisoner of war until September 1953.

By August 4, Walker's forces had been pushed into a small beachhead around the southern port of Pusan. Determined to hold, Walker established a defense in depth, stretching through the hills north of Pusan and west along the Naktong River with the Sea of Japan at his back. Now with the benefit of interior lines, Walker's units could better support each other and more easily move reinforcements to threatened sectors. For the next six weeks, Walker's force held the Pusan Perimeter against determined North Korean attacks while supplies and additional troops arrived in preparation for a breakout. As United Nations forces gained strength, the North Korean Army, unable to replace personnel or destroyed equipment, weakened. Its logistical line was stretched to breaking point as American air strikes further hampered resupply.

Phase II: The United Nations Offensive (September 15-November 2, 1950)

As the Eighth Army defended the Pusan Perimeter, MacArthur planned a risky amphibious assault at Inchon, a port city on the western coast, just south of Seoul. Dubbed Operation Chromite, the landing was intended to relieve the pressure against Pusan by completely severing the North Korean supply line, recapturing the South Korean capital, and then blocking the Communist retreat. MacArthur gave his favorite subordinate, Major General Edward M. Almond, command of the reactivated X Army Corps, now comprising the 1st Marine Division and the Army's 7th Infantry Division, along with a South Korean Marine Regiment and several thousand South Korean troops.

A naval task force representing nine nations supported the landing. Naval guns in coordination with carrier-based air attacks bombarded communist-held coastal defenses. Underwater demolition teams cleared mines and other obstacles to the landing, and ships and amphibious assault craft ferried the Marines to their landing points. On September 15, two Marine regiments secured Wolmi Island just outside the causeway into Inchon. Later that afternoon, two more Marine regiments landed at Red Beach and Blue Beach, where they had to scale high seawalls. Protected from enemy air attack by air superiority and encountering only scattered enemy resistance, the Marines had surrounded Inchon by the following morning. Four days after the landing, the 1st Marine Division was advancing toward Seoul while the 7th Division moved to block Communist troops retreating from Pusan. On September 29, Seoul was liberated for the first time in the war.

The Eighth Army broke out of the Pusan Perimeter on September 19 and began pushing north, battling North Korean forces all along the way. A week later, the Eighth Army linked with the southern elements of X Corps. In October, United Nations forces began advancing north toward the Yalu River, at the northern border between North Korea and China. The Eighth Army followed a western route up the peninsula, while X Corps was taken by sea to the port of Wonsan, on the eastern coast of North Korea. South Korean units led the advance through much of the Wonsan Campaign, seizing the North Korean capital, Pyongyang, on October 19 before American forces reached the city.

With a promise of 'home by Christmas' and hoping to avoid the severe conditions of the Korean winter, MacArthur ordered his commanders to press north as quickly as possible. The Eighth Army advanced in two columns, while General Almond moved northward and slightly inland from Wonsan. It looked as if the war would soon be over, with the Korean Peninsula reunited under a non-Communist government.

Phase III: The Communist Chinese Forces (CCF) Intervention (November 3 1950–January 24, 1951)

With United Nations forces at or at least very near the North Korean border with China, CCF forces entered North Korea in mid-October; but the level of Chinese involvement was at first uncertain. Late in October one of X Corps' South Korean elements advancing toward the Changjin (Chosin) Reservoir encountered a Chinese force. The battle lasted several days, under brutal conditions, until the 7th Marine Regiment broke the Chinese line near the reservoir. On November 6, the Chinese broke contact. During the same period, near the Chongchon River in the west, Chinese forces pushed the Eighth Army back under severe attack. Russian-designed MIG-15 fighter jets had also entered the air war.

During the next few weeks, MacArthur tried to assess the strength of Chinese forces in Korea. Despite rising estimates, he was convinced that

Figure 13.2 An integrated weapons squad fighting with the 2nd Infantry Division north
    of the Chongchon River, November 20, 1950. Photo by PFC James Cox.
Source: National Archives.

the Chinese were too weak to mount a major offensive and that United
Nations forces should continue the push north. The Eighth Army recovered and continued its two-pronged advance, while X Corps turned
slightly northwest toward Walker's command. Walker launched the
United Nations counter-offensive on November 24. During the following
night, the Republic of Korea II Corps took the brunt of a strong counterattack by China's XIII Army Group. On November 27, X Army's 1st
Marine Division and elements of the Army 7th Division were attacked by
China's IX Army Group near the Changjin Reservoir. Declaring that the
conflict was now 'an entirely new war,' MacArthur ordered Walker to
retreat along whatever escape route possible and instructed Almond to
withdraw to the eastern port of Hungnam for evacuation south.

Hoping to check the attack, Walker moved his reserves forward, but
they could not stop the Chinese. Walker withdrew south across the
Chongchon River, where the American 2nd Division fought a ferocious
delaying action at Kunu-ri. Through the last few days of November, the
division suffered nearly 5,000 casualties while screening the rest of the
Army's retreat toward Seoul. Under pressure from the Chinese advance,
the Eighth Army's withdrawal turned into a headlong flight to safety as
officers lost control and units disintegrated. Desperate to lighten their

loads, soldiers discarded weapons and equipment as they fled. By mid-December, the longest retreat in American military history was over.

Walker regrouped his force, forming a defensive line around the South Korean capital. On Christmas Eve, Walker died when his jeep collided with a truck. Two days later, General Matthew B. Ridgway took command of the Eighth Army and immediately began reorganizing his shaken and disheartened force. Having commanded the 82nd Airborne Division in World War II, Ridgway was an experienced combat leader who understood that soldiers were intolerant of 'tall talk' and hyperbole, and he made a point of addressing them straightforwardly and respectfully. The soldiers' natural skepticism of officers quickly gave way to trust and respect for the new commander.

MacArthur had limited expectations of what Ridgway could do with the demoralized troops, asking only that he hold Seoul as long as possible. On January 4, 1951, the Eighth Army evacuated the capital only slightly ahead of attacking Chinese troops, destroying bridges across the Han River as it retreated. Ten days later, Ridgway established a defensive line just below the 38th parallel. When the Chinese broke off their offensive, Ridgway began to think that the Communist armies could be defeated with current force strength. Taking advantage of the enemy's inability to supply extended offensives, Ridgway decided to fight a war of maneuver. When the Communists attacked, Ridgway ordered delaying actions, and when the weakened enemy pulled back, he attacked.

While the Eighth Army was retreating southward, soldiers and Marines fought for their survival at the Changjin Reservoir. To the east of the reservoir, a 3,000-man task force under Lieutenant Colonel Don C. Faith, Jr., was approaching the Yalu River when it was attacked by a much larger Chinese force. Between November 17 and December 1, Task Force Faith fought a retrograde action toward American lines at Hagaru-ri, west of the reservoir. Unable to drive vehicles across the frozen reservoir, Task Force Faith made its way along a road that was frequently under attack, its progress further checked by enemy-constructed roadblocks. Winter gear had not reached the combat troops, so the men wore only summer uniforms as protection against temperatures of 30 degrees below zero. Despite airdrops, food and ammunition were in short supply. Task Force Faith was decimated; fewer than 400 men survived the ordeal. Faith died during the battle from wounds received while leading an attack against a roadblock.

To the west of Changjin, the 1st Marine Division was spread out along a road leading from the coast to the reservoir, a deployment that allowed the enemy to isolate and surround individual formations. Led by Lieutenant General O. P. Smith, the Marines and soldiers who had reached Hagaru-ri started back toward the port of Hungnam. Unwilling to convey a sense of defeat to his men and at the same time accurately describing the situation, Smith responded to a question about the withdrawal: 'Retreat hell! We're attacking in a different direction!' Indeed, over the next two weeks Smith's men, with the help of air support, fought their way through frigid temperatures and enemy attacks to the coast, where they were evacuated by sea to South Korea.

When 1951 began, MacArthur had predicted that without substantial reinforcements or direct attacks against mainland China, United Nations forces would likely be pushed out of Korea. However, when Army Chief of Staff General J. Lawton Collins visited South Korea in mid-January, the new situation convinced him the fight was still on. Before leaving, Collins announced, 'We are going to stay and fight.'

Phase IV: First United Nations Counter-Offensive (January 25–April 21, 1951) and Chinese Spring Offensive (April 22–July 8, 1951)

The UN counter-offensive, Operation Thunderbolt, began on January 25. Aided by air support, elements of the Eighth Army pushed north on either side of the Han River, retaking Inchon, Kimpo airfield, and Suwon before establishing a defensive line a few miles south of the capital in early February. For three days, beginning on February 13, United Nations forces and the Chinese battled for Chipyong-ni, a crossroads southeast of Seoul near the Han River. The fighting was close range and bloody, resulting in the first tactical defeat for the Chinese since intervening over two months before.

A few days after Chipyong-ni, Ridgway launched an offensive, Operation Killer, aimed at forcing the Chinese back north of the Han River. By the beginning of March, the CCF had abandoned its positions south of the river. Operation Ripper, a general offensive to recapture Seoul, followed Killer. When the United Nations counter-offensive ended, Eighth Army had regained control of the capital and established a defensive line slightly north of the 38th parallel.

Having regained control of South Korea, the Truman administration decided to pursue a negotiated end to the war. The objective had changed from preserving an independent South Korean state to unifying the Korean Peninsula and then back to protecting South Korea. These changing war aims were a classic case of military success on the battlefield driving the political objectives of the war, rather than the other way around.

Before the president could make an offer, however, MacArthur announced that he was prepared to negotiate an armistice. Worse, he threatened to attack China if the Communists refused peace talks. MacArthur then began to lobby a friend, Republican Congressman Joseph W. Martin, to support his position. Throughout the war, the relationship between MacArthur and Truman had been strained, mainly because the general stretched his authority. For Truman and the Joint Chiefs of Staff, MacArthur's threat to expand the war was the last straw.

Moreover, MacArthur's letter to Martin, who led the opposition to Truman's policies in the House of Representatives, openly challenged the

Figure 13.3 The Korean War.

authority of the president as commander-in-chief. In fact, MacArthur believed that as theater commander he was entitled to act on his own, without consulting even the president. To preserve civilian control of the Army, Truman relieved MacArthur, naming Ridgway as his successor. Lieutenant General James A. Van Fleet took over the Eighth Army. Although Truman's action caused him serious political trouble, it resulted in better relations between Washington and the Far East Command. MacArthur returned to the United States, exalted by many—including Congress—as a great American hero rather than as an egocentric military commander who had caused a severe crisis of American civil–military relations.

MacArthur enjoyed widespread respect and popularity, and public reaction to his relief was immediate and intense. Truman received thousands of letters criticizing him for firing MacArthur. The Senate Armed Forces and Foreign Relations Committees began hearings into Truman's decision in May 1951. Lasting seven weeks, the hearings gave MacArthur the chance to declare publicly his belief that the United States must commit to the destruction of communism by military force. The military implications of his suggested policies made many Americans question their initial disapproval of his dismissal. In addition, the hearings allowed the Joint Chiefs of Staff an open forum in which to expose the flaws in MacArthur's proposals and to explain the risk he posed to civilian control of the military. Disillusioned with a man they had once revered, Americans soon lost interest in the hearings.

Shortly after Van Fleet took command, Chinese and North Korean forces launched a spring offensive. Ordered to retake Seoul, the Communist armies pushed the United Nations troops southward several miles from the capital before Van Fleet's force stopped their advance. Enemy units had to withdraw and regroup as they ran low on supplies. In mid-May, the Chinese and North Koreans renewed their offensive, this time directing pressure against weak points in the eastern part of the defensive line. Despite forcing a breach, the enemy could not make headway against the Eighth Army's determined stand. Pulling back, the Communists established their own defensive line opposite the Eighth Army, just north of the 38th parallel.

The stalemate presented an opportunity for ending the war. Toward the end of June, the Soviets and Chinese proposed negotiating an armistice. Although the South and North Korean governments wanted to continue fighting until reunification, their patrons were not willing to risk domestic and international political costs for what had become a strategically questionable war. Negotiations began on July 10 in Kaesong, in far western North Korea just north of the 38th parallel. Vice Admiral C. Turner Joy led negotiations for the United Nations command opposite Lieutenant General Nam Il, Chief of Staff of the North Korean People's Army. They quickly agreed that combat would continue until they decided upon armistice terms. From then on, the conflict became a war of fighting while negotiating. The war turned into an intense clash of patrols and small but bloody battles in which places like Pork Chop Hill and Bloody Ridge repeatedly changed hands. The closing phase of the Korean War lasted two years, forcing soldiers to endure two more frigid Korean winters and two more sweltering Korean summers as peace talks dragged on.

Phase V: Fighting While Negotiating (July 9, 1951–July 27, 1953)

Eastern portions of the defensive line had United Nations forces positioned north of the 38th parallel. Beginning at Seoul, the western section of the line lay below the parallel. Joy contended that the current position was geographically more secure and thus easier to defend. Communist negotiators, however, insisted that the division between North and South must revert to the prewar border. When Joy would not concede, the

Communists broke off negotiations on August 23. Hoping that military pressure would bring them back to the negotiating table, Ridgway launched a new offensive to extend United Nations-controlled territory.

Van Fleet ordered X Corps to advance the eastern position a minimum of five miles north. In mid-August, elements of Almond's corps began an attack against a group of three hills and the ridges that connected them, in an area that American soldiers nicknamed 'The Punchbowl.' Starting in mid-August, the 2nd Infantry Division battled heavily entrenched North Korean troops for control of a key ridge. Known as Bloody Ridge, the territory changed hands several times throughout the battle, each time taking a heavy toll on both forces. In close combat, American infantrymen cleared the Communist defenders from their entrenchments, finally pushing them from the ridge in early September. The western portion of the line was also advanced several miles to increase the security of the South Korean capital and its rail lines.

Negotiations began again at the end of October when the Communists abandoned insisting on the original demarcation line as the postwar border. Instead, the delegates agreed that the border would be the current line of contact if the war ended within a month. Peace talks quickly came to another halt over disagreements about conditions for exchanging prisoners of war. By that time, the opposing forces had thoroughly dug in, creating conditions reminiscent of World War I. Negotiators continued to assume that their forces' present positions would determine the postwar division of Korea.

Van Fleet redeployed his forces to strengthen strategically important sections of the line, such as the region around Seoul. He also rotated battle-weary units out of the line, relieving them with National Guard units from the 40th and 45th Infantry Divisions. Concurrently, air and naval pressure against the North intensified, particularly around Pyongyang. Although fighting continued, the summer and early fall of 1952 were comparatively quiet. In October, however, combat briefly heightened as each side hoped to expand its territorial control before the war ended. Eastern units again experienced the heaviest fighting. Communist forces were keen to take White Horse Hill to control the main highway to the city of Chorwon. The South Korean division defending White Horse held its ground over several days against strong Chinese attacks. Similar contests in October and November also did little to improve either side's position. Unable to exert sufficient pressure against the enemy on the ground, the United Nations command further expanded the air war against North Korea.

Lieutenant General Maxwell D. Taylor became Eighth Army commander in February 1953 when Van Fleet retired from the Army. Despite a significant exchange of sick and wounded prisoners of war in April, armistice negotiations continued to creep along, stymied by disagreement over repatriation of prisoners. Although less frequent and generally not as intense, fighting continued. The contest for Pork Chop Hill was typical of the combat during the last months of the war. On the night of March 23, the Chinese attacked and won control of the hill from its American defenders. The next morning, the Americans returned with reinforcements and reclaimed Pork Chop. In a bloody attack on April 16, the Chinese again took the hill. Both sides then bombarded it with artillery and brought in reinforcements. Before dawn the next morning, American troops attacked Chinese positions. After a day of bloody fighting, including bayonet attacks, the Communists were driven off. On the morning of April 18, however, the Chinese attacked again but were finally forced off Pork Chop. Over the next several weeks, both sides punished the hill with artillery; and on July 6, the Chinese infantry again attacked. For the next five days, each side brought in reinforcements; the Americans ultimately committed five battalions to the fight. Expecting an armistice at any moment and unwilling to commit more troops to the contest, Taylor abandoned the hill to the Chinese.

Disagreement between the negotiators was not the only reason reaching a peace agreement was difficult. Rhee was unhappy about ending the war without the Korean Peninsula being reunited under his authority. In the middle of June, negotiations were thwarted again when Rhee freed nearly 30,000 North Korean prisoners who did not want to return north. Although he claimed that the prisoners had escaped, his actions nearly derailed the peace talks altogether. Also, as a result of Rhee's ruse, the Chinese began attacks against Pork Chop Hill as well as other points. United Nations forces lost control of the area around Pork Chop and nearly lost several miles of territory along the western section of the front line.

The last combat action of the Korean War took place on July 26, 1953. On the following morning, July 27, negotiators signed an armistice. Although Stalin had died in March and new Soviet leadership had somewhat softened Cold War divisions, the Soviet dictator's passing probably did not affect the eventual armistice. Although North Korea gained some territory that it had not controlled in November 1951, it lost nearly 1,500 square miles overall. Delegates also agreed to a demilitarized zone extending two kilometers on either side of the line of demarcation to serve as a buffer against attack by either nation against its neighbor. The Korean War had cost over 37,000 Americans killed and more than 100,000 wounded. South Korea lost over 250,000 killed, over 400,000 wounded, and at least one million civilians killed. Together, some 1.3 million Chinese and North Korean troops died in the conflict. Because no peace treaty formally ended the war, the United States continues to maintain over 30,000 troops along the Demilitarized Zone between North and South Korea, which remains one of most heavily militarized places in the world.

Conclusion

Although it lasted little more than three years, the Korean War profoundly affected American strategic thinking. The Korean War changed the way

American policymakers approached the Cold War world. American containment policy originally formed around providing economic aid to countries threatened by Communism, but substantial military underwriting was now required to support allies and threatened nations alike. The Korean War had made military force a permanent part of American containment policy, leading to the first large standing Army in American history. Moreover, although national security policy and military planning remained focused on the Soviet threat to Western Europe, the Korean War irreversibly involved the United States in Asian affairs. American policymakers' understanding of the threat posed by the communist forces in Vietnam, and the decision to commit American combat troops in that war, were heavily influenced by the Korean War.

Further Reading

Barlow, Jeffrey. *Revolt of the Admirals: The Fight for Naval Aviation, 1945–1950.* Dulles, VA: Potomac Books, 1998.

Blair, Clay. *The Forgotten War: America in Korea, 1950–1953.* New York: Times Books, 1987.

Brands, H. W. *The General vs. the President: MacArthur and Truman at the Brink of Nuclear War.* New York: Doubleday, 2016.

Demarest, Heidi B., and Erica D. Borghard. *U.S. National Security Reform: Reassessing the National Security Act of 1947.* New York: Routledge, 2018.

Grimm, Kevin E. *America Enters the Cold War.* New York: Routledge, 2017.

Halberstam, David. *The Coldest Winter: America and the Korean War.* New York: Hyperion Books, 2008.

Holm, Jeanne. *Women in the Military: An Unfinished Revolution.* New York: Presidio Press, 1992.

Kaufman, Burton I. *The Korean War: Challenges in Crisis, Credibility, and Command.* 2nd ed. New York: McGraw-Hill, 1997.

Pearlman, Michael D. *Truman and MacArthur: Policy, Politics and the Hunger for Honor and Renown.* Bloomington, IN: Indiana University Press, 2008.

Stueck, William. *Rethinking the Korean War: A New Diplomatic and Strategic History.* Princeton, NJ: Princeton University Press, 2004.

Taylor, Jon E. *Freedom to Serve: Truman, Civil Rights, and Executive Order 9981.* New York: Routledge, 2012.

Witt, Linda, et al. *'A Defense Weapon Known to Be of Value': Servicewomen of the Korean War Era.* Lebanon, NH: University Press of New England, 2005.

14 Challenges of the Cold War

Introduction

The Korean War had shown how difficult it could be to achieve limited objectives in the fight against Communism without the use of nuclear weapons, without a congressional declaration of war, and without full mobilization. It had also once again exposed the delicate balance between military command in the field and civilian control of policy objectives, as well as the difficulties of matching military objectives with war aims. NSC-68 had been put to the test, but the new Eisenhower administration wanted to make significant economic, political, and strategic changes to containment doctrine. The Kennedy administration would also alter containment to meet changing strategic conditions. A nuclear and conventional arms race intensified throughout the 1950s and early 1960s, as did inter-service rivalry and competition over limited budget resources. The Cold War entered its most dangerous period, challenging the traditional American way of war.

Strategic Contours

President Eisenhower had ended the stalemate in Korea and preserved the independence, though tenuous, of the South Korean republic by the armistice agreement of July 1953. He had rejected General Douglas MacArthur's recommendation to use tactical nuclear weapons in North Korea as well as Secretary of State John Foster Dulles' suggestion that the war expand to include attacks in Manchuria and a naval blockade of the Chinese coast. Far from being squeamish about the use of nuclear weapons, Eisenhower instead saw little strategic value in their use in the Korean situation. Likewise, widening the war risked alienating European allies, not to mention starting another world war. The strategic objectives in Korea did not warrant either course of action. The Soviets, Chinese, and North Koreans also understood the concept of limited war for limited objectives. Yet, nuclear weapons had proven useful without being used. Though the American atomic arsenal far outmatched and outnumbered the Soviet one, the mere existence of such power served as a deterrent against expanding the Korean War and had made leaders on both sides think twice about ways and means to attain those objectives.

Perhaps the biggest problem facing national security policymakers in the 1950s involved the question of exactly how to use nuclear weapons to achieve policy objectives. Nuclear weapons rapidly reached such destructive levels that 'winning' a nuclear war had become a questionable concept. Even the tactical use of nuclear weapons came under military, diplomatic, moral, and ecological scrutiny. The very idea, however, that the most destructive weapon ever developed potentially could be of no use seemed unfathomable. In this paradoxical paradigm, American and Soviet leaders struggled to find a strategic role for nuclear weapons.

The United States decided to maintain a sizable nuclear arsenal as a deterrent to Soviet aggression. Advances in the Soviet arsenal now required that the United States maintain the nuclear capacity to survive a first strike by the Soviet Union and deliver a retaliatory strike to 'win' a nuclear exchange. To achieve strategic superiority, the Truman and Eisenhower administrations poured money into the development of new nuclear weapons and more effective means to deliver them. Massive defense budgets, anticipated in NSC-68, in turn, caused intense competition among the services, especially the new Air Force, for budget resources. The Air Force reaped the benefits, having the best means to deliver nuclear weapons. Beginning with B-47A Stratojets, then the B-52 intercontinental bomber, the Air Force's Strategic Air Command (SAC) maintained around-the-clock air delivery capability, which it continued through the end of the Cold War.

Ground forces also benefited, though not without going through some rough budgetary and doctrinal adjustments. Despite the limited nature of the Korean War, the guerrilla nature of the French Indochina conflict, and increasing numbers of small wars for national liberation around the globe, the United States Army continued to focus on general war with the Soviet Union in Europe.

NATO and Preparing for War in Europe

The United States and its European allies in NATO differed on their concept of war in Western Europe. American war planners considered the potential size of a mobilized Soviet army, Soviet nuclear capability, American nuclear availability, and non-nuclear defense in planning for a Soviet invasion of Western Europe. NATO's original purpose of deterrence through collective security eroded as it became more apparent that Western Europe, primarily Germany, would be a nuclear rather than a conventional battleground. The United States had hoped NATO countries could provide a temporary non-nuclear defense of Europe before American nuclear capability would have to be used to stave off a Soviet invasion. Even as late as 1954, American military planners projected that only about eight percent of the American nuclear arsenal could be used in Europe. The remainder had to be held in reserve for a direct attack on the Soviet Union and China. American tactical nuclear weapons had developed well beyond similar Soviet capabilities, so planners assumed that nuclear weapons would be used on Soviet military assets rather than Russian cities.

Europeans, understandably, did not relish the destructive horror of another non-nuclear conventional conflict in Europe, nor did the absolute horror of a nuclear exchange in central Europe appeal. While the United States pressured NATO countries to build up conventional forces, Europe grew concerned with the growing American reliance upon nuclear weapons in Europe. As the nuclear option became more apparent, many NATO countries saw little point in spending limited resources on conventional forces that were rapidly growing obsolete. By 1955, with a rearming Germany now a member of NATO and American nuclear capability increasing, American planners thought that NATO's conventional forces could stall a Soviet attack, forcing Soviet divisions to concentrate their mass to break the NATO defensive line. This concentration of Soviet forces would, in turn, allow American tactical nuclear weapons to pulverize massed Soviet forces. If Soviet nuclear capability was far behind that of the United States, American planners did not fear a similar Soviet strike upon bunched NATO forces.

In response to Germany's entry into NATO, the Soviet Union formed the Warsaw Pact, organizing its Eastern European satellites into a military alliance to stand toe-to-toe against the United States and NATO. The alliance had been and remained a voluntary association, which made broad acceptance of American strategic concepts consistently problematic. The new Warsaw Pact, on the other hand, answered directly and instantly to the strategic whims of the Soviet Union. Lines of communication and chains of command in NATO could be convoluted and cumbersome, while Warsaw Pact nations had a single chain of command that both originated and ended in Moscow.

Eisenhower's New Look

The war in Korea, commitments in Europe, the defense buildup in the United States, and investment in new military technologies placed an incredible strain on the American federal budget and economy. When Dwight Eisenhower took up residence in the White House in 1953, he brought with him decades of military and diplomatic experience, and a concern that the Cold War not only might make the American economy dependent upon defense spending, it could indeed break it. With the advent of the hydrogen bomb and the means to deliver this most destructive of weapons, using military force to achieve victory in the Cold

War seemed less likely. Instead, decades of spending, arms races, and asymmetrical conflicts appeared the more likely course of this new type of conflict. Even though planners continued to focus on a climactic battle in Europe and the buildup of nuclear and conventional forces, Eisenhower demanded that defense expenditures be brought down to levels that would not overburden the American economy. However, he did little to address the need for conventional responses to non-nuclear conflict.

Projections by the United States held that the Soviets might have a hydrogen bomb by 1957. Once they got it, the Joint Chiefs of Staff argued, a nuclear exchange would be more likely. Admiral Arthur Radford, Chairman of the Joint Chiefs of Staff, even proposed a preventive war against the Soviet Union, thereby using the American nuclear advantage rather than waiting until the Soviets achieved parity. He worried about the possibility of a nuclear war or a lengthy stalemate that would drain American economic resources. Although Eisenhower wisely dismissed Radford's preemptive war, he wanted a way to cut costs while maintaining a strong military deterrent to prevent a Soviet attack.

Cutting costs became a critical component of a new defense strategy. With increased defense budgets and massive spending in the Korean War, inflation had wracked the American economy. While strategic planners doubted that the Soviet Union could defeat the United States militarily, a lengthy military buildup could give the Soviet Union an economic advantage. The American economy could ultimately collapse under the protracted strain of the Cold War. To avoid such a scenario, the United States had to cut military spending, yet stay stronger than its adversary for the long haul—perhaps for decades.

In early 1953, the Joint Chiefs of Staff gave Eisenhower a means to cut costs and maintain the strategic initiative. Reasoning that nuclear weapons were much cheaper to build and maintain than conventional forces, the Joint Chiefs argued that the only way to cut costs was to reduce conventional forces. This approach could work only if nuclear weapons were deployed and used without restraint. The deterrent effect could be maintained only if the Soviet Union believed that any aggression on its part would result in massive American nuclear retaliation. The United States had to be willing to use its nuclear arsenal. The question was, as it remains, does the United States have the will to use nuclear weapons?

Eisenhower brought these concepts together in NSC 162/2 in October 1953. This guideline for the use of military force to achieve national strategic objectives radically altered how nuclear weapons might be used. NSC 162/2 allowed for the use of nuclear devices whenever military strategy dictated. In the future, according to the document, in limited regional wars, such as in Korea, the United States would have a clear nuclear option. Now the United States could use nuclear weapons in limited war, general war, or whatever situation it saw fit. Such a policy for using nuclear weapons allowed for both a reduction in conventional forces and a strong deterrent against the Soviet Union, which now had to consider that the United States would use nuclear weapons in a variety of situations. In NSC 162/2 the United States had a deterrent policy for both general and limited war, and the country could save money by cutting conventional forces.

Project Solarium, an intensive study of American strategic alternatives, helped Eisenhower pull together these new strategic concepts. The other options under consideration included continuing the containment policy developed under the Truman administration, adding massive retaliation to containment doctrine, and focusing on regional military, diplomatic, and economic success to discourage the Soviet Union and its communist allies. Using the Joint Chiefs' move toward a more nuclear and less conventional force, the nuclear guidelines in NSC 162/2, and Solarium's massive retaliation alternative, Eisenhower formulated a new strategic framework to fight the Cold War. His framework became known as the New Look.

Secretary of State John Foster Dulles made the New Look public in January 1954. In a speech to the Council on Foreign Relations, Dulles warned of the increasing economic burden caused by the Cold War rivalry with the Soviet Union and announced that the United States must seek strength and deterrence at a cost that the American economy could safely absorb. By increased reliance upon airborne nuclear weapons, the United States could and would respond to a crisis with massive force when, where, and by whatever means it chose. Massive retaliation became part of the New Look. The great dilemma, however, that the nuclear New Look created was that by relying on such an overwhelming destructive capacity for all contingencies, the actual deployment of nuclear weapons might become obsolete because the destruction caused would likely far outweigh the objectives gained. But in 1954, such a strategy could work because the Soviets' ability to retaliate with nuclear weapons was weak. If the New Look and massive retaliation could deter the Soviets, American planners reasoned, the Soviets would resort to political and economic strategies to subvert American influence. To counter such strategies, the United States had to maintain a healthy economy; thus, the New Look served both ends.

Eisenhower began cutting. The Army went from 20 combat divisions in 1954 to 15 in 1957. With over 40 percent of its force deployed in Europe and other overseas posts, the Army had little capacity for a major conventional war outside the European continent. The New Look reduced the Navy's 765,000 sailors and 1,126 combat ships to 650,000 men and 1,030 combat ships. The Marine Corps' three divisions operated at reduced strength, going from 244,000 to 190,000. As the primary delivery arm for the American nuclear arsenal, the Air Force avoided drastic cuts and even gained continental defense wings. However, the service lost several transport and troop carrier wings. During 1957, the Air

Force turned to an all-jet bomber force for SAC as the new B-52 bomber filled out all SAC wings.

The New Look intensified inter-service rivalry. All services invested in ballistic missile research, resulting in duplicated effort and capability. Intermediate-range ballistic missiles (IRBMs) such as the Air Force's Thor missile, the Navy's Polaris nuclear submarine program, and the Army's Jupiter missile system each gave the United States missile delivery capacity in Europe and Alaska. Polaris went further, allowing for a mobile retaliatory strike force via nuclear-powered submarines.

The 1957 launch of the Soviet Sputnik satellite by an R-7 rocket, however, brought intercontinental ballistic missiles (ICBMs) to the forefront. If the Soviets could place a small satellite in space, they certainly could deliver a nuclear warhead by rocket to a target in the United States. The American Atlas, Vanguard, and Titan ICBM programs had apparently fallen behind Soviet capabilities. While the United States countered Sputnik in 1958 with a modified Jupiter IRBM, the Soviet Sputnik launch spurred the services into action, each promoting its own ICBM program as the answer to stay ahead of the Soviets. Even the Air Force admitted that ICBMs could eventually make SAC obsolete. A B-52 could be shot down; an Atlas ICBM could not, and the Atlas could potentially deliver a much larger warhead than could a single B-52.

Aside from several private and public investigations into why the United States was behind the Soviets, Sputnik resulted in two crucial long-term developments for the United States. First, Congress passed the National Defense Education Act, which provided funds for university graduate programs in the sciences and engineering and revised public school curriculums to offer more science courses at the elementary and secondary levels. Second, Congress passed the Defense Reorganization Act of 1958. To overcome duplication of effort and expense, and to minimize competition among the services, the Defense Reorganization Act gave the Secretary of Defense new and extraordinary powers. The secretary now could assign new weapons systems to an individual service, alter service functions and capabilities, and exercise direct command via the Joint Chiefs of Staff over inter-service commands. The latter command function added a new and controversial layer of civilian control over the military.

Congressional hearings and Eisenhower's own investigation, the Gaither Committee, still expressed alarm in response to Sputnik. Various findings urged Eisenhower to increase second-strike capability, to invest more in missile technology, and to address the strategic dilemma posed by limited war under the New Look. The Gaither Committee recommended an accelerated ICBM program, warning that the United States might not close the missile gap until 1960 or 1961. Later studies of Soviet capabilities revealed that there was indeed no missile gap. Eisenhower did not overreact. He understood the incredible difficulties in building a viable ICBM platform and knew that Soviet ICBM capabilities were undoubtedly exaggerated. He instead followed up on commitments to place IRBMs in Europe and Turkey, knowing that the Soviet Union would still not risk war even with ICBM capability because of the massive American first- and second-strike delivery capabilities.

The Rise of Civilian Strategists

Sputnik also accelerated critiques of the New Look among academics and other think-tank strategists. The Army hired civilian strategists to argue its case for a non-nuclear alternative to the New Look. The United States, the Army claimed, must have an option other than nuclear weapons. Henry Kissinger, a Harvard professor, supported the return of a conventional alternative. Herman Kahn, of the Air Force's RAND think-tank, argued that managed conflict escalation could achieve political objectives. With only a nuclear option, controlled escalation might not be possible. A non-nuclear alternative had to exist to respond to a non-nuclear threat by the Soviets. A credible response did not have to be massive, but it certainly had to be appropriate. In 1959, retiring Army Chief of Staff Maxwell Taylor wrote a scathing critique of the Eisenhower New Look in a book called *The Uncertain Trumpet*. He was one of the leading proponents of a new strategic concept called Flexible Response that would replace the New Look in the Kennedy administration.

Other critics of the New Look included Robert Osgood, who argued for conventional warfare capability, and Bernard Brodie, who argued that the United States, like all military powers, was bound by its past. That very past restricted fresh strategic thinking in the missile age. Brodie offered the most in-depth critique of the strategic dilemmas presented by the New Look. Deterrence as a strategy ran counter to the use of the offensive in Western warfare. The offensive in the nuclear age, however, meant a preemptive strike to destroy the enemy's second-strike capability. Deterrence, according to Brodie, was primarily a preventive war in disguise. He rejected the use of tactical nuclear weapons in limited war situations, noting that containing limited wars in the hope of preventing an all-out war would be very difficult if nuclear weapons were used on the regional level. The nuclear age, Brodie argued, had made constrained war so vastly different from what it was in the past that fighting limited wars would require a revolution in strategic thought.

Whatever strategists thought about the New Look, few disagreed with the need for a coherent continental defense system to protect the United States from a Pearl Harbor-like attack by the Soviet Union. Working with Canada, in 1951 the United States established an early warning radar system, called Distant Early Warning (DEW), across subarctic Canada and Alaska. The Continental Air Defense Command coordinated air interceptors and ground anti-aircraft defense networks. The new Nike

Figure 14.1 Atlas Ballistic Missile on display at the San Diego Aerospace Museum, Gillespie Field, El Cajon, California. Photograph by Eric D. Bier.

Source: Wikimedia Commons.

Ajax anti-aircraft missile provided accurate long-range defense capability with batteries strategically located around the United States.

SIOPs

Eisenhower also saw the need to overcome the growing rivalry between the services in nuclear attack targeting. Each service had its own strategic and tactical plans for first-strike and retaliatory nuclear attacks, both. As a result, each service planned to act against the same targets in the Soviet Union, China, North Korea, and in other communist states. Eisenhower wanted to eliminate waste and redundancy as well as potential command problems that would arise during a nuclear attack. The president knew from personal experience that the lack of a unified attack plan could cause chaos, which would be fatal for the United States in an all-out nuclear strike.

In 1957, Eisenhower ordered the Joint Chiefs and the Secretary of Defense to begin work on a Single Integrated Operational Plan (SIOP) for a nuclear attack, to be put in place by 1962. SIOP-62 was one of the most secret of the American war plans. When presented with an early draft of SIOP-62, Eisenhower claimed that it 'frightened the devil out of me.'

SIOP-62 provided for a preemptive attack if early warning detected an imminent Soviet nuclear assault on the United States. Plans called for the delivery of over 3,200 nuclear devices on over 1,000 targets in the Soviet Union, China, and communist satellite states in Eastern Europe and Asia. Such an attack, the plan predicted, would destroy over 150 cities and kill hundreds of millions of people around the world. Even the retaliatory option in SIOP-62 included over 1,700 nuclear bombs delivered on over 700 targets. This was a plan to win a nuclear war.

SIOP-62 combined the nuclear capabilities of the Army, Navy, and Air Force for the first time in a cohesive attack plan. Polaris submarines, Strategic Air Command, ICBMs—all would be unleashed on the Soviet Union in a coordinated, devastating assault. The first drafts of the plan alarmed military leaders. Overkill seemed to be the most common complaint. How many 80-kiloton devices did it take to destroy a target? The target list did not discriminate between communist countries at war with the United States and those that were not. Would the United States still strike them all?

Kennedy tried to make SIOP fit his Flexible Response strategy by allowing the military to pick and choose targets. SIOP-63 allowed more discretion, including options to strike only military targets, but still maintained the capacity for the complete destruction of the Soviet Union and China.

Regional Challenges

The New Look strategy, with its preoccupation with massive retaliation as a deterrent, could not influence events in several regional Cold War crises.

Indochina, Quemoy and Matsu, the Middle East, Berlin, and Cuba are a few of the places that became hotly contested Cold War arenas. The loss of a U-2 spy plane over the Soviet Union in 1960 only intensified the warming of the Cold War. The United States used a variety of tools to approach these crises to achieve political objectives without risking broader conflict. Far from being representative of the New Look, these regional conflicts instead reflected the increasing diversity of Cold War strategy.

Indochina

The United States had supplied military aid to France in its fight to maintain the pre-World War II colony of Indochina (Vietnam, Laos, and Cambodia) since 1950. The United States had earlier supported Viet Minh leader Ho Chi Minh's efforts to fight Japanese occupiers in the region during the war, but despite this close association Ho's communist connections and American diplomatic maneuvers to keep France supportive of NATO dictated severing the tie with the leader of what was now an insurgency against French rule.

The communist takeover of China in 1947 dramatically changed the French war against Ho's Viet Minh insurgents. With supplies freely flowing across the Chinese border, Ho's guerrillas became a real army. To counter the growth of Ho's forces, the United States supplied the French with excess war materiel from its own war in Korea. French reverses, however, negated much of this American aid. Before 1951, French commanders relied on static garrisons, which the Viet Minh overran. Attempts to draw the new Viet Minh army into a climactic set-piece battle never materialized. In 1951, the French tried a new strategy. Using mobile forces and massive firepower, the French scored early successes; but the Viet Minh proved adaptable and adjusted to the new French approach.

As the communist nature of Ho's movement became more apparent, and the Cold War intensified, the United States came to see Indochina as a critical Cold War battlefield to preserve the region against further communist aggression. North Korea was already under communist control, and the threat to South Korea remained. The Domino Theory embraced by Eisenhower and others in the national security establishment held that if one country fell in Southeast Asia to the Soviet or Chinese sphere, then others could soon follow. The momentum of communist expansion would then be too great to stop. Moreover, the region's abundance of rubber, tungsten, and rice made Southeast Asia economically important.

By 1953, French domestic support for the war in Indochina had evaporated. High casualties, especially among the officer corps, and no sign of progress toward defeating the Viet Minh and establishing semi-independent states under a French union made the war unpopular. Still, the Eisenhower administration increased military aid and called for the French to replace unimaginative commanders with more dynamic generals. One of the new French commanders, General Henri Navarre, hoped to force the Viet Minh army into a decisive battle. To do this, he boldly established a base of operations deep inside Viet Minh-held territory in a valley called Dien Bien Phu. At first, Navarre wanted to conduct aggressive operations from Dien Bien Phu against Viet Minh supply lines along the Laotian border. The rough mountainous terrain, however, convinced Navarre instead to use the large base he had established on the valley floor as bait to entice the Viet Minh into a mass assault. With the Viet Minh concentrated in a small area, Navarre reasoned, he could annihilate them with air strikes and artillery positioned around Dien Bien Phu.

As the diplomatic landscape evolved in early 1954, the Viet Minh found themselves in a position to force the French out of Vietnam for good. Talks at Berlin and Geneva would favor the Viet Minh if they could defeat the French at Dien Bien Phu. Well-supported by the Soviet Union and China, the Viet Minh assaulted the French outpost. With this, the Viet Minh should have fallen into Navarre's trap, but the French failed to stop the incredible buildup of Viet Minh artillery and anti-aircraft guns in the hills surrounding the outpost.

As the Viet Minh overran the surrounding artillery positions, the French government begged the United States to militarily intervene to save Dien Bien Phu. The French asked for bombing, ground troops, even nuclear weapons; but Eisenhower rejected French pleas for help. Dien Bien Phu is close to the Chinese border, and the president feared that American intervention there might trigger a wider war, as had occurred in 1951 when American forces approached the Chinese border in North Korea. Moreover, Eisenhower wanted congressional approval before placing American troops in harm's way. Such authorization would take time, which the French did not have. The risk of uncontrolled escalation and the fact that the region simply was not strategically important enough to warrant direct American military intervention convinced Eisenhower to let Dien Bien Phu fall, which it did on May 7, 1954. Exhausted, the French stopped military operations in Indochina and sought a settlement at the peace talks in Geneva.

The United States also wanted an end to the war and hoped that the Geneva settlement would open the door to political and economic ways to halt communist expansion in Southeast Asia. The agreement promised country-wide elections in Vietnam in 1956, but these did not take place. This set the stage for the United States to take over France's colonial aspirations in the region in pursuit of its own Cold War objectives. At Geneva, the Soviet Union pressured the Viet Minh to accept the agreement because it also feared that the conflict could widen into a general war. Perhaps the threat of massive retaliation had influenced the end of the French Indochina War after all.

Militarily, French withdrawal from Indochina gave birth to a new regional collective security arrangement among Southeast Asian nations and the United States. The Southeast Asia Treaty Organization (SEATO) included the Philippines, Australia, New Zealand, France, and Great Britain, in addition to the United States. SEATO obligated signatories to guarantee the security of Pakistan, Malaya, and Thailand as well as the new states of Laos and Cambodia. Like NATO, SEATO relied on a conventional regional deterrent augmented by the New Look of the United States.

The French Indochina War exemplified the limited regional conflicts that increasingly characterized the Cold War. Regional revolutionary wars went beyond military means to include social and psychological resistance, ideas that rallied populations to such effective levels that popular guerrilla armies successfully challenged conventional forces. Occurring just as the New Look was formalized, the war in Indochina should have signaled to military strategists that limited regional conflicts required hybrid non-nuclear responses. Still, the United States had restrained its military response at Dien Bien Phu and had reached an agreement that, although it did not resolve the issue of Vietnamese independence and unification, at least provided the conditions for a future peaceful resolution. Unfortunately, this was not to be.

Quemoy and Matsu

Fresh from the Korean War, the United States again came close to open war with China in 1954 and again in 1958 over the contested islands of Quemoy and Matsu. Claimed by Taiwan, the tiny offshore islands had strategic value in blocking an amphibious invasion of Taiwan from mainland China. China shelled the islands briefly in 1954, prompting Eisenhower to invoke the New Look by threatening the use of nuclear weapons against China and petitioning Congress to authorize the defense of Taiwan if China moved to take the islands. While the United States was obligated by treaty to defend Taiwan (the treaty also gave the United States the power to veto any attack planned by Taiwan against China), Sino-Soviet agreements could easily be activated if the United States got into another war with China. Under these agreements, the Soviet Union could use such a scenario to start a war in Europe. Quemoy and Matsu were much less strategically important than Europe, and Eisenhower, his nuclear threat aside, hardly saw the value in going to war over the two islands—especially after so recently getting out of Korea and refusing to aid the French at Dien Bien Phu.

The Chinese shelled the islands again in 1958, this time in response to Taiwan's move of nearly a quarter of its army to the islands. American military planners advised that the islands could not repel a Chinese invasion unless bases along coastal China were first destroyed in a nuclear attack. Taiwan had tried to back the United States into a strategic corner by risking so much of its army. Although the United States had not acted in 1954, Taiwan gambled that it would, nevertheless, take the threat to the islands seriously and come to Taiwan's aid. The gambit nearly worked. Eisenhower ordered the Navy to escort Taiwanese supply ships to the islands and allowed Taiwanese Air Force jets to be armed with American missiles. A joint Army–Marine strike force of several thousand troops joined the Taiwanese Army on the islands. Fearing nuclear war over two small islands, the Soviets pressured the Chinese to back down, which they did.

Quemoy and Matsu demonstrated how close to the brink of nuclear war the nuclear powers seemed willing to go. Of course, as with the New Look, such brinkmanship depended on the certainty that saner heads would prevail, and one side would back down.

The Middle East

Postwar nationalism and conflict between Arabs and the new Israeli state, combined with increased oil production in the area, made the Middle East an intensely contested region in the early Cold War. Soviet interest in Iranian oil production gave the United States due cause for concern. Eisenhower worried that Soviet expansion via Iran might jeopardize the entire Middle East and cut Western access to the region's oil. Eisenhower approved a CIA-sponsored coup, organized and carried out by Kermit Roosevelt, to overthrow Iranian leader Mohammed Mossadegh in 1953 to prevent the spread of Soviet influence in Iran. The new government, under the Shah of Iran and supported by $45 million in American aid, had severe economic problems to overcome. Eisenhower sent Herbert Hoover, Jr., son of the former president, to negotiate a new oil deal with the Shah's government. In the end, the agreement gave the major American oil companies a virtual monopoly on Iranian oil production and distribution. National security interests in the Cold War apparently overrode American antitrust traditions.

In 1955, the Baghdad Pact (Turkey, Iran, Iraq, Pakistan, and Great Britain) provided a tenuous American-supported collective security system in the region. The United States did not directly participate in the alliance for fear of upsetting its already delicate relationship with Middle Eastern nations. With NATO in place in Western Europe and SEATO in Southeast Asia, the Baghdad Pact group provided yet another collective security alliance on the periphery of Communist China and the Soviet Union. Containment had indeed taken many forms.

The Suez Crisis of 1956 was resolved without American military interference, but just barely. Egyptian President Abdel Nasser ordered the nationalization of the Suez Canal in July 1956, prompting angry protests from Great Britain and France. Nasser took this drastic step in retaliation against the United States for pulling financial support for the massive Aswan Dam project. Eisenhower decided to withdraw support in response to Nasser's attempt to attract Soviet interest in the project. Egypt planned to use toll proceeds from the canal to finance the dam, but Great Britain and France opposed this plan. The West likened Nasser to Hitler and brought up the haunting specter of Munich as justification for standing firm against Nasser's brazen act.

Eisenhower consistently ruled out military action throughout the crisis. Fearing the effect of military force on world opinion, not to mention his own reelection bid in the 1956 presidential campaign, Eisenhower sought a peaceful solution to the crisis. For Nasser, Egyptian nationalism was at stake. For Great Britain and France, their role as imperialist leaders in the region had been jeopardized, as had the stock certificates of stockholders in the Suez Canal Company. Despite the best efforts of Eisenhower and Secretary of State Dulles, armed conflict erupted when the British bombed Egyptian bases and the Israelis, under a secret agreement with the British and French, attacked the Sinai and the Gaza Strip.

Furious, Eisenhower worried that the Suez conflict could explode into a world war. On November 5, the Soviet Union warned that it would launch missiles against French and British cities unless they immediately stopped their attack on Egypt. With American forces around the world on full alert, Eisenhower feared the worst. Then the Soviets suggested a joint American–Soviet military intervention to end the fighting. Although not a serious proposal, it nevertheless made great communist propaganda, allowing the Soviets to look like peacemakers. As suddenly as the crisis began, it ended. Bombarded with negative domestic and worldwide public opinion, the British and the French decided to obey the United Nations resolution calling for immediate cessation of hostilities. Cessation of hostilities made the Soviet Union look like the savior of Egypt, if not the Middle East. But, to prevent the expansion of Soviet influence in the region, the United States now had to fill the void left by Great Britain and France. Because of Eisenhower's refusal to use military force in this situation, however, the crisis had been contained.

One significant result of the Suez crisis was the Eisenhower Doctrine. In January 1957, Congress authorized the president to defend any Middle Eastern nation attacked by a communist state and provided $200 million in economic and military aid to Middle Eastern nations. Initiating the Eisenhower Doctrine, however, required a government to request assistance. Countries like Egypt and Syria would probably not ask for American help, and in many areas of the Middle East, Arab nationalism threatened stability much more than did the expansion of communism.

The Eisenhower Doctrine was put to the test in 1958. Egyptian-backed rebels began attacks in Lebanon and assassinated the King of Iraq, prompting Jordan and Lebanon to request American assistance. Units of the American Sixth Fleet, the Marines, and the Army moved into Beirut without firing a shot. British airborne forces landed in Jordan, supplied by the United States Air Force. American troops in Turkey stood ready to move into both Lebanon and Jordan. Bolstered by American and British forces, the Lebanese and Jordanian governments restored order, allowing American and British forces to leave after only two months. Eisenhower had again avoided massive military action in the confused world of nationalism and the Cold War. The New Look seemed to be evolving into something different.

U-2 Shootdown

American U-2 spy planes had flown intermittent top-secret high-altitude missions over the Soviet Union since 1952. Knowing that Soviet air defense systems could detect the aircraft but not shoot them down, Eisenhower approved the flights. With effective spy satellites still years away, the U-2 provided the only means to photograph Soviet capabilities and movements. Even with this supersonic aircraft and the poor state of Soviet air defense capabilities, the infrequency of flights made it difficult to fully assess what the Soviet Union was doing inside its borders. The U-2 could, however, accurately photograph not only Soviet bombers sitting in the open on Soviet airfields but also open Soviet missile silos. Though imperfect, U-2 missions provided the first real independent assessment of Soviet air and ground forces.

The Soviets desperately wanted to stop U-2 flights, but until 1960 their air defense network did not have an anti-aircraft missile capable of reaching the high-altitude flights. Just two weeks before the Paris summit between the United States and the Soviet Union aimed at rapprochement was scheduled to begin, the Soviets got their wish. On May 1, 1960, a Soviet surface-to-air (SAM) missile shot down a U-2, piloted by Francis Gary Powers. For the United States, the timing could not have been worse.

Assuming Powers was dead, the Eisenhower administration at first denied any wrongdoing, claiming the flight had been a weather reconnaissance mission that had strayed into Soviet airspace. A few days later, the Soviet Union announced to a stunned United States that Powers was alive and had admitted the true nature of his flight mission. The Soviets tried Powers for espionage and sentenced him to ten years in prison. He was exchanged, however, in 1962 for a Soviet operative held in the United States. Embarrassed, the Eisenhower administration had to backtrack and admit the existence of the U-2 program. Eisenhower, to his credit, took full responsibility. In Paris, Soviet Premier Nikita Khrushchev grandstanded in protest of the U-2 spy missions and walked out of the summit before substantive talks got underway. Although Eisenhower stopped U-2 missions over the Soviet Union, the United States continued flyovers of other communist states. By the early 1960s, satellites had advanced enough to provide useful data. Moreover, they could not be shot down.

Figure 14.2 To bolster the cover-up that the U-2 piloted by Francis Gary Powers was on a NASA weather research mission and had strayed off course, a U-2 was quickly painted in NASA markings and put on display for the news media at the NASA Flight Research Center at Edwards Air Force Base on May 6, 1960.

Source: National Aeronautics and Space Administration.

Kennedy and the Cold War

The nonexistent missile gap became the chief issue of the 1960 presidential election and having been chided for being weak on communism in 1952, mainly because of Truman's conduct of the Korean War, the Democrats now attacked the Republicans on military preparedness. Eisenhower's loss of Cuba to rebel leader Fidel Castro, the growing debacle in Indochina, the Soviet shootdown of an American U-2 spy plane, and other humiliations pointed to what critics claimed was the inherent weakness of the New Look. The all-or-nothing option could not operate in a Cold War that now demanded limited war approaches to regional nationalist conflict. Kennedy's victory over Eisenhower's vice president, Richard Nixon, in 1960, brought a new national security strategy and policy-making style to the White House. Gone were Eisenhower's weekly National Security Council meetings and formalized decision-making process via a military-style staff system. Instead, Kennedy relied heavily on advisors, systems analysis, and informal decision making. Having been elected on a campaign highlighting the crisis of

Communist expansion in the world, Kennedy could not divorce his rhetoric from geopolitical realities of the new so-called third force player—nations or coalitions that exercised influence exceeding their economic and military strength—in the Cold War.

Building a Flexible Response

To better prepare the United States to deal with this new phase of the Cold War, Kennedy appointed the dynamic former chief of Ford Motor Company, Robert S. McNamara, to head the Defense Department. McNamara brought to the vast bureaucratic defense establishment a slashing style, built upon maximum business efficiency, called the planning-programming-budgeting system. McNamara disagreed with Eisenhower's over-reliance on nuclear retaliation. To replace the New Look with Flexible Response, the Department of Defense had to prepare the armed services to appropriately respond to the range of threats that now characterized the Cold War. To do this, the services had to be streamlined, re-equipped, and adequately trained, all at the lowest possible financial cost. Such a task was most fitting for a businessman like McNamara. Centralization, cost-cutting, and long-range planning became the principal means of McNamara's Department of Defense to achieve Flexible Response.

McNamara continued to gradually replace fixed-wing bombers with missiles as the primary means to deliver large nuclear warheads, but he also dramatically increased the armed services' conventional capability to respond to regional crises, such as Cuba and Vietnam. To maintain American nuclear superiority and retaliatory capability, McNamara increased the number of ICBM silo sites and nuclear submarines with Polaris missiles. Through modest budget increases, McNamara expanded the size of Army, Navy, Marine, and Air Force conventional forces and added new specialized units and equipment.

In the Army, for example, Kennedy's pet project for an elite guerrilla-style unit and the use of helicopters for ground combat support became a reality. Army Special Forces already existed, but under McNamara and Kennedy, the elite force became experts in small-unit guerrilla tactics and nation-building strategies, which, when combined, came to be known as counterinsurgency. Army Special Forces, also then known as the Green Berets, became the elite force of the American military, and soon each service enhanced their rough equivalents. New equipment also changed the battlefield. For example, the Army and Marines had used helicopters during and since the Korean War mainly for reconnaissance and medical evacuation, but now both services gave rotary aircraft a central combat role. Air assault and air mobility, based on the French model, seemed ideally suited for small, regional conflicts in rugged terrain, such as that in Vietnam. McNamara's Army–Air Force Strike Command gave joint capability to new concepts of air mobility on the battlefield.

Through McNamara's micromanagement of the Department of Defense, Kennedy gained a military force that could maintain massive retaliatory capability yet conventionally respond to minor crises with a variety of tools, including the use of force, nation-building, and military advising. While the services experienced growing pains under McNamara's program, they were arguably better organized, equipped, and prepared to meet the new challenges of the Cold War. Crises in Berlin, Cuba, and Vietnam made mixed use of this new Flexible Response approach.

The Berlin Crisis

The trickle of East Germans sneaking through the West Berlin gap into West Germany was reaching flood stage by early 1961. Khrushchev threatened to close the border completely, with military force if necessary. Kennedy and Khrushchev met in June 1961 in Vienna to discuss the crisis. The Soviets wanted a treaty restoring Berlin to their control, while the Western powers wanted to maintain the four-power status of the divided city. Khrushchev issued an ultimatum to a berated Kennedy, demanding a settlement by December or he would seal off the city from the West, an act that would assuredly provoke a war in Europe. Failing to understand the growing split between the Soviet Union and China, and still clinging to his missile gap campaign rhetoric, Kennedy lost the initiative in the Berlin crisis and left himself with few diplomatic and military options.

A speech by Kennedy in July implied that the United States might take no action if West Berlin was not attacked or disturbed by Soviet attempts to stop the flood of refugees into West Germany through Berlin. On August 13, 1961, East German laborers began constructing the Berlin Wall, arguably the most potent symbol of the Cold War. It gave Kennedy a way out of the crisis. Khrushchev stopped threatening West Berlin. With the wall up, only a few brave East Germans dared attempt to escape to the west side of the city.

Kennedy ordered an attack plan drawn up in case of a Soviet move against Berlin. A small attack force of low-flying bombers could get past the weak Soviet early warning detection system and knock out Soviet ICBM silos in the western part of the country before the Soviets could get a missile off the ground. Unlike SIOP and its hundreds of targets, striking a mere 42 targets could so weaken the Soviets that they would not be able to continue offensive operations against Berlin and West Germany. In November, Khrushchev withdrew his ultimatum for a December settlement. He had achieved his objective. The Berlin Wall plugged the hole in the dike meant to keep East Germans on the Soviet side of the Iron Curtain. The Soviet Union had displayed the ability for achieving limited objectives through means that limited American retaliatory action.

Missiles in Cuba

Kennedy took a black eye in the Berlin Crisis that added to the one he received earlier in the failed Bay of Pigs invasion aimed at overthrowing

Figure 14.3 United States Army tanks face off against Soviet armor at Checkpoint
　　　　Charlie, Berlin, October 1961.
Source: United States Army.

the Soviet-allied Cuban leader Fidel Castro. In response to the American
deployment of nuclear missiles in Turkey and Europe, Khrushchev boldly
decided to deploy similar weapons in Cuba in 1962. The Soviet operation
to deploy the missiles to Cuba, Operation Anadyr, was secret and risky.
Khrushchev feared American naval interference if American spy satellites
recognized missile parts on the decks of Soviet freighters headed to Cuba,
so he ordered the parts hidden underneath tractors and other agricultural
machinery. Soviet naval captains had orders to scuttle their vessels if
American naval forces threatened to board them.

Word of the deployment leaked, and before long, American U-2
overflights had detailed photographs showing the construction of missile
launch platforms as well as the missiles themselves. In October 1962,
Kennedy ordered plans for an invasion of Cuba—not by CIA-supported
rebels, but by U.S. armed forces. The Joint Chiefs and Secretary of State
Dean Acheson supported immediate military action to destroy the missiles
already being assembled in Cuba. As an alternative plan, Kennedy also
discussed a naval blockade of Cuba to stop further delivery of Soviet
weapons and equipment. The president's brother, Attorney General
Robert Kennedy, and Secretary of Defense McNamara argued in favor

of the blockade. On October 22, a Soviet anti-aircraft missile shot down a U-2 spy plane over Cuba, killing its pilot Air Force Major Rudolf Anderson, Jr., of Greenville, South Carolina. Castro cabled Khrushchev, demanding an immediate nuclear assault on the United States. Soviet commanders in Cuba had at their disposal tactical nuclear weapons for battlefield use that were ready to fire. Kennedy placed the United States military around the world on highest alert. That evening, Kennedy made a dramatic television address to the world announcing the blockade or 'quarantine,' as he called it, of Cuba.

To describe the situation as tense does not begin to appreciate conditions in October 1962. Nonetheless, the crisis was resolved. Using diplomacy while threatening the use of force, Kennedy managed to broker a deal in which the United States agreed to withdraw American missiles from Turkey—they were supposed to have been removed a year earlier but had not been. Further, Kennedy promised not to invade Cuba in exchange for the Soviets' agreement to withdraw their missiles from Cuba. This offer also gave Khrushchev a face-saving way out. Kennedy's willingness to risk global nuclear war over Cuba surprised Khrushchev, who thought Cuba not worth such a price. Kennedy had maintained tight control of American commanders around Cuba to minimize the potential for an accidental attack. An unintended consequence of this control was the establishment of a tradition of executive interference with local commanders, bypassing the regular chain of command.

The crisis represented a point of maximum danger in the Cold War, but it also highlighted the difficulties in the evolution of Flexible Response from the old New Look. For many Americans, if not for people around the world, the resolution of the Cuban Missile Crisis made it appear that Kennedy had saved humanity from a nuclear holocaust and resurrected his prestige.

Conclusion

By the end of 1963, Kennedy was dead from an assassin's bullet and his vice president, Lyndon Baines Johnson, was president. Kennedy had already placed over 15,000 military advisors, including hundreds of Green Berets, in South Vietnam to help train and equip South Vietnamese military forces to fight the North Vietnamese-supported insurgency there. Cuba remained a thorn in the side of the United States, as Castro survived CIA attempts on his life. NATO's stability was uncertain. France threatened to withdraw, and there were continuing disagreements over nuclear versus conventional strategies and obligations. China was moving out from under the shadow of the Soviet Union to act as a communist force. Thus, despite a nuclear test ban treaty signed by the United States and the Soviet Union in 1963, the Chinese successfully tested a nuclear bomb in 1964. Clearly, the Cold War was in full swing.

The American military had grown—dramatically—in size, capability, and purpose since the Korean War. Eisenhower had made the United States the most robust nuclear power on the planet. Kennedy then balanced nuclear power with non-nuclear capabilities. McNamara's management style eliminated waste and created a financial balance between weapons programs and personnel. Military leaders debated the merits of nuclear force versus limited conventional response. Nation-building and counterinsurgency were just two of the many new strategies and policies added to the American military's arsenal of unconventional capabilities. While the threat of nuclear war remained, the United States found itself fighting small wars in remote places. After spending more than a decade preparing to fight a nuclear and conventional war in Europe, ironically the United States became embroiled in a lengthy unconventional conflict in Southeast Asia that would shake the military, indeed the nation, to its very core.

Further Reading

Allison, Graham T., and Philip Zelikow. *Essence of Decision: Explaining the Cuban Missile Crisis*. 2nd ed. New York: Addison Wesley, 1999.

Gaddis, John Lewis. *Strategies of Containment: A Critical Appraisal of Postwar American National Security Policy*. New York: Oxford University Press, 1982.

Gavin, Francis J. *Nuclear Statecraft: History and Strategy in America's Atomic Age*. Ithaca, NY: Cornell University Press, 2012.

House, Johnathan. *A Military History of the Cold War, 1944–1962*. Norman, OK: University of Oklahoma Press, 2012.

Kempe, Frederick. *Berlin 1961*. New York: G.P. Putnam's Sons, 2011.

Lehman, John. *Oceans Ventured: Winning the Cold War at Sea*. New York: W. W. Norton, 2018.

Linn, Brian M. *Elvis' Army: Cold War GIs and the Atomic Battlefield*. Cambridge, MA: Harvard University Press, 2016.

Munton, Don, and David A. Welch. *The Cuban Missile Crisis: A Concise History*. New York: Oxford University Press, 2011.

Nichols, David A. *Eisenhower 1956: The President's Year of Crisis—Suez and the Brink of War*. New York: Simon & Schuster, 2011.

Robin, Ron Theodore. *The Making of the Cold War Enemy: Culture and Politics in the Military-Intellectual Complex*. Princeton, NJ: Princeton University Press, 2003.

Trauschweizer, Ingo. *The Cold War U.S. Army: Building Deterrence for Limited War*. Lawrence, KS: University Press of Kansas, 2008.

Westad, Odd Arne. *The Cold War: A World History*. New York: Basic Books, 2017.

Windrow, Martin. *The Last Valley: Dien Bien Phu and the French Defeat in Vietnam*. Cambridge, MA: Da Capo Press, 2004.

15 Vietnam

Introduction

Until the recent war in Afghanistan, Vietnam was America's longest war. The most socially divisive American conflict since the Civil War and a still controversial conflict, Vietnam continues to cast a shadow over American public life and popular culture, reflecting its role as the defining event for the 'baby boom' generation that came of age during the 1960s and 1970s. The conduct of the war at the highest levels was characterized by hubris and bad assumptions that marked a culminating point in American Cold War policy and international behavior. The ultimate defeat in 1975 of South Vietnam prompted serious introspection within the armed forces and, ironically, led to a far-reaching renaissance in American military power.

Early American Involvement

The United States became involved in Vietnam by way of World War II then broader Cold War concerns mostly relating to Western Europe. Like Korea before them, the French colonial territories of Indochina were of little interest or importance to the United States until Japan occupied French Indochina early in World War II. Following the war, in the spirit of American espousals of self-determination for subjugated peoples in the colonial world, Vietnamese nationalist and communist Ho Chi Minh declared Vietnam's independence in Hanoi. Initially open to Vietnamese nationhood, the United States quickly supported French attempts to reimpose colonial rule in exchange for French support of the new NATO alliance in Western Europe. By 1950, the United States was financially underwriting the French war to regain Indochina, while Ho Chi Minh and his rising general Vo Nguyen Giap enjoyed the support of communist China as well as the blessing of the Soviet Union.

The French Indochina War, as it came to be known, dragged on for several years, taxing both the financial and military resources of France, which had yet to fully recover from World War II, as well as the patience of the French public, which grew increasingly wary of the cost in money and lives. The French defeat at Dien Bien Phu in May 1954 effectively ended the fighting in Indochina, leaving communist forces in nominal control of the north, while French forces tenuously held the south. the Geneva Conference that spring was far from satisfactory for either side, as Vietnam was divided into north and south with the promise of elections for possible unification in 1956. These elections never took place. In the aftermath of the Korean debacle and other Cold War-related developments, the American leaders believed the United States could ill afford any loss to the communist world.

The French soon withdrew, leaving the United States to fill the subsequent power vacuum in the south to deny the newly created country, the Republic of Vietnam (or South Vietnam), to the communists in the north, who established the Democratic Republic of Vietnam (or North Vietnam). Ho Chi Minh and the communists represented the nationalist aspirations of a large proportion of the Vietnamese people and the search for credible alternatives and a legitimate client state in the south was to be an enduring problem for American policy throughout the conflict.

Direct involvement in Vietnam was a gradual process, beginning in earnest during the Eisenhower administration. The United States and its allies increasingly backed Ngo Dinh Diem, an authoritarian Catholic in an overwhelmingly Buddhist country. Diem's government had enjoyed considerable success in the second half of the 1950s in defeating internal threats to stability from both communist and non-communist sources. The Diem government's heavy-handed methods on communist sympathizers and others who challenged his policies fed instability in the cities as well as rural areas. The American equipped and trained the Army of the Republic of Vietnam, known as the ARVN, slowly pressured communist networks in the south, leading Hanoi to restart the revolutionary struggle to unite the country under communist rule in 1958–1959. This move was not without organizational and political friction, as the National Liberation Front (NLF) and its armed insurgents the People's Liberation Armed Forces (PLAF) often considered themselves semi-autonomous from their benefactors in the north. Collectively known as the Viet Cong, the NLF carried out an effective if not brutal insurgency against the government of South Vietnam. American military leaders in Vietnam and political decisionmakers in Washington often failed to understand the complex relationship between the NLF and the North Vietnamese government, and further were slow to appreciate the competitive support on the part of the Soviet Union and communist China for North Vietnam in its war of unification and national liberation.

At several points between 1960 and American commitment of combat forces in 1965, the United States was faced with the choice to reinforce Diem and his sycophants or to withdraw support. Each time, the United

States did just enough to stave off imminent disaster without arriving at a clear strategy for a permanent and acceptable solution. The image of a quagmire, frequently invoked in accounts of the war, owes something to this less than ideal process.

The American military that fought the war initially entered the conflict at the peak of effectiveness, self-confidence, and apparent technological superiority, and was structured to stand against Soviet forces on the plains of Central Europe. Despite the creation of Special Forces capabilities, notably the 'Green Berets,' and some enthusiasm within the Kennedy administration for what has been termed 'the cult of counterinsurgency,' it was not especially well shaped for the challenges posed by revolutionary guerrilla war in mainland Southeast Asia.

Greatly influenced by its experiences of the Second World War, the American military increasingly emphasized the roles of firepower, mass, and technology as solutions to the problems posed on the battlefield. There was a strong belief in the efficacy of airpower throughout the American military, but particularly within the Air Force. Consistent with its general doctrine, the Air Force proposed a campaign of strategic non-nuclear bombing on primary industrial and military targets in North Vietnam. The Army organizationally and doctrinally exploited the potential arising from the helicopter, using it on the battlefield in tactical situations through the creation and evolution of air mobility and the conversion of the Army's 1st Cavalry Division to an air-mobile role.

The American war can be divided into four broad phases. From the mid-1950s until the end of the American commitment, a substantial training and advisory effort were mounted to create, develop, and sustain the Republic of Vietnam Armed Forces, especially the ARVN. Until the deployment of large numbers of American combat troops and the decision to Americanize the war in 1965, the advisory war represented the major American effort in the country. Between 1965 and 1969, American combat units led by General William C. Westmoreland, the commander of the American Military Assistance Command Vietnam (MACV), fought a 'big-unit' war against communist forces while using the ARVN to mostly manage pacification efforts. The third phase, between 1969 and 1972, followed the election of President Richard Nixon, who had campaigned on a promise to end the war, or, at least, American involvement in it. This third period saw the Vietnamization of the conflict with the United States turning over responsibility for much of the war's conduct to the ARVN and the South Vietnamese government. American troop levels dropped significantly, and Westmoreland's successor, General Creighton W. Abrams, faced the difficult challenge of fighting while turning the war over to the South Vietnamese, all as peace talks moved at a glacial pace in Paris.

American forces had been withdrawn from major ground combat by 1972. The final phase, from American withdrawal until the fall of Saigon in 1975, saw the South Vietnamese solely responsible for their own defense with only nominal financial and materiel support from the United States. Increasingly embattled by a resurgent enemy no longer wary of American airpower and ultimately abandoned by their American patrons, the corrupt South Vietnamese government and its rapidly decaying military had little chance against the North's well-supplied and well-trained conventional forces.

The Advisors' War

The advisors' war is the aspect of American involvement least known or understood. Military advising was the part of the MACV effort that brought American personnel into the closest and most sustained relationships with their South Vietnamese counterparts. These American advisors often had the most contact with the pacification and counterinsurgency tasks that were central to the guerrilla struggle in the villages.

Especially in the southern Mekong River delta and in the central highlands working with the Montagnard hill people, American military advisors often found themselves outside the formal military structure and relatively isolated from other Americans. Those advisors who worked within the Vietnamese military were often prized by their Vietnamese counterparts for access to American fire support that they could seemingly instantly provide.

Advisors also trained the ARVN. In keeping with the Korean War experience, the Vietnamese military was fashioned in an American image, designed initially to counter or repel a conventional military invasion of the south along the lines the North Koreans had attempted in 1950. This was not the nature of the threat they faced, however. Such assumptions ignored the nature of this hybrid war and that Vietnam was, in the parlance of the time, a 'third world' country. No did American perceptions of the conflict appreciate the cultural contradictions of the role of war in Vietnamese tradition and society. Thus, MACV built an ARVN ultimately ill-suited for the conflict it faced.

Diem's ouster and murder in November 1963 ushered in a period of chronic political instability and revolving-door governments installed and removed by coup and countercoup. American attempts to sustain a viable non-communist South Vietnam were unraveling; this was especially apparent to the advisors on the ground, some of whom became staunch critics of how the advisory effort was conducted and of the unrelenting and increasingly unrealistic optimism with which higher authority presented it. By 1963, there were 16,000 American military personnel in Vietnam, and while they enjoyed success in some areas—especially in arming and training the hill tribes—their efforts elsewhere appeared futile. For example, in the Battle of Ap Bac, in January 1963, a large ARVN air-mobile force supported by armored personnel carriers attempted a rather straightforward operational envelopment of two PLAF battalions. Lack of coordination, failure to respond to enemy resistance, and poor combat leadership resulted in heavy casualties among the attacking force and the loss of several armored vehicles and American helicopters. The attack signaled to American military and political leaders that perhaps the ARVN and South Vietnamese government were incapable not only of crushing the Viet Cong insurgency but of defending the country as well. This realization led to the Kennedy administration's decision to support a coup against Diem led by ARVN generals in October 1963, which resulted in the deaths of Diem and his brother Nhu.

President Lyndon Johnson faced difficult decisions during 1964, a presidential election year. Johnson himself, though generally remembered as a war president, was in fact focused on domestic issues arising from his Great Society program, but his presidency was increasingly overshadowed by the war in Southeast Asia. It is sometimes suggested that the Johnson administration always did enough not to lose the war, yet never enough to win it outright; this misunderstands the real nature of the struggle in South Vietnam, which in the end could be won only by the South Vietnamese themselves and the underappreciated range of domestic constraints under which Johnson labored.

Advisors, training, and material assistance had not produced the desired results, and in late 1964 Johnson decided to escalate American involvement. In response to an attack on an American destroyer in the Gulf of Tonkin by North Vietnamese patrol boats, in August 1964 Congress overwhelmingly passed the Tonkin Gulf Resolution, which authorized Johnson to take whatever measures he saw fit to defend Americans and American interests in Vietnam and to uphold American obligations to the Southeast Asia Treaty Organization. Johnson ordered increased American air support of ARVN operations as well as a separate air campaign to compel the North Vietnamese government to the negotiating table.

Americanizing the War

Ap Bac and the overthrow of Diem convinced the Johnson administration that the South Vietnamese could not win their war on their own. The Americans would have to fight it for them. In February 1965, PLAF forces attacked the American base at Pleiku, killing several American military personnel and wounding dozens more. Other attacks and terrorist assaults followed that, instead of warding off the United States from further involvement, only served to deepen the Johnson administration's resolve to escalate the war. American Marines landed at Da Nang in March 1965 to defend the airfield there. Before long, Marine patrols began the first so-called search-and-destroy missions from the airfield to seek out enemy units and engage them through superior American firepower before the enemy could attack the airbase. American forces were now in combat in South Vietnam.

To convince the North Vietnamese government to enter negotiations through military force but doing so gradually to not alarm the Soviet Union or communist China, Johnson initiated Operation Rolling Thunder in March 1965, which until its conclusion in 1969 dropped over seven million tons of bombs on North Vietnam, a pre-industrial and mostly agrarian country. Essentially a campaign of graduated escalation, it was intended to convince Hanoi that continued support for the insurgency in the south would have serious consequences within the north. This assumed that the communists were susceptible to such argument and vulnerable to such pressure. Neither was the case. For the communists, this was a war of national unification and independence, war aims that were not susceptible to negotiation. For the United States, limited war theory guided the American approach to Vietnam, hoping to achieve political objectives using graduated military force while keeping the conflict contained in Vietnam and thus avoiding an expanded war like that of Korea in the early 1950s.

Washington fundamentally misunderstood its enemy and the nature of the war the United States was embarking upon. In response to the bombing, North Vietnamese actually intensified the operational tempo of the PLAF and regular North Vietnamese forces, the People's Army of Vietnam (PAVN), in the south. PLAF and PAVN units pointedly attacked American facilities and the bases from which some of the bombing missions were being launched for the first time. Far from coercing the North Vietnamese government to the negotiating table, Rolling Thunder had the opposite effect. With Chinese and Soviet assistance, the airspace over North Vietnam became one of the most intense air defense environments in the world. American losses steadily mounted as the bombing campaign and North Vietnamese defense against it escalated.

During the Great War for Empire, British General James Wolfe maintained that war is an option of difficulties—an apt appraisal of the alternatives Johnson faced in Vietnam just over 200 years later. Johnson did not want the war, and his senior advisors do not appear to have believed, in private, that it could be won. Enemy activity increased in intensity and effectiveness, and American officials in Saigon grew pessimistic about the ARVN's combat performance as well as South Vietnam's future. At the same time, Johnson did not wish to encourage opposition in the United States by being seen to have 'lost' Vietnam in the manner that Truman was alleged to have 'lost' China in 1949. Withdrawal, therefore, was not an option.

In Saigon, Westmoreland enthusiastically advocated committing American ground combat troops to the fight, and between April and July 1965, Johnson approved force requests that amounted to nearly 200,000 American soldiers with additional troops offered from South Korea, Thailand,

Figure 15.1 A U.S. Marine Corps Vought F-8E Crusader takes off from Da Nang Air Base in 1967. Photograph by Staff Sergeant Bill Fisher.

Source: United States Marine Corps.

Australia, New Zealand, and the Philippines in response to pressure from Washington. The 'American' war had begun in earnest.

Considerable divisions existed within the American command authority over the war and its conduct, and this did little to assist in the formulation of coherent and effective strategy. The most important of these differences centered on the Secretary of Defense, Robert S. McNamara. Brought in by President Kennedy from the Ford Motor Company to rein in the defense budget and make the Pentagon more efficient and responsive, McNamara surrounded himself with 'whiz-kids,' bright young technocrats schooled in systems analysis and with neither military experience nor respect for those who had it. McNamara himself treated the Joint Chiefs of Staff with thinly veiled contempt, while the vociferous demands for quantification of results helped to drive the 'body count' culture that emerged as a result of the November 1965 Battle of Ia Drang, in which American forces first squared off against the PAVN in a large-scale engagement. The Chief of Staff of the Army, General Harold K. Johnson, agonized over whether to resign in protest at the misconduct of the war and subsequently regretted that he had not done so.

With heavy losses through combat and even heavier ones through desertion, the ARVN was incapable at this stage of holding its own against

PLAF and the PAVN forces. Consequently, Westmoreland's decision to fight the war with American Army and Marine units was probably justified for a time. In 1965–1966 the big-unit war, pursuing an aggressive and capable enemy across the length and breadth of the country, staved off collapse and bought time to rebuild South Vietnamese capabilities. Too little advantage was taken of this opportunity, however; the attitude frequently seemed to be that the South Vietnamese were ineffective. Nor did the big-unit approach have much to offer the process of pacification, which while important to Westmoreland many Americans regarded as a 'second order' task fit only for the ARVN while the Americans fought the 'real' war.

But the Americanized war was expensive in casualties. American combat units suffered significant losses while undoubtedly inflicting them as well. With such a heavy though not exclusive emphasis on kill ratios, MACV reasoned that eventually the PLAF and PAVN would be unable to replace their losses, hitting a 'crossover' point where losses outweighed continuing the war. While this may have made perfect logical sense to an American mindset, such an assumption completely ignored the agency of the enemy, who, it must be remembered, 'gets a vote.'

Moreover, attrition required substantial firepower, and innocent non-combatants often became caught in the crossfire. In addition to casualties, massive American firepower from air strikes, artillery, and naval vessels in the South China Sea destroyed homes, business, and farm buildings. Such an approach also revealed Westmoreland's and MACV's poor understanding of the nature and challenge of revolutionary war and indeed risked alienating local populations. Military force was only one part of the security equation in counterinsurgency warfare, but in this phase of the war, it received more emphasis from Westmoreland and his superiors, perhaps because it was the one aspect of warfare that they best understood and were most familiar with.

There were, in fact, four different ground wars in Vietnam at any one time, and where a soldier operated primarily determined the nature of his operational experience. The most intense combat environment was in the northern provinces adjoining the 17th parallel, where the Marine Corps and the best of the ARVN formations, such as the airborne, were deployed. The mountains and thick jungles of the interior also saw sustained heavy combat, where much of the fighting was done by the Montagnards, tribesmen whom the South Vietnamese regarded as inferiors but whom many American soldiers and Marines highly regarded. The more densely populated central and southern regions brought combat units into close contact with villagers, many of whom were wounded or killed by American firepower and a willingness of the Viet Cong to use civilians to shield their own fighting units. Finally, the Mekong River Delta in the south came closest to the classic image of a war fought by black-pajama-clad PLAF units. Much of the fighting in this area was done by the ARVN, accompanied by American advisors. Generally, the Americans stayed out of the cities, such as Saigon and Hue, leaving security there to the South Vietnamese—although there were exceptions to this, such as during the Tet Offensive in 1968.

Hanoi matched the American force buildup in the south, despite suffering heavy casualties at the hands of American firepower. Regular PAVN units and formations were deployed in increasing numbers, in part to replace casualties among the PLAF and match the combat capabilities of American units. The slogan adopted by many soldiers from North Vietnam—'born in the north to die in the south'—acquired a grim certainty in this period of the war.

The PLAF and PAVN made extensive use of rocket and mortar attacks, especially against the few massive but vulnerable American bases located across South Vietnam. With deadly tactical skill, they also used mines, snipers, ambushes, and bunker systems, but were also willing to engage in set-piece conventional actions of their own choosing, especially in the northern provinces. Tactically, enemy units often attempted to close with and 'hug' opposing units to negate American advantages in fire support, especially from helicopters and other aerial platforms. Using heavier, crew-served automatic weapons, they inflicted significant casualties upon American helicopter units and their crews. Regular northern units and provincial Viet Cong formations, in particular, were not an enemy to be taken lightly.

Although the ARVN was created in imitation of its American patron, it had some significant differences and limitations. Corruption, political patronage, and incompetence were real problems right up to the fall of Saigon in 1975. There were, however, a growing number of honest and competent officers in senior command positions, especially after 1968, to whom Americans generally paid less attention. Indeed, there were many courageous and tenacious ordinary ARVN soldiers and junior officers for whom the war never ended and who did not enjoy the comparative luxury of a 12-month tour of duty. Their performance often went unnoted or worse was derided by stereotypes from American troops. After 1975, the ARVN became a 'forgotten' army.

At its height, the ARVN numbered more than half a million men, with perhaps as many again in a variety of part-time militias, irregular units, and other paramilitary formations. Desertion was undoubtedly a problem, but it is worth noting that very few ARVN deserters went over to the other side, while perhaps as many as 90,000 PLAF and PAVN regulars rallied to the southern government during the war. Associated with this, the majority of ARVN divisions were regionally based, and soldiers operated in the same provinces from which they were conscripted and in which their families continued to reside. Aside from concern for their families, many soldiers felt an obligation to help with the harvest and similar tasks. When the communists launched their final offensive in 1975, many ARVN soldiers took action to safeguard their families, in some cases attaching them to units as these withdrew, which further contributed to

Figure 15.2 The War in Vietnam.

the general disorder that was part of the enemy's overall plan. As a result of all this, the ARVN suffered from a low level of strategic mobility, which limited its effectiveness in conventional operations when these again came to dominate the war in its final stages.

The Bombing of North Vietnam

The air campaign over North Vietnam occasioned great controversy within the United States, and indeed internationally. Using global propaganda, the North Vietnamese government and its allies skillfully exploited the attacks to put pressure on Washington to cease the bombing—a sign, perhaps, that it was more effective than apologists for Hanoi sometimes cared to admit. Operation Rolling Thunder remains controversial, particularly for critics of the way the war was conducted who point to the gradualism and severe target restrictions of the air campaign as crippling mistakes. Moreover, such limitations did not apply to the enemy, who were fighting for the unlimited objective of national liberation. The strategic thinking behind the 'sending of signals' and the process of bombing halts followed by renewed intensification of the campaign was undoubtedly flawed.

Even with restrictive rules of engagement and attempts to limit damage and civilian casualties, the technology of the time could not eliminate collateral damage. This was seized upon by America's critics at home and abroad, aided and abetted by those—such as Jane Fonda—who lent themselves to enemy purposes through highly publicized visits to Hanoi, where they made naïve and ill-considered criticisms of the bombing in particular and more generally of American objectives in the war. Johnson halted the bombings in October 1968, following his decision to withdraw from the 1968 presidential election campaign in March of that year, as a sign of good faith to begin peace talks with North Vietnam.

The importance of helicopters in the ground war in South Vietnam has been noted already, but fixed-wing aircraft played an equally important role in providing air support to American and allied ground forces. Transport aircraft provided an extensive network of logistic support and resupply flights that, together with the close air support provided by attack aircraft, made the skies over South Vietnam some of the busiest in the world.

Close air support missions dropped vast quantities of explosives and napalm on enemy positions, while an extensive program of aerial defoliation, using chemical agents collectively known as Agent Orange, stripped vast acreages of the rural countryside to deny the enemy the overhead cover provided by jungle and forest. In a further demonstration of their versatility beyond their strategic purpose, B-52 bombers were used in Arc Light missions, dropping bombs from great and undetectable altitudes upon otherwise well-hidden enemy positions. Along the Ho Chi Minh

Trail, for example, B-52s caused frequent damage and considerable effect on enemy morale.

Blue and Brown Water Operations

Winding from the North Vietnamese border with Laos southward through Cambodia and then into South Vietnam at various points, the Ho Chi Minh Trail itself was the result of another success against the enemy's war effort, this time at sea. The maritime war had several components: blue water; brown water; harbor and port defense, especially in the waters around the port of Saigon; and naval activities ashore.

Operation Sea Dragon commenced in October 1966 and involved offensive operations against shore targets in North Vietnam designed to complement Rolling Thunder. Operation Market Time, directed against seaborne infiltration of supplies and personnel southward along the coast, proved so successful in stemming the flow of logistic support from the north by 1967 that it led the Communists to find other, safer means of resupplying the south along the Ho Chi Minh Trail and through the supposedly neutral Cambodian port of Sihanoukville.

The brown-water riverine war, encompassed by Operation Game Warden, utilized vessels of the United States Navy, the South Vietnamese Navy, and the United States Coast Guard against PLAF movement along South Vietnam's internal waterways, assisted by the Coastal Groups, South Vietnamese paramilitaries more commonly known as the 'junk force.' The riverine war was dangerous and intense, and enemy contact and casualties were frequent.

The air and naval wars were always an adjunct to that fought on the ground. In 1967, the size of the forces on each side continued to grow, the intensity of the fighting was maintained, and the enemy usually retained the tactical initiative. American forces grew that year from 385,000 to 486,000, though the number of allied maneuver battalions only increased from 256 to 278. Despite the emphasis on large-scale search-and-destroy operations, the PLAF and PAVN usually evaded American and ARVN forces when they desired to do so, initiating contact up to company level (and sometimes higher) and frustrating Westmoreland's grand designs. The fighting in the five northern provinces of I Corps was especially fierce, but throughout the country, the casualty rate for American forces more than doubled over that suffered in 1966: over 9,000 combat deaths and over 60,000 wounded. Enemy battle deaths were estimated to have reached nearly 90,000 for the year.

The Tet Offensive

Westmoreland's optimistic reporting on the situation on the ground in the fall of 1967, together with the ferocity of the combat and the heavy losses imposed on the enemy, made the impact of the Tet Offensive at the end of January 1968 all the more powerful. Distracting attention through sustained operations along South Vietnam's borders and against the Marine outpost at Khe Sanh, North Vietnam moved sizable forces against the cities and major urban centers throughout South Vietnam. Orchestrated largely by Le Duan, the General Secretary of the North Vietnamese Communist Party and therefore the head of the North Vietnamese government, the so-called 'Great Offensive, Great Uprising' involved PLAF units to strike provincial capitals, the cities, and other military and political targets across South Vietnam while prepositioned main force PAVN units would sweep in to secure these objectives. Simultaneously, Le Duan believed the people of South Vietnam, long tired of the corrupt and ineffective South Vietnamese government, would rise up to support the PAVN and PLAF forces, which together would cause the South Vietnamese government to collapse. With no client government to support, Le Duan reasoned, the United States would abandon Vietnam. The Tet Offensive was intended to provide the final stage in protracted revolutionary warfare along the Maoist model—the nationwide popular uprising that would sweep away the Americans and their 'puppets' in Saigon. It was a bold and audacious plan, one that both Ho Chi Minh and General Giap objected to as too risky. Ho's position, however, had become mostly ceremonial by late 1967, and Giap did not have the political support to oppose the extremely powerful Le Duan. Thus the plan went ahead.

Tet, the festival of the lunar new year, is the most important holiday in the Vietnamese calendar and had routinely been marked by brief holiday truces among the combatants; in the lead-up to the offensive, much of the ARVN was on leave. To mount such a broad attack on Vietnam's most revered holiday was a risk in and of itself. Security was paramount for success, perhaps too much so, as many PLAF units knew little of their objectives or tasks until days if not hours, before the offensive began.

Still, enough communication had been intercepted to alert MACV that something big was in the offing. Although Westmoreland remained convinced, as Le Duan intended, that the isolated Marine outpost at Khe Sanh was the primary objective of North Vietnamese strategy, he was persuaded to station additional American units in the vicinity of Saigon just before the offensive was launched, greatly enhancing MACV's capacity to respond quickly to the assaults on the capital.

Due to miscommunication, some attacks commenced a night early, but the main thrust began in the early hours of January 30 as planned. PLAF and PAVN units struck 36 of the 44 provincial capitals across South Vietnam, as well as five of the six major cities, 64 district capitals, and numerous South Vietnamese and American bases and military facilities, including 23 airfields. From the American perspective, the most significant shock involved the breaching of the compound wall at the American

Embassy in Saigon by a small detachment of Viet Cong sappers, most of whom were killed in the ensuing firefight with American military police units. Television images of this small aspect of the great offensive that was unfolding repeatedly played on news broadcasts in the United States fatally undermined Westmoreland's confident assertion at the end of the previous year that 'the end comes into view' in Vietnam.

The most significant aspects of the Tet Offensive were, in fact, the things that did not happen. The populace did not rise up in support of the National Liberation Front as Le Duan had hoped. The ARVN did not desert, nor did it collapse; in fact, the ARVN fought surprisingly well during Tet. The Saigon government did not lose its nerve or its capacity to respond. Soldiers and police fought fiercely and well, and in many instances, they ejected or exterminated the attackers in short order. Saigon was mostly cleared of the enemy within a week of the offensive's launch, but intense fighting in Saigon's crowded slum districts led to widespread destruction and significant civilian casualties. The old imperial capital of Hue, in the north, was largely destroyed and thousands of its citizens killed or rendered homeless. At least 3,000 'enemies of the people' were rounded up in the city by the NLF and murdered, then buried in mass graves. American Marines and several ARVN units fought a fierce battle

Figure 15.3 A corpsman give medical attention to a wounded Marine during the battle for Hue, February 1968.

Source: National Archives and Records Administration.

to retake the city in scenes reminiscent of urban fighting during World War II.

The two most significant and long-term outcomes of Tet were the fatal undermining of American resolve and the near destruction of the Viet Cong. Because the American and South Vietnamese military response to the Tet Offensive nearly destroyed the Viet Cong, after mid-1968 the proportion of North Vietnamese regulars in South Vietnam increased dramatically and continued to do so for the remainder of the war. In late 1965, they had made up 25 percent of the enemy force in-country; by June 1968 this had grown to 55 percent, and to 70 percent overall if northerners drafted into Viet Cong units were included. It has been suggested subsequently that the destruction of the indigenous southern movement in 1968 enabled Hanoi to tighten its control over the revolutionary movement in the south.

Predictably, Westmoreland responded to the Tet Offensive by demanding an additional 205,000 American troops. Johnson had little choice but to deny the request. Under intense political pressure at home and himself realizing the futility of the war in Southeast Asia, Johnson shocked the nation in a speech on March 31, 1968, by first opening the door for negotiations with North Vietnam and then announcing he would not run for reelection. By mid-year, Westmoreland had returned to the United States to take up the post of Chief of Staff of the Army, replaced in Vietnam by General Creighton W. Abrams. President Johnson, facing certain defeat if he ran, declined to be considered for the Democratic Party nomination for another term as president.

Americans killed in action exceeded 500 per week in February and March 1968, and although enemy losses were staggering—over 45,000 in the first three weeks of February alone—support for the war in the United States declined still further and never recovered. While American media objectively reported the fighting during Tet, even praising the courage of American and South Vietnamese troops, by late February some, such as CBS News correspondent Walter Cronkite, began questioning what many referred to as a 'stalemate.' Troubling images, such as Associated Press photographer Eddie Adams' photograph of Saigon police chief General Nguyen Ngoc Loan summarily executing suspected Viet Cong fighter Nguyen Van Lem with his sidearm on February 1, 1968, caused many Americans to question their support of the war. Tet had been a military defeat but a political victory for North Vietnam and became the turning point in the American war.

The Tet fighting foreshadowed the intense and relentless combat to come that year. Over 16,800 Americans were killed in Vietnam in 1968, making it the deadliest year of the war. That same year, over 27,000 ARVN perished. In the United States, domestic support for the war began to crumble.

Fighting While Negotiating

Richard Nixon came to the presidency in 1969 with the intention of with-drawing from Vietnam, but of doing so 'honorably.' This was much easier said than done both from a practical standpoint and because of political complexities both at home and abroad, certainly in Vietnam. In fact, as many Americans were killed in Vietnam under Nixon's administration as had died under the Johnson administration. On several occasions, Nixon appeared to widen the war, dangerously in the view of his detractors, as he sought a means to get out of Vietnam while leaving the South Vietnamese with a reasonable chance of holding the communists at bay.

General Creighton Abrams paid much more attention to training and equipping the ARVN, building up the regional and popular force militias in the villages, and doing general pacification tasks aimed at strengthening the authority and legitimacy of the government in Saigon at the expense of the NLF. Considerable advances were made in these areas, and it has been argued that a greater emphasis on them earlier in the American war would have produced stronger long-term results. While this is an intriguing prospect, it overlooks two things. First, the much-weakened state of the NLF after 1968 made it easier to pacify in the countryside than had been the case in 1966–1967. Second, and perhaps more importantly, the implacable resolve in Hanoi to win the war and unify the country proved unshakable.

Changes in the Draft

Intense fighting continued while the ARVN was modernized and the Americans increased resources for pacification efforts. At the same time, the Nixon administration intensified the peace talks with the Communists in Paris that Johnson had initiated in mid-1968; President Nixon also announced a timetable for gradual troop withdrawals in June 1969. Consequently, changes also occurred in the draft. After World War II and in part because of the Cold War, Americans temporarily disregarded their traditional dislike of involuntary military service and supported a large standing army made up of conscripts. By the 1960s, however, glaring social inequalities and questions concerning American involvement in Vietnam combined with draft boards dominated by white elites to make selective service more difficult to accept. Indeed, the draft was biased against working class and rural whites and minorities. The college defer-ment was particularly controversial. In 1967, President Johnson attempted to placate anti-draft protesters by making small changes in draft legislation, but his failure to reform conscription only sparked increased dissent. During the 1968 presidential campaign. Nixon argued in favor of a smaller all-volunteer military, but he also signaled his reluctance to make drastic changes as he cautioned against ending selective service until American military involvement in Vietnam had concluded.

After he was elected president, Nixon tried, as Johnson had, to mollify anti-draft protesters with small gestures such as ordering a study of terminating the draft. Ultimately, however, increased agitation prodded Nixon to reform local draft boards by increasing minority membership and excluding service personnel and anyone younger than 30 years of age from board membership. Shortly after that, Nixon tried to make the draft seem fairer by instituting a draft lottery and dismissing the increasingly unpopular Selective Service chief, General Lewis B. Hershey. Yet, the president could do little to appease opponents of the draft until American forces began leaving Vietnam and draft calls became smaller. From then, anti-draft agitation declined. Although some lawmakers worried that protesters would renew their outcry when Congress extended the draft in 1971, restricting reauthorization to only two years and including a pay raise for enlisted service members diluted anti-draft sentiment. More importantly, no draftees were sent to Vietnam after mid-1972 as the American withdrawal accelerated.

Dissent

To restrict the enemy's capacity to operate effectively within South Vietnam, Nixon authorized moves to interrupt the Communist resupply system running through 'neutral' Cambodia, with massive air attacks against the sanctuaries and base areas commencing in March 1969. Following a coup against Prince Norodom Sihanouk by pro-American elements in the Cambodian armed forces, a joint American–ARVN force of 20,000 troops launched ground and air assaults against the enemy base areas across the Cambodian border in May 1970. Militarily, this inflicted considerable losses, but in the United States the Cambodian incursion reinvigorated the antiwar movement and added to the domestic political problems of the Nixon administration.

Domestic opposition to the war flared as Nixon ordered the FBI to increase surveillance on antiwar groups in the United States. National Guard troops shot and killed four students on the campus of Kent State University in Ohio during an antiwar demonstration in protest of the Cambodian Incursion. At the same time, press reports and congressional investigations revealed the brutal massacre of hundreds of Vietnamese civilians at My Lai in March 1968 by troops in the Americal Division. The cover-up of the My Lai killings and the fact that only one soldier, Lieutenant William Calley, was convicted for the atrocity only exacerbated the American public's disenchantment with the war. Even Vietnam veterans began protesting the war through groups such as Vietnam Veterans Against the War. The so-called Winter Soldier hearings in Detroit in early 1971 made public allegations of atrocities committed by American forces in Vietnam.

The American commitment to Vietnam was always controversial, though in its early stages opposition was primarily confined to political groupings on the Left and traditional peace activists such as the Quakers. Support for military regimes in the Republic of Vietnam became increasingly difficult to sell to the American public as the casualty rates rose, U.S. servicemen came home to local cemeteries all over the country, and the aims, purpose, and outcomes of the war remained unclear, at best. President Johnson inherited a commitment arguably not of his making and decidedly opposed to his own inclination to build the 'Great Society' at home; but it was on his watch that the war was inexorably lost, at least in American living rooms and on American campuses.

Loss of confidence in American purpose in Vietnam transcended social class and political affiliation. Antiwar sentiment can be divided roughly into two parts: the active antiwar movement that was the visible face of the era on campuses, on the streets, and outside draft offices, and the growing disenchantment felt by many respectable Americans who abhorred the more violent activities of the first group while nonetheless withdrawing their support for the prosecution of the war. Demonstrations against official policy grew from the major peace marches in 1965 to the large-scale mobilization of protesters outside the Pentagon in October 1967 and culminated in the use of troops during the protests at Kent State and elsewhere in March 1970 that resulted in the deaths of four students, shot by the Ohio National Guard.

Dissent was widespread, sometimes intense, and was fueled by extensive media coverage, though certainly not caused by it. Popular culture reflected this, though one should beware of assuming that antiwar sentiment was all-pervasive. The political environment under Nixon became increasingly volatile—something that the President encouraged by his policies and behavior—but the sentiment in the country was frequently one of profound weariness with a war that was clearly lost. The divisions produced within the country as a result of the war remain with Americans still, as the public debate over recent conflicts in Iraq and Afghanistan suggests.

Getting Out

The United States was caught between conflicting pressures to end its part in the war, reassure its allies in Southeast Asia and the Pacific, and create a viable South Vietnam that could survive after the withdrawal of American ground troops. The results remained mixed. A measure of political stability had been established with the reelection of Nguyen Van Thieu to the presidency in 1971, but the poor performance of the ARVN during Operation Lam Son 719 in Laos the same year suggested that it was incapable of defeating the Communists on its own. On the other hand, when the North Vietnamese launched a major, countrywide offensive at Easter in 1972, the ARVN performed credibly, especially at places such as An Loc. The key, however, was the steadfastness of American advisors and the close air support they controlled—factors that would soon be removed.

Nixon authorized further heavy bombing against targets in North Vietnam; Operation Linebacker effectively targeted communications and transportation infrastructure and heavily damaged the economy. North Vietnamese willingness to conclude an agreement, albeit one that favored their position within the south, was encouraged through further air attacks at Christmas in 1972 through Operation Linebacker II, which finally brought about the signing of the Paris Peace Accords in January 1973. South Vietnam was promised immediate American military support in the face of any further northern aggression, and substantial continuing military aid.

While giving the United States a way out of the war, the Paris agreements ironically brought no peace to Vietnam and left substantial Communist forces in place in the south, from where they were able to undermine attempts by Thieu's government to maintain its authority and legitimacy. Nixon's domestic political troubles arising from the Watergate scandal and his ensuing resignation, together with the passage of the War Powers Resolution in 1973 that significantly limited a president's ability to use military force, robbed South Vietnam of any remaining hope of survival in the face of mounting northern military activity.

What was initially planned as a limited offensive in April 1975 quickly gained momentum in the face of command confusion in Saigon, rapid local successes on the part of the enemy, and disintegration of the ARVN. While some units fought to the last—such as the 18th Division at Xuan Loc that barred the road to Saigon for almost two weeks—the collapse was generally rapid. On April 30, having replaced Thieu in the hopes of furthering some form of negotiations, President Duong Van Minh surrendered his country. American embassy staff and remaining military personnel, along with aid workers and others still in South Vietnam, were dramatically airlifted out of the country to nearby Navy vessels. President Gerald R. Ford requested further aid for South Vietnam, but Congress balked. The Vietnam War was finally over.

The Impact of Vietnam

Vietnam was the last American war to be fought by an army heavily reliant on conscripts, giving way to the all-volunteer military after 1974 that was very much part of the reaction to that war and its costs. The burden of service was not equally or equitably shared, however. The average age of soldiers in Vietnam was 19 (compared to 26 in World War II). Ethnic and racial minorities and the economically disadvantaged were over-represented in the ranks because of the draft and misguided programs such as Project 100,000. Thus they were subsequently over-represented among the casualties. The sons of the middle class and opinion-forming elites had numerous options to avoid service in Vietnam, and many took them. College deferments, leaving for Canada, or loitering in the National Guard were alternatives to active duty.

Although they represented 12 percent of the American population, African Americans made up 31 percent of the rank and file in infantry battalions in 1965. Their casualty rates for the war as a whole reflected their proportion in the population at large, 12 percent; but, especially early in the war, the casualty rate was disproportionate: 24 percent in 1965, 19 percent in 1966, and 13 percent in 1968. Class, education, and region were also factors in determining who served, and who did not. Southerners were over-represented, with 28 percent of soldiers originating there, while those from low-income backgrounds were twice as likely to serve in the military and to see combat, as were those from families with higher incomes.

The war's effect on the American military as an institution was corrosive over time and required considerable corrective action after the withdrawal from Vietnam before being restored to a semblance of organizational health. Low morale and increasing drug use among soldiers not only in Vietnam but among troops in Europe and the United States as well signaled severe problems for the military. The advent of numerous 'fraggings,' assaulting or killing a superior officer or non-commissioned officer with a fragmentation grenade or other means, in Vietnam alarmed senior leadership in the Army and Marine Corps. Racial problems also highlighted disciplinary and organizational breakdowns in the military, especially the Army. While reflective of the racial issues in the United States during the 1960s, these spilled over into American forces in Vietnam. Riots at the Army's Long Binh jail in South Vietnam and the Marine brig at Okinawa, while caused by several factors, were primarily the result of racial inequities in the military. The military later tried to blame these problems on the draft, establishing a narrative that found fault with a sub-par, unmotivated pool of young men infected by the anti-authority movement of the 1960s. Swearing off the draft as a means to fill out its ranks, the services instead embraced, not without some concerns, the all-volunteer force model.

The other issue that remains at the forefront of the Vietnam experience is the 1,589 servicemembers listed as missing in action, or MIA. It is impossible to determine precisely how many Americans the North Vietnamese took prisoner, but the majority of them were aircrew shot down inside North Vietnam. Between February and April 1973, a total of 566 Americans were released and repatriated; this left a further 2,483 who were officially unaccounted for. Over time this number has slowly decreased, as remains are recovered with the cooperation of the Democratic Republic of Vietnam, especially after relations were normalized in 1995. Since that time, both the United States and Vietnam have worked together to recover remains of American soldiers. Through DNA testing, positive identification of many missing servicemembers from the Vietnam War and other conflicts is possible. In fact, the remains in the Tomb of the Unknown Soldier for Vietnam at Arlington National Cemetery were

Figure 15.4 The Hoa Lo Prison, dubbed the 'Hanoi Hilton' by the American POWs held
there during the Vietnam War.
Source: United States Air Force.

identified through DNA technology. There may never be another
Unknown Soldier.

Still, a cottage industry playing upon the fragile hopes of loved one,
quickly developed peddling information that some Americans were still
alive, held as captive in remote camps across North Vietnam. No evidence
supports this, but the issue was quickly embedded into the American postwar narrative. Admittedly, the lack of cooperation by Hanoi after the war
through the early 1990s in determining the fate of those missing fueled the
conspiracy industry that surrounds the issue, which did little to help the
families of MIAs. None dispute, however, that the treatment of American
prisoners of war was barbarous, including the widespread and sustained use
of torture and attempted exploitation for propaganda purposes.

Conclusion

Vietnam was America's longest war and its most divisive since the Civil War.
The cost in blood alone was considerable: 58,318 dead and over 300,000

wounded, with countless other lives blighted by the war and its aftermath. Over 5,000 American women served in Vietnam, mostly as nurses. Eight lost their lives, including one, Lieutenant Sharon Lane, who was killed when an enemy rocket hit an Army hospital at Chu Lai in June 1969. PLAF and PAVN killed are estimated at more than one million, with millions more wounded. ARVN combat deaths exceeded 250,000, with more than half a million wounded. Conservative estimates for civilian deaths in both North and South Vietnam are well over 600,000 and perhaps as high as 1.2 million. Added to this tragic figure are the millions who lost their homes, their livelihoods, and their families. Over two million Vietnamese fled the country after the fall of Saigon in April 1975, creating a world-wide refugee crisis. Many were able to emigrate to the United States.

The war made the United States unsure of itself, strained relations with European allies, put the American military into turmoil, and left the American people disgusted and then increasingly apathetic to America's role in the Cold War world. It took an immense effort for the American military to recover from this war—and for the American people to regain their confidence in America's military institutions.

Further Reading

Clodfelter, Mark. *The Limits of Airpower: The American Bombing of North Vietnam.* New York: The Free Press, 1989.

Daddis, Gregory. *Westmoreland's War: Reassessing American Strategy in Vietnam.* New York: Oxford University Press, 2014.

Elliott, David W. P. *The Vietnamese War: Revolution and Social Change in the Mekong Delta, 1930–1975.* New York: Routledge, 2006.

Hagopian, Patrick. *The Vietnam War in American Memory: Veterans, Memorials, and the Politics of Healing.* Amherst, MA: University of Massachusetts Press, 2011.

Jones, Howard. *My Lai: Vietnam, 1968, and the Descent into Darkness.* New York: Oxford University Press, 2017.

Lewy, Guenter. *America in Vietnam.* New York: Oxford University Press, 1978.

Longley, Kyle. *Grunts: The American Combat Soldier in Vietnam.* Armonk, NY: M. E. Sharpe, 2008.

Milam, Ron. *Not a Gentleman's War: An Inside View of Junior Officers in the Vietnam War.* Chapel Hill, NC: University of North Carolina Press, 2009.

Moïse, Edwin. *The Myths of Tet: The Most Misunderstood Event of the Vietnam War.* Lawrence, KS: University Press of Kansas, 2017.

Nguyen, Lien-Hang. *Hanoi's War: An International History of the War for Peace in Vietnam.* Chapel Hill, NC: University of North Carolina Press, 2012.

Spector, Ronald H. *After Tet: The Bloodiest Year in Vietnam.* New York: Free Press, 1993.

Stur, Heather Marie. *Beyond Combat: Women And Gender In The Vietnam War Era.* Cambridge: Cambridge University Press, 2011.

16 Reform and Adjustment for a Changing World

Introduction

Rebuilding the post-Vietnam American military while still fighting a Cold War against the Soviet Union in a geopolitical environment that saw an increasing number of conflicts across the developing world was indeed a great challenge for the United States. Force structure, procurement, and doctrine would have to adapt to this changing world from the 1970s through the 1990s. From the low point of the immediate post-Vietnam years, the American military would see the fulfillment of its rebuilding in the triumph of American combat arms in the Gulf War of 1991. With the end of the Cold War, however, and a tendency to use military force in situations that were peripheral to American interests, the American military continued to be challenged.

Toward an All-Volunteer Force

Indeed, during the immediate post-Vietnam years military morale reached its lowest levels since perhaps the early years of the American Revolution, and popular support of the defense establishment was at a twentieth-century nadir. As a result, the Department of Defense had to accept the end of the draft, alter enlisted personnel policies, and learn to fight with a leaner, all-volunteer force.

Military leaders were intensely skeptical of an all-volunteer force. Global military commitments required large armed forces, and motivation for volunteerism was not what military or political leaders expected following the Vietnam debacle. During the war, substantial numbers of draft-eligible men volunteered to serve in the armed forces, hoping to avoid assignment to combat units. By the early 1970s, over 50 percent of volunteers admitted that they enlisted because they expected to be drafted and believed that enlisting would allow them to choose a non-combat specialty. Without the draft, the Army feared motivation to voluntarily enlist would evaporate. The Army also worried that ending conscription would endanger national defense because the military would have to lower intelligence standards for recruits to meet manpower requirements. Some military leaders also opposed an all-volunteer force for fear that the aggressive recruiting campaigns required for volunteerism would cheapen the image of the armed services.

Nevertheless, in 1969 the Army began to study the viability of an all-volunteer force. The study, Project Volunteer in Defense of the Nation, or Provide, concluded that although an all-volunteer force was possible, it would increase military costs because volunteers would expect higher pay and better benefits than draftees had received in the past. Also, the report suggested that the Army would have to recruit more women if it wanted to meet enlistment needs.

The White House and the Department of Defense also conducted their own separate studies. In March 1969, Nixon appointed the Commission on an All-Volunteer Armed Force, known as the Gates Commission after its chairman, former Secretary of Defense Thomas M. Gates. The Department of Defense study group, Project Volunteer, convened in April of the same year also with the goal of deciding how the services could best develop an all-volunteer force. Both the Department of Defense study, which was heavily influenced by Provide, and the Gates Commission report agreed that an all-volunteer force was feasible.

Nevertheless, there were significant differences between the reports regarding how to implement an all-volunteer force. The Gates Commission concluded that merely increasing enlisted pay was sufficient to spur enlistments, while Project Volunteer argued that although better pay was important, a successful all-volunteer force also required better working and living conditions for enlisted service members, as well as an intensified recruitment effort for both enlisted members and officers.

Secretary of Defense Melvin Laird presented the Department of Defense recommendations to Nixon in March 1970. Draft authorization was due to end in 1971, but Laird recommended that draft authority continue and draft calls be decreased, in tandem with the reduction of the American presence in Vietnam, until there was a 'zero draft.' Temporarily retaining the draft offered insurance against the military's probable failure to meet recruitment needs in the near term. Laird also proposed a 20 percent pay increase for junior enlisted personnel, more and better on-base housing, improved housing allowances for personnel who lived off post and making junior enlisted service members eligible for on-base housing. Moreover, Laird recommended that the military provide health care for service members' families and that the government pay moving expenses for families of married service personnel who were transferred to new duty stations. Laird further urged improved educational and training programs, and an increase in civilian hiring to reduce the amount of support duty that enlisted members had to perform. In addition to these quality-of-life improvements, Laird wanted to expand each service's recruiting program. Nixon accepted these proposals and asked Congress to add $2 billion to the 1972 budget to fund them.

Unfortunately for the military, the Army and Department of Defense studies were classified, leading the public to assume that the Gates Commission had implemented the changes despite the opposition of military leaders. Even the *Army Times* inaccurately reported that the Pentagon resisted not only the all-volunteer force but also improvements for service life. While the armed forces preferred the certainty of personnel provided through selective service, the services recognized the inevitability of an all-volunteer force and began planning for the end of conscription.

Making the most of the draft's two-year extension, the Army explored the best way to implement the proposed changes. Under a 1971 program dubbed Project Volunteer Army, or VOLAR, commanders surveyed enlisted personnel and officers to discover what would increase retention and reenlistment. Resulting reports found that a bit less 'army' in the Army would go a long way toward retention. While less kitchen duty, a set work week, less stringent uniform regulations, and generally less Army 'red tape' had superficial appeal, better and fairer opportunities for job advancement and promotion, enhanced inducements to reenlist, and improved base housing and facilities would increase retention rates among enlistees as well as officers. By the end of 1972, at several Army posts, including Fort Benning, Fort Bragg, Fort Carson, and Fort Ord, experiments with these and other changes recommended from the survey reports resulted in higher morale and increased reenlistments. To encourage recruits to choose combat service, the Army began offering proficiency pay for enlisted personnel who met specific performance standards. The Navy, Marines, and Air Force instituted enlistment bonuses for recruits who chose a combat specialty. Each service also added recruiters and increased budgets for recruitment, including contracts with Madison Avenue advertising firms for television and commercials and radio spots. Despite leftover negative attitudes from the public toward military service, the American military took the initiative in making military service appealing to young people in the 1970s.

Reforming Training, Rethinking Doctrine

Soldiers sent to Southeast Asia had been trained in a World War II-era system that provided rapid basic training before men were shipped out as individual replacements to under-strength units. Conceived in expectation of mass mobilization and large numbers of draftees, the training plan met the personnel needs of a military fighting a worldwide war. The armed forces, particularly the Army, concluded that an outdated training scheme had contributed to the breakdown of unit cohesion and discipline in Vietnam. Ending the draft meant that the military could no longer plan around a large, quickly mobilized pool of recruits. Also, the Joint Chiefs were convinced that the American military was at a technological and numerical disadvantage to the Warsaw Pact. A better-trained, more professional military would help reduce that handicap.

In the past, a small professional military quickly trained conscripts in the basics of soldiering, following a prescribed syllabus through all levels of training. Completing an exercise or spending the required amount of time on any given subject, rather than going through an assessment of performance, determined when a service member or a unit had completed training. To help offset reduced enlistments, the armed forces intensified training based on an evaluation of performance. In the Army, for example, the new Training and Doctrine Command, or TRADOC, took over training and professional military education. At each level of training and education, soldiers and their units were assessed according to performance rather than task completion. The Air Force and Navy adopted similar approaches.

Withdrawing from Vietnam also prompted doctrinal changes. For more than a decade the Army had directed its resources toward the hybrid war effort in Southeast Asia. As a result, it was both doctrinally and technologically outpaced by potential enemies that maintained robust conventional forces. Determined to catch up, the American military focused its intellectual energy on restructuring and modernizing its forces.

Planners identified two likely scenarios for future conflict—a 'small' war in a less-developed country fought by light infantry and a conventional big-unit war in Western Europe employing mechanized forces. The Nixon Doctrine also influenced the way the military prepared for the future. In July 1969, President Nixon told reporters while visiting Guam that unless Asian nations were threatened with nuclear attack, the United States expected their governments to fight their battles without American assistance. Over time, Nixon's statement was refined and eventually indicated that the American military should be prepared to fight one-and-a-half wars. That is, the United States should be able to simultaneously fight a small war and a large conventional conflict. Although the first scenario seemed most likely, the 18-day Arab–Israeli War fought in October 1973 brought home to the Army that a mechanized war could potentially be the most challenging conflict to fight.

Doctrinal changes were also influenced by new technology, which had become much more lethal and efficient than it had been ten years earlier. Israel's destruction of Egyptian and Syrian tank forces with a light, infantry-borne antitank weapon, the M72 LAAW, for example, demonstrated not only the power of new military hardware but also the vulnerability of armor fighting without support from other combat arms. Clearly, a well-trained, well-equipped smaller enemy posed a serious threat to even the largest, most modern armed force. How much greater a danger, then, was the Soviet Union? While the American military had been fighting a hybrid counterinsurgency–conventional war in Southeast

Asia, the Soviet Union had modernized and restructured its forces. After a decade of being overshadowed, conventional warfare based on large-scale operations once again became the Army's doctrine *du jour*.

Planning for conventional war, however, did not mean a return to pre-Vietnam era ideas. In the past, the United States had been almost proudly ill-prepared for war, typically making a poor early showing while mobilizing and training its fighting force. Powerful new weapons now made fighting while preparing too risky; the end of conscription made it virtually impossible. The modern battlefield demanded that the United States win its first battle or risk losing the initiative. Improved technology required a better-educated, more intensively trained soldier, while the end of the draft meant that the country had to fight with a leaner force.

General William E. DePuy, commander of the new Army Training and Doctrine Command, took the lead in articulating an updated doctrine. Called AirLand Battle, this post-Vietnam doctrine was not actually new. At its core, AirLand Battle emphasized the long-standing essential elements of tactics and strategy. However, improvements in technology and air warfare techniques made it clear that airpower was vital to successful ground warfare and the new doctrine recognized airpower's vital role. In DuPuy's iteration, AirLand Battle relied on the primacy of the defensive. By 1977, DuPuy's successor, General Donn A. Starry, revised Army doctrine to focus on the offensive and the so-called 'indirect approach.'

By 1982, the lessons of the Arab–Israeli War were fully absorbed, and AirLand Battle was again revised—this time emphasizing winning the first contact against a numerically more substantial force. Moreover, in part because of American technological capability, armor began to contest the infantry's status as 'queen of battle.' Yet, neither arm could fight effectively without the other. Thus the symbiotic relationship between infantry and armor prevented the tank from making the infantryman obsolete. Indeed, superior technology was essential to a leaner, more lethal all-volunteer force. As a result, the military introduced a number of new or upgraded weapons systems, including the Army's M-1 Abrams tank and M-2 Bradley infantry fighting vehicle; the Air Force's F-15E dual-role fighter and B-1B multi-mission bomber; and the Navy's nuclear-powered aircraft carriers and more-advanced carrier-based aircraft such as the F/A-18 and the S-3, a submarine hunter.

Just as a smaller military encouraged increased interest in technology, it also spurred movement toward reducing the 'tooth to tail' ratio. Divisions were reduced to two active brigades and when needed, a reserve brigade would bring the division to full strength. Also, the Army began to redesign its organization around the light infantry division. Initially, restructuring emphasized the use of technology, such as a light armored vehicle, and smaller more easily transported units. A smaller, less cumbersome division meant that the United States could more rapidly deploy to trouble spots around the globe, thus alleviating an increasing concern after the Iranian hostage crisis and the 1979 Soviet invasion of Afghanistan.

Adoption of light infantry divisions sometimes prompted intense debate over rapid deployment among critics who feared that lighter divisions could not stand against more heavily armed adversaries, and proponents who argued that the deployability of a light division offset its lack of armor. Opponents also worried that when first introduced, light infantry divisions trained only for low-intensity conflict. More severe critics charged that the United States was fielding a 'hollow' force. Nevertheless, the emphasis on lighter and more rapidly deployable divisions continued.

The Cold War and the Military

Under President Jimmy Carter, a graduate of the Naval Academy, the American military suffered significant yet necessary budget cuts. The inflation-ridden economy of the 1970s made such measures unavoidable. The Carter administration also took a non-interventionist approach to conflict in the developing world and had tried to reduce nuclear armaments in intensive talks—such as the Salt II negotiations—with the Soviet Union. Carter, for example, cut the B-1 bomber program and curtailed naval ship construction to reduce defense spending.

While making these cuts, the Carter administration also realized that American nuclear power, particularly the capacity for a gradually escalating nuclear conflict, had fallen far behind that of the Soviets. The United States needed more versatile means to deliver nuclear warheads. Carter's Presidential Directive 59 called for more multipurpose nuclear capabilities to allow for a more flexible nuclear response. The Air Force's MX intercontinental ballistic missile and the Navy's Trident missile provided some flexibility, while platforms for nuclear weapons, such as the Navy's Ohio class submarine and the Air Force's cruise-missile-capable B-52s, offered more versatile means of delivery.

Carter came into office hoping that a foreign policy focused on human rights and peaceful initiatives would give the United States a moral edge in the Cold War, an approach he believed would appeal to nonaligned nations of the developing world. Such an approach, however, proved a disappointment because the developing world seemed to be exploding with ethnocentric nationalism and religious extremism. Soviet aggression in Afghanistan, while only indirectly related to the Cold War, convinced the Carter administration to reconsider its foreign policy. By 1979, Carter embraced a more aggressive approach to world affairs; by 1980, the United States, under Carter's guidance, became the policeman of the Persian Gulf. This change in foreign policy, in turn, entailed a national security strategy with more inherent risk. As Carter left office in 1981, defense budgets were already on the rise to meet the changing geostrategic world.

When Ronald Reagan became president in 1981, American foreign policy took an even more dramatic turn. Convinced that communism was an inherently expansionist ideology that could be defeated only by strength, Reagan determined to prevent the Soviet Union from further spreading its influence, especially in the Middle East and Central America. Reagan took a hardline approach toward the Soviet Union, using extremely aggressive rhetoric while pushing a massive military buildup through Congress, arguing that this more aggressive stance would achieve 'peace through strength.'

During the Reagan presidency, the military budget increased by an average of eight percent per year. Increased defense spending was part of a multipronged strategy aimed at forcing the Soviet Union to bankrupt itself by trying to keep pace with the American military buildup, as forecast 30 years previous in NSC-68. Increased defense budgets also gave service members long overdue pay raises, bringing them nearer parity with their civilian peers, helping with some of the issues outlined in the VOLAR study. In addition, Reagan's unabashed patriotism helped renew pride in military service. Increased defense budgets also meant new procurement, which upgraded American weapons and equipment while reinvigorating the defense industry.

One of Reagan's most controversial moves was his proposal for a space-based missile defense system called the Strategic Defense Initiative, which critics nicknamed 'Star Wars' after the blockbuster 1977 George Lucas film. In theory, armed satellites orbiting the globe would destroy nuclear missiles fired at the United States before the weapons entered the earth's atmosphere. Rather than counter these American defense budget increases and technological developments with its own buildup, the Soviet Union pursued arms reduction negotiations, especially after the reformist Soviet General Secretary Mikhail Gorbachev came to power in 1985. In 1988, the United States and the Soviet Union completed the Intermediate Nuclear Forces Treaty, the first nuclear arms treaty that eliminated weapons rather than setting limits on their numbers.

The developing world continued to edge toward the forefront of this renewed Cold War. Under the Reagan Doctrine, the administration provided support to anti-communist groups around the world, including the mujahideen fighting against the Soviet invasion of Afghanistan and the Contra rebels in Nicaragua. In many instances, support did not include the commitment of American troops, but in some cases Reagan did not hesitate to use military force, even though the objectives were not always primary to American interests. The Reagan administration's support of the Contras precipitated the most damaging scandal of the Reagan presidency, the Iran–Contra Affair, during which Marine Lieutenant Colonel Oliver North and National Security Advisor Robert McFarlane orchestrated secret arms sales to Iran during its war with Iraq, channeling the proceeds to the Contra rebels in Nicaragua.

Desert One, Lebanon, Grenada, and Defense Reorganization

The seizure of 52 American hostages from the American Embassy in Tehran by Islamist militants in November 1979 provided the final chapter of the Carter presidency while exposing the limits of American military power. The failure of the attempt to rescue these hostages in an overly elaborate and ambitious operation dubbed Desert One (officially as Eagle Claw) contributed to Carter's defeat by Reagan in the 1980 presidential election. The Desert One debacle led to necessary and overdue reforms in the way the United States organized and conducted joint operations. The operation resulted in eight dead and four wounded, the loss of some aircraft, and the further public humiliation of Carter's Middle Eastern policy. An internal investigation noted failures in command and control and planning, but most importantly the inability of the services to operate effectively in a joint environment. The birth of the 1986 Goldwater–Nichols Act and other pressures toward 'jointness' and interoperability came from the specter of burning aircraft and frustrated intent in the sands near Tabas in Iran.

Other operations exposed similar issues. As part of a multinational force, Reagan ordered the Marines to Beirut in August 1982 to help enforce a United Nations-brokered agreement ending the Israeli retaliatory invasion of Lebanon. Despite a reasonably peaceful beginning to the operation, the assassination of the newly elected Lebanese president caused Israel to deploy troops throughout West Beirut in mid-September. In just a few days, approximately 800 Palestinian noncombatants living in refugee camps in Beirut were slaughtered. Appalled, Reagan announced he was sending in more Marines, and by year's end over 1,800 had been deployed. While the Marines were primarily intended to aid the Lebanese government in regaining its authority, their presence also pressured Lebanese officials to accept Israel's terms for a withdrawal. The Marines had been placed in a dangerous political situation that their presence only exacerbated.

The Marines established a protective perimeter around Beirut International Airport and by February 1983 were frequently the focus of Israeli and Palestinian military pressure. Despite an agreement to end the war, signed by Lebanon and Israel in May, by late August the Marine perimeter was frequently under fire from various factions. On the 29th, two marines were killed and 14 wounded during a mortar and rocket attack. Violence escalated as the Navy bombarded terrorist targets in Beirut from ships in the Mediterranean. More Marines died in skirmishes with Lebanese militias.

At that point, Congress stepped in and placed an 18-month deadline for the withdrawal of the Marines, a deadline Reagan had been reluctant to impose. Because the Marines were now openly supporting the Christian-dominated government, they were more frequently subject to attack by hostile Palestinian militias. Tragically, in October 1983, two truck bombs broke through security barriers and destroyed the Marine barracks at the airport, killing 241 people, including 220 Marines. Failures in security, joint communication, and intelligence had left the Marine barracks open to such a devastating attack. Despite congressional pressure for an immediate withdrawal, Reagan tried to maintain a military presence in Beirut. The increasing violence finally forced Reagan to order the Marines to leave Lebanon for good in early 1984. Their presence had been virtually ineffective in maintaining order and had arguably made the situation worse. Moreover, the absence of a centralized command for the operation resulted in a lack of strategic cohesion and purpose. Arguably, the intervention in Lebanon was doomed to disaster from the start.

The disaster in Lebanon and other uncertain diplomatic and military steps in the Middle East frustrated the Reagan administration and the Pentagon. An operationally ugly but nonetheless successful assault on the tiny Caribbean island of Grenada, however, somewhat eased the anxiety. The government of Grenada had been overthrown, and its leader killed by socialist revolutionaries supported by Cuba on October 19, 1983, endangering American students attending the island's medical school. Shocked at this violence in the Caribbean and needing a foreign policy success, Reagan ordered an assault on Grenada to rescue the American students and end Cuban influence on the island. In Operation Urgent Fury, each service insisted on playing a role, which resulted in an operational plan more focused on service participation than on effectively achieving mission objectives. With little time for planning a rather complicated joint operation, plenty could go wrong—and plenty did.

The operation began on October 25 and ultimately involved over 6,000 Marines, soldiers, and Special Forces over six days. Rigid rules of engagement severely limited the use of airpower to support troops on the ground. Artillery was likewise limited to reduce collateral damage and minimize civilian casualties. Nineteen American servicemen were killed in the operation, while at least 50 soldiers of Cuba's and Grenada's armed forces died. Although the American military personnel performed well under such extenuating circumstances, the conduct of the operation was hardly 'joint,' exposing serious planning, coordination, and communication problems that had plagued the armed services in previous operations.

The apparent poor performance of the American military since Vietnam— the botched operation to rescue the American hostages in Tehran, the Marine barracks tragedy, and now the Grenada operation—convinced many in the military and in Congress that a thorough overhaul of the defense establishment was necessary. The problems seemed to emanate from a convoluted command structure, corrosive inter-service rivalry, and an ineffective Joint Chiefs of Staff. Under the leadership of Senator Barry Goldwater and Congressman Bill Nichols, Congress passed the Goldwater–Nichols Defense Reorganization Act in 1986 to address these issues.

Figure 16.1 82nd Airborne artillery personnel load and fire M102 105 mm howitzers during Operation Urgent Fury. Photograph by Staff Sergeant M. J. Green.
Source: Department of Defense.

The most significant defense legislation since the 1947 National Security Act, Goldwater–Nichols made the Chairman of the Joint Chiefs of Staff the principal military advisor to the president as commander-in-chief of the armed forces. Whereas previously the chairman operated somewhat like a general manager for the service chiefs, he now could voice his own opinion directly to the president. The chairman was also included in the operational chain of command, which now ran from theater commanders to the chairman and then to the president. Theater commanders were also given complete control over all assets, regardless of service, under their authority. Operational command had been streamlined and made more efficient—truly 'joint.' Also, the chairman now oversaw his own joint staff, made up of officers from each service. Joint billets were no longer a hindrance to promotion; instead, they were now mandatory for promotion to general officer. The service chiefs became the primary managers of recruitment, training, and weapons and equipment procurement.

The overall objective of Goldwater–Nichols was twofold. First was to make the American military 'joint' in its operational doctrine and regional command structure. The second was to give the Chairman of the Joint Chiefs of Staff direct access to the president, who is commander-in-chief. Critics charged that loyalty to one's service would always undermine jointness and that giving the chairman of the Joint Chiefs of Staff so much power lessened the influence of the service chiefs and eroded civilian control of the military. Changing decades of service primacy in favor of joint command would take time, and the role of the Chairman of the Joint Chiefs of Staff would depend a great deal on the personality and command style of the individual holding that position. Coming military operations, however, would show that Goldwater–Nichols had been the correct approach to remake the American military establishment.

'No More Vietnams'—Operation Just Cause

By the time Reagan left office in 1989, the American military establishment was well on its way to rejuvenation. Reagan's successor, George H. W. Bush, took office only months before the Berlin Wall fell, a harbinger of the full collapse of the Soviet Union that left the United States as the world's sole superpower, thus ending the Cold War. Like Reagan, Bush looked forward to a world in which freedom and democracy were the norm; also like his predecessor, Bush was determined to protect freedom, world stability, and American dominance.

Just six weeks after the fall of the Berlin Wall, the United States invaded Panama to remove the narco-militarist dictator Manuel Antonio Noriega. Although the United States had often intervened in Latin America, it had typically been to prevent the spread of communist influence into a region that held great geostrategic importance. By 1989, however, conditions had changed. The Soviet Union was no longer the threat it had once been, and the Panama Canal would soon be returned to Panamanian control. The Panamanian dictator Noriega was heavily involved with trafficking drugs into the United States and frequently violated American–Panamanian treaties. Panama, under Noriega's regime, had also become a center for arms smuggling and money laundering.

In 1988, the United States declared its 'war on drugs,' and a Florida court issued indictments against Noriega for drug trafficking and money laundering. The United States determined to remove him from power. Both the Reagan and Bush administrations attempted to foment *coups d'état* and supported political opposition to Noriega. When these measures failed to topple his regime, the United States tried economic sanctions and issued military threats. For Noriega, open defiance of the world's only superpower only enhanced his authority. On December 15, 1989, Noriega's handpicked legislature declared him the winner in a rigged presidential election, as Noriega's thugs harassed and beat opposition candidates. The Bush administration had seen enough.

Four days later, on December 19, the United States launched Operation Just Cause, a carefully planned invasion designed to simultaneously strike several strategic objectives and capture Noriega while limiting civilian casualties and keeping American residents in Panama safe. At the time of the invasion, there were already 13,000 American troops in the American-occupied Panama Canal Zone as part of Southern Command; another 14,000 were airlifted into the country for the initial assault. Despite efforts to keep the invasion secret, the heavy show of American force around the Canal Zone alerted Noriega that American military action was imminent.

Just Cause was the first instance of the so-called Powell Doctrine. Named for the newly appointed Chairman of the Joint Chiefs of Staff, Army General Colin Powell, the Powell Doctrine was actually a corollary to the Weinberger Doctrine, named for Reagan's Secretary of Defense Casper Weinberger. Weinberger had outlined six prerequisites for the United States to commit to using military force. These were a direct response to the disaster in Lebanon and the earlier failed attempt to rescue the American hostages in Tehran, if not the Vietnam War. First, the United States should not commit forces to combat unless vital national interests of the United States or its allies were clearly at risk. Second, American troops should be committed only unreservedly and with the clear intention of winning. Third, American combat troops should be committed only with clearly defined political and military objectives and be given the capacity to accomplish those objectives. Fourth, the relationship between the objectives and the size and composition of the forces committed should be continually reassessed and adjusted to assure victory. Fifth, American troops should not be committed to battle without the support of American public opinion and Congress. Last, the use of force should be considered only as a last resort, after diplomacy and other means have failed. To this Powell added emphasis on the use of overwhelming force to ensure American military victory. During the 1950s and 1960s, use of force had essentially replaced diplomacy as the primary tool in American national security policy. Now, use of force would ideally take a back seat to diplomacy and economic sanctions. Under the Weinberger–Powell Doctrine, there theoretically would be no more Vietnams and no more Lebanons, as meeting all of these conditions would be extremely difficult. Powell especially wanted to rein in the apparent trend of reaching for the hammer before allowing the other tools of national security policy a chance to work.

In the predawn hours of December 20, 1989, Operation Just Cause began with the operational debut of the new F-117 Stealth bomber, which attacked a Panamanian Defense Force barracks. Infantry and armor forces stationed in the Canal Zone moved in to support airborne troops who had flown all the way from the United States. Special Forces, including Delta Force and Navy Seals, were tasked with finding and securing Noriega, which they did on December 24. The operation had been a success, due mainly to the superb integration of the various services into a single joint plan. In an operation involving over 23,000 service members from all services, only 23 were killed and 324 wounded. At least 314 Panamanian Defense Force troops were killed and perhaps as many as 300 Panamanian civilians, unfortunately, lost their lives in crossfire and the bombing.

Just Cause had shown that joint planning and joint operations could work. It also confirmed that if the local population is supportive of intervention, things will proceed much more smoothly than if it is not. The American military seemed to have recovered and rebuilt from its Vietnam experience. The all-volunteer American military had become a lethal and effective fighting force.

The Gulf War

The most significant test of the all-volunteer force and the advent of 'jointness' was the Gulf War of 1991 that expelled Iraqi leader Saddam Hussein's military forces from Kuwait. The total joint commitment to planning, buildup, and execution, integrating air, land, and naval forces, was a stunning success of American combat arms, but one that was partially possible due to changes in the post-Cold War environment.

The long Iran–Iraq War of the 1980s had left Hussein's Iraq with spent treasury and over $90 billion in debts to Middle Eastern nations, notably Saudi Arabia. To compensate, Hussein ordered the invasion of his wealthy southern neighbor Kuwait on August 2, 1990, where he hoped to secure Kuwaiti oil fields and production facilities as well as access to deep-water ports. Kuwait's army was no match for the large, well-equipped, experienced Iraqi military. When three armored divisions of Iraq's elite Republican Guard invaded, the Kuwaiti military was already off-balance from pre-invasion probes by Saddam's army. Within only a few days 11 Iraqi divisions had occupied the small country and were threatening the Kuwaiti border with Saudi Arabia. Iraqi control of Kuwaiti oil fields had already shaken the global oil market; a worldwide economic disaster would follow if Saddam also gained control of Saudi Arabian oil production.

On August 7, at President Bush's direction, the United States Central Command, or CENTCOM, began deploying forces to protect Saudi Arabia. CENTCOM was, and remains, one of several Unified Combatant Commands enhanced by the Goldwater–Nichols Defense Reorganization Act and given operational control over all American forces in specified geographic regions. At the time of the Gulf War, Army General Norman H. Schwarzkopf commanded CENTCOM. Because Bush and his military advisors wanted to project that American actions were strictly defensive, the initial military deployment under CENTCOM's Operations Plan 1002–1090 was code-named Operation Desert Shield. The subsequent operational plan for the combat phase was called Desert Storm.

Navy battle groups that regularly patrolled the Mediterranean Sea and the Indian Ocean immediately diverted to patrol the Gulf of Oman and the Red Sea. Formed around the aircraft carriers *Independence* and *Dwight D. Eisenhower*, the two battle groups were the first American forces to arrive on station. A third carrier battle group joined the naval force the following month. In addition, *Missouri* and *Wisconsin*, World War II-era battleships that had been recommissioned during the Reagan administration, were sent to the Persian Gulf. On August 8, two F-15 squadrons arrived in Saudi Arabia from Langley Air Force Base, Virginia. Within a month there were approximately 800 aircraft in the Persian Gulf, including Marine and Army air assets. Also, on August 8, the first ground forces joined Desert Shield when a brigade from the 82nd Airborne Division, part of the XVIII Airborne Corps, arrived in Saudi Arabia.

Few expected a single brigade to turn back the Iraqi invasion of Kuwait; instead, the paratroopers comprised a task force intended to deter an Iraqi attack against Saudi oil fields along the Saudi gulf coast, directly south of Kuwait. By the end of August, most of the XVIII Airborne Corps had deployed to Saudi Arabia. It took almost two months, however, before troop strength was sufficient to stop an Iraqi attack against Saudi Arabia, in part because the military buildup of the 1980s ignored logistical concerns in favor of high-tech weapons systems and personnel issues. As a result, military transport, especially sealift, was at a premium, and units were often initially deployed without spare parts or adequate ammunition. At the very least, Schwarzkopf reasoned, the presence of such a substantial American force, numbering 500,000, would make Saddam think twice before moving against Saudi Arabia.

While the United States was deploying forces to the Gulf region, it was engaged in diplomatic efforts to politically isolate Iraq. Both the United Nations Security Council and the Arab League passed numerous resolutions condemning the invasion of Kuwait and demanding that Iraq withdraw. The most critical United Nations measures were Resolutions 660 and 678. Approved by the United Nations Security Council on August 2, Resolution 660 demanded that Iraq leave Kuwait and declared United Nations determination to ensure Iraqi compliance. Hoping to avoid war, diplomats attempted negotiations with an ultimately intransigent Iraq for a peaceful settlement. Its collective patience nearly exhausted, on November 29, the United Nations Security Council passed Resolution 678, which set the withdrawal deadline for January 15, 1991, and authorized the use of all necessary means to restore order and peace to the region. Military action against Iraq now had United Nations sanction.

While the United Nations and the Arab League pursued a diplomatic resolution, the United States continued military preparations, including the formation of a worldwide coalition against Iraq. Although some nations were less than enthusiastic toward non-Arab interference, Secretary of State James Baker eventually convinced 33 nations from Europe, Asia, Africa, and North and South America to join the American-led coalition. In keeping with the Weinberger–Powell Doctrine, President Bush also had to convince the American public that intervention in the Iraq–Kuwait crisis was justified. Since the war in Vietnam, Americans had generally been wary of foreign military adventures. Moreover, a vocal minority of Americans against the war was convinced that the administration's real purpose was to assert more significant influence over Middle Eastern oil production, which was admittedly a vital American interest. Bush administration arguments in favor of intervention, however, emphasized Saddam's human rights abuses, his 'naked aggression' against Kuwait, and the oil-based Saudi–American friendship.

As military preparations neared completion, negotiations for a peaceful settlement continued. Neither Iraq nor the United States, however, were willing to compromise on Kuwait. To rally Arab support by linking his invasion of Kuwait to Arab nationalism, the Iraqi dictator refused to leave Kuwait unless Syria withdrew from Lebanon and Israeli troops left the West Bank and other areas contested by the Palestine Liberation Organization. Arbitration having failed, on January 12, 1991, Congress authorized military intervention after three days of intense debate. Coalition nations quickly fell into line in support of using military force.

In advance of the ground attack, Schwarzkopf ordered an air campaign directed against strategic targets within Iraq. Civilian targets were off-limits, but that did not eliminate civilian casualties or 'collateral damage' because objectives marked for destruction were sometimes surrounded by civilian structures. Nevertheless, the Air Force designed a carefully controlled campaign intended to immediately acquire air superiority and then to inflict as much damage as possible, as quickly as possible, on Iraqi command and control as well as advance Iraqi ground forces while keeping civilian casualties to a minimum. Purposely contrasting the Gulf War plan against the Rolling Thunder air campaign against North Vietnam, the Air Force dubbed their concept Instant Thunder. It seemed that the spirit of Billy Mitchell had returned, as Air Force planners believed that Instant Thunder had the potential to force Saddam's compliance before the ground war ever began.

Beginning on January 16, 1991, the air phase of Operation Desert Storm began with strikes against the Iraqi capital city of Baghdad and Iraqi air capabilities. During the first day of Desert Storm, American Air Force, Navy, and Marine aircraft, along with coalition air assets, flew over 1,300 missions and met with only half-hearted attempts at air combat by the Iraqi Air Force. On the second day of Instant Thunder, air attacks began against Iraq's military and governmental infrastructure and against Iraqi ground forces scattered across southern Iraq and the Iraqi–Saudi border. Desperate to break up the coalition allied against him, Hussein fired Scud surface-to-surface missiles against Israel and Saudi Arabia. If Israel entered the war, Arab members of the coalition would leave the anti-Iraq alliance, and attacks against Saudi targets might convince the Saudi royal family that its friendship with the United States was too dangerous. Equally intent on keeping the coalition together, the United States hurried Patriot anti-air and anti-missile batteries to Israel and Saudi Arabia. Thwarted by delivery of the Patriots, which had mixed success in knocking incoming Scuds out of the sky, Saddam began dumping crude oil into the Persian Gulf. This gambit wasted oil and caused severe environmental damage but had no effect on the war.

Over the following month, near-constant airstrikes repeatedly hit military and naval facilities, power stations, communication centers, transportation networks, and Scud missile launchers. Of these targets, the Scud missile launchers perhaps represented a crucial waste of Allied air assets, as the mobile launching units were difficult to locate and target in what became known as the Great Scud Hunt. When the ground war began on February 24, the Iraqi military was in disarray; its command and logistics system had broken down, and much of its frontline equipment was destroyed. Although the Republican Guard retained cohesion, discipline, and fighting morale, most of the Iraqi conscript army was severely shaken and demoralized.

Iraq launched its only organized offensive of the war during the night of January 29. Late in the evening, Air Force surveillance aircraft registered troop movement in southern Kuwait, as two Iraqi divisions prepared to attack the evacuated Saudi Arabian city of Khafji. Iraqi forces quickly overran the nearly deserted city, as well as several American outposts along the Kuwait–Saudi Arabia border. Two Marine reconnaissance teams became trapped inside Khafji during the battle for the city. Although their positions were precarious, the Marines expertly directed artillery and air strikes on enemy forces. Within 48 hours a pan-Arab force recaptured Khafji, taking minimal casualties in the process. By February 1, the Battle of Khafji was over. As many as 2,000 Iraqis had died, over 400 Iraqi soldiers had been taken prisoner, and the rest of the invading force had expeditiously withdrawn to Kuwait.

Although the Battle of Khafji received little media attention at the time, the poor Iraqi showing prompted Schwarzkopf to reconsider the professionalism of the Iraqi military. After Khafji, Hussein's forces seemed less formidable. Moreover, in the American military's most intense combat since Vietnam, the Marines had performed admirably. Unfortunately, Khafji also resulted in the worst incidence among American forces of deaths caused by friendly fire.

Most significantly, Khafji later gave airpower proponents an opportunity to argue that air forces could subdue ground forces. At Schwarzkopf's direction, the Air Force took the lead in repelling the Iraqi assault, permitting attacks deep into Iraqi-held territory and eliminating the need to redeploy American ground forces. Air attacks destroyed Iraqi transport columns, disrupting the flow of troops and supplies and making it impossible for the attack to unfold as planned. According to an Air Force study conducted after the war, Khafji was conclusive proof that airpower could control the battlefield.

Plans for the ground campaign fully exploited Iraqi anxieties and weaknesses. Although Iraq's coastline is relatively short, extending less than 40 miles along the Persian Gulf, it offered an entry into Iraq and threatened the nation's two deep-water ports. A disinformation campaign

Figure 16.2 The Gulf War.

deceived the Iraqi military into believing that an invasion would begin with an amphibious assault by the 5th Marine Expeditionary Brigade. Saddam also expected an attack through Wadi al Batin that runs along the Kuwaiti border and into Saudi Arabia and deployed eight divisions in defensive positions to counter both threats. Combined with the entrenched defenses Iraq positioned along the wadi, approximately 20 percent of Saddam's military strength was unavailable to deflect the actual ground assault. The Marines landed in friendly territory, and the 1st Cavalry Division conducted only a short feint up Wadi al Batin before withdrawing, freeing the units for the supporting attack launched by the 1st and 2nd Marine Divisions and for the sweeping main attack from Saudi Arabia spearheaded by VII Corps, a combined American–British formation.

Positioned along the Saudi–Kuwait border, the 1st Marine Expeditionary Force had to attack into Kuwait across two heavily defended, heavily

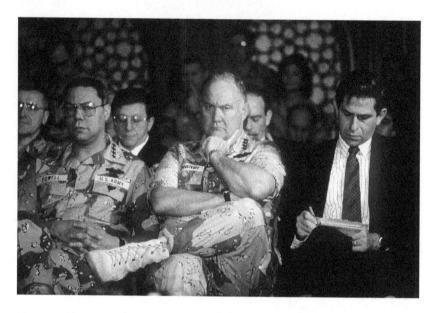

Figure 16.3 General Colin Powell (left), General Norman Schwarzkopf, Jr., and Under-Secretary of Defense Paul Wolfowitz (right) listen at a joint American–Saudi press briefing during Operation Desert Storm.

Source: Department of Defense.

mined areas. Engineers and tanks fitted with mine plows quickly breached the minefields, eventually clearing 20 lanes through which the Marines could advance toward Kuwait City. Along the way, they took 10,000 Iraqi prisoners and seized control of Al Jaber Airfield. By the third day, the Marines had repulsed an Iraqi counterattack and isolated Kuwait City.

The nearly 150,000 soldiers of the VII Corps faced the vaunted Republican Guard as they made their great sweep across the desert north of the Kuwaiti border. VII Corps quickly breached Iraqi-built obstacles and eliminated the first Iraqi line of defense while opening lanes of advance. Other units enveloped Iraqi positions to the west. In short order, one British and three American divisions launched an armored assault against the reinforced Republican Guard. M1A1 Abrams tanks and M2 Bradley fighting vehicles made quick work of the elite Iraqi force. Enemy targets were either destroyed or surrendered. From the air, Air Force A-10 Warthogs struck Iraqi armor up and down the battlefront. Although VII Corps thoroughly defeated the Republican Guard units and took thousands of prisoners, large numbers of Republican Guardsmen escaped.

By February 27, Kuwaiti forces made their way back into Kuwait City, which the Iraqis had abandoned. By February 28, the remaining Iraqis, including the vaunted Republican Guard, were in full retreat toward

Figure 16.4 Destroyed vehicles along the 'Highway of Death.'
Source: Department of Defense.

Baghdad. As Iraqi units fled in chaos back to Iraq in stolen cars, trucks, and whatever vehicles they could manage, American A-10s pummeled the traffic jam of over 1,200 vehicles of all sorts packing the main highway north out of Kuwait. The ground phase was basically over, and the images of hundreds of destroyed vehicles raised questions concerning needless killing. While Iraqi troops perished in the attack, the casualties did not match the troubling pictures of smoldering cars and trucks. Most Iraqi troops abandoned their vehicles at the first sign of coalition aircraft, knowing the fire quickly to come. What the media dubbed the 'Highway of Death' in part led President Bush to order the halt of ground operations. Though far from totally defeated, Saddam had to accept the destructive end to his Kuwait adventure. If anything, the end of the Gulf War highlights the difficulty of war termination.

Ground combat in Operation Desert Storm lasted a mere 100 hours. Early casualty predictions for American and coalition forces had been high, in the thousands. Army and Marine Corps units suffered only 122 combat deaths, including 35 from friendly fire, and 131 non-combat deaths. The Air Force lost 20 killed in combat and six dead from accidents. The Navy had only six killed in action and eight non-combat deaths. These numbers include 15 American servicewomen killed during Desert Shield and Desert Storm. Only 278 Americans were wounded in the war. Twenty-one Americans, including one woman, were captured and later released by the Iraqi military. Melissa Rathbun-Nealy was the first American woman taken prisoner of war since World War II. One Navy F/A-18 pilot was listed as missing in action. Lieutenant Commander Michael Scott Speicher was shot down over western Iraq on the first day of the air war, but his body was not recovered. His remains were discovered in August 2009 after Marines operating in Al Anbar province were led to a grave by Bedouin tribesmen. Specialists at Dover Air Force Base examined the remains and confirmed identification as Speicher. Coalition casualties included 92 dead and 318 wounded. Iraqi losses were estimated at 10,000 military killed and 2,000 civilians dead.

Although the United States had confronted a larger but inferior army, success in the Gulf War convinced many in military and civilian circles that the American military had banished the ghosts of Vietnam. The Gulf War had been the largest mobilization of American military power since the Korean War and had been fought according to standards set by decades of planning for a similar type of conflict against the Soviet Army in Western Europe and adjusted by the 1986 Goldwater–Nichols Act. American troops returned home to much fanfare, including a ticker-tape parade in New York City and a presidential review in Washington, where President Bush declared 'we kicked the Vietnam War syndrome once and for all.'

Peacekeeping and Nation Building

As the United States basked in the glory of victory in the Gulf War and contemplated the peace dividend of the end of the Cold War, the power vacuum created by the sudden end of 40-plus years of Soviet–American conflict contributed to a variety of wars and conflicts around the world. Some were admittedly peripheral to American interests, while others were more vital. In the 1990s, the military found itself involved in rather complex peacekeeping and nation-building missions in places like Somalia, Bosnia, Haiti, and Kosovo. One of the influences in these missions was the new president, William Jefferson Clinton, who exhibited a mix of Wilson's idealism and Carter's humanitarianism that held that the role of the United States as the sole superpower should be to restore order in places where chaos still reigned.

American involvement in Somalia began in the last years of the Bush administration. Warlords who controlled humanitarian aid and food distribution had ruled Somalia since 1989. In early January 1991, American Marine and Naval units evacuated over 400 Americans from Mogadishu in a very complex operation called Eastern Exit. Using 20-year-old maps, the rescue force had difficulty even locating the American embassy compound but was able to secure the area—amid violent looting—to complete the evacuation. Throughout the next two years, the situation in Somalia deteriorated even more, finally forcing the United Nations to step in with a large peacekeeping force. Hundreds of thousands of Somalis had died from starvation and disease as rival warlords battled for control of this town or that. In Mogadishu, warlord Mohamed Farrah Aidid waged relentless gang warfare on his rivals.

In April 1992, the United Nations sent in a small security detail to protect relief workers and guard aid warehouses and transport in Mogadishu, but this token force had no effect on the warlords. In July, two United Nations relief aircraft were stopped at gunpoint at the Mogadishu airport and looted. Red Cross relief flights began arriving in August 1992; to protect them, Army helicopters sent from Mombasa hovered above the airport. The Red Cross had at first forbidden any ground security, but when a 500-strong Pakistani infantry unit arrived, the Red Cross relented and allowed the airport to be secured. Not long after, the first of 3,000 United Nations peacekeepers began arriving.

By December, the United Nations authorized an American-led peace-keeping force representing a variety of nations. With warlords hijacking relief trucks as they left the safe confines of the airport, little aid reached the population that so desperately needed it. President Bush authorized American forces to provide for the secure distribution of relief, while the United Nations hoped the Americans would disarm the rival gangs.

By the spring of 1993, Aidid and other gang leaders increased their attacks on United Nations and American personnel. A new United Nations Quick Reaction Force began conducting offensive operations to bring the warlords to heal. Aidid was its chief target. In July, a multinational force attacked Aidid's compound without success, while angry Somalis violently protested against the United Nations, including one instance where a mob killed four foreign journalists. A car bomb killed several American soldiers in August. In late August, Secretary of Defense Les Aspin ordered the Joint Special Operations Force to Somalia to remove Aidid from power. Task Force Ranger, as it was called, was not under United Nations command, but instead remained directly under CENTCOM control.

The nadir of American involvement in Somalia occurred in October when American Special Forces got hard intelligence of Aidid's exact location. As troops took off in Blackhawk assault helicopters and moved into Mogadishu by road in several Humvees, the assault began. Things went awry when Somalis shot down one of the Blackhawks. The remaining force became pinned down in the city center, surrounded by thousands of armed Somalis. After 17 hours of fierce combat that cost the lives of 18 American soldiers and perhaps over 1,000 Somalis, a relief force extracted the besieged Americans. Subsequent television news footage of dead American servicemembers being dragged through the streets of Mogadishu by angry mobs caused public support for the operation to evaporate almost overnight.

President Clinton, who took office in January 1993, ordered the American force to withdraw from Somalia by March 1994. Also in

March, Clinton signed Presidential Directive 25, which stated that American participation in peacekeeping operations must be contingent upon the conflict's threat to international security or whether directly serving American interests. Arguably, the tragic events in Somalia had done neither.

A 1991 military coup that exiled Haitian President Jean-Bertrand Aristide provided the United States with reason enough to intervene in Haiti in 1994, continuing a long tradition of intervention in the Caribbean island nation's affairs. United Nations embargoes and other sanctions against the military government of Haiti failed to bring about the return of legitimately elected government. In the face of congressional, public, and international disapproval, the Clinton administration nonetheless ordered over 5,000 American troops and Marines to occupy Haiti in September 1994. In Operation Uphold Democracy, American and international forces met next to no resistance in gaining control of the country. President Aristide was returned to power in October after the military junta agreed to a general amnesty passed by the restored Haitian assembly. Token American and international forces remained in Haiti through 1998, maintaining order and conducting nation-building tasks.

The United States became involved in peacekeeping operations in the Balkans in the 1990s, where decades of authoritarian rule had given way to ethnic-based governments and civil war. The most horrific aspect of these conflicts was the widespread use of ethnic cleansing among rival peoples in the former Yugoslavia. In Bosnia, United Nations peacekeepers entered the fray in 1992 to protect relief workers. Their impact was negligible, as the Serbs continued slaughtering Bosnian Croats, sometimes slaughtering entire villages. The United Nations peacekeepers struggled to provide security, much as had the Marines in Lebanon in 1983.

The United States stayed out of the conflict in Bosnia until 1995, when President Clinton ordered tactical air strikes against the Serb capital of Belgrade to stop the bloodshed. Wanting to avoid a ground war in the Balkans, Defense Department officials testified before a wary Congress that such a force might require more than 400,000 American troops fielded against well-armed and experienced armies in Serbia, Croatia, and Bosnia. Chairman of the Joint Chiefs General Colin Powell was adamantly opposed to intervening in a conflict that, though fraught with human tragedy, was in his mind militarily untenable and peripheral to American interests.

Fortunately, NATO had taken the lead in providing air cover and aid protection in the beleaguered region. Beginning in 1993, American Air Force planes assisted in patrolling over the Adriatic Sea and Bosnia, while the Navy kept a carrier battle group in the Adriatic Sea to interdict merchant ships smuggling arms into the former Yugoslavia. What followed were two years of escalating violence between NATO and Serb forces. Finally, in August 1995, NATO air bombardment hit Serb targets around Sarajevo and other locations, forcing the Serbs to the peace table. The Dayton Peace Accords of November 1995 ended the fighting in Bosnia and put in place a NATO peacekeeping force of over 60,000 troops.

Meanwhile, in Kosovo, armed nationalists began threatening Serbians living in Kosovo. Serbia responded, starting an even more horrific ethnic cleansing than had occurred in Bosnia. By 1999, the violence had escalated even more. In March, Clinton approved NATO air bombardment of Serb targets in Kosovo and Serbia. This initial bombing only intensified the fighting on the ground, where Serb forces decimated Kosovar villages. Horrified, Clinton nonetheless refused to send in ground forces to stop the fighting. Airpower would have to do what it had promised it could do since the 1920s—break the political will of a people and bring a government to its knees. NATO bombing began to focus on Belgrade itself, the Serbian capital, hitting command and control targets, electric power plants, bridges, and other vital infrastructure. Some said the scene in Serbia recalled the height of strategic bombing in World War II.

After enduring 78 days of bombing, Serbian leader Slobodan Milosevic agreed to a peace settlement wherein Kosovo was divided into occupation zones. Milosevic was apprehended in 2001 and charged with war crimes by the International Criminal Court at The Hague. He died in the fifth year of his trial in 2006. The United States had used NATO for the first time in a major military operation and had significantly shied away from United Nations involvement. The tragedy in the former Yugoslavia was immensely complex but humanitarian and security concerns finally motivated the United States and NATO to take action that arguably had been needed years before, finally ending the bloodshed.

Conclusion

American troops remain a part of the NATO peacekeeping force in the Bosnia–Serbia–Kosovo region. Nation building became the new focus of the NATO mission, as American forces assisted in establishing law enforcement and government administration. American forces conducted similar operations in Haiti in 1994 to ensure fair elections. After the Gulf War, American pilots patrolled the southern and northern thirds of Iraq, occasionally destroying surface-to-air missile batteries and radar stations in response to Iraqi violations of the Gulf War ceasefire agreements. It seemed that the great American military establishment, made so by decades of Cold War, was now relegated to dealing with so-called small wars. With such a future in mind, successive secretaries of defense reconfigured force structure, procuring different weapons systems, and downsizing personnel. The new American military would have to be leaner, faster, and more lethal to deal effectively with these conflicts.

Such a force, however, was ineffectual if the United States lacked the political will to use it. American political and military leaders appeared convinced by the unpleasant experiences of the 1990s to be ever more cautious in using force in the new post–Cold War world.

Further Reading

Adkin, Mark. *Urgent Fury: The Battle for Grenada.* Lexington, MA: Lexington Books, 1989.

Bacevich, Andrew J., and Efraim Embar, eds. *The Gulf War of 1991 Reconsidered.* London: Taylor & Francis, 2003.

Benis, Frank M. *U.S. Marines in Lebanon, 1982–1983.* Washington, DC: U.S. Government Printing Office, 1987.

Bowden, Mark. *Blackhawk Down: A Story of Modern War.* New York: Atlantic, 1999.

Bowden, Mark. *Guests of the Ayatollah: America's First Battle in the War against Militant Islam.* New York: Atlantic Monthly Press, 2006.

Burg, Steven L., and Paul S. Shoup. *The War in Bosnia-Herzegovina: Ethnic Conflict and International Intervention.* Armonk. New York: M. E. Sharpe, 1999.

Clark, Wesley K. *Waging Modern War: Bosnia, Kosovo, and the Future of Combat.* Cambridge: Public Affairs, 2002.

Corum, James, and Wray R. Johnson. *Airpower in Small Wars: Fighting Insurgents and Terrorists.* Lawrence, KS: University Press of Kansas, 2003.

Gordon, Michael R., and Bernard E. Trainor. *The Generals' War: The Inside Story of the Conflict in the Gulf.* Boston, MA: Little Brown, 1995.

Hutchthausen, Peter. *America's Splendid Little Wars: A Short History of U.S. Military Engagements: 1975–2000.* New York: Viking Press, 2003.

Locher, James R. *Victory on the Potomac: The Goldwater-Nichols Act Unifies the Pentagon.* College Station, TX: Texas A&M University Press, 2002.

Olsen, John A., and Edward N. Luttwak. *Strategic Air Power in Desert Storm.* London: Taylor & Francis, 2003.

Stevenson, Jonathon. *Losing Mogadishu: Testing U.S. Policy in Somalia.* Annapolis, MD: Naval Institute Press, 1995.

17 Into the Twenty-First Century

Introduction

At the close of the twentieth century, the United States enjoyed unrivaled power in the world that some called the American 'unipolar moment.' By the mid-1990s, the collapse of the Soviet Union and the end of the Cold War with an unambiguous victory for the liberal-capitalist West left the United States militarily unchallenged. To a considerable extent, the globalizing world economy was driven by the American economy, while American popular culture reached around the world. In many parts of the globe, especially in the developing world, American and Western interests were considered synonymous and indistinguishable.

The 2000 presidential election brought former Texas governor George W. Bush, a Republican, to office with an administration whose senior members had, in many cases, spent the previous two decades defining and honing the neoconservative views on American power. The most influential among them—Vice President Dick Cheney, who had been Bush's father's secretary of defense in the Gulf War, and Secretary of Defense Donald Rumsfeld, who also served as secretary of defense under President Gerald Ford from 1975 to 1977—believed implicitly in using American power to further American global dominance and check potential rivals and other national security threats. Secretary Rumsfeld also firmly believed in the need to transform the American military to reflect American strengths in technology and global reach while at the same time directing defense spending into areas other than conventional military capability, such as space-based missile defense. Rumsfeld called this program to make the American military lighter, leaner, and more lethal 'transformation.' The major loser in this process was ultimately the Army. At one early stage, for example, Rumsfeld suggested reducing Army strength from ten divisions to eight. All the services stood to lose specific projects and capabilities. Vice President Cheney came to office convinced that the regime of Saddam Hussein in Iraq remained an existential threat to American security at home and to American interests in the Middle East.

9/11 and the End of Unrivaled Power

Weaponizing hijacked airliners fully loaded with passengers and fuel, on the morning of September 11, 2001, al-Qaeda terrorists struck the World Trade Center in New York City and the Pentagon in Washington, D.C., shattering post-Cold War assumptions of domestic security that accompanied the Bush administration into office. Two Boeing 767s struck the World Trade Center's 110-story Twin Towers, dramatically collapsing both, while a Boeing 757 hit the Pentagon's western facade, plowing deep into the building's five 'rings.' A fourth aircraft crashed in western Pennsylvania after passengers courageously attempted to overwhelm the hijackers. The attacks that morning killed almost 3,000 people—including all on board the aircraft, hundreds of people in and near the World Trade Center and Pentagon, and tragically over four hundred first responders trying to get people out of the buildings—and injured several thousand more. The attacks caused billions of dollars of property damages, and billions more in economic losses as the United States government shut down all civilian and commercial air traffic across the country for several days. The New York Stock Exchange remained closed for an unprecedented entire week, causing a ripple effect of losses among the major exchanges around the world. If al-Qaeda intended to strike the heart of American financial and military power, then the terrorists accomplished that mission with spectacular devastating effect. Not since Pearl Harbor had a foreign entity attacked American soil with such surprise and impact.

Many of the features of post-Cold War American national security were challenged by the attacks. The vaunted air defense system that had been fashioned to counter Soviet air and missile attacks in the Cold War was impotent in the face of hijackers flying fully laden passenger aircraft into buildings, while the fundamental premises of the Revolution in Military Affairs (RMA) lay in tatters. There had been massive failures in intelligence, as the most devastating attack on American soil since World War II had been carried out by only 19 terrorists armed with little more than cheap box-cutters.

Although the impact of the destruction of the World Trade Center was immense, the attacks represented a culmination in developments going back a decade or more. Terrorism was not new, even on American soil. The deadly bombing of the Alfred P. Murrah Federal Building in Oklahoma City in 1995 and the 1993 attempt to bomb the World Trade Center had both suggested American vulnerability, while many of America's allies in Europe and Asia had battled domestic and transnational terrorism for decades.

Moreover, even before the end of the Cold War, anti-Americanism had been on the rise, especially in the developing world and in parts of Western Europe. Militant fundamentalism had also been a growing problem for many governments in the Muslim world for decades; in theological and intellectual terms, fundamentalism was grounded in Wahhabism and took its political inspiration from radical movements such as the Muslim Brotherhood, which had been active since the 1950s. Al-Qaeda and its leader, Osama bin Laden, both resulted from American policy that had fostered the anti-Soviet mujahideen in Afghanistan during the protracted Soviet occupation of that country in the 1980s. The radical fundamentalist turn in Afghan politics that saw the Taliban come to power was in part a result of meddling in the internal politics of Afghanistan by Pakistani intelligence services over several decades.

On September 11, 2001, all these disparate elements finally successfully came together with devastating effect. Characterized by one early analysis as a meeting of 'Saudi money and Egyptian brains,' the attacks set in motion a series of responses culminating in the war in Iraq—Operation Iraqi Freedom—which, like so much else surrounding the 'War on Terror,' was already under active consideration when the destruction of the Twin Towers gave it an impetus that it had hitherto lacked.

The damage from the attacks was far more psychological and financial than it was physical—it tends to be overlooked that the actual number of casualties inflicted that day was many times fewer than it might have been as tens of thousands of people successfully evacuated the World Trade Center before it collapsed. In fact, for the first time in American history, local law enforcement and firefighting units were on the front lines of an attack on the United States. The impact, nonetheless, was global. President Bush had little trouble persuading the international community that the attacks had been planned in Afghanistan, that the chief perpetrators of the outrage remained there protected by the Taliban, and that it was just and appropriate for the United States and its coalition allies to launch a major offensive—Operation Enduring Freedom—into Afghanistan to kill or capture those responsible for the 9/11 attacks.

Operation Enduring Freedom

The campaign to remove the Taliban illustrates both the strengths and weaknesses of the American military and the American way of war. American capacity to project and maintain combat power at great distances from the continental United States was seemingly effortless. The absence of existing advance bases and airfields in Afghanistan and in surrounding states was quickly negated through swift diplomacy with small and impoverished neighboring nations eager to become clients of the United States and using carrier battle groups and the strike aviation capabilities they deployed. Advances in precision-guided munitions, combined with improved targeting systems employed by Special Forces elements on the ground, significantly increased lethality and helped minimize though not eradicate casualties to civilians and friendly forces. So-called 'blue-on-blue' incidents still occurred, as did errant strikes that killed and wounded innocent civilians, tragic events exploited both by al-Qaeda and the Taliban for propaganda purposes. Additionally, the logistical effort was vast and highly successful, as it had been during the Gulf War in 1990–1991.

The campaign was orchestrated and commanded through Central Command (CENTCOM), based in Tampa, Florida, under the command of Army General Tommy Franks. The initial attack began on October 7, 2001, with concentrated air strikes against a wide range of targets mounted by B-1, B-2, and B-52 bombers, tactical strike aircraft, and Tomahawk cruise missiles launched from American and British naval vessels. Within months, however, mission-creep altered the original objectives and strategic approach of Enduring Freedom. Initially, a special operations-focused campaign relying mainly on airpower to strike al-Qaeda strongholds, large unit operations slowly took precedence as the CENTCOM was also tasked with destroying the Taliban. Doing so, then, required the military to also engage in nation-building in Afghanistan. The Taliban controlled around 80 percent of the country, which provided excellent cover for al-Qaeda cells in the desolate mountains that cover much of Afghanistan and neighboring Pakistan. Taking advantage of the chaotic, tribalized politics of Afghanistan, therefore, was an essential factor for American success.

Contrary to subsequent claims, there was considerable heavy ground fighting against al-Qaeda and Taliban forces. But much of this was done by the Northern Alliance of tribes opposed to Taliban rule, aided by Special Forces and CIA teams rather than American regular forces, allowing the impression to form in some quarters that American airpower had been the overwhelming and decisive factor in the early success of the war. In fact, CENTCOM fielded only relatively small ground elements, initially from the Army's 101st Airborne and 10th Mountain Divisions and Marine Expeditionary Units, because the anti-Taliban forces inside the country were ready and willing to fight. Coalition allies, principally the United Kingdom, also supplemented American forces. Ultimately, contributions of various kinds from 68 nations, of whom 27 supplied military capabilities of one form or another, aided this initial campaign in the War on Terror.

The provincial center of Mazar-i-Sharif fell on November 9, the old capital of Kabul on November 13, and the Taliban capital of Kandahar on December 13. In the challenging terrain of eastern Afghanistan from December 6–17, American and Allied special forces units and Northern Alliance fighters made a concerted push to kill bin Laden and al-Qaeda leadership believed to be hidden in a complex series of caves known as Tora Bora, located in the White Mountains. While the Battle of Tora Bora failed to find bin Laden, over 200 al-Qaeda fighters were killed in the intense fighting. Al-Qaeda and Taliban power centers unraveled quickly in the face of steady, intense pressure on the ground and from the air, aided by the fact that the regime's only reliable fighters—al-Qaeda members known locally as 'Afghan Arabs'—were widely hated by the local population. Remaining resistance was quickly driven to the rugged and inhospitable southeastern fringes of the country along the porous border with Pakistan, and coalition operations, such as Anaconda in February 2002, contained and then eliminated many die-hard groups of fighters.

An interim government was established on December 22, 2001, and the American command element was replaced by the International Security Assistance Force (ISAF) headquartered at Bagram Air Base near Kabul. ISAF covered all coalition forces deployed but still relied heavily on American personnel and logistical support.

The early operations in Afghanistan were in many respects so successful that they disguised the fact that no absolute solution had been obtained. While a new Afghan government, under the leadership of Hamid Karzai, struggled to unify the seemingly infinite factions and tribes, the Taliban and al-Qaeda remained military and politically potent. Indeed, while the Taliban was severely damaged, small groups loyal to the former regime continued to operate in the country. While al-Qaeda's senior command structure was partially destroyed and its remaining capability severely degraded, Osama bin Laden remained at large and the nature of the organization was such that the removal of its leaders in Afghanistan did little to impair its effectiveness elsewhere—as subsequent events in Iraq and terrorist attacks in Western Europe and Southeast Asia demonstrated.

Taliban forces reorganized in the mountains and, much like the Viet Cong in the American war in Vietnam, relied on small-unit tactics and acts of terror while avoiding open combat with ISAF forces. In 2003, under the leadership of Mullah Omar, the Taliban escalated attacks against ISAF and Afghan government targets. At the behest of the United States, NATO took command of ISAF. Fighting reached new levels of intensity during the 2003–2005 period, especially near Kabul and along the border with Pakistan. Casualties to end of 2005 reflected this: 252 American personnel killed and 393 wounded, with 127 coalition troops killed and 381 wounded. Afghan casualties, military and civilian combined, approached an estimated 40,000.

The operations in Afghanistan suffered from the switch in focus to Iraq and the rapidly increasing difficulties that American and allied forces encountered there. The criticism of the Bush administration—that it embarked on a large and uncertain enterprise in the Middle East before completing the task in Central Asia—is undoubtedly correct. Gains made in Afghanistan were quickly eroded, the Taliban was able to rebuild and significantly increase the scope and intensity of its operations, and the task that the allied forces then faced after the withdrawal from Iraq was far more difficult than perhaps it need have been. The balance between the two theaters gradually shifted, marked by a surge in Afghanistan that roughly corresponded to the troop withdrawals in Iraq.

After two years of inconsistent results and setbacks, in the first six months of 2008, the United States dramatically increased its forces in Afghanistan from roughly 26,000 to over 48,000. This infusion of American personnel was part of a 'surge,' similar to that undertaken in Iraq in 2007. British troop numbers also increased while they, the Canadians and, of the non-NATO allies, the Australians continued to make significant combat contributions in the southern provinces. The conflict in Afghanistan had shifted to a big-unit war, but gains remained minimal and often offset by continued problems with errant strikes killing innocent civilians.

The war spilled into Pakistan in September 2008, a response to the ease with which Taliban groups maintained sanctuaries in the tribal border regions between Afghanistan and Pakistan, causing considerable friction between the United States and Pakistan. The Taliban likewise intensified operations in the region, making attacks upon NATO convoys running between Peshawar and Kabul. The United States subsequently stepped-up its operations against targets in Pakistan, which required delicate negotiations with the Pakistani government and resulting in occasional confusion as to rules of engagement on both sides of the border. American drone strikes against al-Qaeda leadership assets located in Pakistan and, most symbolically, a Navy Seal Team raided a compound in Abbottabad on May 2, 2011, killing Osama bin Laden, who had been living quite brazenly right under the eyes of the Pakistani authorities.

American troop numbers continued to increase to a high of 90,000, this out of an ISAF total of 132,000. In July 2010, General David Petraeus assumed command after the relief of General Stanley McChrystal for insubordinate public comments critical of the Obama administration. A second 'surge' again had mixed results, as 2010 proved to be the most violent year since the war began. Afghan provinces, such as Waziristan and Helmand, saw dramatic increases in insurgent attacks, often in the form of improvised explosive devices (IEDs). American and Allied forces now balanced big-unit and special forces operations with a renewed emphasis on counterinsurgency efforts, a move that reflected Petraeus's belief that winning the 'hearts and minds' of the Afghan people should not fall victim to the mistakes of Vietnam. Petraeus hoped to achieve the sort of significant short-term success that would justify a partial troop withdrawal from Afghanistan. Although President Obama signaled in June 2011 that troop withdrawals would commence with the aim to be out of the region by 2014, the security situation remained problematic when Petraeus departed in August 2011 to assume the directorship of the Central Intelligence Agency.

The administrations of Presidents Barack Obama and Donald J. Trump have withdrawn some American forces only to see more sent to Afghanistan to shore up the struggling Afghan government against resurgent Taliban forces. As late as 2018, the Taliban remained active across much of Afghanistan. Poppy production, the historical foundation of the Afghan

Figure 17.1 U.S. Soldiers with 2nd Battalion, 327th Infantry Regiment, 101st Airborne Division return fire during a firefight with Taliban forces in Barawala Kalay Valley in Kunar province, Afghanistan, March 31, 2011.

Source: Department of Defense.

drug trade, also remained significant. The war has cost as many as 170,000 civilian lives. Numerous atrocities have been committed by soldiers on all sides, including American troops, such as Sgt. Robert Bales, who was convicted of killing 16 civilians, including nine children, in the March 2012 'Kandahar Massacre.' As for the combatants, over 2,400 American forces have been killed in Afghanistan, including 45 women servicemembers. Almost 20,000 Americans have been wounded in Afghanistan. Over 1,000 coalition forces have died in the conflict, with over 60,000 Afghan security forces also killed. Taliban and al-Qaeda losses are estimated at over 60,000 killed.

Despite considerable effort in recent years, the weak link in the Afghan security environment remains the Afghan forces themselves. Substantial gains were made in improving and expanding the Afghan National Army, but much less attention was paid to the quality and training of the Afghan National Police, and this remains one of several weak elements in the attempt to build a viable nation-state with a functioning civil society. Corruption and nepotism remain widespread, and these, along with popular resentment at the presence of foreign forces and the inflicting of civilian casualties by ISAF operations, provide a steady stream of recruits for the Taliban.

Operation Iraqi Freedom

The justifications of the Bush administration for waging renewed war on Iraq—the elimination of weapons of mass destruction and the threat that Saddam Hussein allegedly posed to the United States—were much less clear-cut and compelling than those that justified the war in Afghanistan. There is no question that Saddam's Iraq had used chemical weapons against both the Kurds and Shiites within the country and against Iranian forces during the Iran–Iraq War of the 1980s, and there is equally no doubt that the regime had expressed the intention to acquire nuclear and biological weapons in the future. But Iraq did not possess these in 2003, and in the failure to verify their existence, the international coalition of opinion that the Bush administration sought to build rapidly fell apart. In marked contrast to the international support for military action in Afghanistan, the 'coalition of the willing' for Iraq consisted primarily of American and British forces with minor additions from Australia and a handful of other countries such as Canada, Poland, and Spain. Relations with many European nations, notably France, reached new lows.

The war in Iraq also offered a test for Secretary of Defense Donald Rumsfeld's much-vaunted transformation policies, which occasioned heated debate within the Pentagon and elsewhere. Operation Desert Storm had been fought by a large force that had taken months to deploy and an enormous logistic effort to sustain. In contrast, central to Rumsfeld's idea of transformation was a belief that American military operations should be pursued with a greater emphasis on the technological superiorities that the United States could deploy and a corresponding lesser reliance on personnel, which is easily the largest single expense in the defense budget. These ideas shaped the American approach to the Iraq War.

Although the total size of the American forces deployed in Operation Iraqi Freedom topped 460,000, the numbers deployed forward for combat and the war on the ground in Iraq were very much smaller. This size discrepancy was the hub of the argument between Rumsfeld and the Army, including Army Chief of Staff General Eric K. Shinseki. Along with Secretary of the Army Thomas White, in February 2003, Shinseki testified before the Senate Armed Services Committee that the deployment in Iraq was far too low to handle both combat and post-combat operations. For this break with Rumsfeld, Shinseki was ultimately sidelined and publicly humiliated by the Secretary of Defense before his term of appointment ended, while White was forced to resign.

Drawing on the experience of recent operations in Kosovo and elsewhere, Shinseki and others argued that the forces deployed on the ground would be insufficient to deal with the demands of occupation and reconstruction that would inevitably follow even a short and successful campaign. Rumsfeld, they argued, had grossly underestimated the force necessary for the inevitable 'then what' that follows all combat phases of warfare. In line with 'transformational' thinking, however, and reflecting the infatuation with technological solutions to military problems, CENTCOM and General Franks had devised a war plan calling for an initial decapitation strike—dubbed 'shock and awe'—that would destroy the Iraqi command authority, including Saddam, and make full-scale ground operations either unnecessary or less central to the campaign to follow. The promise, drawing on flawed premises concerning the efficacy of precision operations from the air in the former Yugoslavia in the 1990s, was not realized. The attacks did have the effect of destroying much of the civilian infrastructure of the country—notably the electric power grid—without any plan for quickly rebuilding it early in the occupation phase that would follow. It was one of several decisions that in hindsight would have been better not made.

One way of viewing the conflict between the United States and Iraq involves two short but intense periods of open warfare, in 1990–1991 and 2003, separated by a decade of low-level conflict involving sanctions; weapons inspections; the enforcement of 'no-fly' zones in the north and southeast of the country, dubbed Operations Northern and Southern Watch; and an increasingly tense diplomatic standoff. American aircraft also regularly targeted the Iraqi command and air defense networks, routinely bombing these in response to Iraqi provocations and attempts to violate the no-fly status of Kurdish and Shiite areas within the country. The sanctions program, mostly enforced at sea by a multinational naval force, aroused considerable controversy internationally due to its effect on the civilian population—especially women and children, whom Saddam's regime ruthlessly but effectively exploited for propaganda purposes.

The inconclusive outcome of the shock-and-awe strike was followed, inevitably, by the opening of a coalition ground offensive into Iraq staged from Kuwait. An intended simultaneous northern invasion using the American 4th Infantry Division had to be abandoned when the Turkish government refused Washington permission to stage it from Turkish territory; the division had to be rerouted through the Gulf states and took no part in the initial invasion or subsequent operations until close to the end of hostilities. British forces in conjunction with American Marines seized the oil fields, the port of Umm Qasr, and the city of Basra in the south, while the American Army's 3rd Infantry Division moved to envelop Baghdad and the 1st Marine Division secured the Rumaylah oil fields and the critical city of Nasiriyah. The 82nd and 101st Airborne Divisions and the 1st Armored Division were also fed into the operations, securing cities and facilities that consolidated and extended the advance while diverting Iraqi forces that might otherwise have interfered with the move on Baghdad. On April 5 and for several days after that, American troops staged 'Thunder Runs' into parts of the Iraqi capital, using Abrams tanks and Bradley infantry vehicles to test the defenses and draw out Iraqi

Figure 17.2 The Iraq War.

defenders. Control of the airport and a strong foothold inside the city were established in this way, with the capital finally secured on April 9. Saddam fled into hiding, and his regime was declared at an end.

The collapse of Saddam's authority was rapid, aided by a careful campaign to exploit disaffection at senior levels of the military involving bribes and various agreements. This should not obscure the absolute mastery that coalition forces quickly acquired over their opponents, especially those in the vaunted Republican Guard divisions that were expected to fight hardest in defense of the regime. The superiority exercised over the Iraqi forces was generally one-sided. The Iraqi air force, for example, took no part in defensive operations, while morale among many Iraqi troops was low and declined rapidly, with soldiers refusing to fight or surrendering to the advancing coalition forces. On a positive note, all this helped to ensure the success of a conventional campaign that lasted just 21 days and involved remarkably low coalition casualties (American 138 dead, UK 42 dead). Nevertheless, losses among the civilian population (figures are contested, but range from 1,200 to 5,000 dead) and among the Iraqi armed forces (figures again are disputed and range from 2,300 to as high as 20,000) were high.

President Bush dramatically declared what turned out to be a premature end to 'major combat' on May 1, 2003, by landing aboard the carrier *Lincoln* in a Navy S-3B Viking to make the announcement to cheering sailors and network news cameras. The vacuum created by the rapid collapse of the regime was clearly not anticipated, as demonstrated by the widespread looting and disorder that quickly followed across the country and that coalition forces were powerless to stop. Moreover, some civilian planners in the Pentagon had predicted Iraqis would welcome American and coalition forces as liberators akin to the Allies liberating Nazi-held territory during World War II. This was not the case, as Iraqis largely stayed indoors and watched the invaders from under cover. A leaner and transformed 'Rumsfeldian' military might have been enough to win the conventional operation of the opening phase of the war, but it was incapable of successfully reestablishing order and security, rebuilding infrastructure and central authority, and engaging in the range of national reconstruction tasks that now presented themselves.

Moreover, there were insufficient forces to deal with the rapidly growing and wholly unexpected insurgency that now faced occupation authorities. The United States made serious mistakes early in the occupa-tion, which compounded structural deficiencies in American forces and in United States policy in Iraq more generally. After decades of Baathist repression, the Iraqis saw no reason that they should now be an occupied country, and even those who detested the former regime and had no sympathy for the radical jihadists felt little gratitude for the coalition forces that remained in their country. Like many in the developing world, ordinary Iraqis had been sold on the idea and image of American bounty and the American dream, and they were frustrated when none of it seemed to quickly come their way. The complete lack of preparation for military government on such an extensive scale and the needs of national reconstruction, together with the wrong-headed insistence that rebuilding would be undertaken by the private sector on a for-profit basis under-written by Iraqi oil revenue, brought inordinate delays and mismanage-ment and increased suspicion of American intentions.

The gravest error was the wholesale disbandment of the Iraqi military and the initial refusal to have any engagement with former Baathists. Ordered by the head of the new Coalition Provisional Authority Paul Bremmer with the tacit approval of the Bush administration, disbanding the military threw hundreds of thousands of trained soldiers onto the street, making them unable to provide for their families, thus creating a source of recruits and other support for the growing insurgency. De-Baathification also robbed the

Coalition Provisional Authority of an invaluable security resource—officials who possessed local knowledge, knew the language, and were able, at least in theory, to soften the image of the 'occupation.' While there was evil in the ranks of the Baath Party, many of these party officials were already dead, including Saddam's sons, or in American captivity. Lumping all former party members into one category suggested how much the Americans had to learn about the country for which they now exercised responsibility—and about the best ways in which to combat a modern insurgency.

The extended nature of rebuilding Iraq and the declining security situation that, in turn, made reconstruction more difficult, led to an urgent need for more American troops on the ground. The failure of the Bush administration to build a wide-based coalition before the war now made itself felt, with many American allies refusing to become involved in a war they had thought ill-advised and unnecessary. The increasing shortfall in personnel had to be corrected by mobilizing the National Guard and the Reserves for extended tours of duty in Iraq.

The Reserves would have been called forward in any case, and here again, history came round to demonstrate the law of unintended consequences. As part of the rebuilding of the military following the defeat in Vietnam, the armed forces made the decision to locate many combat support functions in the Reserves. Doing so would mean that no president could take the regular military into a major war again without taking the reserves to fight, as well as protracted operations would now be unsustainable without at least a partial mobilization. The downsizing of the active-duty military in the 1990s also meant greater reliance on National Guard units to provide personnel for duty in Iraq, and elsewhere, with unfortunate consequences. Casualties mounted, deployments were extended with little warning, and reenlistment rates dropped while both recruitment and retention in the active-duty military experienced significant problems due to injuries and a growing perception in parts of the American population that the task in Iraq was thankless and possibly unsustainable. Another question arose with discipline among Guard and Research units. The most infamous of these was the heinous abuse of Iraqi prisoners at Abu Ghraib prison. Photographs emerged of military police personnel, many from Reserve units, committing acts of physical, psychological, and sexual abuse in violation of international protocols. Several were discharged while others were convicted by military courts. The most senior officer implicated in the scandal, Brigadier General Janis Lapinksi, was ultimately relieved of command and demoted to colonel. Fourteen others, including a colonel and lieutenant colonel, were given either non-judicial punishments or jail sentences relating to prisoner abuse at Abu Ghraib. Media investigations into Abu Ghraib revealed that the Department of Defense and Department of Justice had approved the use of torture in Iraq as well as at the military detention facility in Guantanamo Bay Naval Base in Cuba.

Because of the high operational tempo and compact deployment rotation, in 2004, there was some discussion about reintroducing the draft, although by the end of 2005 this had come to nothing and was probably politically impossible in any case. In the same year, senior officers within the National Guard and Army Reserve publicly commented that the continuing war in Iraq had severely damaged both organizations to the point that it might take a generation to recover. The impact on the existing stocks of ground-force equipment, from individual items to combat vehicles, also placed sustained pressure on equipment refurbishment and replacement systems, especially in the Army and Marine Corps. Navy and Air Force airframes suffered significant wear and tear as well.

By the end of 2005, American forces in Iraq had suffered 2,182 killed and 16,155 wounded. Iraqi civilian deaths had climbed to around 30,000, while dozens of foreign journalists, aid workers, and contractors were killed in shootings or by car bombs, or kidnapped and gruesomely murdered at the hands of jihadists with the proceedings broadcast on social media platforms. The nature of the insurgency was complex, involving both radical fighters external to Iraq, former Baathists increasingly recruited from the disaffected Sunni population, and other Iraqis angered by the continuing occupation.

The operational tempo to some extent belied the label of insurgency and its defining characteristic in 2004–2005 was sustained close combat on a protracted scale. The new Iraqi National Army (INA), recruited mainly from veterans of Saddam's Iraqi army, gradually improved in size and capability but remained for the most part unready for independent operations. National elections were successfully held in 2005, and the trend to sectarian violence and civil war intensified, with Iraqi soldiers and especially civilians incurring heavy casualties in the ensuing fighting. In June 2006, Abu Musab al-Zarqawi, the leader of al-Qaeda in Iraq, was killed while the Iraqi government proceeded with the execution of Saddam and several his key lieutenants. Meanwhile, President Bush received the report of the Iraq Study Group, which he had tasked with advising on a way forward in the growing chaos in that country; by the end of 2006, insurgent attacks had intensified to over 950 per week.

The result was the deployment of some 20,000 additional combat troops in a surge under the command of the newly appointed General David Petraeus. Coupled with a change in emphasis in operations and, crucially, the emergence of the Anbar Awakening, which saw a move by Sunni Arab tribes toward active cooperation against al-Qaida, this surge brought about some decline in civilian deaths and sectarian violence, although ethnic cleansing of urban districts by both Sunni and Shia forces also may have contributed to this. At the same time, Petraeus placed a renewed emphasis on training and upgrading the INA. Relative success was reflected in the INA operations in Basra and against the Shia stronghold of Sadr City in Baghdad in March 2008. Although the Iraqi forces

Figure 17.3 Army soldiers of the 5th Battalion, 20th Infantry Regiment take cover during a firefight with guerrilla forces in the Al Doura section of Baghdad on March 7, 2007.

Source: United States Army.

sustained heavy casualties, the Shia militias opposing them were forced to accept negotiated settlements (though the durability of these was open to question).

Domestic pressure in the United States for a withdrawal from Iraq was matched by similar pressure within Iraq for the American forces to leave. In December 2008, the United States and Iraqi governments negotiated a status of forces agreement, and in the following month control of the Green Zone was transferred to the Iraqis. That month's nationwide provincial elections were characterized by assassinations and intimidation, but there was a strong sense that the American phase of the war was winding down, and in June 2009 American forces withdrew from Baghdad altogether, followed by the final withdrawal of combat forces in August 2010. A robust advisory and training effort remained in place, however.

The Iraq War was controversial and divisive, and the costs of the Bush administration's decision to widen the war on terror in that manner will take many years to calculate. U.S. forces lost 4,476 dead and more than 32,000 wounded; Iraqi losses are set at 26,000 insurgents killed, with civilian dead anywhere between 125,000 and 654,000. The total cost to the U.S. economy alone is estimated at $3 trillion, with some critics pointing to the additional strains it placed on the U.S. economy as contributing to the severity of the global financial crisis that emerged in 2008–2009.

In addition to the casualties in Afghanistan, almost 4,500 American servicemembers have been killed in Iraq, including 98 women. Hundreds of coalition troops also lost their lives in Iraq, with thousands wounded. The Iraqis have suffered most. Over 200,000 Iraqis have suffered violent deaths in Iraq since the American-led invasion in 2003. Despite the violent nature of both conflicts, a higher percentage of wounded survived their injuries than in any previous American war. Almost 87 percent survived their wounds, compared to 76 percent in the Vietnam War, due to improvements in triage, medical transportation, trauma surgery and other advancements in combat medicine.

Consequently, many survived wounds that would have caused death in previous conflicts. Hundreds suffered amputations, many more than one limb. But as in past conflicts, advancements in prosthetics have improved quality of life for these soldiers. The same can be said for head wounds and other internal injuries. One Pentagon study estimates that over 360,000 veterans suffered some level of traumatic brain injury, such as a concussion.

Nevertheless, while these physical injuries could be overcome, many of these wounded, as well as others not physically injured, suffered from the emotional and psychological effects of their deployments. Post-Traumatic Stress Disorder, or PTSD, affected over 12,000 per 100,000 service members who served overseas. Suicide rates among service members and veterans became a national concern. The subsequent demand for medical services from both active-duty service members and veterans has greatly pressed the medical services of the armed services and the Veterans Administration and will continue to do so. Disability benefits for veterans of these wars will make up a significant portion of the American defense budget for decades to come.

Challenges for the Future

The impact of both the Iraq and Afghan wars, as well as the broader Global War on Terror, on the armed forces has been profound, if not overwhelming. The United States has spent well over $1 trillion on these wars since September 2001. Multiple deployments and the high operational tempo broke personnel as well as equipment. The Department of Defense has faced difficult choices for budget priorities for procurement, recruiting, and providing upgraded housing, schools, and other facilities for active-duty service members and their families.

The operations in Afghanistan and Iraq demonstrate both the potential and the limitations of advanced technology as applied to the battlefield. Like the Jeep in World War II, the Huey helicopter in Vietnam, and the High Mobility Multipurpose Wheeled Vehicle (commonly referred to as the HUMV) in the Gulf War, the Mine-Resistant Ambush-Protected vehicle, or MRAP, became a ubiquitous symbol of transport in the Iraq and Afghan wars. Despite massive spending on sensors, satellites, and other mechanisms of electronic intelligence, a foot patrol captured Saddam Hussein. Unmanned Aerial Vehicles, known as UAVs or Drones, performed reconnaissance from thousands of feet to several feet to see around the corner of a building. Combat-capable UAVs, such as the Air Force MQ-9 Reaper, were also used to attack targets with precision-guided missiles. Legacy weapons systems, such as the B-52 bomber and the A-10 assault aircraft, proved their worth and resilience in Iraq and Afghanistan as they had in the Gulf War in 1991. But other systems and platforms, such as the F-22 Raptor and the Joint Strike Fighter, have derailed the acquisitions budgets of the armed forces, and as per-unit costs climb and initial orders are scaled back to fit within projected expenditure limits, new platforms may appear in such limited numbers as to undercut their intended roles and missions.

The potential job losses and local and regional economic impact of program cancellations and scale-downs make these highly sensitive political issues. The same has proved correct of attempts to rationalize force structure and deployments through the base closure program begun in the 1990s. Also, as American forces outstrip even their closest allies—such as the British—in terms of technological and cutting-edge capabilities, their ability to cooperate satisfactorily on, around, and over the battlefield becomes increasingly compromised, thus making coalition warfare even more difficult.

The demands of operations since 2001 have brought into sharp relief several issues that were already present, if less starkly delineated. The all-volunteer military always faces problems in recruiting and retaining the best-quality personnel whenever the domestic economy is booming, jobs are plentiful, and salaries are healthy. Without compromising the quality of either enlisted or commissioned personnel, the armed forces must work harder to broaden the demographics of those to whom they seek to appeal. As happened with the racial integration of the military from the Korean War onward, women have found increasing opportunities within the military as more specializations have opened to them in the absence of sufficient numbers of skilled males.

This has led to an ongoing argument about the involvement of women in combat, a function that officially remains closed to them despite female combat casualties in Iraq and Afghanistan. Political and social conservatives maintain that the involvement of women in combat will fatally undermine capability and commitment on the part of their male counterparts. Proponents of the role of women in combat-designated units point to the increasing combat role of some female personnel in Iraq. Women often made up as much as 50 percent of the logistical and other support units deployed in Iraq, which, especially in 2003–2004, were regular targets for jihadist ambushes increasingly wary of engaging regular Marine and Army combat units. Women did not serve in actual combat units in Iraq, but a portion of them indeed served in combat, and some acquitted themselves well. In June 2005, Sergeant Leigh Ann Hester, serving with the 617th Military Police Company of the Kentucky National Guard, became the first woman since World War II to be awarded the Silver Star for her part in fighting off an ambush on a supply convoy in March of that year.

Women are neither as congenitally incapable of combat as opponents maintain, nor are they as widely and regularly exposed to close combat as proponents suggest. Nevertheless, Secretary of Defense Leon Panetta authorized women servicemembers for combat units in January 2013, allowing women for the first time in American history to serve in the infantry. Women, of course, had already broken barriers as combat pilots in the Air Force. Since 1993, the Department of Defense has allowed women to pilot combat aircraft, even though women flew in Desert Storm in 1991. On the ground, recently there have been several 'firsts' for women gaining access to combat roles. In 2015, although several women washed out, Captain Kristen Griest, who had already served in Afghanistan with the 101st Airborne Division, and Lieutenant Shaye Haver became the first women to complete Army Ranger School training. Griest later became the Army's first female infantry officer, commanding Bravo Company of the 2nd Battalion, 505th Parachute Infantry Regiment. In 2016, the first women, ten in total, completed the Army's Infantry Basic Officer Leader's Course at Fort Benning, Georgia. In 2017, Lieutenant Marina Hierl completed the Marine Infantry Officer Course to become the first female infantry officer in the Marines, while Private First Class Maria Duame became the first Marine enlisted female to enter the infantry that same year. In 2018, several female Marines completed the Marine Combat Training Course for non-infantry. In another breakthrough for women and minorities, in 2018 Lorna Mahlock became first African American female brigadier general in the Marine Corps.

With these increased roles for women since the inception of the All-Volunteer Force, problems remain, not the least of which is sexual harassment and assault. The 1991 Tailhook scandal and a rash of sexual assaults at the Air Force Academy exposed in 2003, among other high-profile incidents, revealed to the public the crisis of sexual harassment and assault in the American military. By 2010, unfortunately, both issues had reached epidemic proportions. Several Department of Defense reports and external studies attest to the problem, noting that as many as 30 percent of female service members claimed to have been sexually assaulted and as high as 80 percent have been sexually harassed, in both cases mostly by fellow servicemembers. Studies also revealed that reporting such incidents is culturally discouraged and damaging to career advancement. Over 50 percent who reported incidents experienced some form of retaliation for doing so. Though new Department of Defense directives mandating

Figure 17.4 U.S. Army Reserve Maj. Lisa Jaster, center, became the third woman to graduate from the U.S. Army's elite Ranger School, October 16, 2015, in Fort Benning, Georgia. At that time, Jaster joined just two other women, Capt. Kristen Griest, left, and 1st Lt. Shaye Haver, right, in gaining the coveted Ranger tab. Photograph by Paul Abell.

Source: U.S. Army Reserve.

additional training on harassment and assault and Congressional support for greater resources for both the military and Veterans Affairs, sexual assault and sexual harassment remain a severe problem in today's military.

Another sociopolitical flash point concerning military service relates to homosexuals and those who classify themselves as transgender. President Clinton famously fell afoul of traditional opposition to acknowledge gay service in the military at the beginning of his first term in 1993. The 'Don't Ask, Don't Tell' policy, as it became known, theoretically protected homosexual personnel so long as they adhered strictly to its guidelines. But the policy was clear that 'homosexual conduct is not compatible with military service,' implying that openly gay service members would promptly be discharged. The policy was clearly open to abuse. The issue had both civil rights implications and very practical operational capability implications, with well-publicized instances of soldiers with much-needed language skills in Arabic, for example, being discharged because of sexual orientation. President Obama came to office with a clear policy of opening service to homosexuals, which was signed into law in December 2010 and enacted when the Congress repealed the earlier legislative restrictions in September 2011. The Chairman of the Joint Chiefs, Admiral Mike

Mullen, personally endorsed the changes, and extensive training and orientation efforts were undertaken within the services to ensure compliance. From 1993 through the repeal of Don't Ask, Don't Tell in 2010, over 13,000 servicemembers were discharged because of their sexual orientation.

More recently, the service of transgender servicemembers has come under question. Various bans on transgender service had been in place since the early 1960s, but by the 2000s changes in social attitudes in the United States brought challenges to preventing transgender individuals from service. Finally, in 2016 Secretary of Defense Ashton Carter, after a year of studies and small steps toward ending the ban, ordered the services to allow transgender personnel to openly serve. Any discharges of servicemembers with gender dysphoria had to be because the condition interfered with performance of their specific duties. Further, Secretary Carter authorized Department of Defense benefits to support medical procedures to change sexual identity. However, President Donald J. Trump reinstated the ban on transgender service in June 2017, causing protests in several cities as well as by dozens of retired and current general officers. Several court filings challenged the ban, resulting in court-ordered stays against the ban until the cases play out. The issue remains unresolved.

Another issue that has arisen is the role of the military in responding to national disasters, such as Hurricane Katrina in 2005. While states can call out their respective Guard units for emergency response, natural disasters, such as Katrina, encompass such scale and destruction that a larger, better-equipped federal agency is needed to coordinate search and rescue, recovery, and rebuilding operations. The American military is really the only federal agency that can undertake such a massive undertaking. States, however, do not wish to relinquish control over their Guard units while conducting operations within their borders. The debate over the old tradition of state control and *posse comitatus* was again brought to the fore because state and federal civilian agencies failed to respond effectively to Katrina, after which the military finally came in and seemingly restored order, bringing much-needed aid to people in desperate situations. The American military's role and capacity to provide relief in international disasters, as evidenced in the 2004 tsunami in Indonesia and the 2010 earthquake in Haiti, also remains a critical asset to American security interests.

The broader military establishment faces some pressing challenges in the early twenty-first century. It remains heavily committed across the world in operations, and it is smaller than at any time since the Vietnam War. Because of downsizing in the 1990s, the Army alone declined from 780,000 to 480,000, and the senior levels of the Pentagon expressed strong opposition in 2004 to congressional attempts to increase the strengths of the services. The National Guard is a finite resource, while regular repeat deployments for active-duty personnel to Iraq, Afghanistan, or elsewhere will inevitably have an impact upon service families and raise various quality-of-life issues that in turn will significantly impact retention rates. The much debated and universal questions of who serves and why are likely to come into sharper focus in the ensuing years. The weakness of the U.S. economy in the aftermath of the financial meltdown of 2008–2009 had significant medium-term implications for the American military across the board. Yet, in 2019 the Trump administration submitted the largest proposed defense budget in American history.

Conclusion

Since the end of the Cold War, the American military, like the United States that it serves, has struggled to find a clear and pressing role in the world. The 1990s had offered a confusing mix of messages as to likely future roles for the armed forces: peacekeeping, counterterrorism, the front line of the drug wars in Central and South America; none of these roles accorded with the military's own view of its traditional and expected role in national security. The Army, for example, has never been comfortable with peacekeeping as a mission. Indeed, the United States is often regarded as lacking the temperament for either peacekeeping or counterinsurgency, each of which requires patience, a long-term view, and an understanding that armed force is only one part, and usually the lesser part, of the security function involved.

For many years, it appeared that counterterrorism had become a core mission for the variety of special forces organizations within the various armed services, but in the War on Terror, again, much of the fight belongs to police and intelligence agencies and only secondarily to the active-duty military. Military involvement in the War on Drugs during the Reagan presidency, for example, was often seen as a misuse of capabilities and raised some difficult constitutional and civil–military relations issues when transferred to American soil. Since the 1990s, non-state actors, such as al-Qaeda, Somali pirates, and cybercriminals have presented a tremendous challenge for the national security of the United States. Recent Department of Defense studies even list global climate change as a national security threat. During the same period, China has become more of a peer military power and Russia is resurgent. North Korea remains a critical threat to American interests in Asia.

These different threats require a military establishment of diverse capabilities, procurement, and personnel. But it is essential to understand that the American military establishment is a massive bureaucratic organization. Change can be slow, even glacial. Too often, the services want to reset to a comfortable mission following a conflict that required less than comfortable operations. Thus, for example, following the Iraq War and as the Afghan conflict winds down, the Army is moving away from studying and preparing for counterinsurgency and moving more toward big-unit warfare. The danger is, however, that the global threat environment is far too complex for a military too narrowly focused. Can the United States be prepared for every type of war? Does it need to be? If so, how does it equip, train, and recruit to meet these myriad security challenges? These are questions that dog the modern American military.

The American military's past shows that this democratic nation has somehow managed to overcome security challenges in part by building an adequate military establishment to meet them. This has not been done without cost or mistakes, however. Civil–military relations, funding priorities, force structure, weapons procurement, doctrinal debates, incorporating cutting-edge technology, changes in American society and culture, and a focus on having an all-volunteer force, be it militia or regulars, have always tested American military effectiveness.

A standing military in a democratic republic remains a delicate thing and will perhaps stay so for the United States due to the very nature of its governing system and political principles. Challenges abound. What security threats will the United States face over the next century? How will the United States procure weapons systems, adapt its force structure, and fund the increasingly expensive and diverse mission to provide not only for its own security but also that of others? And how will it do these things without resorting to politically unpopular conscription, increased taxation, and base consolidation—and without alienating allies? These are the most difficult questions.

The American military has evolved, dramatically, from what was initially intended. Its history has been storied and gallant but also littered with tragedy and troublesome issues. Nonetheless, it has defended the United States successfully for over 230 years, and it will most likely continue to do so.

Further Reading

Bacevich, Andrew J. *The New American Militarism: How Americans are Seduced by War.* New York: Oxford University Press, 2005.

Bacevich, Andrew J. *America's War for the Greater Middle East: A Military History.* New York: Random House, 2016.

Bailey, Beth, and Richard H. Immerman, eds. *Understanding the U.S. Wars in Iraq and Afghanistan.* New York: New York University Press, 2015.

Bristol, Douglas W., Jr., and Heather Marie Stur, eds. *Integrating the U.S. Military: Race, Gender, and Sexual Orientation since World War II.* Baltimore, MD: Johns Hopkins University Press, 2017.

Filkins, Derek. *The Forever War.* New York: Knopf, 2008.

Gall, Carlotta. *The Wrong War: America in Afghanistan, 2001–2014.* New York: Harcourt, 2014.

Herspring, Dale R. *Rumsfeld's Wars: The Arrogance of Power.* Lawrence, KS: University Press of Kansas, 2008.

Jones, Seth. *In the Graveyard of Empires: America's War in Afghanistan.* New York: W. W. Norton, 2009.

Ricks, Thomas E. *Fiasco: The American Military Adventure in Iraq.* New York: Penguin Press, 2006.

Ricks, Thomas E. *The Gamble: General David Petraeus and the American Military Adventure in Iraq, 2006–2008.* New York: Penguin Press, 2009.

Weiss, Eugenia L., and Carl Andrew Castro, eds. *American Military Life in the 21st Century: Social, Cultural, and Economic Issues and Trends.* Vol 2. Santa Barbara, CA: ABC-CLIO, 2019.

Index